David Turner has been a member of the German Department at the University of Hull since 1963. He is the author of *Roles and Relationships in Otto Ludwig's Narrative Fiction* (1975) and numerous articles on German literature from the eighteenth to the twentieth century.

MORAL VALUES AND THE HUMAN ZOO
THE *NOVELLEN* OF STEFAN ZWEIG

Hull University Press

MORAL VALUES AND THE HUMAN ZOO
THE *NOVELLEN* OF STEFAN ZWEIG

by

DAVID TURNER

Senior Lecturer in German
University of Hull

HULL UNIVERSITY PRESS
1988

© D. Turner 1988

British Library Cataloguing in Publication Data

Turner, David
    Moral values and the human zoo : the *Novellen* of
    Stefan Zweig.
    1. Short stories in German. Zweig, Stefan, 1881-1942
    I. Title
    838'.912

    ISBN 0-85958-476-3

Phototypeset in 11 on 12pt Times and printed by the
University of Hull.

For my wife Margaret

Contents

Acknowledgements

Some of the material in this volume grew out of papers given at various symposia held during 1981, the centenary of Zweig's birth. I am grateful to the organisers of those symposia, to those whose financial assistance enabled me to take part in them, and to others who guided me through some of the Zweig material available during the course of those visits. I would like to mention in particular Professor Marion Sonnenfeld, Mrs Yvonne Wilensky, Mr John Saulitis, and Mrs Joanne Schweik of the State University of New York College at Fredonia; Dr Fritz Cocron of the Austrian Institute, New York; Dr Mark H. Gelber of the Ben Gurion University of the Negev, Beer Sheva; Dr Mordekhai Nadav of the Department of Manuscripts and Archives at the Jewish National and University Library, Jerusalem; Professor J.P. Stern of the Institute of Germanic Studies, London; Dr Bernhard Stillfried of the Austrian Institute, London; Dr Eva Alberman of London; and my own university.

Some of the material has appeared, in a different form, in various journals and collections of essays: 'The Function of the Narrative Frame in the *Novellen* of Stefan Zweig' in *Modern Language Review*, vol. 76 (1981) pp. 116-28; 'The Choice and Function of Setting in the *Novellen* of Stefan Zweig' in *Neophilologus*, vol. 66 (1982) pp. 574-88; 'A World beyond Space and Time: some implications of a recurrent motif in Stefan Zweig's *Novellen*' in *The Hebrew University Studies in Literature*, vol. 10, no. 2 (1982) pp. 225-46; 'The Humane Ideal in Stefan Zweig's *Novellen*: some complications and limitations' in *Stefan Zweig: the world of yesterday's humanist today: proceedings of the Stefan Zweig symposium*, ed. Marion Sonnenfeld, (Albany, 1983) pp. 157-67. I am grateful to the editors of the journals and to the State University of New York Press for permission to use that material.

I should also like to express my thanks to the British Academy for a generous publication subvention; to Professor Edward McInnes for his encouragement during the writing of the study; and to Margaret Jarvis, Catherine Ready and my wife, Margaret, for invaluable help in the preparation of the typescript.

List of Abbreviations

For ease of reference the following abbreviations have been used throughout:

EE   *Erstes Erlebnis: Vier Geschichten aus Kinderland (= Die Kette: ein Novellenkreis: der erste Ring)*, Leipzig, 1925

A   *Amok: Novellen einer Leidenschaft (= Die Kette: ein Novellenkreis: der zweite Ring)*, Leipzig, 1925

VdG   *Verwirrung der Gefühle: drei Novellen (= Die Kette: ein Novellenkreis: der dritte Ring)*, Leipzig, 1927

K   *Kaleidoskop*, Vienna, Leipzig, Zurich, 1936

S   *Schachnovelle*, Stockholm, 1943

VdG²   *Verwirrung der Gefühle*, Frankfurt a.M., 1960

INTRODUCTION

Stefan Zweig has been one of the most widely-read authors of the twentieth century. His works have been translated into many languages, from Albanian to Yiddish, Catalan to Bengali, Romansch to Esperanto.[1] And of all his works the *Novellen* are indisputably among the finest as well as the most popular. They are, in the words of one critic, his 'eigentliche Domäne'[2] and, in the words of another, his 'wesentliche künstlerische Leistung'.[3] They sold, moreover, in vast numbers. It has been calculated that in the fifteen years between the end of the First World War and Hitler's assumption of power over half a million volumes of his *Novellen* were bought by the public.[4] Yet these central works of one of the most famous modern writers in the German language have received very little critical attention. Readers who are interested in Zweig's life-story can call not only on the memoirs of the author himself, *Die Welt von Gestern*, and the account given by his first wife, Friderike,[5] but on a very full and carefully researched biography by Donald Prater, particularly in its expanded German version.[6] Those who are seeking a general introduction to the man and his works are well served by Joseph Strelka's recent study.[7] Those who are concerned with the nature of his humanism will find it subjected to scrutiny from different angles in numerous essays.[8] Those, on the other hand, who are looking for similar comprehensive treatment of the *Novellen* are likely to be disappointed. Apart from scattered reviews, which appeared when the various volumes were originally published, there are a few articles which offer interpretations of individual works or examine isolated aspects of the *Novellen* as a whole;[9] but the only serious attempts to examine the *Novellen* collectively and in detail have been made in a handful of unpublished doctoral dissertations, difficult to obtain and uneven in quality.[10]

It sometimes seems that Zweig's very popularity has worked to his disadvantage in this regard, giving rise to the suspicion that he cannot possibly have taken his role as a creative artist seriously enough. Many commentators therefore, notably American reviewers, have been eager either to relegate him to the rank of a mere writer or to defend him as a true artist.[11] Meanwhile, from most of the established figures of German literature who were Zweig's seniors his *Novellen* have had a cool reception. In their letters to him, as often as not thanking him for the arrival of a complimentary copy, they managed to make a few encouraging

3

remarks, but these rarely extended to more than a sentence or rose above the level of generalities. A post-card from Arthur Schnitzler, written in pencil and dated 29 November 1922, thanks him 'für die liebenswürdige Übersendung Ihrer Novellen, mit denen eine werthvolle Bekanntschaft zu erneuern ich mich herzlich freue', before going off on to a different topic.[12] A letter from Thomas Mann of 21 February 1923 thanks him for the gift, presumably of *Amok*, which he describes as 'meisterhaft, mit vollkommener Klugheit und Sicherheit erzählt', and as a 'glänzende Repräsentation europäischer Prosa'.[13] And a letter from Hugo von Hofmannsthal dated 10 November 1926 thanks him for some unspecified kindness and then concludes with the unconnected comment: 'Ihre Novellen haben wieder einen außerordentlichen Erfolg. Ich gratuliere Ihnen dazu und freue mich mit Ihnen'.[14] Of their literary accomplishment it says nothing. In their correspondence with other people these writers were not so insincere as to contradict the opinion expressed to Zweig himself. They simply ignored his *Novellen*.[15]

I do not propose to speculate on what their true assessment was, nor to continue the argument about whether Zweig should be classed as a 'Dichter' or merely as a 'Schriftsteller', an argument which is usually conducted on the basis of assertions or nebulous criteria and on the unspoken but unsubstantiated assumption that the two terms refer to entirely different kinds of activity.[16] Instead I shall treat his *Novellen* as fictional creations worthy of critical study and leave it to others to classify their author as they will. I am encouraged in the undertaking by the fact that at various times notable practitioners in the art of narrative from a number of countries, Romain Rolland in France, Maxim Gorky in Soviet Russia, and, more recently, John Fowles in England and Max von der Grün in Germany, have been happy to commend Zweig's stories to their public.[17]

In singling out Zweig's *Novellen* I am, of course, excluding — except for the purpose of occasional comparison and contrast — his one completed novel, *Ungeduld des Herzens*, the novel-fragment which has been published posthumously as *Rausch der Verwandlung*, and the handful of legends, which inhabit a different fictional world and are for the most part narrated in a markedly different tone. I shall also concentrate on what may be regarded as his most important *Novellen*, those whose publication he himself endorsed. Others which appeared only in newspapers or not at all during his lifetime, together with those contained in the early volume *Die Liebe der Erika Ewald*, which even a sympathetic Hermann Hesse found to be the work of a writer not yet fully mature and accomplished[18] and which Zweig himself preferred not to publish again later,[19] will receive only marginal attention.

If the best of his *Novellen* are among his finest and most characteristic achievements altogether, what gives them their special quality? And what marks them out as peculiarly his?

Their most arresting feature is their exploration of the varied manifestations of the human psyche. That is the foundation on which they are built; and it is there that any understanding must begin. In Part I therefore I shall seek to uncover the often complex and obscure inner workings of Zweig's characters, observing in particular those elements which repeatedly exert their fascination over him. In doing this I shall resist the temptation to use the works as raw material for the psychoanalysis of the author — a risky undertaking even for the trained analyst. I shall keep in mind rather that they are literary creations, which have their own logic and pursue their own objectives.

These *Novellen* are not only the products of a fascinated observer of the human psyche; they are also, unmistakably, the work of a humanist, whose values and beliefs inform his fictional creations no less than his essays and biographies, even though the mode of expression may be more oblique. These values will be examined in Part II. Here, however, it will no longer be a matter of aesthetic judgement, of the author's success or otherwise in creating psychologically convincing characters. Moral criteria will also be involved: we shall want to know not only what values are implied, how they are implied, and whether they are incorporated in the events and characters of the fictional world, but whether these values are reasonable, coherent, and such as command our approval.

Unlike the legends, the works under consideration are set in a world which their author knew, a world which his readers have no difficulty in accepting as a facsimile of the real world, even where they are too young to remember it personally or not widely enough travelled to have seen it for themselves. If the choice of both temporal and spatial setting is not arbitrary, it will be interesting to learn not only when and where a given work is set, but what significance attaches to the setting and what, if any, relation this bears to the psychology of the characters and the human values implied. This will be the main task of the investigation in Part III.

It is impossible to proceed as far as this without already entering into some discussion of narrative rhetoric. Distinctions between form and content dissolve in the face of the material presented. Accordingly, in Part IV, when we turn our attention to the two most prominent features of that rhetoric, the imagery and the narrative frame, we shall not be leaving behind the issues that have occupied us hitherto. For these stylistic and structural devices are much more than just devices; they are means whereby the author makes the often strange and disturbing psychology of his characters real and understandable to us and guides our responses, so that, ideally, they may be in tune with the human values embodied in each work. They are indeed one of the chief sources of our knowledge about the characters' psychology and the author's values.

Each of these four parts represents an extended essay which, as it approaches the *Novellen* from its own particular angle, may claim a measure of autonomous coherence and may even be read in isolation. Nevertheless, there is an important element of progression from one part to the next; and the degree to which the individual parts complement, reflect, or qualify each other means that the picture derived from any one in isolation would be incomplete.

Zweig's *Novellen* do not present the same intellectual difficulties as those of Hofmannsthal, Thomas Mann, Kafka, or Musil. Yet, as the evidence of some reviews suggests, the relative ease with which they may be read can also lead to a superficial reading, a failure to appreciate their complexities. There are good reasons for reading the texts both carefully and critically. In making the human psyche — and more specifically the unconscious — such a major part of his fictional world Zweig is confronting something which is not readily accessible to rational understanding, exploring an area where motive forces are often hidden from view. When, as frequently happens, the characters are called upon to do much more than express their feelings in occasional snatches of dialogue and have to give an extended account of some extraordinary experience, the reader must be alive to all the many opportunities for inadequate understanding, self-deception, dissimulation, and

6

rationalisation.[20] It is not only the self-assessment of the characters, however, which needs to be carefully weighed; the narrators too, particularly (though not exclusively) when they write in the first person, are no more infallible. The concept of the unreliable narrator has now become quite familiar,[21] but, as John M. Ellis has more recently shown, it is not that there are, in principle, two different kinds of narrator: one who may be trusted implicitly and another who may not. It is his argument rather that 'the attitude of the narrator is offered to us as part of the thematic material, not as a key to it; something for us to think about and evaluate, not to accept as the attitude of the work as a whole'.[22] In Zweig's case we shall repeatedly have cause to challenge his narrator's interpretation of events; and at times we shall be driven by the organisation of the whole to question the narrator's very outlook on life. If, therefore, careful scrutiny is called for at all times, it becomes particularly important where either the narrator or one of the characters offers some evaluative comment on what occurs.

Although a close reading of individual texts has formed the basis of my investigations, I have chosen to examine the texts collectively and from the four angles outlined above.[23] I shall of course have failed in my task if this does not lead to a better understanding of individual works. Nevertheless, my overriding concern has been to bring out their family likeness and at the same time to indicate something of their creator's development. I have also tried to set them in the wider context of Zweig's writing as a whole. Although the demands of narrative fiction are different from those of drama, biography, essay, and private correspondence, it was the same mind that brought them all to life. And just as these other writings shed light on the matters raised in the *Novellen*, so too the *Novellen* in their turn contribute significantly to the full understanding of the author's mind, its concerns and values, its strengths and weaknesses.

The works with which we are chiefly concerned not only form part of the total *oeuvre* of one very prolific writer; they also belong to the tradition of a particular literary form. In conclusion, therefore, I shall endeavour to assess their relation to the tradition of the German *Novelle*, a task for which the earlier chapters, over and above their inherent interest, will serve as a necessary preliminary.

PART ONE

THE PSYCHOLOGICAL FOUNDATION

It was Romain Rolland who provided the most telling formulation of Zweig's psychological curiosity. In an introduction to the French translation of *Amok* he described his Austrian friend as a 'chasseur d'âmes'.[1] The metaphor seems to imply something of the predatory instinct which may be present in the attempt to lay bare the inner workings of a human quarry. Yet the evidence of the stories themselves suggests that Zweig is to be regarded as a hunter with a less sinister purpose: to capture the widest possible variety of human specimens for his psychological menagerie.

In his introduction Rolland went on to indicate what he clearly saw as the essential influence on this psychological approach. For him Zweig was 'le poète armé de la clef redoutable du Dr. Freud, dont il fut l'admirateur et l'ami de la première heure'.[2] Certainly, the importance of Freud cannot be overlooked. It was to him that Zweig dedicated his study of Kleist, Hölderlin and Nietzsche (*Der Kampf mit dem Dämon*); having occupied himself more closely with psychoanalysis, even to the extent of consulting Freud in his surgery,[3] he devoted an extensive study to him, the crowning piece of the volume *Die Heilung durch den Geist*; and after Freud's death in London he delivered a funeral oration, praising the man who had pioneered the exploration of the human psyche: 'Und wo immer wir versuchen, in das Labyrinth des menschlichen Herzens vorzudringen, wird sein geistiges Licht weiterhin auf unserem Wege sein'.[4]

Although this close personal and intellectual involvement with Freud is reflected in many of the *Novellen*, the temptation is to overestimate its importance by ignoring either the role of other influences or the occasional need for a very different psychological approach. Robert Neumann, for example, sums up Zweig's writing in these words: 'Bei näherer Betrachtung erweist sich sein ganzes Werk [. . .] als romantisch angewandte Psychoanalyse. Es ist lesbar gemachter Freud'.[5] That is much too simple. It should

11

not be forgotten that Zweig grew up in a Vienna where an interest in art and the individual psyche generally provided an outlet for those unable or unwilling to engage in public affairs.[6] Of particular significance for the emergence of his own psychological approach was his acquaintance with the stories of Schnitzler, whom Freud was to call his double,[7] with the novels of Dostoyevsky, who has come to be regarded as an anticipator of Freud,[8] and, in relation to child psychology, with the writings of the Swedish reformer and educationist, Ellen Key. Nor should one overlook those fascinating fictional portraits by Zweig where the Freudian approach seems entirely inappropriate. Depth psychology is an inadequate tool where, as with Jakob Mendel (*Buchmendel*) and Czentovic (*Schachnovelle*), there is no depth.

Even where Freud's theories of the mind seem very relevant it is cautionary to observe what actually happens when the father of psychoanalysis applies his own theories to one of Zweig's works. In a paper entitled 'Dostoevsky and Parricide' he offers a 'Freudian' interpretation of *Vierundzwanzig Stunden aus dem Leben einer Frau*, which does little justice to the published work. Not only does it shift the emphasis from the main character, Mrs C., to the Polish gambler; it goes on, without any further evidence, to interpret his involvement with her as the fulfilment of a wishful fantasy (of his or Zweig's?) to be initiated into sexual life by his mother in order to be saved from the consequences of masturbation, an addiction for which his gambling is the present substitute.[9] Even the sensitive and discriminating literary historian can be seduced by the undoubted similarities between Freudian insights and Zweig's stories into unwarranted speculative reconstruction, burdening the adult characters with childhood traumas which are nowhere hinted at in the texts and have as little substance as the much-debated children of Lady Macbeth.[10] To do justice to Zweig's *Novellen* as works of literature it is wise not to regard them merely as applied psychoanalysis, but at the same time to bear in mind the degree to which Freud's theories of the mind may provide a useful intellectual framework.[11]

In the grouping of those *Novellen* which went to form the three volumes of *Die Kette (Erstes Erlebnis: Vier Geschichten aus Kinderland; Amok: Novellen einer Leidenschaft*; and *Verwirrung der Gefühle)* Zweig intended to indicate a typology of psychological problems. The division is not entirely satisfactory. It necessarily disregards any overlap; more especially, it places *Vierundzwanzig Stunden aus dem Leben einer Frau* in the wrong company; and of course it is not designed to accommodate the considerable number of *Novellen* which appeared elsewhere. Nevertheless, it does invite both reader and critic to think in terms of classifications within the psychological menagerie. Taking our cue from Zweig, then, while acknowledging the limitations of any system of grouping, we shall consider the psychological content of his *Novellen* under the following heads: the problems of adolescence; the eruption of the unconscious; single-mindedness; inner conflicts; the battle of the sexes; intellectual feats and deficiences; the psychology of self-revelation; the psychology of curiosity.

I

The Problems of Adolescence

Leaving aside *Die Liebe der Erika Ewald*, it is above all the volume *Erstes Erlebnis* which concerns itself with those special difficulties confronting young people on the threshold of adult life. Among the early reviews of the collection is one by Theodor Reik, a disciple of Freud, writing in the first issue of *Imago*; he commends the volume as one of the most important literary works of recent years from the psychological point of view, one which makes even Thomas Mann's *Buddenbrooks*, Hesse's *Peter Camenzind* and *Unterm Rad*, Strauß' *Freund Hein*, and Musil's *Die Verwirrungen des Zöglings Törleß* pale by comparison. Reik has no difficulty in establishing links with Freudian theories and insights: the role of sexual curiosity; the uncertainties of adolescents; their conception of the sex-act as a fight; the damaging effect of any sense of betrayal by the older generation. And he concludes his review with these words: 'Mit "intuitiver Psychoanalyse" hat der Dichter Titanenkämpfe der kindlichen Psyche, die sich allen Erwachsenen und oft dem Kinde selbst verborgen im Unterbewußtsein abspielen, ans helle Tageslicht gehoben.'[1] If Zweig's understanding of adolescence was not entirely intuitive, it seems unlikely that it derived directly from Freud. In part, no doubt, it was based on his own experience of growing up in an atmosphere of sexual concealment in late nineteenth-century Vienna.[2] Later his personal experience also received confirmation from the ideas of Ellen Key, whom he first met in 1907 after corresponding with her for some years previously and whose widely-read book *Das Jahrhundert des Kindes* emphasised the sensitivity of children, the importance of encouraging their independence and, perhaps most significant in

14

the present context, the need for openness in dealing with sexual matters: 'Die Verschleierung hingegen verleitet und verroht. Für die durch diese Geschädigten wird die Bibel ebenso sinnenreizend sein, wie irgendwelche Nacktheiten der neuen Literatur. Aber auf das ruhige Gefühl der Selbstverständlichkeit des Natürlichen läßt sich eine echte Unschuld gründen.'[3] It was to Ellen Key that Zweig dedicated the volume *Erstes Erlebnis*, which explores that vulnerability of adolescents, the uncertainties that arise from their dim awareness of a world which lies, or is kept, just beyond their reach.

The opening story of the collection, *Geschichte in der Dämmerung*, with its impressionistic, neo-romantic traces, inhabits the same world as some of Hesse's early stories, particularly *Heumond* from the collection *Diesseits* of 1907, which likewise explores the emotional uncertainties of adolescence, depicts a love that vacillates between two women, and uses setting and atmosphere to reflect the mental states of its young hero. In his treatment of the theme Zweig makes explicit use of the phrase 'jenes erste Erlebnis' to describe his fifteen-year-old hero's first encounter with the opposite sex, an encounter which is said to determine his future inability to find a proper relation to women and love (EE,56). The roots of Bob's difficulties lie in a solitude which is a product of his uncertain position as an adolescent. At the Scottish castle of his sister he is excluded from the company both of the gentlemen, who withdraw to smoke and play cards, and of the ladies, whose talk turns to hushed whispers as soon as he enters the room and who treat him condescendingly as a messenger-boy. Even his three female cousins, who are not much older than he and were once his playmates, seem already, in their cool dignity, to belong to a different world from that of his inner restlessness. For the first stirrings of his sexuality have as yet found no object, but express themselves in vague longings and melancholy, dreams of women, or surrogate sensual contact with trees and breezes.

In this restless state, as he walks through the castle grounds at night, he is suddenly and passionately embraced by an unidentified young woman. Although there is an element of ambivalence even in this first encounter, to the extent that his emotional intoxication soon gives way to the assertion of his will in the need to know who it was, to have a name for his happiness, this only becomes disturbing during their second meeting, in which there is a clear conflict between a surrender to sensual delight and a desire for knowledge. He may be flattered by the sensuality of her embrace, but his anger at her refusal to reveal her name is such that he sadistically digs his nails into her flesh. There are also other expressions of uncertainty in Bob's response — the alternation between the desire to know and the desire to preserve the mystery, between fear of what he takes to be Margot's dissimulating calm during their day-time meetings and jubilation at the beauty of her disdainful pride — but it is the degree to which his love is coloured by bitter anger, sadistic cruelty, or the desire to dominate[4] which is ultimately more decisive. For despite occasional lapses into their psychological opposites (reconciliation, masochism, self-abasement) these emotions persist.

When Bob learns that the young woman who embraced him was not Margot but her sister Elisabeth, he is no longer able to transfer his love to the proper object:

> Hätte Elisabeth damals sich ihm gezeigt, er hätte sie geliebt, denn in jenen Stunden war er ja noch kindhaft in seiner Leidenschaft, aber jetzt hat sich in tausend Träumen der Name Margots zu tief in ihn eingebrannt, als daß er ihn weglöschen könnte aus seinem Leben. (EE,52)

Zweig seems to imply a certain typicality in Bob's subsequent failure to marry. Yet most of what he has presented derives from the rather special circumstances of mistaken identity. It is, above all, Bob's mistaken belief that the passionate young woman who embraced him is identical with the cool, haughty, and supposedly dissembling Margot which intensifies his confusion, his anger, and his cruelty. Through no fault of his own he stands in a false relation to reality.

What is interesting in Zweig's portrayal, however, is the extent to which, in his immaturity, Bob magnifies this false relation. It could be argued that the frequency with which his anger and frustration become directed at his own self[5] or find only a substitute outlet, as he spurs his horse (EE,30), kicks the dog (EE,32), or strikes out at the trees (EE,34), is one example of this, but it is less significant than his increasing reliance on imagination. Even just before his critical fall, as he climbs the tree to peer in at Margot's window, he is caught up in a fantasy of her presence (EE,39). After the fall a relation born largely of ignorance

16

becomes the cherished foster-child of a wilful imagination. He welcomes his long convalescence because he is relieved of all obligations and can indulge in reverie, in the romantic notion that he is suffering for Margot's sake, bears a permanent scar, or is even dead and mourned by her (EE,44). Not only does he wish away the visit of other women, but when she herself comes to his room and behaves differently from the Margot of his dreams, he chooses to close his eyes to the real person, preferring to cultivate his fantasy image (EE,46-7). Because all this predates the discovery of his lover's true identity, it makes the transition to reality impossible. Bob retains his love for Margot, though now with the desperate longing for what is unattainable (EE,52).[6]

When, after his recovery, he visits the scene of that first embrace in the garden, he senses the presence of an invisible wall, behind which stands his childhood and in front 'ein anderes Land, fremd und gefährlich' (EE,55), presumably the adult world. While it may be true that, by the time he leaves his sister's castle, he has attained manhood in his physical features, he is still prone to outbursts of childish weeping (EE,56) and, more especially, fails to overcome that immature psychological reliance on the imagination, so that in later years, as a quiet, correct, widely-travelled Englishman, he appears lacking in feeling, because he ignores the smiles of women. For as the narrator puts it, musing on the fate of such men, 'wer denkt, daß sie die Bilder, auf die ihr Blick stets geheftet ist, innen, verflochten ihrem Blute tragen, das stets um sie lodert wie ein ewiges Licht vor dem Bilde der Madonna?' (EE,57).

In *Geschichte in der Dämmerung* the perspective adopted is exclusively that of Bob, so that the painful confusions of Elisabeth, who, objectively, is just as much a victim of misunderstanding as the hero, are barely touched upon. In the second, much shorter story, *Die Gouvernante*, an entirely female perspective is presented. Since *two* young people are now involved, dialogue can replace 'erlebte Rede' as the chief means of revealing their excited state of mind.

In *Die Gouvernante* the secretive silence of the older generation on sexual matters, which performs a minor role as part of the social background in the first story, now occupies a central position and is the major contributory factor in the girls' adolescent difficulties. During the course of the story, as their governess's pregnancy is revealed, as she is rejected by the putative father, their cousin Otto, is dismissed by their outraged parents, and finally commits suicide, the girls are confronted by a wall of silence, half-truths or lies. Yet factual ignorance is accompanied in the sisters by a keen intuitive awareness,[7] an awareness of some connection between their cousin and the governess, of the injustice done to the governess, and above all of the 'Atmosphäre der Lüge und des Verschweigens' (EE,77) which surrounds them. They have left behind the carefree enjoyment that belonged to their childhood; they are full of an inner restlessness to penetrate the secret which is being kept from them; they have become mistrustful and silent, turned in on themselves, and answer the dishonesty of their environment by a nervous stealth, an unnatural dissimulation.

As with Bob in *Geschichte in der Dämmerung*, there is an element of immature uncertainty in their responses, as they vacillate between anger at their treament and shame at their own deception, between the desire to know and the fear of what they might discover. In one respect, however, their reaction to their treatment by the adult world moves in the direction of greater assurance. What, even half-way through, appears as an inner rebellion against the meanness of their mother's behaviour (EE,76-7) eventually breaks out into open revolt. The elder sister goes defiantly to her mother, complaining that they have been kept in ignorance and demanding to know, in provocatively possessive language, 'Wo ist unser Fräulein?' (EE,80). When the mother does admit that their governess has left, the piercing, threatening look of both girls makes it impossible for her to tell them a lie; instead she is forced to flee the room. Even though they no longer speak to each other, Zweig writes of a 'schreckhafte Gemeinschaft' between the two girls (EE,82). By no means the least alarming feature of this is that it is a partnership *against* the rest of the world; it has become an obstacle to social integration.

In parallel with this, their strongly-developed 'Zärtlichkeitsbedürfnis', a product of their newly awakening womanhood (cf. EE,72-3), is also denied an outlet in some relation to the world outside. The road to their parents is blocked by falsity and injustice; the road to the opposite sex proves a *cul de sac* once they discover that the increased attentions of their cousin Otto have been merely a pretext for furthering his affair with the governess. For most of the story, therefore, the governess is the focus of all their tenderness and so serves an important psychological need. It

18

becomes increasingly evident, moreover, that their sympathy with her is so strong because she represents that world of adult womanhood which is soon to become their own. When, without telling them what she is doing, she takes her final leave of them, they burst into tears; and their pitiful sigh, 'Das arme Fräulein', which we have already heard several times, is described as 'schon wieder ein Seufzer ihres eigenen Schicksals' (EE,78), not because they will be without an amiable governess, but because in her their own need for tenderness, their own incipient womanhood has been offended. At the end of the work both the sensual and emotional components in this feeling find their fulfilment in what seems to be the only way open to them: they fall asleep in each other's embrace. They are still, in other words, turned in on themselves.

Die Gouvernante is less certain than *Geschichte in der Dämmerung* about the permanency of the damage done to its adolescent heroines: 'der Zugang zu ihren Seelen ist abgebrochen, vielleicht auf Jahre hinaus' (EE,83). Nor are we given any further glimpse into the future. Nevertheless, it is clear that, like Bob, they have left the world of childhood without achieving a satisfactory transition to the adult world, which remains dark and threatening, an abyss (EE,82 and 84).

Brennendes Geheimnis, the most substantial piece of the collection, which Zweig's friend Raoul Auernheimer described as his 'bisher reifste Schöpfung',[8] devotes considerable space to the psychology of two adult figures, a married woman from the Viennese bourgeoisie, who stands at the critical period of her life when she must make a final choice between the desire for erotic adventure and her domestic role as a mother, and a young nobleman seeking the stimulus of a sexual conquest to counteract his inner emptiness. Both represent types that will recur in subsequent works. The main emphasis, however, is placed on the adolescent problems of the woman's twelve-year-old son, on what is again referred to as an 'erstes Erlebnis' of the unreliable adult world (EE,187).

Despite its concentration on the male adolescent, *Brennendes Geheimnis* has closer links with *Die Gouvernante* than with *Geschichte in der Dämmerung*. The attention which Otto pays to his two cousins as a way of furthering his affair with the governess, a subsidiary motif in *Die Gouvernante*, is developed into a decisive act of exploitation and betrayal in *Brennendes Geheimnis*; and the sense of exclusion from the adult world, coupled with the nervous, passionate desire to penetrate its secret, is once more of major importance, if perhaps less exclusively so than the title might suggest. On the other hand, although the sexual practices of adults again form the content of that secret, the problems of the hero's own sexuality achieve prominence only at the end.[9]

In portraying Edgar's vulnerability Zweig brings out two aspects of the adolescent psyche in particular: the need for affection and the sense of inadequacy. As the story proceeds, it becomes increasingly clear that the young hero has had few friends and received little love at home. His father is a stern, inaccessible man (EE,171); his mother, who appears to have regarded him alternately as a decorative plaything and as a nuisance, understands little of him (EE,109,149). When the work opens, therefore, he is already established as a child with a 'Zärtlichkeits-bedürfnis', a term familiar to us from *Die Gouvernante*, but already used in the earlier *Die Liebe der Erika Ewald*,[10] and here applied twice (EE,96,104) to a psychological need which as yet finds only surrogate satisfaction as he caresses a horse or a St Bernard dog (EE,96,98). The sense of inadequacy, on the other hand, derives from a combination of his upbringing and his transitional stage of development. From the beginning he is acutely aware that, to the extent that he remains a child and is treated as such, his importance as an individual is diminished. He is already finding his boyhood possessions and enthusiasms too trivial to mention in adult company (EE,106),[11] lamenting that his ideas are not taken seriously, and above all feeling embarrassed by the stigma of tutelage associated repeatedly with his being sent to bed early (EE,105,113).

The need for affection and the sense of inadequacy explain why the attentions of the baron make such an impression on Edgar and evoke such a passionate response. He has found an adult friend who treats him as an equal and whom he loves as he has never loved his parents or even God (EE,105). They also help to explain his subsequent emotional reversals and uncertainties. For since the baron is using him as a decoy in the pursuit of his real quarry, Edgar's mother, his emotional response has an illusory basis, which is only gradually revealed. Hence passionate loyalty to the baron and jealousy of his mother, who seems to him to be an intruder seeking to take away his new friend (EE,107,110,123),

20

give way to a hatred of both, when he detects some collusion between them (EE,134,137). Before long he is seeking to woo the affection of his mother, in the belief that the baron alone is responsible for their relationship, a dangerous man from whom she needs to be protected (EE,147-8) and whom he will eventually assault with all the pent-up hatred of betrayed love (EE,160-1), until her blatant lies again turn him against her too. By now he feels entirely deserted in an ugly, hostile, untrustworthy adult world (EE,170). It may be that these emotional reversals owe something to the normal unstable vehemence of adolescence, intensified by recent illness, but the particular direction of his outbursts and their serious consequences derive from his ignorance of the ways of the world or, rather, from the deliberate deception of others.

In many respects *Brennendes Geheimnis* depicts the gradual maturing of Edgar, but it is not an unambiguous development. Nor is his response to it unambiguous. On the positive side, there is a growth of insight both into the behaviour of adults — though its corollary is, of course, a loss of trust and respect (EE,143) — and, on his train journey alone to Baden, into socio-economic realities (EE,176). There is also a growth in self-reliance, as he comes increasingly to break away from the tutelage of his mother and defy her directions. On the negative side, his knowledge of sexual matters remains incomplete. There is no indication that he ever advances beyond his conception of the sex-act as a sort of fight, dangerous to the woman (cf. EE,156). Moreover, he is still liable to burst into childish tears; and the apparent independence of his stalking pursuit of his mother and her would-be lover, for all its undercurrent of sexuality,[12] is qualified by the fact that his movements are closely modelled on his boyhood reading of Karl May (EE,134,156,158). Even his escape to his grandmother in Baden represents not just a (temporary) break with his mother, but a desire to return to the one person who will pamper and protect him: 'Er wollte ja nichts sein als das Kind von vordem, gehorsam, geduldig ohne die Anmaßung, deren lächerliche Übertriebenheit er jetzt fühlte' (EE,172).[13] When it comes to the final reunion with his mother, his protection of her amorous secret and his assumption of all responsibility for the unhappy turn of events may allow him the pride of demonstrating 'wie sehr er schon Mann war' (EE,186), but it is preceded by a scene in which he desires only to

21

beg her forgiveness humbly, to be her child and obey (EE,185), and is followed by a final conciliatory embrace. To the end he remains part-man, part-child.

Reconciliation itself marks a change from the unhappy conclusion of *Geschichte in der Dämmerung* and *Die Gouvernante*, but a more significant difference lies in the unexpectedly hopeful prognosis for the hero's later sexual development. As already indicated, he too has been kept in the dark about the nature of sexuality, with the result that it constitutes the greatest part of the secret he seeks to penetrate. Yet for most of the story it remains the object of merely intellectual curiosity. Only after he has broken free and escaped to his grandmother does it acquire a closer link with his own feelings. The nocturnal activities of the courting couples observed and overheard in the 'Kurpark' at Baden become a source of confusion and yet also of mysterious pleasure to him personally: 'und irgendein schwüles Vorgefühl durchdrang seine Angst mit einem wollüstigen Schauer' (EE,180). It is the first unsettling ferment of his own sexuality. And that makes it more understandable that the reconciliation with his mother at the end should be expressed in a tender embrace in which the erotic element is at least as powerful as the filial. It is undoubtedly this scene which has encouraged interpretations of the work in terms of an oedipal fixation.[14] These, however, require some qualification. In the first place, there is no corresponding suggestion of hostility or guilt towards a father who is perceived as a sexual rival. Even if one were to cast the baron in the role of the father, one would also have to acknowledge that hostility towards his mother for taking away this companion is as pronounced as hostility towards the baron for taking away his mother. Most important of all perhaps: the sexual element in Edgar's love for his mother is apparent in that one scene at the end, where it is clearly presented as a transitional stage on the way to mature relations with the opposite sex, to what Freud would have seen as object-love proper:

> All dies verstand das Kind von damals nicht, aber es fühlte, daß es sehr beseligend sei, so geliebt zu sein, und daß es durch diese Liebe schon verstrickt war mit dem großen Geheimnis der Welt.
> Als sie dann die Hand von ihm ließ, die Lippen sich den seinen entwanden [. . .], blieb noch ein Warmes zurück, ein

Hauch über seinen Lippen. Und schmeichlerisch flog ihn
Sehnsucht an, oft noch solche weiche Lippen zu spüren und
so zärtlich umschlungen zu werden. (EE,188-9)

In some small measure his mother has initiated him into the world
of sexuality, though not as far as adolescents are supposed to wish
according to Freud. It seems certain too that the women he subsequently loves will be chosen for their similarity to his mother. Yet
one could scarcely wish for a clearer statement that his love does
not remain 'fixated' on her. He is now more prepared to enter the
adult world.[15]

Sommernovellette is the shortest and slightest piece of the
collection. It also has something provisional about it, in that both
main strands of the narrative, a young woman's awakening to love
and an older man's unexpected shift from non-committal play to
emotional involvement, are left without explicit conclusion. The
theme of adolescent love, moreover, has to share the limelight with
that second strand on equal terms. Nevertheless, a link is implied
between the fearful yet expectant passion of the older man and
that of some adolescent youth, 'weil beide sich nicht ganz
vollwertig fühlen' (EE,206). Since, therefore, he is passing
through a sort of second adolescence, the collective title 'Erstes
Erlebnis' may be said to apply to his fate just as much as to that of
the girl.

What reduces the impact of her adolescent experience even more
is that it is presented entirely from the outside, constructed from
the older man's interpretation of her gestures and behaviour. She
herself remains a somewhat shadowy figure. There is neither
interior monologue nor 'erlebte Rede' nor yet dialogue (on her
part) to provide more reliable access to her psyche. Nevertheless,
what evidence there is points to a reiteration of problems familiar
from the other three works. Physically, the girl, who is said to be
about sixteen years old, stands at a transitional point, and her
movements have a nervous awkwardness about them. More
important, she has something of that characteristic need for
affection, a longing which lacks direction (EE,196) and certainly
finds no fulfilment from her dull relatives. Like Edgar in
Brennendes Geheimnis, she seeks a surrogate satisfaction by
caressing animals with an excessive passion (EE,196) and, like
him, she is influenced by the literature she has read, which has
filled her head with romantic expectations (EE,197-8).

With that predisposition it is small wonder that she falls victim to the playful ruse of the older man, who writes her a fictional love-letter. Without knowing the author of the letter, she reacts with nervous excitement, embarrassment and an allegedly typical secretiveness. For, we are told, 'es gibt Mädchen, deren Schamhaftigkeit so groß ist, daß Sie mit ihnen das Äußerste wagen können, weil sie so hilflos sind und lieber das Ärgste erdulden, ehe sich mit einem Worte andern anzuvertrauen' (EE,199). This first experience of love brings with it signs of a blossoming into radiant womanhood, but it is accompanied by an unhealthy restlessness and feverishness, and, above all, by the sort of emotional confusion we have come to expect from Zweig's adolescent characters. Once she has (mistakenly) identified the writer of the letter as an elegant young Italian, who corresponds most closely to her romantic expectations, she behaves in contradictory ways: 'es war jenes ewige Spiel zwischen Wollen und Fürchten, Sehnsucht und Scham, in dem doch immer die süße Schwäche die Stärkere ist' (EE,203). It is important to recognise, however, that her psychological uncertainty is in no way dependent on mistaken identity, as was the case with Bob in *Geschichte in der Dämmerung*. It is simply her first, adolescent reaction to the experience of love itself. Indeed it is interesting to note that she never discovers her mistake. The grief and despair which subsequently come over her features and gestures prove — assuming that the interpretation of the older man is correct — to be the natural response to the fact that she must leave for home without being able to confide in her relatives (EE,204).

As to the question of permanent damage, an important element in some of the works of *Erstes Erlebnis*, it must be emphasised that, if it does form part of the conclusion of *Sommernovellette* — and this is only the unauthenticated assumption of the older man — it has nothing to do with a disturbed sexual development. The worst that (perhaps) befalls her is that she contracts a conventional bourgeois marriage in a provincial town, while her holiday experience remains a fleeting memory (EE,204).

When *Erstes Erlebnis* first appeared as part of the larger cycle *Die Kette* in 1922, it was preceded by a sonnet in which, adopting the more personal note of the lyric, Zweig spoke of childhood as a prison from which he wanted to escape into the adult world. At the same time he revealed his ambivalent feelings towards that world once he had entered it, for it brought with it not only excitement and a feeling of expansion, but also a sense of regret and a desire to return to the clarity and security of childhood. The sonnet expresses only some of the issues presented in the stories themselves and so cannot be regarded as an adequate summary of what follows. In 1926, however, Zweig published in the Viennese *Almanach der Psychoanalyse* an introductory essay to extracts from the actual diary of an adolescent girl who had since died. Although he is modest enough not to mention his own volume of stories, it is obvious that this documentary material, whose typicality he repeatedly stresses, is a confirmation of his own fictional portraits without the selective condensation of the conscious artist. For that reason his commentary provides a fuller account of what he was attempting in *Erstes Erlebnis*, as may be judged from the following extract:

> Das Erlebnis dieser Jahre, das Wesentliche dieses Buches ist selbstverständlich das Nicht-mehr-Kind-sein-Wollen. Der Wille, als voll gewertet zu werden, um alle Geheimnisse zu wissen, die alle Erwachsene so krampfhaft vor ihm verbergen. Mit Zorn und Erbitterung notiert die Elfjährige immer, wenn Vater, Mutter oder Schwester sie eine 'Kleine' oder 'Kind' nennen. Mit Ungeduld will sie schon hinauf in die andere Welt, will sie die verschlossenen Türen zerbrechen, hinter denen sie manchmal unverständliche Worte hört und hinter denen für ihr Empfinden das 'eigentliche', das wirkliche Leben liegt. Jedes dieser aufgelauschten Worte hinter den verschlossenen Türen des großen Geheimnisses wird zum Ereignis, zum Geschehnis.[16]

2

The Eruption of the Unconscious

In the long essay on Freud which forms the final section of *Die
Heilung durch den Geist* Zweig draws attention to two facts — the
vulnerability of the child's psyche and the late nineteenth-century
concealment of sexuality on account of its supposed threat to civilisation[1] — which shed a retrospective light on the problems
already presented in *Erstes Erlebnis*. Nevertheless, the essay has a
far greater relevance to adult psychological experiences such as are
dealt with in the two later volumes of *Die Kette*. Of particular
importance is the emphasis placed on the primacy of the
unconscious, that 'barbarian', untutored element which remains
in man, giving the lie to the optimistic belief that reason has
conquered all. It is this whole area of life, below the level of
consciousness, which Freud has managed to illuminate to the
benefit of both theoretical understanding and practical therapy.[2]
And it is this same obscure, dangerous, but authentic 'Unterwelt
der Leidenschaften' which Zweig himself invokes in the sonnet
that stands at the beginning of the volume *Amok*.

The final story of *Erstes Erlebnis*, *Sommernovellette*, has
already given an inkling of the way in which passion can
unexpectedly take possession of even an older man as a result of
his playful and perhaps voyeuristic involvement with a teenage
girl. But this is as nothing compared with the eruptive force which
dominates the lives of characters in later works, nowhere more
devastatingly than in *Der Amokläufer*, which in its very title
provides a model for such irresistible passion.

As with most of the stories of *Erstes Erlebnis*, *Der Amokläufer*
presents a central character who is already psychologically

26

prepared, made receptive by experience to the critical encounter. Living in enforced exile in the tropics after some misdemeanour in Germany and having originally come with romantic dreams of bringing the benefits of civilisation to a primitive people, he has gradually been worn down by the climate and his isolation among natives and animals, so that he feels cut off from his European self, completely demoralised.

The arrival of an English lady, demanding an abortion, provokes an immediate struggle for mastery between the two individuals, a matter to which we shall return later, but which is not the chief characteristic of his running amuck. This takes place only when that open struggle has been decided in favour of the woman, who refuses either to beg for his help or submit to his sexual demands. Only then, after a momentary paralysis brought about by her imperious command not to follow her, is he seized by a mad, unthinking urge to pursue her, an urge which dominates the rest of his life. Although there is a linearity in his pursuit, as there is in the analagous situation of the native who runs amuck ('aber er rennt, rennt, rennt, sieht nicht mehr nach rechts, sieht nicht nach links, rennt nur mit seinem gellen Schrei, seinem blutigen Kris in der Hand in dieses entsetzliche Geradeaus'; A,49), this does not preclude either a contradictory emotional response (A,63-4) or modifications to his immediate aim: first, to provide the necessary medical help to terminate her pregnancy; then, once that is rejected and her life is endangered by a back-street abortion, to save her life; and finally, when that too fails, to preserve her secret from her husband and the rest of the world. Yet each stage is accompanied by the same passionate intensity and concentrated energy and is governed by his overriding thraldom to the woman.[3]

One of the outstanding features of his volcanic passion is the way in which it takes over his conscious will, so that he is no longer in control of his actions. He speaks in terms of 'Besessenheit' (A,49) or 'Bezauberung des Willens' (A,57); he describes himself as 'ein verkaufter Mensch, ein Sklave' (A,53); and repeatedly he conjures up an impersonal 'es' as the motivating force in his behaviour: 'es war zu stark in mir, ich mußte sie sprechen' (A,57); 'da packte es mich plötzlich an und ich lief' (A,58); 'plötzlich schmiß es mich hin zu dem Tisch' (A,61). Although one should not simply equate this 'es' with the Freudian *id* as the collective force

27

of all man's biologically given instincts, it does, nevertheless, share the quality of resistance to conscious control.

That is not to say there are not moments when he is ashamed or is aware of the folly of what he is doing; but, significantly, these feelings or realisations are unable to determine what he does. In describing, for example, the scene when he runs across the room in pursuit of the woman as she leaves the villa of the 'Vizeresident', he remarks: 'ich hatte vergehen können vor Scham . . . noch während ich lief, war mir schon der Wahnsinn bewußt . . . aber ich konnte . . . ich konnte nicht mehr zurück' (A,58-9). In contrast to the woman herself, he loses all self-control. Subject to an inner compulsion, he ignores all civilising restraints, behaves irrationally, even criminally. When he first pursues her after she has refused his demands, he abandons his house without locking up, splinters the wood of his shed in his haste to get out his bicycle, beats her boy, who tries to prevent him, and, when his bicycle has been damaged in the struggle, runs after her in a way unheard-of for a European: wet through and covered in mud (A,45-6). He leaves his post without signing off or appointing a deputy (A,49). After her death the urge to preserve her guilty secret is so powerful that he threatens violence, either to his own person or to his superior medical officer, in order to ensure that the death certificate should (falsely) specify natural causes (A,75-6). Thereafter, thinking he has finished with the woman, he escapes from the colony altogether, travelling like a thief, on a false passport and without leave (A,82).

The doctor's powerful inner compulsion leads not only to uncivilised behaviour, but also to the practical failure of what he feels compelled to attempt. That indeed is why his immediate aims have to be modified. Having followed the Englishwoman from the remote district station to the town, he does the senseless thing in going immediately and without thinking to her house — and is turned away. As he tells the narrator, 'das Stürmische, das Tölpische meines Nachrennens hatte sie erschreckt. [. . .] es war, wie wenn einer einem nachrennt, um ihn zu warnen vor einem Mörder, und der andere hält ihn selbst für den Mörder' (A,51). Similarly, at the reception given by the 'Vizeresident' his ridiculous, intrusive behaviour, which is quite beyond the control of his will, causes her to leave, whereas, if he could only have been discreet, she might have received him the following morning and perhaps permitted an operation under satisfactory medical conditions (A,56-7).

There is a moral dimension to the events recorded in *Der Amokläufer*. The question of man's obligation to offer help is raised several times in connection with the narrator as well as the doctor; medical ethics are involved in both abortion and the falsification of a death certificate. But in Zweig's presentation psychology dictates morality and not the other way round. It cannot be said that the doctor makes a moral choice, either in offering to terminate a pregnancy or in preserving the woman's secret at the expense of legality and honesty. In a real sense the choice is made for him, by a psychological force that is stronger than his conscious will. And as Martha Gschiel points out, the help offered is designed to satisfy his need rather than hers.[4] Consequently, when the doctor, having secured his escape on board ship in the belief that the woman's secret is permanently safe, is again thwarted by the discovery that the husband is now returning to Europe on the same vessel, bringing the body for a possible autopsy, he speaks not simply of a duty that still remains, but of a kind of bondage: 'sie hat mich hierher verfolgt' (A,82); 'sie gibt mich noch nicht frei' (A,83). The compulsion is still inescapable, fatefully so. What was earlier adumbrated in his description of the native who runs amuck — that his end is collapse or death — is realised in his own final act. Rather than allow the lead coffin to be brought ashore, he takes it with him into the depths of Naples harbour.

Die Frau und die Landschaft, the second work in the volume *Amok*, has an unusual complexity for Zweig, but is at the same time very simple in outline. Its complexity resides in a closely-knit web of parallels, amounting at times to a mythical identification, between the experience of the human figures, especially the young woman of the title, and the parched Tyrolean landscape, waiting for the refreshment and fertilising power of the rainfall from heaven. On the other hand, what could be simpler than that, after the waiting, the rain comes or, in human terms, that the longing of the young woman finds fulfilment in a sexual encounter?

Psychologically, the story is much less rich than *Der Amokläufer*. This is partly because the woman's brief encounter with the narrator has no apparent consequences, leaves no apparent trace on her consciousness. It is also because she is presented entirely from the outside, so that all her feelings have to be construed by the narrator from her looks, gestures and few words. But it is as much as anything because only a narrow range of mental activity is indicated. The young woman's experience seems to consist in little more than an awareness of and instinctive response to sensory stimuli.

Even if in a simplified form, however, she, like the doctor of *Der Amokläufer*, is subject to the eruptive force of the unconscious. Like him, too, she is subject to the prevailing weather, in this case a debilitating drought, which leaves her limp and sighing for rain (A,93-4,101). But drought is not merely a cause of her languor; it serves as a parallel to an as yet unfocussed sexual desire which will only find release in an intimate encounter with the narrator. From the very beginning her behaviour is subject to a degree of unconscious control: 'Etwas Nachtwandlerisches und Traumhaftes war in ihrer statuenhaften Gestalt, in ihrem gelösten Blick' (A,94). But she is still able to impose a social restraint, so that even when the narrator detects in her look what he feels in himself, 'die gleiche stille Raserei [. . .], die schmachtende, sinnlose, verdurstende Gier', she manages to hide her feelings behind a mask which he tries in vain to penetrate (A,102-3). That same night, however, he finds her unannounced in his room. She offers no explanation for her presence, and he ventures none. But it is evident that she is now in the grip of that unconscious desire and is therefore incapable of giving any rational account of her actions. She may express some unspecified fear, but her words are directed at nobody in particular and seem to be uttered from a state of sleep. Now there is no resistance to either the desire from within or the narrator's embrace which is its fulfilment. And much as it may deflate his ego to acknowledge it, she is not conscious of what she is doing, still less of his attractions as an individual male. She yields to his embrace as 'eine Unbewußte [. . .], eine Trunkene, eine Kranke, eine Schlafwandlerin ihrer Sinne [. . .], ein Wesen, das nicht wußte, was es tat, das mich vielleicht nicht wollte' (A,112); any pleasure she feels derives not from her will, but from that 'Dämon in ihr, der Herr ihres Blutes war' (A,112); and the more roughly he seeks to rouse her to consciousness, the more she responds 'mit einer sinnlosen Inbrunst' (A,113).

With that her essential experience is over. She collapses into a relaxed, childlike sleep, from which she is roused only by the storm raging outside. Still there is no proper link between her consciousness and what has happened to her. Even though she has gone through a positive physical transformation, which leaves her movements freer, her voice clearer and purer, she is mentally confused and frightened to find herself in a stranger's room. She responds with a look of unbounded hatred and flees in alarm. Once in the company of her parents again, she falls in easily with the superficial manners of her society, its cheerful laughter, its trivial gossip. Catching sight of the narrator, she pauses involuntarily, but it is as though she were seeking in vain to recall what has happened. Her waking self has no knowledge of him. There is neither 'Erregung' nor 'Beschämung', emotions which presuppose a discernible link between the person in front of her and either an anticipated or a remembered passion. Indeed, one might venture to say that the absence of such a link between the outburst of the unconscious and the conscious censor helps to prevent her experience from becoming as devastating as that of the doctor in *Der Amokläufer*.

It will be noticed that this account of *Die Frau und die Landschaft* concentrates on the young woman rather than on her male partner, the narrator. That is because, although he shares many of her experiences — especially that nervous longing in sympathy with the world of nature — and is able to give a fuller description of his feelings, the very awareness which is a precondition of his ability to narrate places restraints on his emotional response to the sexual encounter. He twice experiences an ecstatic communion with nature (A,105-6 and 117), but in his intimacy with the young woman he gets caught up in an attempt to dominate her, which is reminiscent of the first encounter between the doctor and the Englishwoman in *Der Amokläufer* and will be discussed, together with that encounter, in a later chapter.

What the older man of *Sommernovellette* experienced in a minor way — that insignificant, even playful beginnings can have momentous consequences — becomes in *Phantastische Nacht* a major event, which revolutionises the life of the central character. The content of the event is a classic example of the eruptive force of man's unconscious, and its psychological starting-point is here elaborated on, serving both as dramatic contrast to what follows and as an explanation of its necessity. The baron begins in a state

31

of what may, in the strictest sense of the term, be called apathy. At the age of thirty-six he has reached an 'innere Trägheit' which distances him from events and leaves him incapable of any strong feelings. Theatrical sensations, famous books, even his own collection of glassware fail to rouse real interest. He registers no jealousy at the marriage of a once loved woman, no sorrow at the death of a once dear friend (A,130-33).

In his lack of feeling the baron has been likened to the hero of Schnitzler's story *Blumen*,[5] but in general he is more reminiscent of the remote, isolated young aesthete of Hofmannsthal's *Märchen der 672. Nacht,* the more so when one considers some of the social factors which have contributed to his present condition. Having inherited considerable wealth even before the age of majority, he has never been faced by the need to earn a living. Since all his wishes have been satisfied without effort, his inner vitality has slackened and atrophied. And an initial tendency to become a mere observer of events has now become a way of life, a habit encouraged by the city of Vienna, so conducive to 'das Spazierengehen, das nichtstuerische Betrachten, das Elegantsein' (A,128).

As with the young hero of Hofmannsthal's *Märchen*, then, external wealth is accompanied by an inner emptiness, a dissatisfaction which represents the first uncertain stirring of his torpid unconscious:

> Was sich damals unbewußt in manchen Augenblicken der Halberkenntnis in mir sehnsüchtig regte: es waren nicht eigentlich Wünsche, sondern nur der Wunsch nach Wünschen, das Verlangen, stärker, unbändiger, ehrgeiziger, unbefriedigter zu begehren, mehr zu leben und vielleicht auch zu leiden. (A,130)

The substance of what follows is a much more radical answer to those uncertain desires than he can have expected, an outburst of passionate intensity which alters the course of his remaining life. Though unexpected in its power, the eruption is, nevertheless, prepared by a stage of vicarious excitement and provocative play. On an unplanned visit to the Prater race-course his initial scornful aloofness from the unrestrained passion of the crowds gives way to envy and even an enjoyment of their excitement at one remove. For, to quote his own account, 'der anderen Erregtheit ist gerade

32

dem Teilnahmslosen das angenehmste Schauspiel' (A,140-41). Similarly, in surveying the women before him, he is not himself sexually aroused, but derives a secondary excitement from attempts to arouse them with his provocative looks (A,141).

When one particular woman proves a match for his provocation, however, he becomes more directly involved and subject to genuine passion, even if the form this takes is not desire, but rather hatred of her cool coquetry, the mirror of his own attitude, and then a malicious sense of triumph at her humiliation. Nevertheless, it is the chief cause of that humiliation, the vulgar behaviour of her husband in his unrestrained enthusiasm for the turf, which leads to the full emergence of the baron's passion. Having sadistically concealed one of the husband's dropped betting slips and drawn the winnings from it, he seeks to appease his conscience by staking the misappropriated money on a certain loser. For Zweig's purposes the remarkable thing is not that the horse wins and so increases the ill-gotten gains, but that the baron becomes passionately involved in the race, impatient for its start, angry at the progress of rival horses, overwhelmed by an unprecedented ecstasy at the success of his own horse (A,157-61). So intense is the passion that it produces physical symptoms, a feverish pulse, perspiration, even a suggestion of dizziness.

On discovering that racing is over for the day, he reacts not with the indifference of one registering a fact, but with the anger of one cheated of further opportunity for intense experience. An irreversible change has taken place within him. He has recovered the ability to feel deeply: 'Auch in mir [. . .] glühte also noch jener geheimnisvolle vulkanische Kern alles Irdischen, der manchmal vorbricht in den wirbelnden Stößen von Begier' (A,165). And the joy it brings cannot be taken away from him. Indeed the inner turmoil is such that it needs some outlet beyond his own narrow individuality; it strains after communality, which attracts him first in the form of those unrestrained pleasures which the civilised gentleman would have repudiated: 'das zog meinen neuen Instinkt magisch an, als empfände ich zum erstenmal im Animalischen, im Triebhaften, im Gemeinen eine Verwandtschaft mit mir selbst' (A,171). This in turn leads to an adventure in an underworld of sensuality and criminality, an encounter with a poor prostitute and her accomplices,[6] in which he is confronted by the memory of the instincts he once indulged in adolescence, but through which he

33

experiences a previously unknown sympathy with these social outcasts. What is important here, however, is that this sympathy is depicted not as a moral force, but as an ungovernable passion:

> [. . .] überkam mich mitten in dem gespannten Empfinden ein ganz weiches, flutendes Mitleid mit diesem erbärmlichen, zertretenen Stück Leben. (A,189)

> Und in diesem Augenblick überkam mich plötzlich — und es war, als ob die innere Gärung alle Dauben in meiner Brust plötzlich sprengte und heiß das Gefühl in mein Blut überliefe — ein so unendliches, ein brüderliches Mitleid mit diesen beiden Menschen. (A,196)[7]

In much the same way as with the doctor in *Der Amokläufer*, the volcanic force of the baron's passions brings him into conflict with the law, the military code, and the etiquette of polite society — to say nothing of the dictates of a not very exacting conscience. It leads him to steal and exploit the proceeds of his theft, to elbow his way brutally through a crowd and snatch a chair away from a lady, to court the company of prostitutes and criminals, and to refrain from handing them over to the officers of the law when this is quite within his power. And when his residual conscience does stir, it proves ineffective. The instinct to rid himself of his first illegally acquired winnings, the manifestation of a 'Sauberkeitsgefühl' instilled into him in childhood (A,155), is thwarted by a second lucky win. His self-recriminations evaporate from lack of conviction. Just as he earlier felt not desires, but the desire for desires, now, conversely, he feels not shame, but only the wish to be ashamed, while deep down he is happy and proud of his foolish deed (A,165).

The eruption of passion occasionally brings with it a characteristic ambivalence of response, a mixture of pleasure and horror (A,106,169,183), but its most persistent concomitant is a loss of conscious control. From the very beginning there has been in the baron's psychology a tendency to abdicate responsibility in the exercise of his rational faculties, to drift and give himself over to relaxing, cradling movements. And this seems to merge into his new experience, as he enjoys the voluptuousness of leaving all to chance or the movement of the crowd (A,170-1) or yielding to the magnetic attraction of an unknown human encounter (A,186). In fact, however, a similar pattern of behaviour has now acquired an entirely different significance. It is no longer a symptom of apathy; it has become rather the symptom of such powerful urges that the conscious self is no longer in command. Accordingly, the baron frequently describes his new state in terms of intoxication (A,169,172,190,204), for it is as though there were some foreign substance at work within him that both created a sense of elation and impaired his ability to control his actions. More particularly, he emphasises how little his will is now able to assert itself. He makes excited movements involuntarily (A,159); he is surprised to find himself shouting fanatically, as though the voice belonged to another (A,160); or he is subject to some impersonal force operating within him (A,150,161,162). But he makes the point most explicitly in describing the scene where he follows the prostitute into the obscurity of the Prater trees:

> Magnetisch stieß es mich nach, ich ging nicht bewußt, sondern strömte gleichsam, von geheimnisvoller Macht gezogen, hinter ihr her. [. . .] Am liebsten hätte ich mich irgendwie losgerissen, . . . aber mein Wille hatte keine Macht mehr über mich. [. . .] Ich konnte nicht mehr zurück und wollte vielleicht gar nicht mehr, und jetzt, wie sie vertraulich sich an mich drückte, faßte ich unwillkürlich ihren Arm [. . .] Die Schwerkraft des Verbrecherischen, die sich nachmittags im Abenteuer auf dem Rennplatze an mich gehangen, riß mich weiter und weiter hinab. (A,188-91)

Although this force appears autonomous, it is not external to him; it is nothing less than his own rejuvenated unconscious.

By contrast with *Der Amokläufer*, the eruption of the unconscious in *Phantastische Nacht* does not end in disaster. To the baron is granted what is denied the young hero of Hofmannsthal's *Märchen*: he is permitted to see the poverty of his earlier life and live. It cannot be said that, having learnt the lesson of his apathy, he mends his ways. Renewal comes more as an unexpected gift; it is the unplanned re-assertion of unconscious energies. But perhaps the most positive aspect of it — beyond its alleged persistence — is its ultimate absorption into his conscious life, which in the concluding pages is no longer overwhelmed by the unconscious, but enhanced by it, endowed with a greater awareness of all life.

The remaining stories of *Amok* do not accord well with the

35

pattern already established. This is particularly true of *Die Mondscheingasse*, where the dominant psychological feature is a battle of the sexes. But in *Brief einer Unbekannten* too, where an eruption of instinctive forces is certainly the starting point, the characteristic quality of the work derives from the single-mindedness of a consciously willed devotion, which must be discussed elsewhere. In *Vierundzwanzig Stunden aus dem Leben einer Frau*, however, placed somewhat inappropriately in the volume *Verwirrung der Gefühle*, Zweig returns to a classic statement of that eruption of the unconscious first laid down in *Der Amokläufer*.[8] Here it is expressed above all in the narrator's assertion that 'eine Frau in manchen Stunden ihres Lebens jenseits ihres Willens und Wissens geheimnisvollen Mächten ausgeliefert sei' (VdG,19), though the fate of the young Polish gambler with whom Mrs C. becomes involved and the vehement arguments of the hotel guests in the narrative frame are proof enough that eruptive passions are not an exclusively female phenomenon.

As in the earlier examples, the author is careful to provide the psychological background which makes the unexpected outburst intelligible. As a woman of forty Mrs C. suffers from a sense of inner emptiness, since the course of nature has robbed her of a meaningful role in life (VdG,32). The husband with whom she shared twenty-three years of her life has died, and her two sons, who have now grown up and left home, no longer need her care. Consequently, when the unconscious forces do erupt in her, they follow channels already worn by the sexual and maternal instincts which now find no outlet. To this extent the events of those remarkable twenty-four hours in her life are more readily understandable than the sudden elopement of Mme Henriette in the narrative frame, the scandal which sparks off the discussion of volcanic experience and provides Mrs C. with the occasion to tell her story. For Mme Henriette has both husband and children who still need her care.

The eruption of unconscious forces in Mrs C. is further prepared, much as it was in *Phantastische Nacht*, by a brief period of vicarious excitement, a sort of voyeurism quite common in Zweig. Where the baron derived a stimulus from the excitement of other race-goers, Mrs C., revisiting the places formerly frequented by her husband, seeks to rouse her emotions by observing the passion of other gamblers in the casino of Monte Carlo. As she remarks to the narrator, 'für den Erlebnislosen ist ja leidenschaftliche Unruhe der anderen noch ein Nervenerlebnis wie Schauspiel oder Musik' (VdG,32).

The emotional intensity which seizes her, however, follows a different direction and has no immediate relation to the passion for gambling. Although she displays remarkable empathy as she observes the young Pole at the roulette-table, it is, above all, the passion of his despair which she shares. When, having lost all, he leaves the casino, she follows him, not so much from curiosity as from fear that something desperate is about to happen. It is the reflex action of a woman confronted by a child in danger (VdG,48). By the following morning, however, a closer personal tie is indicated. Having discovered no other way to save the young man from suicide than to take him to a cheap hotel and spend the night with him, she awakens to a sense of shame which impels her to slip silently away. But then, unable to resist one final look at him, she is struck by 'ein ganz kindliches, ganz knabenhaftes Gesicht' (VdG,64). What she feels is not merely the general satisfaction of having acquired a purpose in life, but a quite specific maternal pride: 'Und ich sah nun [. . .] mit einem mütterlichen Blick auf diesen Schlafenden hin, den ich noch einmal — schmerzvoller als meine eigenen Kinder — in das Leben zurückgeboren hatte' (VdG,65-6). It is as though he had become a substitute child for her;[9] and it comes as no surprise that during the course of this new day, in his excited enjoyment of the Riviera landscape through which they drive and in his gratitude for her act of rescue, he repeatedly strikes her as childlike (VdG,69 and 76).

A more significant change comes over her relations with the young man, however, when the sexual instincts supersede the maternal. Having insisted that he leave the Riviera, with all its dangerous temptations, she is in fact disappointed that he should prepare to obey her so meekly, that he should accept the role of her child, as one might also put it. As she admits to the narrator only with great difficulty and hesitation, she is disappointed that he does not cling to her passionately, that he treats her as a saint and not as a woman (VdG,83). She, for her part, is burning to run away with him, to abandon all for his sake; and he fails to respond appropriately (VdG,84). Subsequently, when it emerges that he has used her gift of money to return to his gambling rather than take the train home, her fury is that of a woman scorned, not — as he mistakenly supposes when he complains that he is not under her tutelage (VdG,97) — that of a parent who has been disobeyed. Watching him at the roulette-table, she notes especially the way in which he caresses the money (VdG,92). In thinking thus she unwittingly reveals that the true cause of her anger is sexual betrayal, the sense that the eruption of her unconscious instinct has not been matched by an equivalent response.

The intensity with which the unconscious erupts in Mrs C.'s life can be gauged by the vehemence of her response when these impulses are thwarted, a vehemence which surprises the reader by its contrast with her calm, tactful manner during the arguments of the narrative frame. Both when the young Pole resists her early attempts to rescue him and when he later offends her womanly self-sacrifice, she reacts with an anger which sometimes verges on madness, as the following succession of nouns may indicate: 'Wut', 'Zorn', 'Manie', 'Raserei' (VdG,58-9), 'rotblickende Wut' (VdG,91), 'Welle von Wut' (VdG,95), 'Zorn' (VdG,96).

The suggestion of madness may also be related to what is again the most insistent feature of the erupting unconscious: the loss of conscious control, which inevitably entails a loss of full responsibility. At times it is a matter of some impersonal force within Mrs C. which impels her to act, whether she will or not: 'Aber dann riß es mich fort, ich mußte ihm nach: ohne daß ich es wollte, schob sich mein Fuß. Es geschah vollkommen unbewußt, ich tat es gar nicht selbst, sondern es geschah mit mir' (VdG,46). At times it is a matter of involuntary acts which she finds herself performing without knowing it, as, for example, when she exchanges her mourning for brighter clothes (VdG,68), or when a groan escapes her at the prospect of losing the young man for good (VdG,85). But essentially, these are all manifestations of the same phenomenon, the emergence of an unconscious force so powerful that it leads a life of its own, independent of or in defiance of the will, not susceptible to rational understanding or even clear perception.

Inevitably Mrs C. experiences great difficulty in applying her mind to the devising of plans appropriate to the success of what she feels impelled to do. And in one important respect she takes action which the reader immediately realises is irrational as well as dangerous to her enterprise. For who in her right mind would advance money to an acknowledged gambler, even on the understanding that he will use it to redeem pawned valuables (VdG,81)? Inevitably also, though her conscience occasionally asserts itself, it soon yields to an affirmation of the course which those unconscious forces have impelled her to take. Returning to her own hotel after the night spent with the young Pole, she ignores the astonishment of the porter. For, as she says to the narrator, 'nichts mehr von Scham und Ärger über das Geschehnis drückte auf meine Sinne, sondern [. . .] ein unvermutet neues Gefühl von der Notwendigkeit meines Daseins durchblutete die erfüllten Adern' (VdG,67-8).

Yielding to these unconscious impulses, moreover, repeatedly brings her into conflict with the social conventions and moral attitudes instilled into her since childhood. It makes it possible for her to listen calmly and without indignation to the story of the young man's crime (VdG,72); it makes her prepared to incur public gossip, to dishonour her own and her children's name (VdG,83); it causes her to be rude, even brutal to a solicitous cousin (VdG,87). What is then remarkable, however, is that, once her womanly pride has been injured by the insults and final rejection of her protégé, she immediately reacts with an intense horror, which is not the considered decision of her social self, but has all the unconscious energy and irrationality of the Freudian super-ego, impelling her to flee the Riviera, return non-stop to her home in England, there to take a bath and wash away from her body not just the dirt of the journey, but everything that seems to cling to her from the passion of that possessed, unworthy young man (VdG,100). The outcome for her is neither the catastrophe of the doctor who ran amuck nor the prolonged elation of the baron in *Phantastische Nacht*, but a nagging sense of guilt which gradually loses its sharpness but remains with her for almost a quarter of a century. For the death-wish which momentarily asserts itself proves in the end less powerful than the instinct for survival.

Vierundzwanzig Stunden aus dem Leben einer Frau is chiefly the story of Mrs C.'s experience. But, as already indicated, the young Pole who is the catalyst in her reaction is himself subject to the force of eruptive passion in another form. At the point in his life when he is set to embark on a sober diplomatic career he is casually introduced to gambling and immediately becomes enthralled by it. There is no need to go into his story in detail, but it is worth noting that the symptoms of his passion do not differ greatly from those of Mrs C.: there is the same inability to exercise rational control (cf. VdG,39); the same indifference to social convention, which in his case leads to crime. Even his temporary rescue by Mrs C., who serves as a mother-figure,[10] does not bring a return to rational calm. He swings rather to the opposite extreme and becomes effusively passionate, even ecstatic in his gratitude (VdG,74,77-9). His emotional instability is such that the nervous reluctance with which he takes the money advanced by his protectress seems only too well-founded. Certainly, it comes as more of a surprise to her than it does to the reader that he is soon to be found back at the roulette-table, unable to resist that 'Raserei des Spiels', now more passionately intent than ever, lost to the world around him, violent and abusive in his rejection of her last desperate bid to save him from his ruinous passion (VdG,91-7). We may leave it to Freud and devoted Freudians to interpret this obsession as a disguised expression of the compulsion to masturbate.[11] It does have a sexual component, as the passage describing the way he caresses the money already suggested. But understood simply as gambling, it is evidence enough of the uncontrollable energy of the erupting unconscious.

Of Zweig's remaining stories only *Leporella* and *Schachnovelle* place a major emphasis on the eruptive force of the unconscious. In *Angst*, where excitement is a crucial ingredient in the heroine's experience, it comes not as an unwilled eruption, but as the desired fulfilment of a more or less conscious need. And it is psychological conflict above all which defines the peculiarity of the work. Although *Der Zwang* often describes its hero acting involuntarily and under some compulsion, it is the conflict between this compulsion and the attempts to assert his own freedom which gives the work its characteristic psychological profile. Even *Verwirrung der Gefühle*, where passion erupts in various forms — the professor's homosexual proclivities, the amorous adventures of his young pupil, and the intellectual enthusiasms of both — is primarily concerned to portray the inner conflicts of its two central characters, as indeed its title suggests.

With *Leporella*, however, Zweig returns to what was arguably his most cherished psychological theme. As Klawiter remarks, the story could well have been grouped together with those of *Amok*.[12] And interestingly, although it first appeared in 1929 in

the volume *Kleine Chronik*, it was written according to the manuscript in 1924,[13] only two years after the publication of *Amok*.
What distinguishes it from the stories of that earlier collection,
however, is its choice of a dull-witted peasant-woman as a central
character. There will be occasion to consider her restricted
mentality later in another context. For the present it is important
to note that the psychological background in this work is not
presented as an explanatory preparation for the eruption that
follows, as though there were some particular receptivity or unfulfilled need. The most that can be asserted is that Crescenz's limited
experience, which does not extend beyond that of domestic servant
and spinster, and her blinkered outlook, especially her avarice,
determine the direction which her passion takes.

In the opening paragraph Zweig places her among the
'unbewußte Kreaturen Gottes' (K,47), by which, presumably, he
means to indicate that she lacks the rational faculties and social
awareness of the characters discussed so far in this chapter. It
might, therefore, be expected that the unconscious forces within
her would assert themselves much more readily. Yet this is not the
case. If events follow a less dramatic course than in those earlier
works, it is not because the volcanic energy is less great; it is rather
because it has to force its way not through a brittle crust, but
through a thick layer of sluggish matter. The author expresses the
idea metaphorically in passages such as the following:

> So begann durch diesen zufälligen Anstoß nun Schicht um
> Schicht ein Ziehen und Bewegen in ihrem innern Erdreich, bis
> endlich, erst klotzhaft und dann immer deutlicher, ein neues
> Gefühl sich ablöste. (K,52)

The whole disastrous chain of events is set in motion by no more
than a trivial coincidence. Having left her Tyrolean village in
search of better pay in the capital city, Crescenz falls into a pattern
of unchanging routine and narrow horizons in the service of a
baron and his hysterical wife, until a census brings to light
unexpected links between her native village and the baron, for
whom, it appears, she has once, many years earlier, prepared a
meal. From the horse-play that follows, which she misconstrues as
a form of courtship, there develops an absolute devotion to the
baron, what the manuscript of the story calls an 'Eruption der
Zugehörigkeit'.[14] It takes the form of a fanatical attention to his

41

every need and then, as an offshoot, what Zweig describes as 'ein vorerst dumpfer, allmählich aber unverhüllt und nackt vorspringender Haß' towards his wife, the woman who lives and sleeps with him, but who seeks to humiliate him (K,53).

Although an undoubted sexual element is indicated in both her devotion and her jealousy — Strelka speaks in terms of an Electracomplex[15] — it finds satisfaction, like much else in her activity, in a surrogate form. Once the baroness has been dispatched to a sanatorium to seek a cure for her overwrought nerves, Crescenz, emotionally and physically neutered by years of spinsterhood, finds her fulfilment in the procuring of girls for the satisfaction of her master's sexual needs, thereby earning her nickname 'Leporella':

> In ihrem eigenen abgerackerten, durch jahrzehntelange Arbeit geschlechtslos gewordenen Körper längst nicht mehr bedrängt, wärmte sie sich wohlig an der kupplerischen Lust, nach ein paar Tagen schon einer zweiten und bald auch der dritten Frau in den Schlafraum nachblinzeln zu können. (K,58)

Vicarious, voyeuristic passion, which for the baron of *Phantastische Nacht* and Mrs C. of *Vierundzwanzig Stunden aus dem Leben einer Frau* was merely a preliminary to more immediate experience, becomes the peak of fulfilment for Crescenz, especially since it satisfies her two complementary needs: to serve the baron and to offend his wife.

Her fanaticism assumes a criminal form, however, only when the baroness returns. Although Crescenz has gained some degree of mental as well as physical agility, this does not extend to the ability to think beyond her immediate concerns. She is so narrowmindedly possessed by the need to serve her lord and master that she gives no thought to the possibility of his wife's return, which comes, therefore, as a bolt from the blue. Her response to the news is again no sudden outburst. Nevertheless, what issues from her sluggish inner stirrings — a sinister hint to the baron that something could be done about his (and her) difficulty — is described as a violent discharge (K,61). Since the suggestion cannot immediately be translated into action, her pent-up fury finds a surrogate outlet in her domestic activities, as she pounds the meat and scrubs the pots and pans (K,63). But once the baron has taken his leave, to seek a similar surrogate release for his anger in hunting, the way is clear for Crescenz to express her feelings in a more direct manner, by killing the baroness. So, at least, we are led to assume. For Zweig does not describe the act, leaving us to deduce the truth from the news of the baroness's 'suicide' and our knowledge of Crescenz's mentality. As someone whose frustrations could only be vented in an act of physical violence, she has been likened to Hauptmann's Bahnwärter Thiel.[16] Despite the similarity — and one might add that she too reverts to a strange mental calm after the deed — it is important to note that Crescenz lacks that powerful element of guilt and inner conflict which characterises Hauptmann's hero and that her mental calm at the end is a matter of moral indifference rather than morbid apathy.

Mention has been made of her avarice as well as her (obliquely expressed) sexual insticts. What remains to be explored is an unusual link between the two which Zweig seems to imply. Having repeatedly stressed her blinkered interest in the accumulation of money and having once remarked on the tenderness with which she handles the banknotes (K,49), he introduces the word 'Habgier' in what seems initially to be a very different context. He uses it first to describe the tenacity with which she seizes hold of her new-found devotion to the baron, a devotion which immediately displaces her earlier restricted concerns: 'Und mit jener bäuerischen Habgier, die das einmal Ergriffene nie mehr aus den harten Händen läßt, zog sie dieses neue Element tief hinein unter die Haut bis in die verworrene Triebwelt ihrer stumpfen Sinne' (K,53). Later he takes up the same notion to explain the intensity of the hatred and sexual jealousy with which she greets the unexpected return of the baroness from the sanatorium: 'Ihr habgieriges Gefühl empfand sich durch diese Rückkehr widerrechtlich bestohlen' (K,62). In the absence of explicit comment it is difficult to know whether Crescenz's sexual jealousy is to be regarded as a transformation of her earlier avarice or, conversely, whether the avarice is a displaced form of sexual gratification. Possessiveness is common to both. And unless one adopts a Freudian approach *a priori*, only the passion which erupts in the later, more clearly sexual context may be said to indicate that the sexual element is the original driving force.[17]

Zweig's last story, *Schachnovelle*, has a much greater psychological complexity, not only because it presents two main characters, but also because the more important of these, Dr B., embodies three interrelated psychological concerns: sensory deprivation, inner conflict (to which we shall return later), and the erupting unconscious, which is ultimately the decisive issue in both the inset narrative and the frame.

It has been argued that the author's chief aim here is to demonstrate the effects of brainwashing,[18] a view which may be accepted only to the extent that the emphasis is placed firmly on the word 'effects'. For the isolation from virtually all human contact and sensory stimulus which Dr B. endures at the hands of his Nazi tormentors serves as the psychological starting point in much the same way as Mrs C.'s widowhood in *Vierundzwangzig Stunden aus dem Leben einer Frau*. The main differences lie in the severity of the deprivation, in the fact that its causes are anything but natural, and in the prominence given to unfulfilled sensory rather than instinctive needs. The lack of new stimulation for sight and hearing affects after all that area of mental life which would normally form a relation between the external world and the ego, the conscious part of the self. Nevertheless, in Zweig's presentation at least, sensory stimulus appears to be more of an instinctive need, akin to hunger. Hence Dr B.'s theft of the book which turns out to be a chess manual, though requiring considerable conscious effort, is governed above all by a compelling appetite (S,72).

Important as this instinctive attempt to feed his starved senses is, it does not yet represent the characteristic eruption of the unconscious. The excitement caused by his new possession can be channelled into the rational acquisition of chess techniques and a mental discipline designed to counteract the psychological torture of his oppressors. But the excitement wanes once he has learnt by heart all the games of the masters reproduced in the manual. It is not simply that the element of novelty and surprise has gone, as it has long since in his physical surroundings; it is also the case that he has exhausted the potential of what for characters in some of the earlier works served only as a preliminary stage of vicarious excitement. The problem for him is how to progress beyond his role as an observer of other men's confrontations (S,87), which demands some exercise of his mental powers, but 'ohne jeden Einsatz von Erregung' (S,86). The use of the word 'Einsatz' to describe the personal involvement he so misses is instructive. In recalling the world of gambling, it reminds us that it was through observing the passion of others who had placed their bets that the baron of *Phantastische Nacht* and Mrs C. themselves encountered a passion strong enough to impel them to stake their own public standing. For Dr B. the way forward — a no less dangerous way — is not opened up by fate or chance. It is a course of action consciously adopted, though still very much governed by his enforced isolation: he decides to play games of chess against himself.

It will be necessary to discuss the inner conflicts to which this leads in a later chapter. For the present it is important only to underline that this new personal involvement quickly results in an outburst of passionate intensity, which is beyond his powers to resist and is concentrated entirely on chess. While much of the vocabulary Zweig employs to express the intensity is familiar from earlier works, some introduces a more powerful suggestion of mental and even physical pathology. He speaks, for example, of 'gefährliche Erregtheit', 'fast manische Erregung' (S,88), 'eine Besessenheit', 'ein Spielzwang, eine Manie, eine frenetische Wut' (S,89), 'fiebrige Ungeduld' (S,90), 'eine Schachvergiftung', 'diese monomanische Besessenheit' (S,91). The crisis of what medical opinion later diagnoses as 'eine akute Irritation der Nerven' (S,96) lies so far beyond the reach of Dr B.'s conscious apprehension that he has to rely on the report of other people to know that it involves a violent assault on one of his warders, whom he confuses with an imaginary chess opponent.

That brings us to a rather special ingredient in the eruption of his unconscious. Although he is not very explicit on the point, it emerges quite forcibly that the games of chess he plays against himself do more than fill an intellectual vacuum. They serve a much more primitive psychological need. In his most revealing comment he depicts himself as 'ein Mensch, der seine aufgehäufte Wut längst gegen irgendetwas entladen wollte'. He then continues: 'Und da ich nichts anderes hatte als dies unsinnige Spiel gegen mich selbst, fuhr meine Wut, meine Rachelust fanatisch in dieses Spiel hinein' (S,88). His feelings for the Nazis have previously found an outlet in appropriate action, but his imprisonment has robbed him of all such opportunity. If, in the case of Mrs C., it was the sexual and maternal instincts that were frustrated, with Dr B. it is more a matter of the aggressive instinct. But, as with

45

her, the eruption that follows is the more violent for the frustration; and it is directed first against himself and then against his warder.

This psychological crisis, the climax of the inset narrative, ends in hospital treatment and then in his expulsion from Nazi-dominated Austria. But it is repeated in the narrative frame during the games of chess which Dr B. plays on board the ship taking him into exile. And not unnaturally, it is accompanied by many of the same symptoms as before, especially an insatiable thirst and a distracted pacing up and down, which unconsciously restricts itself to the dimensions of the room where he was formerly imprisoned (S,91,107,111). Since his first nervous collapse he has been warned not to play chess again. When he does nevertheless become involved, it is the result of an involuntary intervention in a game between the chess champion, Czentovic, and a group of amateurs, a reflex action which, in the author's very formulation, is reminiscent of the way in which Mrs C. first goes to the aid of the suicidal Polish gambler in *Vierundzwanzig Stunden aus dem Leben einer Frau*. It is described as 'eine reine Instinkthandlung, [. . .] ein impulsiver Zugriff, wie man, ohne zu überlegen, ein Kind faßt, das sich über ein Geländer beugt' (S,100). Matters only become dangerous when he has been persuaded to engage in a second private encounter with Czentovic, against both his own better judgement and the advice of the narrator, who has seen the warning signs of that passionate 'Spielfieber'. As in his earlier imprisonment, there is an external provocation, the malicious delaying tactics of his opponent. They lead not merely to uncivil behaviour and unnatural excitement, but to passionate hatred, directed now at someone who is conceived of as a real enemy (cf. especially S,110-11). Dr B.'s need to triumph becomes so intense that his imagination advances far ahead of the real game; it is as though he had forgotten his immediate opponent 'in dieser kalten Form des Wahnsinns, der sich plötzlich in irgendeiner Heftigkeit entladen konnte' (S,114). This explosion does indeed occur when he utters a victorious cry of 'check' which bears no relation to the realities of the game in front of him.

As will be expected from earlier parallels, as will perhaps be evident from some of the passages quoted more recently, Zweig is concerned to present the operation of a psychological force which is independent of and often more powerful than the conscious self.

It may express itself in the guise of an irresistible compulsion, of what Dr B. calls 'eine Besessenheit, deren ich mich nicht erwehren konnte' (S,89), or as involuntary acts such as his first intervention and his later impatient but unconscious drumming on the table (S,112). It may be experienced as the activity of some external power or even another person. For, once he has embarked on a game in his solitary confinement, he is overtaken by a wild force, which causes him to run to and fro with clenched fists, and he hears his own voice call out 'check' or 'mate' as though it belonged to someone else. Or, finally, it may continue to function in its own way, irrespective of whether his senses are feeding his brain with information about the external world. That is why, in his imprisonment, he sometimes wakes up to find that he has been continuing to play chess unconsciously in his sleep (S,89) and why, in his final game against Czentovic, he becomes caught up in an imaginary game, from which he has to be roused like a sleepwalker (S,116).

This final turn of events means that, unlike his earlier counterparts, Dr B. does not in the end live out the full consequences of the passion that erupts from within. He is held back at the last moment by a solicitous narrator, through whose kindly admonitions he is able to recover the full awareness and conscious control that are needed for a dignified apology and a renunciation of chess for good.[19]

3

Single-Mindedness

It was one of the features of the man who ran amuck that he was driven straight on, looking neither to the right nor to the left (A,49). Similarly, the passion which erupted in the life of Dr B. was described as a 'monomanische Besessenheit', since it was focussed entirely on the game of chess (S,84). In a later chapter we shall have to consider characters like Jakob Mendel and Czentovic, whose peculiarity is a highly-developed but one-sided mental ability. The single-mindedness with which we are here concerned, however, is to be distinguished from both of these psychological types. It differs from the former in its emphasis on the conscious will at the expense of uncontrollable unconscious forces and from the latter in the primacy given to zealous commitment rather than mental skill. It appears at its grandest in *Brief einer Unbekannten*, in a form which is well characterised by the title of an American review of the English translation: 'Unwavering Devotion';[1] but it also appears, less romantically, in the all-sustaining enthusiasm of the art-collector in *Die unsichtbare Sammlung*.

In *Brief einer Unbekannten* Zweig again provides insight into the state of mind and social background of his nameless heroine in order to make her devotion understandable. In the first place, there is about her home surroundings, if not outright poverty, then at least a social and cultural limitation, which is more acute than that experienced by the otherwise similar heroine of the earlier story, *Die Liebe der Erika Ewald*,[2] and which makes her immediately susceptible to the attractions of someone who has a servant at his disposal, displays elegant manners, and is surrounded by *objets d'art* and leather-bound books (A,216-18). It is by no means the least important factor in her devotion to the young writer that she perceives in him a means of escape, if only vicariously, into a nobler, brighter sphere. In the second place, there is an element of emotional deprivation. The heroine has grown up in obscurity, in an apartment with no name-plate on the door and no visitors (A,214); her father has long been dead, and her mother, in her 'Pensionistenängstlichkeit', is a stranger to her (A,223). It may even be that she is unconsciously seeking a substitute father. For before she has met their new neighbour, the young writer, in person, she pictures him as some kindly but reverend old man (A,218). Whether or not this may be regarded as a classic case of the Electra-complex,[3] it is clear that the young man fills an emotional void in her life.

An additional factor, however, is the heroine's age. She is only thirteen at the time when the young writer comes into her life. Yet although there are traces of those adolescent problems presented in *Erstes Erlebnis* — a certain naiveté in sexual matters, some emotional confusion — the decisive quality of her response is a fanatical adherence to her chosen object, such as will be repeated in the idolisation of the actor Peter Sturz by two teenage girls in the posthumously published story *Die spät bezahlte Schuld*,[4] such also as would be unlikely in a woman of greater maturity. From the first arrival of their new neighbour she fastens her attention on him 'mit der ganzen bohrenden Beharrlichkeit einer Dreizehnjährigen' (A,220) and then never wavers from her slavish devotion for the remaining fifteen or sixteen years of her life (cf. A,222).

The death-bed letter which she writes to her unknowing lover is a catalogue of this devotion: from her immature reverence for every object he handles to her later insatiable reading of every book he writes, from the hours of waiting outside his door or window to the rejection of an advantageous marriage to a kindly and generous man. And the hardships and humiliations she endures in this single-minded devotion stand in sharp contrast to the comfortable life of her lover and his many amorous adventures.

This single-mindedness does not of course mean that there are not moments of adolescent shyness which make her run away from the encounter she so much desires (cf. A,225,235). Nor does it preclude some change in the acknowledged content of her feelings. To begin with there is allegedly a sexual innocence in her response, a lack of sensuality in her first wish to see him and cling to him (A,229), though this does not prevent an early awareness of some erotic element in his first look, 'diesen umfangenden, an Dich ziehenden, diesen umhüllenden und doch zugleich entkleidenden Blick' (A,221). Before long, however, as her body begins to develop, she herself begins to perceive the sexual content of her feelings: her passion becomes 'frauenhafter'; her sole thought is to give herself to him physically (A,223); and when she sees him in the company of another woman, she feels not only hostility, but envy of their bodily intimacy, a sure sign of her own adulthood (A,235-6). Yet the undoubted shift towards sexuality marks only an enrichment of her devotion and in no way affects its direction or tenacity.

With the birth of their child, on the other hand, it might appear that the direction of her devotion changes, since her love for the man becomes less passionate and painful, as she surrenders herself to this new life which needs her and will be all hers to hug and kiss (cf. A,250). In fact, however, the son functions as a reincarnated lover; and the sacrifices she makes for him — including a form of high-class prostitution — are not distinguished in her mind from sacrifices made for the father. As she puts it in her letter, 'Du verachtest mich nicht, ich weiß, Du verstehst alles und wirst noch verstehen, daß ich es nur für Dich getan, für Dein anderes Ich, für Dein Kind' (A,252).[5] The single-mindedness of her devotion is in no way impaired; and even the sexual component is not entirely abandoned.

Unwavering loyalty of this magnitude presupposes strong feelings. Nevertheless, although there are moments when she is subject to ungovernable unconscious impulses, the overriding impression given is of a conscious determination, expressed above all in the frequency with which she uses the noun 'Wille' and the cognate verb 'wollen'. The following are some of the outstanding examples:

> Aber in mir wuchs ein eiserner Wille. Mein ganzes Denken und Trachten war in eine Richtung gespannt: zurück nach Wien, zurück zu Dir. Und ich erzwang meinen Willen, so unsinnig, so unbegreiflich er den andern scheinen mochte. (A,233-4)

Nur Dich einmal sehen, nur einmal Dir begegnen, das war
mein einziger Wille, [. . .] ich wollte Dir ja begegnen, ich
suchte Dich, ich wollte von Dir erkannt sein nach all den
sehnsüchtig verdämmerten Jahren, wollte von Dir beachtet,
wollte von Dir geliebt sein. (A,235)

Aber ich wollte mich nicht binden, ich wollte Dir frei sein in
jeder Stunde. (A,253)

On several occasions, moreover, it is necessary for her to exercise
great conscious control over impulses which run counter to the
demands of her devotion. She twice has to steel her will to combat
the involuntary urge to run away from a direct confrontation with
the object of her love (A,235,236). And at their last meeting, when
he again fails to recognise her, it costs her a considerable effort of
will to fight off a wild desire to reveal her identity (A,261-2), which
would threaten the integrity of her devotion, the pride she feels in
what she has single-mindedly and single-handedly achieved.

It may be open to argument whether shame, as a socially
inculcated phenomenon, belongs to the conscious or unconscious
part of the self.[6] But conscious or unconscious in origin, it is
characteristic of the shame which the heroine of *Brief einer
Unbekannten* feels from time to time that it is overcome, whether
immediately or in retrospect, by the exercise of her will or the
conscious affirmation of whatever her devotion leads her to do.
Typically, on the first night she spends with her lover she consciously suppresses the hesitation of her virginal modesty in order
to preserve the secret of her love and protect him from the possible
shock of realisation (A,242). In discussing this central aspect of the
heroine's life Martha Gschiel makes a useful but untranslatable
distinction between 'eine unselige Leidenschaft', which does not
apply to the young woman (though it might be an apt description
of the doctor's experience in *Der Amokläufer*), and 'ein seliges
Leiden', which does provide a neat summary of her story in its
combination of joy and sorrow.[7] The only proviso it is necessary
to make is that 'Leiden' is to be understood as pain or sorrow and
not as passivity. For it is her active pursuit of a course which is
both thrilling and grievous that endows this woman with her
special character.

By comparison, the single-mindedness at the heart of *Die
unsichtbare Sammlung*, which first appeared in 1927, operates on

a much smaller scale and is much less costly to the central character. The object of devotion in this case is an invaluable collection of etchings and prints which the 'Forst- und Ökonomierat a.D.' has gradually built up over the years and which he shows to the visiting art-dealer with the pride and enthusiasm of a child — or rather thinks he shows, for the collection has had to be sold off by the members of his family in order to make ends meet, while he, in the blindness that has overtaken him, remains unaware of the truth.

In his own way the collector too has made conscious personal sacrifices for the sake of his ruling passion. As he tells his visitor with some satisfaction: 'in sechzig Jahren kein Bier, kein Wein, kein Tabak, keine Reise, kein Theater, kein Buch, nur immer gespart und gespart für diese Blätter' (K,85). And now in his blindness he seems deliberately to exclude other matters from consideration and is interested only to hear his daughter read from the newspapers about the auction of art-works (K,80). If his undoubted singleness of purpose appears less heroic or noble than that of the young woman in *Brief einer Unbekannten*, it is not merely because its cost to him is smaller, but because it has none of her selflessness. He makes sacrifices for *his* collection, but, as we shall see later, fails to note the sacrifices which others are forced to make.

4

Inner Conflicts

In both *Der Amokläufer*, where the doctor becomes subject to uncontrollable unconscious forces, and *Brief einer Unbekannten*, where the heroine's conscious will is the dominant force, a remarkable linearity of action ensues, which brushes aside all opposition. In many of Zweig's stories, however, it is the very opposition of mental forces which is the chief concern, even though the nature of these forces may vary from work to work. The title of the collection in which two of the works concerned appear, *Verwirrung der Gefühle*, is clearly intended to convey something of that inner struggle. But its Kleistian overtones are probably more appropriate to some of the emotional uncertainties already encountered in *Erstes Erlebnis*. Here it is a matter of more radical psychological tension, which can sometimes lead to the very edge of madness.

Angst was first published in 1920, but was written in 1913 and so belongs more to the period of *Erstes Erlebnis*.[1] Since it is in no way concerned with the problems of adolescent sexuality, however, it could hardly find a place in that collection. In its presentation of the confused responses of a married heroine who has taken a lover in order to seek some new stimulus it does follow on from the portrait of Edgar's mother in *Brennendes Geheimnis*; but in its description of her early emotional inertia it is more reminiscent of the portrait of the baron at the beginning of *Phantastische Nacht*. Irene's marriage, however, is by no means as unequivocally boring as that of Edgar's mother. The worst that can be said of it is that it offers an unchallenging as well as unchallenged happiness, 'acht Jahre stillpendelnden Glücks', as the narrator describes it at one point (K,137-8). It is this above all which provokes the need for adventure, yet also represents an attractive haven from all the unwanted consequences of adventure — and thereby paves the way for the happy solution. For, unlike *Phantastische Nacht, Angst* is not the story of unconscious forces which erupt out of such emotional lethargy, but the account of the psychological conflicts that ensue once the heroine has embarked on her adventurous course. Her adulterous love-affair is already established when the work opens and constitutes only one element in the inner struggle that follows, a struggle that comes to take on different, though interrelated forms.

It expresses itself, first, as a conflict between the desire for adventure and the desire for bourgeois security, one of several points at which Zweig seems indebted to Schnitzler's *Die Toten schweigen*.[2] This is a conflict of desires and is not to be confused with a conflict between inclination and duty.[3] The moral aspect of Irene's behaviour seems to receive little consideration. Nor is it to be confused with the question of whether she is more attracted to her lover than to her husband. When the story opens, the lover has already lost something of his novelty, and the affair has been accommodated in the regularity of her bourgeois life, so that 'das Abenteuer schien ihr bald so banal wie der erlaubte Genuß' (K,133). Still she seeks some form of adventure and is prepared to look for it elsewhere, in the pleasure of walking confidently through the streets with the eyes of other men on her (K,134-5). Even the fear which plays such a prominent part in her anguish can also be part of the adventurous excitement, as Zweig himself knew from his own sexual escapades.[4] It has been argued indeed that for Irene 'fear is itself an erotic experience'.[5] Such fear was already there at the beginning of her affair, in her lover's covetous look: 'Sie erschrak und fühlte gleichzeitig die Wollust aller Angst' (K,131-2). And it is still there when the affair has lost its initial stimulus, in her encounters with the supposed blackmailer, which she at one point welcomes because the fear it engenders is at least a genuine feeling, as powerful and stimulating as anything she has recently experienced (K,133).[6] Yet matters are rarely simple in Irene's mind. Fear is more often an extremely disturbing experience and can itself call into question the worth of her adventure. Accordingly, part of her response to the lack of stimulation she finds in her affair is to weigh the sense of adventure against the price she has to pay, the risks she has to take. Since she has been spoilt by nature and upbringing, she is ready to sacrifice her lover for peace of mind and bourgeois comfort (K,133). And when only a short time afterwards she is oppressed by the prospect of a never-ending threat from blackmail, it is not because it inhibits her search for adventure, but rather because now it threatens 'das äußerlich würdevolle Gebäude ihres häuslichen Glückes' (K,137).

In the conflict between her desire for adventure and her desire for a calm, bourgeois security fear performs an ambiguous role, since danger is after all a part of adventure. Elsewhere, however, fear is more clearly negative, especially so when it functions as the opponent of the heroine's desire for sensual pleasure and uninhibited freedom in what may be seen as the second form which her inner conflict takes. After enjoying a sense of bodily freedom in her supple gait as she walks through the open streets and after relishing the sensual delight of her own beauty (K,134-5), Irene is so stunned by a further encounter with the blackmailer that she imposes a kind of house-arrest on herself. More properly, it is her fear which creates its own prison — note the reference to 'diese unsichtbaren Gitterstäbe von Grauen' (K,139) — from which she then seeks an escape at a social gathering, where she can enjoy herself free from care, give herself over to the sensual excitement of the dance and thereby avoid the need to think about the causes of her fear. She is cut short in her wild intoxication by her husband, whose presence inhibits her dancing and who, from now on, appears as a further source of threat, so that she feels hemmed in on two sides (K,140-1). The full significance of this conflict, however, is best seen in Irene's changing attitudes to nakedness, which is an expression at once of the sensual delight in her own body, of an abandonment of social convention, and of the undisguised assertion of her selfhood. As she dances, therefore, she experiences an unconscious desire to tear off her clothes. Although she does not in fact yield to the desire, her response to her husband's look is an involuntary movement to cover her breast (K,141). In the dream she has that night — a condensed form of this conflict between sensual abandonment and fear — the latter assumes the form of a pursuit by the blackmailer, who gradually tears off her clothes and exposes her to the mockery of onlookers (K,142-3).[7] Zweig has depicted in her a continuing battle between

55

the instinct to be herself and seek uninhibited pleasure and a fear of letting her true self be seen, a sense of shame which may be initiated by the external threat from a supposed blackmailer, but has a momentum of its own, magnifying that threat and turning her kindly husband into an equally frightening figure.

Whether experienced positively or negatively (the more frequent case), fear operates throughout the story as an almost entirely instinctive force, beyond the control of the heroine's conscious self. Indeed all the inner conflicts so far considered take place between opposing desires or impulses. On the other hand, the third form which her inner conflict takes is that of a struggle between her instinctive fear and the best efforts of her rational powers. As usual with instinctive forces in Zweig, the fear manifests itself in a loss of awareness and in the involuntary nature of her acts; or else it makes itself felt as a power independent of her will, almost external to her. But perhaps its more memorable aspect in *Angst* is the way in which it expresses itself physically: in sensations of heat and cold, for instance, in a dizziness, a trembling, or a bodily paralysis, in an increased pulse-rate or an inability to breathe. In its conflict with Irene's rational faculties fear frustrates not so much her desire for adventure or sensual delight as her desire for bourgeois security, which has conscripted the conscious mind in its service. Even when the story opens her usual ability to parade a succession of well-thought-out lies in explanation of her absence is frustrated by the power of her fear, which has made her neglect such preparation and forced her into clumsy improvisation (K,129). And despite her subsequent, calmly considered determination to preserve her composure in any further encounter with the blackmailer, to deny everything and turn the tables on her accuser, the actual meeting proves different, with Irene in the uncontrollable grip of her fear (K,135). The more she becomes weakened by this unequal struggle, the more it becomes a matter of seeking to preserve face, to appear cheerful at home and at the same time conceal the effort that this 'nutzlose Selbstvergewaltigung' (K,152) takes. The conflict is never resolved in the sense that either her rational faculties or the unconscious forces of fear win an outright victory. All that happens is that, when the impulse to confess her guilt becomes too powerful to be resisted by any force, the basis of the conflict is removed.

That brings us to the fourth form which Irene's inner conflict assumes: a conflict between the urge to confess and the fear of speaking out. Although her sense of shame is naturally strongest in front of her husband, he also offers the best hope of forgiveness and restoration. It is her realisation of this which makes the conflict possible and, incidentally, distinguishes her from the heroine of Schnitzler's *Die Toten schweigen*, whose final confession comes quite unexpectedly and against all her wishes. The anguished cry for help which rouses Irene from the dream mentioned earlier may cause her to fear that she has betrayed herself in her sleep, but when she feels the gentle caresses of her husband on her naked arms, she is seized by the desire to fling herself on his firm body and cling to him until all is confessed and forgiven. Under the bright light, however, shame and fear gain the upper hand and she simply makes excuses (K,144-5). Later, when her husband's understanding treatment of a misdemeanour by their daughter opens up the way for her own confession, the urge to confess — shown above all in her impassioned embrace of the daughter who admits her guilt — has again to contend with the sense of shame, before him more than before anyone else (K,154-6). Finally, when her husband inquires about her missing engagement ring, an inner expression of relief that the ordeal of secrecy will soon be over is immediately opposed by an instinct which drives her to summon all her conscious powers for a last prevarication (K,161).

In the second of these incidents Irene speaks of the shame that inhibits confession in terms of embarrassment at undressing in front of others (K,155) and thereby recalls that contradictory attitude to her own nakedness already discussed. Yet, while it is not difficult to see a similar shame at exposure in both confession and bodily nakedness, it would be wrong to imply a converse parallel between Irene's urge to take off her clothes and her impulse to confess. For the former is an expression of selfhood, the latter, despite its association with physical caresses, an admission of guilt by the self and an acceptance of responsibility to others and public standards. Indeed, without being entirely consistent in the matter, Zweig suggests that it is not only shame but also injured self-consciousness which is at work in preventing her confession. Although one occasion finds her shame stronger because of her husband's considerateness rather than his inquisitorial manner (K,152), other passages seem to imply an element of resistance to superior force. At one point, for example, she is reminded of what he once said about a judge's ability to disarm a lying criminal and of his own psychological passion, which is so suited to his need to get to the bottom of legal cases, but which she now finds personally menacing (K,147). And later, after the episode of the daughter's misdemeanour, it is his very eagerness to receive her confession which seems an obstacle to the making of it (K,157). Consequently, one is left to wonder whether there is not something within her which resists this implied submission to his male authority.

Be that as it may, the struggle between the desire to confess and the instinct to hold back is both mentally and physically debilitating. And so there develops what might be considered the third element in this particular form of the conflict: the impulse to avoid either confession or prevarication, to escape, to be relieved of the necessity for any action. Even as Irene finds herself incapable of confessing after her husband's behaviour towards their miscreant daughter, we also read, as the final statement of this section: 'Und im geheimsten Wunsch ersehnte sie schon, was sie bislang gefürchtet, den erlösenden Blitz: die Entdeckung' (K,157). The outcome might be the same as if she had confessed, but the important difference for her state of mind is that it would have been taken out of her hands. Later, having failed to confess after the discovery of her absent ring and then having exhausted herself in a kind of challenge to fate, she wanders aimlessly through the open streets, almost willing an accident as a means of avoiding the need to decide and enjoying the pleasure of not having to think or perceive clearly (K,162). Following a brief flirtation with the idea of an escape into the world of nature, away from the society she knows (K,165), it comes as no surprise that suicide is her next and last proposed step. For death would be, if not a solution to the problem, then at least a conclusive means of avoiding it, together with the resultant inner tensions.

After all these preliminaries the dénouement of *Angst* comes as something of a disappointment. It is not that one cannot accept the ultimate irresistibility of Irene's urge to confess. Her husband's confession of his guilt and of the part played by the blackmailer he hired has both removed the most urgent threat and brought him down from a position of inhibiting authority. And her inclination to seek refuge from a lingering sense of bitterness and shame in the unconsciousness of sleep establishes an understandable continuity with her former self. The difficulty lies rather in her new sense of happiness in her domestic life and the assertion that any pain she feels is like that of a wound that is healing for ever (K,170). Even if her new perception of a similarity between her son's voice and that of his father might be held to indicate some transference of perhaps sexual feeling from the latter to the former — much as the heroine of *Brief einer Unbekannten* regards her son as a reincarnated lover — can one be assured that her need for adventure and sensual abandonment has finally been laid to rest?[8] In restoring both the marriage and social convention has not Zweig, as one reviewer put it, 'compromised with his material; [. . .] sentimentalised the implications'?[9]

Der Zwang was also first published in 1920, but was written, according to the manuscript, in 1918.[10] Unlike *Angst* it has an undeniable moral dimension; it deals with the question of whether one should take up arms or not, whether one's commitment to mankind as a whole should take precedence over patriotic duty. But this moral problem does not coincide with the central psychological conflict. Ferdinand's reason and moral sensibility have already settled the former in favour of pacifism and international human brotherhood. Yet this does not bring mental peace; it does not prevent him from feeling an irresistible compulsion to obey the call to return from his Swiss exile and face the prospect of military service. Perhaps, then, the psychological issue is whether the individual can maintain the freedom of his moral will against the collective force of state authority. For much of the time Ferdinand does indeed speak in these terms: 'Es ist ein ungleicher Kampf', he says, 'Man kann nicht an wider eine Maschine' (VdG[2],232). Objectively, however, the German military authorities[11] have little real power in neutral Switzerland, as he himself is obliged to admit (cf. VdG[2],235). They pose much less of a threat to the will than the blackmailer of *Angst* for all that she is acting a part. And when, at the end of *Der Zwang*, the hero remains in Switzerland in *de facto* defiance of the summons, it is not because the power of the German authorities is now objectively diminished in any way, nor because his will is stronger than it was at the beginning; it is not the victory of one man's free will over an anonymous collective force.

No, the compulsion at the heart of *Der Zwang*, which enters into conflict with the hero's conscious will, is essentially one that comes from within him. That is why he can say at one point that what he fears is not 'them' so much as himself (VdG[2],231). This power, moreover, possesses many of the symptoms already noted in connection with the unconscious: it results in involuntary actions;[12] it is experienced as the independent functioning of parts of his body;[13] or it expresses itself as some impersonal entity directing what he does.[14] When Ferdinand asserts that it is not he himself who is acting in submission to the authorities, it is not an idle manner of speaking; it is the assessment by his conscious self of a force which seems dissociated from that self, although in fact it originates within the same mind.

Nevertheless, this inner compulsion must be distinguished clearly from those other manifestations of the unconscious discussed earlier; it lacks their tendency to erupt suddenly and with passionate intensity and seems far removed from either the sexual or the aggressive instincts. Although the compulsion may drive Ferdinand to act against his humanitarian and pacifist convictions, it is not because, even unconsciously, he harbours any desire to fight and conquer. Nor is it a matter of simple fear. For its immediate consequence would be an exposure to danger and death. It can best be understood, rather, as the converse of his conscious aims, which require the ability and readiness to confront reality, to make decisions on the basis of rational and moral judgement and then to convert these decisions into appropriate action. The impulse that repeatedly threatens these aims is nothing less than the impulse to run away from responsibility with all its many uncomfortable demands. And it remains in force even when it enlists the support of genuine considerations of human solidarity (cf. VdG[2],224) as well as more obvious rationalisation. Ferdinand himself is of course unaware of its nature; his wife has only occasional flashes of insight; and the author refrains from explicit analysis. Since therefore it is essentially left to the creative co-operation of the reader to perceive and interpret the impulse, some exposition of the factors which lead to this interpretation may be helpful.

Ferdinand has, first, a marked tendency to avoid confrontation with the harshness of reality, even to the extent of seeking to close his mind to an awareness of its unpleasantness. It is not just that he has preferred to set a physical distance between himself and his native country rather than engage in a political struggle for his convictions there. Once his Swiss refuge has been disturbed by a letter from the military authorities, his readiness to return (that is, to submit) is accompanied by attempts to avoid the moral issues and an impatience with his wife for insisting on them. 'Mache mir's nicht schwer. [. . .] Drüben wird mir leichter sein' (VdG^2,247) and 'Warum machst du mir es so schwer, wenn es doch sein muß?' (VdG^2,256) are typical responses. At times he yearns for a kind of mental oblivion, 'Absturz und Vergessenheit' (VdG^2,251). And if the logical conclusion of that is suicide,[15] it too appears on his agenda, conceived of as a plunge into 'den großen Frieden' (VdG^2,254) and, one might add — quoting the similar suicidal thoughts of Erika Ewald — as an escape 'fern von allen Wirklichkeiten'.[16]

Secondly, the mental energies, both affective and intellectual, which might be allied to his moral awareness, are never allowed to bear their proper fruit. His anger at the wretched social conditions of his homeland finds no outlet in public protest, but issues only in impotent gestures: 'mit geballten Fäusten schlich er umher und fühlte, wie er böse und gehässig wurde, sich selbst widerwärtig in seiner ohnmächtigen Wut' (VdG^2,227).[17] And it need hardly be stressed that this is the cause of a further psychological conflict. His failure to meet the demands of his moral judgement is a source of shame, guilt and an anger often turned in on himself.[18] As to his rational faculties, they tend to become exhausted in imaginary encounters and fail to function in live situations. It is made clear that he has a reasoned answer to the letter from the military authorities already worked out in expectation of its receipt. But he never makes use of it. And when he goes to the German consulate in compliance with the letter, he rehearses in his mind an elaborate scenario, which he finds most satisfying and believes will lead to victory over officialdom. Yet the actual interview finds him weak and submissive. We shall not go far wrong in interpreting Ferdinand's imaginary resistance as yet another means of evading the real issue. In a rare moment of insight, commenting on his prepared reply, he confesses to his wife: 'Nie war ich sicher. Alles war Lüge, ein Verstecken vor meiner Angst. Ich habe mich berauscht mit diesen Worten' (VdG^2,230-1).

A third element in Ferdinand's avoidance of confrontation is his distortion of the power-relation between himself and the German authorities. It may be that at home there was little that he could do

61

as an individual against the forces of militarism, but in Switzerland, as indicated earlier, the German authorities have no real power to impose their orders on him. As it turns out, they have little need to. Having avoided an open engagement with the problem, he remains haunted by it, inwardly enmeshed in it, and plagued by a sense of guilt. Since the problem has not gone away, he resorts, no doubt unconsciously, to another method of preventing an engagement: he pronounces the contest unfair and retires. More precisely, using a device which is reminiscent of those described in Adler's individual psychology as mechanisms for counteracting personal inadequacy, he minimises his own power and exaggerates that of the opposition:

'Ich kann es? Nichts kann ich.' (VdG²,248)

'Und sie sind stark, und ich bin schwach. Sie haben ihren Willen, und ich habe Nerven. Es ist ein ungleicher Kampf. Man kann nicht an wider eine Maschine. Wären es Menschen, man könnte sich wehren.' (VdG²,232)

'Wie kann man sich wehren? Sie sind stärker als alle, sie sind die Stärksten der ganzen Welt.' (VdG²,233)

In this he makes use of well-tried rhetorical devices (hyperbole and intensification) as well as the less orthodox stratagem of inconsistency, speaking of the opposition now as people, now as a machine. But whether its plurality or its impersonality is appealed to, the purpose remains the same: to render it unamenable to the will of a single human opponent.

A fourth element in Ferdinand's avoidance of confrontation, perhaps indeed its fundamental ingredient, is a tendency to passivity. It may assume a physical dimension, as it does on his way to the consulate in Zurich, when, hurling himself into a taxi-cab 'wie ein Selbstmörder in den Fluß' (VdG²,238), he recalls that search for oblivion mentioned earlier. But then he relishes a voluptuous feeling at the speed with which the car bears him along to his fate; and, as Zweig explicitly states, 'es tat ihm wohl, passiv dabei zu sein' (ibid.). Once inside the consulate, he finds the same voluptuousness in being borne upwards in the lift, yielding to the mechanical movement, 'als wäre er nicht es selbst, der all dies tat, sondern sie, die Macht, die unbekannte, unfaßbare, die ihn zwang' (ibid.). Evidently, the psychological complement to his physical

pleasure is an abdication of responsibility, the need for a comfort-
ing assurance that all decisions have been taken out of his hands.
The most extreme form which this takes is an attempt to external-
ise his own inner conflict. His knowing wife has left him
completely alone to make up his own mind whether to act
according to his convictions or to comply with the military
summons, to choose between herself or 'them'. Since that decision
is the last thing he wants, he adopts the defence of picturing the
conflict as one between two external and supposedly superhuman
powers, his wife and the authorities:

> er fühlte, daß außen ihr Wille stand, feindlich und bewehrt.
> Und wußte gleichzeitig um jenen andern Willen, der [. . .] ihn
> von sich vorwärts trieb. [. . .] Er fühlte beide Enden seines
> Lebens gefaßt von übermenschlich zerrenden Kräften und
> wünschte nur: es risse inmitten entzwei. (VdG², 250)

Expecting his wife to make the morally acceptable choice for him,
he can use the fact that she now leaves him to his own devices as a
means of placing the blame for his failure on her, while he feels
'vor sich selbst entlastet, daß er dem Zwange nachgab'
(VdG²,254). Even as he leaves the house, still of course without
having come to terms with the problem himself, he is searching for
some other force to do what he cannot bring himself to do, much
as Irene does near the end of *Angst*: 'ob nicht irgend etwas diese
stählerne Maschine des Gehorsams in ihm mit den Fäusten
zerschlagen wollte' (ibid.).

In this respect Ferdinand is also reminiscent of Bob, the young
hero of *Geschichte in der Dämmerung*, at the time of his convalescence, when he enjoys the suspension of social obligations
and gives himself over to sweet reverie. For the hero of *Der Zwang*
is, in fact, seeking to regress to a state of childhood, when others
decided matters for him, and has to be reminded by his wife that
he is after all 'ein mündiger Mensch' (VdG²,247). His attempted
regression, however, is even more radical than Bob's, not only
because he is more advanced in years and the demands made on
him are much weightier, but also because his goal sometimes seems
to lie farther back in time. At one point indeed he appears to desire
a return to earliest childhood, if not actually the womb: 'Er fühlte
sich bereit, allem Zuspruch nachzugeben, nur irgendwie wieder
zurückzugleiten in das Vergangene. Wehmut überwogte die

63

zuckende Unrast, und des Abschieds großes Gefühl erlosch in kindhafter Sehnsucht nach einer kleinen Zärtlichkeit' (VdG²,251). Psychologically, the development of *Der Zwang* consists of a succession of attempts by the hero's will to enforce its rational and moral judgements in the face of a powerful impulse to evade that very responsibility, an impulse which the unexpiated guilt of his earlier evasions has transmuted into an insuperable external power. The first attempt centres on the letter he receives from the military authorities and which he seeks to ignore, although he has been expecting its arrival: 'Wie konnte dies mich unruhig machen, dies Blatt, von dem ich nur weiß, wenn ich will? Und ich will nicht. Ich will nichts als meine Freiheit' (VdG²,228). But when he comes to tear it up, his muscles will not obey, his fingers open the letter as if of their own accord. The second attempt is made in relation to his visit to the consulate in Zurich, when, against the impulse which drives him on, he makes small 'Kraftproben' of his ever-weakening will (VdG²,238) and then, after his arrival, tries unsuccessfully to demonstrate that he is in command of the situation, 'souverän und frei' (VdG²,240). The third attempt concerns the question of whether he should take the train home to Germany. After a refreshing night's sleep he is ready to insist on the primacy of his own freedom as an artist. He even enjoys exercising his will, by throwing his knapsack in the corner, and proposing to tear up his letter as a further test of his will. But again its power evaporates, and he submits to the force he senses emanating from the words set out in front of him (VdG²,253).

After that succession of failures it may come as a surprise that Ferdinand does not in the end return to Germany. The conclusion, however, is ambiguous to say the least. Allowing, for the moment, that what he finally does is morally commendable — and we shall consider that question in a later chapter — does it represent the ultimate and unexpected victory of his will? In fact, his change of direction is largely given to him, as though in response to his well-established tendency to avoid taking decisions for himself. It is noteworthy, in the first place, that the change would not have come about if a train had not arrived, by happy coincidence, bringing wounded prisoners of war on their way back to France. The sight of their injuries suddenly makes him realise the inhumanity he too will be expected to inflict on his fellow-men. In the second place, his response to this call of human brotherhood seems to have little to do with active will. Here it is worth paying special attention to the wording of Zweig's narrative:

> Da kam es über den Zitternden wie ein Blitz. Das sollte er tun? Menschen so schänden, Brüdern nicht mehr ins Auge zu blicken als mit Haß, teilhaftig werden an dem großen Verbrechen durch freien Willen? Mächtig sprang die große Wahrheit des Gefühls in ihm auf und zerbrach die Maschine in seiner Brust, Freiheit stieg hoch, selig und groß, und zerriß den Gehorsam. Niemals! Niemals! schrie es in ihm auf, eine Stimme, urmächtig und unerkannt. Und schon schlug es ihn hin. Schluchzend brach er vor der Tragbahre zusammen. (VdG[2],261)

It is a curious passage. The only reference to free will concerns the performance of military service, on which he has now turned his back. But the most remarkable thing of all is the passivity which Ferdinand displays throughout the paragraph. In only one sentence is he the grammatical subject; in most he is the direct or prepositional object,[19] the one on whom or in whom acts are carried out. An impersonal 'es' is again in command; freedom and emotional truth happen to him; it is not he but they who break the power of the military machine. To the end, then, Ferdinand never re-establishes the supremacy of his moral will; his tendency to passivity has been confirmed, though the shock brought about by his encounter with the wounded soldiers has been powerful enough to overcome the guilt of his earlier evasions. The ending may be morally disappointing, but it carries more psychological conviction than the sudden change at the end of *Angst*.

Untergang eines Herzens, the second story of the volume *Verwirrung der Gefühle*, sets its conflict in the mind of an older man, a Jewish businessman, to whom crisis comes when he is already sixty-five years old. In his patriarchal role and his puritanical attitude to work and pleasure he is reminiscent of Meister Anton in Hebbel's *Maria Magdalena*, but where Anton's response to his daughter's suspected sexual misdemeanour is moral outrage and concern for his reputation, Salomonssohn seems indifferent to moral questions and public opinion and judges his daughter's escapades privately, in terms of the effect they have on the personal relations between the two of them. Above all, the crisis brought about by the discovery of these escapades finds him much less sure of himself, much less single-minded than his counterpart in Hebbel. He is full of inner contradictions.

Some of the details of his early biography, which gradually emerge and serve to make his response to the crisis more intelligible, are also reminiscent of Meister Anton's youth, though without the extreme of deprivation. He is a self-made man, who has come from a simple home and, having been forced by economic necessity to leave school at twelve, has toiled away as a commercial traveller, until he has amassed the money to provide his wife and daughter with luxury and social status (VdG,113). Yet he himself has remained uncultured and still dominated by the advice of his father, that pleasure is not for the likes of them (VdG,117). As we shall see, his money-grubbing life has coloured his attitude to human relations, but as we shall also see, there have been inner tensions which the shock of his daughter's amorous pursuits now brings to the surface. These points are in need of some exposition, because they have sometimes been overlooked, while the central character has been misrepresented as unambiguously altruistic.[20]

The first tension in Salomonssohn is that between his consideration for others and self-interest. The very fact that he is on holiday with his family at Gardone is a consequence of deference to the wishes of his wife and daughter, which have taken precedence over his own need to visit Karlsbad for the sake of his health (VdG,107). And when he suffers a painful attack of the illness which, medically speaking, leads to his death, he refrains from waking his wife so as not to cause her anxiety and instead seeks to find relief alone (VdG,108). The next time he has such an attack, however, he has a greater sense of his impending death and reflects bitterly that he has never really lived, never lived for himself, but has spent his time slaving for other people (VdG,134). This is anticipated by an earlier remark that in working so hard for financial gain he has impoverished himself (VdG,114) and by another passage in which the impression given is that this man, who has lived for work and disapproved of pleasure, harbours a secret, rarely admitted longing to taste the forbidden fruit for himself. Contemplating the beauty of the lakeland scenery, he thinks to himself: 'Hier könnte man glücklich sein. Einmal hab ichs auch haben wollen, auch einmal selber fühlen, wie schön die Welt der Sorglosen ist' (VdG,117).

Growing out of this first conflict between consideration and

66

self-interest is a second, between a sense of pride at what he has been able to provide for his wife and daughter and a resentment at what is after all its precondition: an uneven distribution of work and pleasure. He has been proud to make their lives easy, to work his fingers to the bone to provide contentment for them. And yet his daughter's conduct exposes a festering sore: the sense that all his efforts have merely alienated his wife and daughter and bitter resentment at their carefree pleasure (VdG,112). What offends him here on holiday is essentially a continuation of their whole way of life:

> 'Wieder allein,' dachte er, 'immer allein! . . . Wenn ich morgens ins Büro gehe, schlafen sie noch behäbig und faul von ihren Tanzereien und Theatern . . . wenn ich abends heimkomme, sind sie schon fort auf Vergnügung, in Gesellschaft: da können sie mich nicht brauchen.' (VdG,114)

Such resentment is a clear expression of self-concern. Yet the other side of this conflict too, his pride in what he has provided for his family, is ultimately only a subtler, if costlier, form of self-interest, so that the conflict may be said to be built on a common base.

Much of Salomonssohn's attitude towards his nineteen-year-old daughter, the central relationship of the *Novelle*, may be regarded as a particularised version of the same conflict. But before proceeding to that it is important to note one other contradiction in the way in which he thinks of his daughter. For much of the time he seeks to persuade himself that she is still only a child, his child. He finds it difficult to admit to himself that she is no longer the little girl who pored over her schoolbooks or went to the confectioners to buy sweets; he clings somewhat wilfully to the image he has of her only the day before, begging like a child for a new sweater (VdG,111).[21] At other times he is only too aware of her maturity, of the sexual attraction of her elegant figure. Indeed he observes her physical beauty with an appreciation that seems improper in a father and would be incomprehensible if his feelings for her were simply paternal (cf. VdG,115,121,128).

The more striking conflict in Salomonssohn's feelings for his daughter, however, is that between his pride at this very beauty and his jealousy at the way in which, in his estimation, she prostitutes these gifts in her sexual escapades. Repeatedly we find him observing her lissome movements with an approving eye and then collapsing in bitter anger when the sight of her young male companions or perhaps only his own colourful imagination calls to mind the pleasures which she and one of them have wantonly derived from that body (cf. VdG,115,119-20). Yet these contradictory feelings are perfectly understandable once one has appreciated the complex role he has assigned to his daughter in his emotional life.

To the extent that real life has passed him by in his laborious pursuit of money, she has represented a vicarious enjoyment, valid as long as she does not stray beyond his control. 'Und ein Kind hat man gehabt . . .' he laments at one point, 'aus den Händen ist sie einem gewachsen, ich hab geglaubt, hier fängt man noch einmal an zu leben, heller, glücklicher, als es einem selber vergönnt war, hier stirbt man nicht ganz . . . und da geht sie nachts von einem weg und wirft sich Männern hin' (VdG,134). But there is also more involved. Immediately before these thoughts Salomonssohn has been reflecting on his alienation from his wife in a way which suggests that he suffers a kind of sexual frustration. This is borne out by other reflections (cf. VdG,142), by a passing and unsubstantiated suspicion that his wife too has been dallying with one of the young men (VdG,121), and above all by the numerous occasions on which his imagination wallows in salacious embellishments of his daughter's amours (VdG,111,125,127,128).[22] Against this background it does not seem perverse or unduly Freudian to find further confirmation of sexual frustration in the curious picture which Zweig gives of his hero's impotent rage: 'Der wuchtige Stock, seinen Händen entsunken, pendelte zwecklos zwischen den Beinen' (VdG,126). Salomonssohn's answer to this sexual frustration is to seek some surrogate satisfaction in his daughter, not, to be sure, in actual incest, but in the contemplation of her sexual attraction.[23] If she can no longer be his little girl, she can at least provide sensual stimulus, while he looks on, 'ihr Bild einsaugend mit leidenschaftlichem Blick' (VdG,120). And if other young men disturb this relationship, they immediately become the objects of a very real sexual jealousy.[24] Indeed the wording of his first angry thoughts is entirely appropriate to the role of the cuckolded husband: 'und ich weiß nichts, ich ahne nichts, ich Narr, ich geschlagener Narr' (VdG,112).

With that we come to a further recurrent conflict within Zweig's

Jewish businessman, which is in some respects the converse of that first conflict between consideration and self-interest. It is the conflict between aggression and submission. Although aggression may be related to that self-interest discussed above, however, the submission displayed has none of the positive qualities associated with consideration for others. It is, even in Salomonssohn's own eyes, a sign of weakness. His invariable response to any indication of his daughter's sexual adventures is the urge to take violent measures: to beat his daughter, her male companions or even the door. He even goes to the lengths of buying that stick to make his aggression more effective and enjoyable. But the author makes clear that this very purchase is a sign of weakness, an attempt to buy the strength he lacks (VdG,122). And in practice his violent impulses all evaporate in the presence of his intended victims: he falls into polite small-talk or takes refuge in impotent gestures (VdG,113,121,124,125).[25] With his wife, too, though he musters enough assertiveness at one point to insist that they leave the resort, he is reduced by resistance to the posture of a beggar; and though her continued refusal causes him to clench his fists, ready to strike a blow or explode in angry words, he in fact turns away and staggers off to his room 'wie ein Verfolgter' (VdG,129-32). In his failure to act at moments of real confrontation he is reminiscent of Ferdinand in *Der Zwang*, the difference being that here it is an instinct (aggression) rather than the assertion of reason that is defeated. Both men share the tendency to turn their feelings in on themselves, a tendency which prepares for an ultimate retreat from external reality entirely. And that means that most of the psychological conflicts of *Untergang eines Herzens*, like those of *Angst* and *Der Zwang*, are never properly resolved; the combatants simply withdraw from the field of battle.

The form which Salomonssohn's withdrawal takes is determined by another element in his psychological constitution, one, however, which remains constant throughout those other conflicts. This is his possessiveness, which is seen most clearly in relation to his daughter, to whom he refers as 'mein, mein zartes, behütetes Kind' (VdG,111) or 'mein Fleisch und Blut' (VdG,115-16). His thinking is evidently coloured by a lifetime of commerce, in which what one possesses has been paid for and in which all relationships can be summarised on a balance-sheet. Consequently, in slaving hard to provide luxury for his wife and child he he has robbed himself, 'mich dabei selber bestohlen' (VdG,114), as he puts it; the three young men who dance attendance on his daughter are all seen as 'Tagediebe' in that they do not work for a living (VdG,120,130), while the one who has enjoyed his daughter sexually is seen as a 'Dieb' pure and simple (VdG,128); and when he comes to take his leave of his wife, he departs like a commercial traveller who has 'keinerlei Geschäft mehr' with her (VdG,143). If the financial vocabulary again recalls Hebbel's Meister Anton, it will be noted that the links with moral values have virtually disappeared: it is now a matter of possession, of the affection and loyalty, the quality of life he has or has not bought.[26] Once it is clear to him that it has failed to secure the possession of his daughter, whether as a little girl or as a sexually attractive young woman, he turns to the one thing that cannot be taken away from him, even though it be the bitterest purchase of his labour. That is his illness. If wife and child are alienated, he will die alone, rejecting the sympathy of others:

> 'einzig, was da innen umwühlt, nur das gehört noch mir, das ist *meine* Krankheit, *mein* Tod . . . nur das bin ich . . . das heißt nicht Kommissionsrat mehr und hat nicht Frau und Kind und Haus und ein Geschäft . . . und nur das allein da ist wirklich, was ich mit den Fingern fühle, mein Leib und das Heiße in ihm innen, das weh tut . . .' (VdG,135)

If, as has been suggested, Zweig's *Novelle* owes something to Tolstoy's *Ivan Ilych,* especially in the depiction of a dying man's alienation from and hostility towards his wife and family,[27] it provides a very different focus, not only in the psychological motivation of that hostility, but also precisely in the way which sickness and death become cherished possessions rather than personal enemies.

It might be argued that at least Salomonssohn's first conflict, that between consideration and self-interest, is here decided in favour of the latter, so that when he subsequently avoids other people, it is a question of not being disturbed as much as not disturbing them (cf. VdG,148). Yet it is a sorry, depleted, doomed self whose interest he pursues. And his retreat leaves him in a state more akin to the apathy of the baron at the beginning of *Phantastische Nacht.* His other and more important psychological conflicts are dissolved in an emotional indifference: to his wife's contempt (VdG,141,147), to his sexual frustrations (VdG,142), to his daughter's sexual escapades (VdG,142), to the pleasures of others (VdG,148), even to his own business; in short, to all that earlier excited his anger. Only on the point of death, when he briefly regains consciousness after his operation, is there a last faint flicker of that central conflict in his feelings for his daughter. As she bends over to kiss him, a wan smile comes over his face in recognition of his beloved and beautiful Erna. But it is immediately dispelled by the sickly-sweet smell of her perfume, that reminder of idle pleasure-seeking and sexual sport. And he musters his failing energies to make a last gesture of rejection (VdG,150-1).

Verwirrung der Gefühle, the longest of the three stories in the collection to which it gave its name, depicts the psychological conflicts of two central characters, a first-person narrator, who at the time of his decisive experiences is a young university student, and the professor who is his chief intellectual inspiration. The nature of the conflicts is different in each case, although those of young Roland are very much dependent on those of his professor. For that reason it is advisable to consider the latter first.

The professor is a man of contradictions, but not all of them arise out of psychological conflicts. His change from rhapsodic eloquence to sober factuality is merely a consequence of his subject-matter (VdG,184); his alternation between communicativeness and silence is a function of the company he is with (cf. VdG,185,188). The real psychological conflicts are related in some way to his homosexuality and in particular to the impossibility he has experienced in giving integrated expression to it.

The most obvious of his inner conflicts, the one that some commentators seem to regard as his only conflict, is that between his intellectual pursuits and his erotic instinct, between 'Geist' and 'Trieb' or 'Geist' and 'Blut', as it is variously expressed.[28] Although it is in operation throughout the period of Roland's acquaintance, it remains unrecognised by the innocent young man, who fails to understand the significance of the professor's sudden absences, until these are explained in the final confession. For here is a man who leads a double life, that of an enthusiastic scholar and that of a man in thrall to homosexual passion. The movement from one to the other may perhaps be less rapid than it was, but his present life is essentially a continuation of the 'Doppelschich-

71

tigkeit' which characterised his student days and which Roland summarises somewhat melodramatically as follows: 'indes am hellen arbeitsamen Tag das kristallene Element des Geistigen den Forschenden durchläutert, stößt der Abend immer wieder den Leidenschaftlichen in den Abhub der Vorstädte hinab' (VdG,265).

As Zweig presents it, this split is not inherently or absolutely inevitable. In demanding of his students enthusiasm for their subject before they attempt any analysis, the professor formulates one of the principles of his own intellectual life, that 'aller Geist steigt aus dem Blut, alles Denken aus Leidenschaft' (VdG,174).[29] For him the intellect is not divorced from passion, understood as enthusiastic involvement. Potentially it is even more easily reconcilable with his homosexual passion. It is no accident that he follows the tradition of the Greek *gymnasion* in preferring oral instruction in the company of male students, whose very presence stimulates him into intellectual fervour. And in his relations with Roland he comes close to achieving an integration of both intellectual and erotic strands in one experience, so close that the sufferings of his failure are given an added poignancy. As it is, the morality of his society, the uncertainty of Roland, and his own fear of rejection are sufficient to ensure that he remains in a state of permanent inner division:

> Nie aber war diesem gequälten, verängstigten Herzen die Gnade des reinen Freundes, des Edelgesinnten widerfahren, würdige Erwiderung männlich-übermächtiger Zärtlichkeit: immer mußte er sein Gefühl zerteilen in ein Unten und Oben, in den zart-sehnsüchtigen Verkehr mit den jungen geistigen Gefährten der Universität und jenen im Dunkel gewordenen Genossen, deren er morgens sich nur mehr schauernd besann. (VdG,269)

One might also remark that his failure to integrate the two strands leads not only to inner conflict, but to an added burden of guilt and self-disgust, since he is forced to consort with people whom he would otherwise abhor.

In an earlier section we have already had occasion to note the eruptive force of the professor's passion. Of greater importance for Zweig's purpose, however, is the protracted conflict which arises out of the attempts of his conscious will to bring this instinctive energy under control. In adolescence the rejection and mockery of his schoolfellows have led to isolation and created a sense of shame powerful enough to enable him to maintain control. But once he goes to Berlin as a student, his 'lang-beherrschte Neigung' seeks satisfaction in degrading street encounters (VdG,264). The next decade and a half are spent there-fore in a persistent struggle between his instinct and the attempts of his conscious self to master it (cf. VdG,265). At the same time his will is further engaged in the battle to keep this very duality from public knowledge and in doing so fosters that division between intellect and instinct already considered. Even his marriage is designed to help master what is called his 'fehlgänger-ische Neigung'. In contrast to Freud, who argued that male homo-sexuals tended to seek feminine characteristics in their love-object,[30] Zweig here presents a man who seeks to dupe his homo-sexual instinct by choosing a woman with boyish physical charac-teristics, only to find that his original desire has an overwhelming will of its own (VdG,266) and that in the presence of his male students, who have a great affection for him, the struggle to control himself is as demanding as ever (VdG,267).

His relations with Roland constitute a special form of this same conflict. As the young hero perceives matters, his professor blows hot and cold in his affections, alternating between responsiveness and ironic distance, between gratitude and indifference, between the intimate 'Du' and the remote 'Sie' (VdG,204-5,217,227 and 230). But this is only the public face of a very different conflict, in which his feelings for Roland remain constantly warm: the conflict between a desire to give full rein to his feelings and the need to hold back, for fear of offending Roland or being rejected by him (VdG,260,270,271). More than with any other student he has been placed in a position of mental anguish: 'Hart zu sein gegen zudrängende Neigung, unablässig mit der eigenen Schwäche in nie endendem Kampf' (VdG,267). Not surprisingly, it is after the interruption of their greatest intimacy, when the professor comes closest to the integration of his intellectual pursuits and his erotic instincts, that he again departs on one of his degrading escapades (cf. VdG,230-7). Again the relation between the present conflict and the first is underlined.

The ending of *Verwirrung der Gefühle* brings no resolution. Roland's departure merely removes the most immediate and urgent cause. Yet the passion of his professor's farewell embrace,

73

the abruptness with which he then turns away, and the convulsive energy with which he resists any further sympathetic approach are clear evidence that the inner conflict is as strong as ever (VdG,273-4).

In discussing Roland, some commentators have tended to ignore or play down the element of inner conflict. Having considered the incurable dichotomy in the older man, Gschiel goes on to speak of the second theme of the story as 'die Wandlung des jungen Menschen durch die Begeisterung'.[31] And Klawiter, who draws a provocative parallel between Roland and Aschenbach in Thomas Mann's *Der Tod in Venedig*, asserts that the main concern of the story is to 'reveal the incalculable creative force that can flow from sublimated *eros*'.[32] Both views contain some truth; and certainly Roland's starting-point in narrating the story is the need to acknowledge his indebtedness to the professor for the stimulus of his friendship. Nevertheless, the substance of what he narrates concerns his own inner struggles. The title refers to him at least as much as to his mentor — more, if one judges by the frequency with which the word 'verwirrt' and cognate forms are applied to him.

As already indicated, his conflicts are to some extent determined by those of his professor, although they assume a very different form. The first cause, however, lies farther back, in the habits of childhood given further shape by a reaction against the pedantic and puritanical restriction of his provincial upbringing. He has developed the custom of hurling himself fanatically into one thing at a time until all its possibilities have been exhausted (VdG,160). Consequently, his early adult life becomes a succession of contradictory enthusiasms — sensual indulgence, scholarly austerity, physical sport, intellectual fervour — each of which he pursues to excess and often to the detriment of his health. Like the conflict between instinct and intellect in his professor, this conflict within Roland is not a matter of opposing psychological forces pulling the mind in different directions at the same time. In some respects he is a single-minded character, but only temporarily. He follows one course without balancing 'Gleichzeitigkeiten' (VdG,161) and is then liable, like a pendulum, to swing in the opposite direction as soon as he has reached the extreme point. Zweig's essay on Kleist describes a similar swing from book-learning to enthusiasm for the primitive and unconscious.[33] The similarity is the more remarkable when one bears in mind that the phrase 'Verwirrung der Gefühle' was first used in connection with Kleist.

Increasingly, as the story progresses, the movement of this mental pendulum is affected by the second conflict within Roland, his changing feelings towards his professor. At times he is magnetically attracted or passionately devoted (cf. VdG,170-1,188), at other times mistrustful or full of hateful anger (cf. VdG,183,206,234-5). And while the former gives impetus to his passionate pursuit of learning, the latter helps drive him to sensual excess, if only to spite his mentor. Yet Zweig leaves the reader in no doubt that these changes are not signs of fickle affections. They constitute a secondary conflict, entirely dependent on the contradictory behaviour and therefore on the inner struggles of the professor. The link is made very clear in an almost hysterical outburst to the professor's wife, in which he complains: 'wie er mich zurückgestoßen und verfolgt und wieder angezogen, wie er sich hart stellte wider mich ohne Grund, ohne Ursache — ein Peiniger, an den ich doch liebend gebunden war, den ich liebend haßte und hassend liebte' (VdG,239).

Essentially, Roland's responses are those of a perhaps rather possessive lover, jealous of the attentions paid to other students (VdG,190) and, since he is unaware of the homosexual background to his mentor's behaviour, jealous also of his unexplained absences (VdG,206). And not the least important motive in the adulterous episode with the professor's wife is a somewhat petty desire to gain recompense for what he regards as personal neglect (VdG,252-3). Even these more unpleasant manifestations, then, are evidence that his affection is still basically unchanged.

Underlying constancy of affection is also the explanation of a further inner uncertainty which Roland exhibits. For it is not just a matter of resentment in apparent conflict with devotion. The acts to which this resentment leads are invariably followed by feelings of shame, which are not dependent on public exposure, as they were when his father earlier discovered him in a compromising situation with a girl, but represent genuine self-hatred. They are present after his complaining outburst to the professor's wife (VdG,238), after his boisterous and loutish excesses (VdG,242 and 245), and above all after his adulterous involvement. In this instance, indeed, they make themselves felt during the very act, though not with sufficient power to outweigh the sexual instinct:

> Manchmal tat mir ihr Wort weh, und ich schämte mich, daß
> ich verstrickt blieb, wo ich verabscheute. Aber der Körper
> unter mir gehorchte nicht mehr dem Willen, er wühlte wild in
> seiner eigenen Lust. Und schauernd küßte ich die Lippe, die
> meinen liebsten Menschen verriet. (VdG,254)

On the part of the wife this is an act of adultery. But for Roland too the motivating jealousy helps to turn it into a betrayal of love which is at least on a par with adultery.

To speak in terms of betrayal of love is to raise the question of the hero's homosexuality and thereby to introduce the final psychological conflict of *Verwirrung der Gefühle*. For some the complication does not exist, because Roland is not homosexual. That, according to Welter, is why the professor does not succeed in integrating the intellectual and instinctive strands in his life.[34] Yet a careful reading of the text indicates some sexual ambivalence in the young hero,[35] which carries less mental agony than other conflicts because it rarely reaches the level of consciousness as a conflict. Certainly, there is no denying his heterosexual activity, both in Berlin and in the small university town where he meets his mentor. Nevertheless, his response to the professor's love reveals considerable emotional uncertainty. In his devoted attachment emotional and intellectual needs are equally satisfied. The scene of their greatest intimacy, when he is first addressed as 'Du', is the fulfilment of his most ardent longing (VdG,227) and he accepts the arm around his shoulder and the loosely held hand, disturbed only by the thought of the professor's eavesdropping wife (VdG,229). It might be objected here that Roland, in his innocence, does not know that this is homosexual love, because he has not yet been told the professor's secret. But that is precisely the point. Before this love has been given a name, he responds to it warmly and, as we have seen, displays a natural jealousy when it appears inconstant. Only when it has been named does he show signs of recoiling.

This is not the first time that Zweig has depicted sexual ambivalence. There is early evidence of it in the young hero of the story *Scharlach* (1908),[36] who sometimes responds like a coy girl or a receptive woman, but at other times plays a more clearly masculine and dominating role. But it is nowhere as pronounced as in *Verwirrung der Gefühle*. Here its presence is underlined by the imagery, to which we shall return in a later chapter, and con-

firmed by Roland's uncertain reaction to the revelation of his
mentor's homosexuality. Having heard the professor's open
admission of love, he makes an involuntary movement away from
him. But his feeling is mixed; it is 'ein Grauen süß und furchtbar
zugleich' (VdG,260). His response to that farewell kiss is similarly
ambiguous:

> Ich schauerte von einem fremd-furchtbaren Empfinden
> zwiefältig gefaßt — hingegeben mit meiner Seele und doch
> zutiefst erschreckt von einem widrigen Wehren des männlich
> berührten Körpers [. . .] (VdG,273)

To the end his inner conflict remains unresolved.

In discussing the eruption of unconscious forces we have already
had occasion to note how, in *Schachnovelle*, the link with an inner
conflict creates acute psychological problems. It is now time to
consider the nature of this conflict in more detail, a conflict which
arises only in the inset narrative, during Dr B.'s confinement by
the Nazis, and is brought about by the very special circumstances
imposed upon him. Unlike the conflicts of Salomonssohn in
Untergang eines Herzens and the professor in *Verwirrung der
Gefühle*, it does not arise out of existing attitudes or disposition. It
comes about only when, in his attempt to counteract the effects of
sensory deprivation and keep his sanity, Dr B. has rehearsed the
chess games of the masters from the stolen manual so many times
that he has exhausted their intellectual stimulus. At this point he
decides to play against himself in games of his own creation. And
the bitter irony is that the very method he adopts to try and avoid
insanity induces insanity in another form.

In taking this decision he is acting against the very nature of
chess. For, as the first-person narrator remarks in the frame, 'Für
Schach ist nun, wie für die Liebe, ein Partner unentbehrlich'
(S,28). More important, he is also acting against the nature of the
mind, which has only one centre of consciousness. Here is a man
who sets about the task of playing two opposing roles, devising
two opposing strategies, without allowing one self to know the
intentions of the other. It might with justification be argued that in
order to play chess against oneself it is not absolutely necessary for
each of two selves to be in ignorance of the other's intentions, just
as one can play a real opponent and still find an intellectual
challenge when his intentions are all-too obvious. Some people do

indeed play against themselves,[37] sitting alternately at opposite sides of the board. Dr B.'s problem is made the more acute, however, because he has no board in front of him. He is forced to construct a mental image not only of the present configuration, but of possible configurations moves ahead — and all from two different perspectives (S,85).

To this extent Dr B. is engaged in an intellectual conflict, a battle of wits which is destructive precisely because the combatants are aspects of one divided consciousness. Yet it is even more dangerous because it is also an affective conflict. Rehearsing the games of the masters was a welcome mental discipline without personal involvement, but creating his own games brings with it a passionate engagement, a desire for victory, an impatience, which is directed only against his other self:

> Jedes meiner beiden Ich, mein Ich Schwarz und mein Ich Weiß, hatten zu wetteifern gegen einander und gerieten jedes für sein Teil in einen Ehrgeiz, in eine Ungeduld, zu siegen, zu gewinnen; ich fieberte als Ich Schwarz nach jedem Zuge, was das Ich Weiß tun würde. (S,87)

The intensity of his involvement is such that he finds himself shouting at his other self and, when one game is over, thirsting for revenge (S,88-91). At the height of his mental illness, having attracted the attention of a warder with his shouting, he hurls abuse at the man and assaults him physically, as though the warder were the opponent who would not move soon enough (S,96). This confusion, this externalisation of an opposing self, is one of a number of hints which serve to confirm the view already advanced in the earlier discussion of the erupting unconscious: that Dr B.'s aggressive passions, which might normally find expression in some appropriate action against his Nazi tormentors, have perforce become directed against himself. He needs to be in the right, and the only opponent against whom he can prove himself is 'dieses andere Ich in mir' (S,88). In such circumstances it is quite understandable that, when a warder enters his room at the climax of his inner excitement, he should transfer his aggression on to an external object, a representative of the forces which are his real opponents. And although there is in practice only an indirect causal link between his act and the resolution of his psychological conflict — his condition is considered dangerous enough for him to be taken to a hospital, where a sympathetic doctor secures his release into exile — there is, nevertheless, a symbolic justice at work. For in externalising his inner conflict he is unconsciously restoring matters to their proper state.

In the earlier discussions of Roland in *Verwirrung der Gefühle* it was noted that his inner conflicts are largely a matter of alternating pursuits. Since Dr B.'s conflict entails the alternate adoption of two opposing roles in a game of chess, it is tempting to underline the parallel. In fact, however, the differences are more striking. Dr B.'s conflict consists in a very rapid alternation. More important, his conflict is not one between different operations of the mind, such as instinct versus intellect, for example. Each side of the conflict has the same constituents: intellect and passion, operating together against the intellect and passion of another self. Dr B. himself speaks of a 'künstliche Schizophrenie' (S,87), but this is a loose description, which would not impress a clinical psychologist, and that, as much as anything, because his condition lacks the dissociation between the intellectual and the affective processes.[38] The difference between Roland and Dr B. can perhaps best be understood by picturing the former's conflict as taking place vertically, the latter's horizontally.

5

The Battle of the Sexes

The conflict examined in the previous chapter took place within the mind of the individual. In this chapter we are concerned with conflicts that arise between one individual and another of the opposite sex. It is one of the peculiarities of Zweig's presentation of sexual relations that they rarely involve an unequivocal affection or a full mutuality as between equals. There is on the contrary an element of struggle, ranging from playful competition to physical hurt and moral domination, in short, a sadism of varying degrees, which may at times swing round and assume a masochistic form. According to Freud, who took over the terminology from Krafft-Ebing, sadism may be seen as the aggressive component of the sexual instinct which has become independent and exaggerated and, by displacement, has usurped the leading position, while masochism appears as an extension of sadism turned round on the subject's own self.[1] To this extent Zweig creates his fictional characters in general agreement with Freud's theories. In detail, however, we shall note differences of emphasis and above all a lack of interest in the causation of these tendencies in the individual's private history.

Sexual conflict of this kind plays its most prominent part in two stories from the collection *Amok: Der Amokläufer* itself and *Die Mondscheingasse*. But it will be helpful to sketch in some of the characteristic features as they appear in other works and, at the end, to consider its perhaps unexpected relevance to *Brief einer Unbekannten*.

Even in the volume *Erstes Erlebnis* there are clear traces of sadism in the adolescent Bob of *Geschichte in der Dämmerung* and

the mature baron of *Brennendes Geheimnis*. In Bob's encounters
with the young woman he takes to be Margot there is a powerful
element of anger and hatred, which, especially in his response to
his failure to penetrate the secret of her name, expresses itself in
the desire to dominate her, at times even in the intended or actual
infliction of pain (cf. EE,23-4,29-30,34). In his adolescent confusion, however, he can also feel regret at the way he has
tormented her and a longing to be close to her, if only to lie near
her door in self-abasement like a dog or a slave (EE,38). With the
shallow, blasé baron of *Brennendes Geheimnis* there are no com-
plicating regrets or reversals to anything resembling masochism.
His approach to Edgar's mother has much of the hunter's instinct
about it, combining cruelty with an element of play, and finding
an added stimulation in the woman's resistance to his dominance
(EE,89,90,93-4,117). Although he uses his social position as a
means to gain superiority, his needs are sufficiently subtle for him
to derive particular pleasure from his ability to make her pursue
him (EE,110,117).

In *Die Frau und die Landschaft* the element of sexual conflict
has a peculiar relation to the overpowering effect of unconscious
forces discussed earlier. Even in the male narrator's response to
the first abortive rainfall there is evidence of a potential for sexual
cruelty. In Zweig's presentation it bears all the marks of sexual
frustration, which provokes the narrator to anger and threatened
violence (A,94-6). Subsequently, once he believes he has detected
in the young woman the same nervous expectancy as in himself, he
becomes involved in a silent struggle, an attempt to force her to
look at him and acknowledge the desire which she is hiding behind
a socially acceptable mask. Yet the look she in fact turns on him is
dark and unconscious, as withering as that of Rilke's 'Schwarze
Katze' (A,101-4). When she does come to his room and shares his
bed, the struggle continues. It is not that she resists his embraces,
but that she yields unconsciously, obeying her instinct, while he
seeks, even roughly, to rouse her to full consciousness. Like the
young hero of *Geschichte in der Dämmerung*, when he tries to
force his beloved to reveal her identity, he is attempting to exercise
power over her, to make her his own when she is in effect in the
possession of unconscious psychological forces (A,113-14). It was
Freud's contention that defloration not only binds the woman to
the man, but unleashes an archaic reaction of hostility.[2] Perhaps

the young woman of Zweig's story shows some awareness of this power-relation. For when she is roused by the storm outside, there is a boundless hatred in her look, and she flees (A,116). It is as though consciousness of what she has done would acknowledge a kind of sexual dependence, which she resists.

In *Phantastische Nacht* there is a brief but pronounced instance of sexual combat in the episode between the baron and the attractive wife of the Hungarian whose betting slip he steals, an instance, therefore, which predates the decisive experience of erupting passions. The woman, who is seen entirely through the eyes of the baron, appears provocative in her coquetry and cold arrogance, angered by her humiliating association with an uncouth husband, yet proudly defiant. Although she is more of an equal participant in the sexual battle than Edgar's mother in *Brennendes Geheimnis*, the baron shares many of the characteristics of his counterpart in the earlier work, especially the element of play or sport which finds additional pleasure in resistance (A,144-6,150),[3] and the role that social status plays in his quest for dominance (A,149). Here, however, the sadism is more pronounced: even if it does not issue in acts of physical cruelty, his imagination delights at the thought of tearing off her clothes and treating her brutally with his looks (A,146-7); and he gloats over the humiliation she suffers by association with her background, regarding even her hatred as a victory, since he has wrested genuine passion from such a cold woman (A,148,150). From the beginning the incident has excited him 'vielleicht mehr im Haß wie in Begehrlichkeit' (A,147). Consequently, no act of sexual intercourse is needed to provide satisfaction; the triumph of her humiliation is satisfaction enough. And an interlude of almost classic sadism is complete.

In *Verwirrung der Gefühle*, too, the sexual battle forms part of an episode, the intimacy between Roland and the professor's wife which develops as a jealous reaction to the professor's apparent coldness. We are not here concerned with the element of hatred towards the latter which informs Roland's relations with the wife and which arises only in response to the older man's confusing behaviour. We are concerned rather with the fight for dominance which is inherent in the relationship between man and woman. Their first contact, which comes before he knows her identity, takes the form of a sporting contest (swimming) full of erotic undercurrents, in which victory and defeat are dominant consider-

82

ations (VdG,192-3). The contest is continued afterwards in the challenging tempo of her walk and is accompanied by a provocatively mocking tone in her utterances and a clumsy attempt on his part to adopt the tone of a student addressing a girl of easy virtue, that is, a social inferior (VdG,194). The battle is interrupted temporarily, not, however, by his discovery of her identity, but by his confession of the cause of his grief, which brings out a maternal tenderness in her (VdG,241-6). Nevertheless, on a second outing to a lake, this time with two other companions, her attempts to provoke him into a swimming race lead to a physical struggle, during which she uses a reed as a whip and her bathing costume is torn, exposing her breast. We scarcely need Freud to remind us of the sexual excitement to be derived from such muscular activity and half-playful romping.[4] It comes, therefore, as no surprise that the events of this day culminate in the act of adultery already mentioned (VdG,249-50).

It is in *Der Amokläufer* that the battle of the sexes first comes to occupy a position of central importance, determining the course which the hero's erupting passion takes throughout the rest of the story. It is here, too, that the masochistic complement to sadism first comes into prominence. As already indicated, Zweig does not examine the childhood or adolescent history of these tendencies in the doctor,[5] but he does provide an earlier instance which gives some insight into his character and at the same time explains why it was that he had to leave Europe in the first place. It emerges that, confronted by a cold, arrogant, domineering woman, he became so enthralled that he misappropriated hospital funds (A,26-7).

The encounter at the heart of *Der Amokläufer* has effects which are both more devastating and more complex, but it must be remembered throughout that it is presented from the man's point of view. When the woman comes to his remote station demanding an abortion, the doctor immediately senses danger in her strength and manly determination, her refusal to beg. Perceiving her as an enemy bent on forcing his will, he yields to some wicked impulse to resist, to compel her to plead with him (A,34-5): '"Sie zur Bitte zwingen", funkelte in mir irgendein Gelüst' (A,37). The battle for dominance has begun; both are full of hatred, she because of her dependence on him for medical help, he because of her refusal to be submissive. For her masterful personality both impresses him and rouses him to resistance (A,38-9).

The struggle already contains a socio-economic component, in that one of the things which angers him is her insistence on performing the role of the lady who can buy his services with money and thereby relegate him to a position of inferiority (A,38 and 40).[6] As yet the sexual component is latent. But once he begins to reflect on the adulterous passion which this apparently cool, haughty woman must have experienced in order to find herself in need of an abortion, sexuality and cruelty begin to coalesce in his conscious mind. It is hinted at first in the striking language he uses to describe the imagined intercourse with her lover, language which recalls the sadistic kiss of Bob in *Geschichte in der Dämmerung*. He pictures them lying 'die Körper ineinander verbissen, wie zwei Lippen' (A,41). But it becomes explicit when he conceives the idea of humiliating her sexually, of forcing groans of voluptuous satisfaction out of this haughty woman. Although he seeks to assure the narrator that there is nothing sexual in this, only the desire to become the master of such arrogance, his words carry little conviction. He goes on to explain that the only women with whom he has had intercourse over recent years have been native women, whose slavish submission spoils his pleasure (A,41). Evidently his sexual needs go beyond the normal tendency to find stimulus in the obstacles placed by conventions;[7] they seek their satisfaction in resistant women, whom he can therefore humiliate, as he now does in his imagination, picturing this Englishwoman in front of him, 'nackt, sinnlich, hingegeben' (A,42).

From here it is only a short step to his (implied) demand for sexual favours in return for the procurement of an abortion, the farthest point which his attempted subjugation reaches. In the face of her defiant response, her scornful laughter, her masterful look, he is devastated; any urge to pursue her and beat or throttle her finds him paralysed by her imperious command to remain where he is (A,43-4). From now on the masochistic component comes to the fore. During the rest of the story he remains in thrall to her, a willing slave, ready to humiliate himself before her, writing her abject letters in which he begs to be allowed to help her. By now, however, the damage has been done. She is prepared to accept death at the hands of a back-street abortionist rather than trust the man who so wounded her pride. Only just before her death, when he vows never to betray her secret, is the conflict between them dissolved in a look of warm gratitude on her part (A,71). Significantly, however, she does not relinquish her position of dominance even in death; or, more precisely, he does not abandon his position of subjugation. It has been suggested by a reviewer of the English version of this story that the brevity of form has imposed a serious limitation, causing the morality of the doctor to dictate his psychology, whereas in life it is usually the other way round. On this view everything turns on the doctor's feeling 'of having shirked his duty to the woman, of having failed through pride and bestiality to help her, so that in compensation he feels an even greater duty imposed on himself by her death'.[8] But if that is not psychology dictating morality, it is difficult to see what is. In fact, when one reads the concluding words of the doctor's narrative, in which he speaks darkly of his final duty, it is clear that he still feels himself to be in thrall to the woman, although she lies dead in her coffin:

> diese Tote, ich spüre sie, und ich weiß, was sie von mir will
> . . . ich weiß es, ich habe noch eine Pflicht . . . ich bin noch
> nicht zu Ende . . . noch ist ihr Geheimnis nicht gerettet . . .
> sie gibt mich noch nicht frei . . . (A,83)

In *Die Mondscheingasse*, the shortest story from *Amok*, a very similar conflict receives a more concentrated expression. Because the sadistic component in the man's behaviour belongs largely to a past which is revealed through a relatively short inset narrative, it is in danger of being overlooked in a present dominated by his cringing servility.[9] And because this present is set largely in what appears to be a brothel, where the woman is employed, the most unusual feature of the conflict — that it concerns a married couple — is also easily forgotten.

According to the by no means flattering account of the husband, the marriage goes wrong because of his impulse to dominate his wife. His chief weapon, which we have encountered already in *Der Amokläufer* and which is briefly adumbrated in *Leporella* in the financial dependence to which the baroness subjects her resentful husband (K,50), is socio-economic superiority. In marrying her, he has taken a much poorer woman, a fact of which he does not hesitate to remind her repeatedly, demanding to hear from her lips expressions of gratitude for her rescue, which serve to deceive his sense of inferiority with assurances of moral superiority (A,286-7). Moreover, the perversity of his love is such that he does not wish away her pride, but derives greater pleasure from the subjugation of a stubborn will (A,287-8).

It is the insistence on her financial dependence which apparently causes her to revolt and leave him, even for a life of degradation — 'apparently', because the story is not entirely clear on this point. In the decisive first instance, when she asks him for money to give to her mother, he does not so much refuse her request as delay his compliance in order to see her beg. The money has already been set aside (A,288). Although he appears niggardly to her, the motive is in fact his familiar need for superiority. During a subsequent attempt at reconciliation, however, what turns her against him is genuine parsimony in the payment of a restaurant bill, a petty concern for money which has no relation to his power over her (A,291). A charitable interpretation of Zweig's intentions might be to argue that the husband's undoubted parsimony is first engaged in the service of his quest for domination of his wife and that any subsequent expression of it, even in a context unrelated to subjugation, is enough to turn her against him once more. The only difficulty with this reading is that the abuse and mockery which she hurls at him in the narrative frame concentrate on his niggardliness and make no reference to the theme of domination.

Be that as it may, once his wife has broken with him, the man swings round to the opposite, complementary pole, in much the same way as the doctor of *Der Amokläufer*. His life becomes a quest to find her, regardless of cost, and it ends in a Mediterranean port in an attitude of degrading servility, as he suffers not only her taunts but her humiliating flirtation with the clients of the establishment. He is, of course, in thrall to her, full of jealous anger at her behaviour, but unable to leave her (A,280). It cannot be said that he derives any pleasure from these humiliations, any more than the doctor of *Der Amokläufer* does, but in the narrator's description of the way in which he responds to his wife's command ('wie mit einer Peitsche aufgeknallt'; A,281) there is a suggestive, masochistic detail.

In the narrative present it is the wife who is in the dominant position and who experiences all the sadistic pleasure, whether from her power to order her husband about like a slave or dog, from her verbal mockery, or from the granting of sexual favours to other men in front of his eyes. In revolting against her enforced subjugation, she is able to enjoy only a perverse sort of freedom, a strange sort of superiority. As she tells the narrator, 'mich soll er doch nicht haben. Alle, nur gerade er nicht!' (A,283). And as her husband explains later, 'Sie dürfen nicht glauben, daß sie so ist, wie sie sich gibt . . . das ist Lüge, und sie tut sich selber weh . . . nur . . . nur um mir wehe zu tun, um mich zu quälen' (A,286). Ultimately, in a manner reminiscent of Roland in *Verwirrung der Gefühle* and even more of the heroine of *Die Liebe der Erika Ewald*, who revenges herself on her lover by giving herself in 'grausame Selbstpeinigung' to the first man who comes along,[10] the wife feels that it is only by degrading herself that she can humiliate her husband.[11]

The battle of the sexes is never finally resolved. With the narrator's refusal of the man's obsequious pleas that he intervene on his behalf, the two central characters are left in a kind of limbo. It is true that the husband issues a warning to the narrator that he will not leave his wife alive (A,293), but, as Klawiter points out, it is doubtful whether he could actually perform the deed.[12] And the flash of metal which the narrator glimpses as he leaves could just as well be money as a knife (A,295).

From sexual battles such as these it seems a long way to the world of *Brief einer Unbekannten*. One might suppose that the unswerving devotion of its heroine could at best serve as contrast to the cruelty and search for domination found in other works. Yet the rapid swing from sadistic to masochistic poles in the central characters of *Der Amokläufer* and *Die Mondscheingasse* is sufficient warrant for a serious questioning of her 'slavish' and 'dog-like' submission (cf. A,222). And on closer examination it does indeed emerge that her attitude to her lover is far from unambiguous. Although there is no evidence of blatant sadism, there are traces of a more subtle form of cruelty and possessive domination, which, together with the self-consciousness she displays about her sacrifices, distinguishes her behaviour from the simplicity and openness of a character like Christine in Schnitzler's *Liebelei*.

These qualities are present in the very existence of the letter which constitutes the main body of the narrative. We shall need to discuss her motives in greater detail later, but here, in the context of the sexual battle, certain questions cannot be avoided. Why, if she prides herself on her anonymity, on living and dying unrecognised, does she write a letter designed to recall her identity to her lover and make him conscious of her sacrifice (cf. A,233 and 237)? Why, if she is not complaining, does she itemise her sufferings so carefully (cf. A,244)? Why, after protecting him from all knowledge of her identity and sufferings during her lifetime, does she burden him with this knowledge after her death, when it is too late for him to make amends? She may argue that a dead woman has no more claim on his love or pity and so will not disturb his comfortable life (A,213), but she has in fact left him with a guilt — or the possibility of a guilt — that can never be expiated. Klawiter goes so far as to assert that, although the letter is unlikely to change the life of the recipient, its probable intention is 'to punish him psychically for the life of physical and mental pain that she has suffered because of him'.[13]

Even when she is indeed protecting her lover by withholding potentially disturbing information, there is an element of psychological ambiguity in her actions. Quite apart from the fact that they sometimes imply an insultingly low opinion of his character — suggesting that, if she were to reveal his paternity, he would not believe her, but suspect her of trying to foist an illegitimate child on him, or that he is by nature incapable of genuine compassion (A,245,246-7) — they also rob him of choice in the matter. She has an image of him according to which he can only survive in carefree ease. It may be an accurate image — we are given little opportunity to discover his own perception of himself — but it is an image accommodated to *her* need for a world to which she may look up, a world above and beyond her narrow circumstances. She also has an image of their relationship as something that must be preserved from all base emotions such as the resentment he might feel at the burden of fatherhood (A,245-6) or the joyless, guilty pity he might experience at her plight, that secret 'Ungeduld, das Unbequeme von Dir wegzuschieben', as she describes it (A,247), looking forward to the theme of Zweig's novel, *Ungeduld des Herzens*.[14] She tells him that it is a matter of pride to her to be remembered only with love and gratitude (A,246). Leaving aside the threat to this aim which the sending of the letter poses, it is worth drawing attention to the role which *her* desires perform in all this. In her apparent self-effacement she asserts her will; her submission to his sexual whims gives her the freedom to dictate the terms of their relationship.

In denying all responsibility to her lover the heroine of *Brief einer Unbekannten* is to some extent placing him in the position of a child. It may well be that, like the hero of *Der Zwang*, he is in any case the sort to evade the difficulties of adult responsibility, but he is given no opportunity to act otherwise. And the manner of his treatment is then continued in the life of their son, who is similarly protected by his mother from all awareness and experience of the unpleasantness of life (A,253). More important than that, the son becomes a surrogate lover in the additional sense that he serves as a means by which she may exercise a possessive dominance over her lover in his absence. One of the reasons why she does not tell him about her pregnancy is the fear that he might persuade her to procure an abortion, which is hateful to her not on moral but on psychological grounds:

> Aber dieses Kind war alles für mich, war es doch von Dir, nochmals Du, aber nun nicht mehr Du, der Glückliche, der Sorglose, den ich nicht zu halten vermochte, sondern Du für immer — so meinte ich — mir gegeben, verhaftet in meinem Leibe, verbunden in meinem Leben. Nun hatte ich Dich ja endlich gefangen, ich konnte Dich, Dein Leben wachsen spüren in meinen Adern, Dich nähren, Dich liebkosen [. . .]. (A,247)

Protectiveness is closely related in her mind to capture and control. Her attempt 'Dich zu halten, den Flüchtigen, in dem Kinde' (A,264) fails not from any relaxation of her domineering power, but because death intervenes. Consequently, with that failure of her surrogate domination, all that is left to her is to impose herself on her lover in her letter and in her apparently modest request that, after her death, he should buy himself flowers on her behalf when it is his birthday.[15] As she puts it, 'ich liebe nur Dich und will nur in Dir noch weiterleben' (A,266). Self-effacement does not mean that she is prepared to disappear and be forgotten entirely. And one may be forgiven for wondering whether to 'live on in him' could not mean an unconscious attempt to dominate posthumously from within.

89

6

Intellectual Feats and Deficiencies

Zweig's psychological interest is focussed predominantly on the affective and instinctive (unconscious) forces of the human mind, though often portrayed in conflict with conscious will and rational faculties, as well as with other passions or other people. He was, however, also fascinated by man's intelligence, especially when it manifested itself in extreme forms. He could wonder at the linguistic versatility of a James Joyce,[1] or the phenomenal memory of people as diverse as Casanova, Balzac, Walther Rathenau, or Frans Masereel,[2] and yet equally at the illiteracy of an unnamed young Italian encountered on board ship.[3] This fascination finds expression in a number of stories, all of which, significantly, fall outside the three volumes that went to form the collection *Die Kette*. With the exception of *Schachnovelle*, they constitute rather the major part of the fictional, but non-legendary material of the collection *Kaleidoskop* of 1936.

Such mental ability (or disability) is a static quality, of itself incapable of propelling the narrative forward. We shall find, therefore, that what dynamic there is derives from its combination with some passion, its conflict with other forces, or the intervention of an external agency.

That the eruption of unconscious forces in *Leporella* should lead to a disturbing and criminal conclusion is due in part to the restricted mentality within which they have to operate. Though not entirely illiterate, as Zweig's Italian acquaintance was, Crescenz never reads, and writes only with difficulty. She is so dull-witted that even to think requires great effort; to grasp a new idea takes considerable time. Such sluggish intelligence explains why her view of life is so extremely blinkered, embracing only 'die fünf gewohnten Begriffe: Geld, Markt, Herd, Küche und Bett' (K,53). For these are matters which need no further mental effort. Most form the content of her daily round, which itself appears demanding enough to exhaust her intellectual and perceptual powers. Only money, which dominates her thinking in the first part of the story, expands her horizons, marginally, beyond the daily round. But even this interest is closely linked with the limitations of her intellect. She hoards money 'mit dem hamsterhaften Instinkt der Bäurischen und Einschichtigen' (K,47). Her naive and fearful misconceptions about the dangers of Vienna are the products of a mind incapable of thinking beyond the need to amass money: 'Betrug und Diebstahl waren die einzigen Gedanken, die ihre klotzige Bauernstirn mit dem Begriff der Großstadt vermörtelten' (K,47-8). Consequently, the experience of the capital city does not have on her the effect it might be expected to have on a young woman from the country: an enlarging of her vision. As the narrator remarks, it brings 'keing Weiterung ihrer innern Welt', but only an increased number of banknotes (K,51).

Crescenz's limited intelligence, so well established on the opening pages of *Leporella*, forms part of the foundation on which the rest of the story is built. It prepares the way for the tenacity, if not the passion, with which she clings to her subsequently conceived plan to serve her master. At the same time Zweig's references to her dull-wittedness are insistent enough to cast doubt on the mechanics of her ultimate, grisly act of devotion. As Martha Gschiel pertinently observes, she hardly seems to have the intelligence to make her murder of the baroness look like suicide.[4]

In *Episode am Genfer See* (1927) psychological analysis is minimal. The work is too short to permit the exploration of a complex mentality, and the central character is observed almost entirely from the outside, with the result that his emotions have to be deduced from his eloquent gestures and facial expressions. What impresses the reader, however, in addition to the sense of alienation in the Russian refugee or deserter, is a quality of mind that might be called either ignorance or innocence, the 'Unbelehrtheit' (K,91), the inconceivable 'Unbildung' of a man whose knowledge scarcely extends beyond his own first name and that of his home village (K,92). His lack of both historical and geographical understanding is comic, yet touching and even challenging. Here is a victim of war who, in the summer of 1918, cannot comprehend the abolition of tsardom in Russia, has no idea of where he has been fighting or how he got there, and fails to appreciate the very notion of a frontier. It is uncertain whether his death by drowning at the end of the story is a conscious act of suicide or the accidental consequence of a naive attempt to swim across Lake Geneva towards home.[5] But it is clear that behind it lies an unbearable sense of alienation which his intelligence is too limited to alleviate. Replying to the suggestion of the hotel-manager that he remain in their Swiss community until the war is over, Boris remarks that he cannot learn the language: 'Ich kann nichts lernen. Ich kann nur auf dem Feld arbeiten, sonst kann ich nichts. Was soll ich hier tun? Ich will nach Hause! Zeige mir den Weg!' (K,95). Hopelessness and restricted intelligence reinforce each other.

Boris and Crescenz are exceptional in their intellectual deficiency. Other characters of Zweig stand out by virtue of some remarkable mental aptitude, although even this may be coupled with a certain limitation. The clearest examples are to be found in *Buchmendel* and *Schachnovelle*, though the aged art-collector of *Die unsichtbare Sammlung* has also, perforce, developed a note-worthy mental skill. Since blindness has overtaken him during the war, his single-minded enthusiasm for his collection has led him to rely entirely on his memory of all its visual details. The reliability of this memory has to be taken on trust, however, for the collection itself has been disposed of by the other members of the family in order to help them survive. Moreover, as the narrator describes the scene in which the old man handles his supposed collection so lovingly, the emphasis shifts from the mental skill, the accuracy of the memory, to a visionary, almost hallucinatory, level of awareness.

In both *Buchmendel* and *Schachnovelle* mental skill plays a much more prominent part. It is also a proven ability, confirmed by what the characters do in public. In the case of the Jewish book-pedlar it is a memory so phenomenal within its chosen sphere that it leads the narrator, a near facsimile of Zweig himself in his predilection for psychological typology, to place him in more famous historical company:

> Unproduktiv und unschöpferisch im letzten [. . .] war dies
> spezifisch antiquarische Gedächtnis Jakob Mendels jedoch in
> seiner einmaligen Vollendung als Phänomen nicht geringer als
> jenes Napoleons für Physiognomien, Mezzofantis für
> Sprachen, eines Lasker für Schachanfänge, eines Busoni für
> Musik [. . .]. (K,105)

The particular content of Mendel's memory is bibliography, which he has mastered so well that he is as reliable as any library catalogue (cf. K,103,105) and more informative, since he is able to quote not only full details of publication, but also the price, new and second-hand (K,104). Of the infallibility of this memory there appears to be no doubt.[6] But of its relation to the senses Zweig gives conflicting evidence. On the one hand, it has a strong optical quality: Mendel is able to retain an eidetic image of any book he has once seen (K,104); and when he provides the narrator with a list of works for a proposed study of Anton Mesmer — a further link between the author and his story-teller — it is as though he were reading from an invisible catalogue (K,102). On the other hand, his method of memorising written material, a secularised application of the method learnt at the Talmud school, which involves a vocalised recitation to the accompaniment of a rhythmic swaying of the body (K,100), seems rather to emphasise the auditory component.

The secret behind this remarkable ability to memorise is absolute concentration, that is, the power to fix the mind on the task in hand and exclude all other matters from attention. His concentration is so complete that, when the narrator goes to pay his first visit to him at the Café Gluck, Mendel fails to notice his arrival, just as another Jakob, the hero of Grillparzer's *Der arme Spielmann*, becomes so absorbed in his music that the arrival of the narrator does not impinge on his consciousness. There will be occasion later to consider the more dubious consequences of Mendel's concentration. For the present it is sufficient to establish only its positive contribution to his prodigious feats of memory.[7]

Memory of this kind, unlike that of the narrator, does not extend far below the surface of consciousness.[8] Nor does it, of itself, involve the affective life of its possessor. Yet the one passion (vanity) which the narrator of *Buchmendel* allows his hero appears only in connection with this mental skill. It expresses itself in pride, in the pleasure he derives from the amazement of those who consult him, and in the offence he takes at the slightest suggestion that he might make a written memorandum (K,103) or at an offer of money for his advice (K,108). His vanity is more than just professional pride. A reference to his 'königlichen Blick' (K,103), comparison with a 'Galeriehofrat' (K,108), and a disparaging contrast with a mere 'Buchhandlungslehrling' or 'Bibliotheks-diener' (K,104) imply a social dimension, a sense of superiority quite foreign to Grillparzer's Jakob and one that accords ill with Mendel's own shabby appearance.

With that the psychological fascination of Mendel is all but exhausted. His specialised genius captures the attention of the narrator (and the reader), but it does not constitute a story. For that we must look elsewhere: to the humiliations and hardships he endures as a passive victim during the latter part of the war and the following years of inflation. Yet even these are not unrelated to his mental skill. As will emerge more clearly in later chapters, his very concentration, the prerequisite for his memory, lays him open to such sufferings. Furthermore, his unhappy experiences in a war-time concentration camp in their turn destroy the memory which is his sole claim to fame.

In the world chess-champion, Mirko Czentovic, who serves as both foil and opponent to the central characater of *Schachnovelle*, Zweig has created a second one-sided genius to stand beside Mendel. And like the Jewish book-pedlar, Czentovic too is conceived of in the context of a psychological classification: among the types of 'intellektueller Überlegenheit' he is the out-sider (S,19), not because of his skill, but because of the lack of culture against which it is set. He is what Alfred Binet would have called an *idiot savant*.

Nevertheless, the particular aptitude which Czentovic possesses is remarkable enough in its own right. From merely observing others play chess he has allegedly acquired the ability to become an active participant and beat the very men he has observed. This, together with the explanation of a rare, early defeat as the result of the fact that he has not witnessed the Sicilian opening from his mentor (S,15), implies a heavy reliance on memory and a gift for mimicry. Yet it is difficult to imagine a chess-player advancing far, let alone becoming world champion, without a highly-developed skill at what psychologists call problem-solving.[9]

It is only when Zweig describes the intellectual limitations which accompany this special gift, however, that the reader's credibility is seriously strained. The 'einseitige sonderbare Begabung' (S,14) of Czentovic is even more radical than that of Mendel. He is a slow learner, even in arithmetic (S,11), and has no intellectual curiosity (S,12). More problematic than that is the repeated assertion that he lacks imagination. He is said to be incapable of playing 'blind': 'Ihm fehlte vollkommen die Fähigkeit, das Schlachtfeld in den unbegrenzten Raum der Phantasie zu stellen' (S,18). Yet it is difficult to accept that anyone can succeed in chess by relying solely on a learnt technique, without the ability to plan moves ahead and construct a mental image of future constellations, which is after all one manifestation of the imagination Czentovic allegedly lacks. With his superior knowledge of chess Jiři Veselý argues that Czentovic simply could not have reached such a standard without being able to play 'blind'.[10] Moreover, in a brief passage of reflection on the philosophy of chess, the narrator too declares that the game is 'mechanisch in der Anlage und doch nur wirksam durch Phantasie' (S,25). In introducing these assertions it seems likely that Zweig was seeking to establish the sharpest possible contrast between Czentovic and the more imaginative Dr B., but in his absolute denial of imaginative powers to the uncouth world champion he overstepped the limits of consistency and credibility.

The narrator speaks of Czentovic as a monomaniac (S,22), a term which can be allowed only as a very loose description. There is no hint of insanity in *him*; and what passion this rather phlegmatic man does display is directed not at chess as a game, as a self-sufficient, autotelic[11] activity, but only at what he gets out of it.[12] He shares something of the avarice of Crescenz in *Leporella*, seeking to make as much money as he can out of tournaments, advertising, or even casual games (S,20); and he takes the professional pride of Mendel to new extremes of unpleasantness.

Reflecting on the peculiar, one-sided genius of Czentovic, the narrator admits that it is difficult to comprehend such a person, 'einen geistigen Menschen, der, ohne wahnsinnig zu werden, zehn, zwanzig, dreißig, vierzig Jahre lang die ganze Spannkraft seines Denkens immer und immer wieder an den lächerlichen Einsatz wendet, einen hölzernen König auf einem hölzernen Brett in den Winkel zu drängen' (S,27). The comment prepares the way for the subsequent account of the insanity that threatens Dr B. when, for a much shorter period of time, he is shut off from all other intellectual activity and has to rely solely on chess to occupy his mind. In the present connection, however, it is worth noting that, as well as threatening his sanity because of the special circumstances under which it has to be performed, his prowess at chess represents an achievement no less remarkable than that of Czentovic. It comprises various mental skills. The first and least amazing of these is memory, by which he comes to learn by heart all the games of the masters printed in the stolen chess-manual. The second is reason, which enables him to understand the different techniques and styles of the players represented (cf. S,80f). The third is imagination, that quality supposedly lacking in Czentovic. Having begun with games on an improvised board, he soon develops the habit of projecting play on to an imaginary board and thence of conducting the games by means of the abstract formulae of chess. The fourth is the more creative skill of problem-solving, which allows him to advance from the mere reproduction of other people's games to the invention of his own (S,82-7). It is a skill which Czentovic too must have possessed in order to progress from the role of passive observer to that of productive player, though in his case it was passed over without comment. In the later stages of Dr B.'s confinement memory, imagination and creative problem-solving are strikingly combined, as he proceeds to play his own games of chess entirely in his head, retaining an awareness of the exact disposition of the pieces at every move. Such mental jugglery is a severe test of the reader's credibility;[13] that it should lead to insanity, as described in the chapter on inner conflicts, does not astonish him in the least.

It is worth emphasising that, while a restricted intellectual life is the permanent corollary of Czentovic's skill, it is only when Dr B. is forced into a position where his mind has nothing else to occupy it that he develops his remarkable gift. In both cases, however, the intellectual feat is inseparable from the intellectual deficiency.

7

The Psychology of Self-Revelation

In varying degrees some nine of Zweig's *Novellen* include an act of self-revelation; they involve a central character who tells his or her own story. This narrative procedure was clearly very congenial to Zweig, perhaps too congenial, since the carping critic has no difficulty in pointing to consequent improbabilities. One American reviewer of *Der Amokläufer* commented on the doctor's 'difficult and slightly artificial role of narrating his own story'.[1] Another, reviewing the translation of *Vierundzwanzig Stunden aus dem Leben einer Frau,* poked fun at the way in which, as he put it, 'an elderly English woman is moved [. . .] to relate an episode in her life to one of the gentlemen guests in 100 pages of finished prose [. . .], a most remarkable feat of writing, but quite a miraculous improvisation for the lady in question'.[2]

In practice, however, the reader is unlikely to be troubled by what is a well-tried convention. Furthermore, Zweig's use of the procedure is not universal or indiscriminate. Some characters are evidently adjudged to be too incommunicative. That is why in *Schachnovelle,* for example, Dr B. is allowed to tell his own story, but Czentovic is not.[3] Even where self-revelation is deemed appropriate, it assumes different forms: it may be spoken or written; it may be addressed to a third person, to the public at large, or to no one at all. The written form might be considered inherently more plausible, since it allows for greater rational control and organisation than a spontaneous verbal disclosure. Yet that too demands a suspension of disbelief; it requires the reader to accept from an uncultured, lower-class woman (*Brief einer Unbekannten*) a standard of German scarcely less high than that of a university professor (*Verwirrung der Gefühle*). All of these difficulties, real or imaginary, lose their significance once it is granted that self-revelation is always subject to editorial revision. In *Verwirrung der Gefühle* the confession of Roland's professor is presented in an abbreviated form and in Roland's words; in *Episode am Genfer See* the account which Boris gives of his background and unhappy war-time experiences is presented indirectly, as an organised summary and translation of his own confused and Russian version (K,90-1); and in *Schachnovelle*, where Dr B. apparently tells his own story in the first person, the primary narrator informs us subsequently that 'Dr B. hatte mir alles viel ausführlicher berichtet, als ich es hier zusammenfasse' (S,101). There seems no reason to suppose that this sort of editorial revision should not also be inferred in those cases where it is not explicitly acknowledged.

In a few instances — the accounts of Boris in *Episode am Genfer See* and Dr B. in *Schachnovelle* — the motives for self-revelation are simple: the characters are either responding to another's desire for information or seeking to explain their present situation. The act of telling performs no further function in their psychological economy. Elsewhere, however, and particularly in those works where the inset narrative constitutes the major part of the total story, Zweig takes pains to motivate the act of self-disclosure and to do so in a way that makes each distinguishable from the others. In some cases it is no exaggeration to say that the psychology of the central character has not been fully understood until the reasons for his or her self-revelation have been appreciated. The narrative act is part of the individual's total psychological experience. That, rather than the attempt to rebut the charge of implausibility, is our warrant for discussing the matter.

Important as the urge to tell may be, it does not follow a straightforward course. It will be recalled that in *Angst* it was one element of the heroine's inner conflicts that the impulse to confess had to contend with a powerful sense of shame. In her case the resolution of the conflict issued in a fit of sobbing and never assumed verbal form, that is, never became a narrative. Yet even where confessions are put into words they are usually the product of a considerable mental struggle.

In *Sommernovellette* self-concealment rather than self-revelation seems to be the governing principle of the elderly dilettante's narration. In the end, however, his meeting with the first-person narrator almost assumes the character of a visit to the psycho-analyst, from whom he disguises the truth, but who finally persuades him to accept consciously what he has hitherto resisted. It is not that the older man has come initially with an urge to confess. The two are casual acquaintances, and the story told arises out of a conversation in which he answers a comment about his failure to communicate his aesthetic appreciation to a wider public by arguing that all experience is over as soon as it is felt and that even literature has only a limited time-span. He then introduces his story with the words: 'Aber ich will Ihnen heute etwas erzählen, wovon ich glaube, daß es eine hübsche Novelle wäre' (EE,194), words which already imply an ambivalent attitude to what he has experienced: on the one hand, the admission of a more than fleeting significance and yet, on the other, the denial of that significance in ironic fictionalisation.

The story he tells deals only with the effect of his spurious love-letters on the adolescent girl and ends at the point when she returns home in anger and despair. 'Das war die Geschichte', he tells the young narrator, 'Wäre es nicht eine Novelle?' (EE,205). With that he is not simply setting his experience at an ironic distance once more. He is holding back an essential part of it: the embarrassing fact that, after playing on the girl's emotions, he himself has become infatuated with her like a young boy. When the narrator indicates that the story as told is too incomplete to form a *Novelle*, the older man talks first of a hypothetical continuation of the girl's life-story, then of some possible elaboration on the young Italian; that is to say, he avoids precisely that conclusion which touches him most nearly. It is left to the narrator to conclude his painful story in an ostensibly fictional completion of what has so far been revealed. This version provokes an unusually vehement denial: 'Verlogen, falsch, unmöglich!' (EE,206). Its vehemence is in fact an involuntary admission of the involvement the older man is con-sciously seeking to hide.

On reflection one sees that this is not the first time he has betrayed what his conscious self has refused to admit. After all, his account begins with a confession that he has misled the narrator: despite his earlier assertions that he never repeats anything — and, one might add, despite his argument that an experience is over as soon as it is felt — he has returned to the same hotel he visited the previous year (EE,195). And during the course of his narration, when he describes the transformation that comes over the girl once she believes herself to be loved, he waxes lyrical in a way that does not escape the notice of the young narrator (EE,201-2). These two circumstances now fall into place as the first unwitting revelations of an emotional entanglement he finds too compromising to admit publicly. Although fictionalisation and suppression of the truth, the weapons he has used to avoid embarrassment, prove inadequate to their psychological task, the sufferer is finally able to admit not only the painful facts but also his act of concealment. This is how he explains it to the narrator:

> 'Aber die alten Leute, die davon das Heimlichste wissen, erzählen nur gern von ihren Erfolgen und nicht von ihren Schwächen. Sie fürchten lächerlich zu sein in Dingen, die doch nur irgendwie der Pendelschlag des Ewigen sind.' (EE,207)

By the end of the story the man has come to terms with his experience, not so much through an act of open self-revelation as through an acceptance of what the narrator reconstructs out of denials and involuntary half-disclosures and then places in front of him.

In *Der Amokläufer* more powerful and urgent emotions are at stake in the doctor's act of narration. If self-revelation is the more immediate urge, the opposing need for concealment is never far away. Strelka indeed makes an overt psychoanalytical link with the 'Spannungsverhältnis zwischen Verdrängungswunsch und Offenbarungsdrang'.[4] The impulse to confess impresses itself on the narrator during his second encounter with the mysterious stranger aboard ship when, confronted by the hungry look in the man's eyes, he realises that here is someone who has to speak (A,21). The compulsion may be explained by two interrelated factors, one external, the other internal. On the one hand, the doctor is suffering acutely from lack of company and therefore opportunity to communicate, a problem which dates back to his years at a remote district station in the East, but is now intensified by his presence on board ship as a virtual stowaway, forced to remain hidden from others. On the other hand, his mind is still preoccupied with the unresolved issue of his relations with the

Englishwoman. That is why he seizes on the narrator's casual reference to man's duty to offer help and repeats it over and over again. For that is the question which still torments him: whether a doctor must be a saviour of all and throw away his life for the sake of others (A,22-3). The story he unfolds helps therefore to satisfy a need to ventilate an issue which has not ceased to exercise his mind even after the woman's death. Moreover, at the climax of his narration, when he has to deal with the woman's horrifying death and in doing so grips his listener's arm convulsively, bares his teeth like an animal, and shrieks rather than speaks (A,67), there can be no doubt that a powerful concrete experience rather than an abstract moral issue is continuing to play on his mind and seeking verbal release.

At the same time the doctor is subject to a contrary need to conceal his story. This is evident in his hesitant beginning, in his short-lived attempt to present the facts as the experience of a third person — a device reminiscent of the fictionalising tendency of the elderly man in *Sommernovellette* — and in the numerous pauses in his narration, which provide the author with a neat means of breaking up the material into easily assimilable sections (quasi-chapters), but also serve to illustrate the present psychological conflict within the central character. For him the pauses afford the opportunity to take in more whiskey, to loosen a tongue which threatens to dry up before the painful events it has to record. In all of this the doctor is apparently not troubled by a point which may well puzzle the reader: that his act of narration goes right against his promise to the Englishwoman that he would keep her secret, the promise he subsequently revives in taking her coffin with him into the depths of Naples harbour rather than have a post-mortem examination reveal the shame of her illegal abortion. One might, of course, argue that he is merely confiding in a neutral stranger, who has already assured him of his discretion in the matter of his presence aboard ship and so may be trusted with more momentous information. Nevertheless — to continue the narrative pretence to its logical conclusion — it must then be admitted that this is a misplaced trust, since the narrator proceeds to tell all the world, even if after a decent lapse of time. Be that as it may, what appears to check the flow of the doctor's story is not anxiety about the woman's secret, but fear of disclosing his own part in the story. As he nears the end of his account, the narrator senses his companion's shame: 'unendliche Scham, sich verraten zu haben an mich, an diese Nacht' (A,83). And the doctor mocks that alleged duty to help others, the maxim by which, as he believes, he has been lured into an admission of his own guilt.

That the doctor does complete his account means that the impulse to communicate proves stronger than the impulse to conceal. (If that were not so, there would of course be no story *Der Amokläufer.*) It does not mean, however, that the act of narration has brought a cathartic release. The first-person narrator has not fulfilled the role of a successful psycho-analyst and enabled the patient to talk away his symptoms. 'Glauben Sie ja nicht, daß mir jetzt leichter sei, seit ich mir die Eingeweide vor Ihnen aufgerissen habe bis zum Kot in meinen Därmen', the doctor tells his listener bitterly and somewhat melodramatically. 'Mein verpfuschtes Leben kann mir keiner mehr zusammenflicken' (A,84). It must also be conceded that, as Strelka puts it, the doctor has not been persuaded to reveal the origin of his 'neurosis' in some childhood trauma.[5] But the reason for that is not some failure of the therapeutic process; it is simply that Zweig does not endow him with a childhood trauma. What he does is to present a character who to the end remains in thrall to the dead Englishwoman and claims only one right for himself: to die as he chooses.

The reader of *Phantastische Nacht* can hardly fail to notice one immediate difference from *Sommernovellette* and *Der Amokläufer* in the baron's account of his volcanic experience. It is not spoken to a listener, but is a written document, handed to the first-person narrator as a work of fiction after its author's untimely death, but accepted by the narrator as a true record. A rather less obvious, though more important, difference lies in the baron's insistence that his narrative is not intended for any public, which, if it were true, would mean that the question of self-revelation could not, strictly speaking, arise. During the four months since his experience he has felt an inexplicable compulsion to depict the events (A,123), but, as he emphasises both at the beginning and at the end of his story, he has written the account only for himself (A,124,206). He has not informed any of his friends (A,206), explaining that he would be unable to make them understand the essential nature of what happened to him and would feel embarrassed at having allowed himself to be overwhelmed by such an accidental occurrence (A,124). If that seems to indicate that the urge to conceal has already been at work in him, what of that opposite impulse to communicate? Can one accept his assurances that he is writing only for himself? In fact his repeated remarks about the difficulty he now encounters in explaining his experience and his apologies for the lack of a literary talent sufficient to his task make no sense unless there is an implied readership to whom they are addressed.[6] In the end one must conclude either that the author has not entirely succeeded in matching his chosen narrative method to the needs of his characterisation or that there is indeed in the baron an urge to communicate of which he himself is not aware. Certainly, the first-person narrator who introduces the document seems to be in no doubt that it represents what he calls a 'seelische Selbstenthüllung' (A,123).

There are two explicit reasons which the baron offers (to whom if not an implied reader?) for documenting his experience: 'es noch einmal nachzugenießen im Gefühl und gleichzeitig geistig zu erfassen' (A,125). At first he speaks of his record as an attempt to come to terms with, have done with the experience — the expression he uses is 'fertig werden' (A,124) — but soon he revises this interpretation, asserting that he wants, not to be rid of it in any way, but to preserve it as a warm, living experience. It is not that he is afraid of losing it entirely, for the events are too clearly imprinted on his memory. He simply wishes to relive the joy by rehearsing the details (A,125-6). In addition to this after-pleasure he also seeks an intellectual understanding of what has happened, and this requires a degree of objective distance. What lives on in his mind has still an intoxicating power over him; the flood of images it produces threatens to confound his undertaking. Rational control is needed to provide order; hence the precise dating and timing of events and the insistence on a strict chronology (A,126). In sum, although the baron's affective life appears to be at odds with his rational faculties, the narrative act is conceived as a means of reconciling both in a fuller apprehension of what he now regards as the turning point in his life.

The inner narrative of *Brief einer Unbekannten* is a further example of the written record. As a letter, however, it differs from the baron's account in *Phantastische Nacht* in that it is consciously addressed to a reader, a very specific reader, over whose shoulders we are then, as it were, allowed to look.

For the woman who composes the letter the most immediate

psychological need it fulfils is to ventilate her emotions, particularly her grief at the death of her son. On three separate occasions she uses the verb 'ausschreien' to give expression to a sense of pent-up feeling seeking release (A,213,249,265). On the first occasion she goes on to say that, if she does not herself fall victim to the fatal influenza which has carried off her son, she may well commit suicide and thereby invites the suspicion that the letter affords an alternative outlet, less injurious to herself. The compulsion to communicate is quite as powerful as that of the doctor in *Der Amokläufer*, and its urgency derives from a similar sense of isolation, less extended in time than his, but equally acute, since the one individual on whom she has come to concentrate all her attention and love is now a silent corpse. It is small wonder therefore that she should seek release in an act of self-disclosure and that this should be directed to the one person who was already embodied for her, by way of substitution, in the now dead child. That is the sense of her reference to the content of her letter as something which 'mein zu Dir hinflüchtender Schmerz Dir verrät' (A,214). And that distinguishes her letter from the narration of the doctor in *Der Amokläufer*, where the verbal catharsis is sought independently of the listener's identity.

As one reads the woman's letters, however, it becomes clear that there is more than grief at the loss of a son which is seeking release. At times it seems just to reach the level of consciousness. For when she has told of her humiliating confinement at the public hospital, she adds an apology:

> Verzeih, verzeih mirs, daß ich davon spreche. Aber nur dieses eine Mal rede ich davon, nie mehr wieder. Elf Jahre habe ich geschwiegen davon, und werde bald stumm sein in alle Ewigkeit: einmal mußte ichs ausschreien, einmal ausschreien, wie teuer ich es erkaufte, dies Kind, das meine Seligkeit war und das nun dort ohne Atem liegt. Ich hatte sie schon vergessen, diese Stunden, längst vergessen im Lächeln, in der Stimme des Kindes, in meiner Seligkeit; aber jetzt, da es tot ist, wird die Qual wieder lebendig, und ich mußte sie mir von der Seele schreien, dieses eine, dieses eine Mal. (A,249)

It has been the pride of her conscious aim to keep from her lover the secret of her identity and her sufferings. But this has evidently created considerable mental tension, and the resentment which has been held in check for so long forces its way through the breach already made by her grief and erupts in a flow of self-disclosure and a carefully documented catalogue of self-sacrifice, which contradicts her open avowal that she is far from seeking to accuse her lover or be a burden to him.

It seems probable that the act of putting pen to paper will have been therapeutic in itself. There is no reason to doubt the woman's assertion that, if she survives the influenza epidemic, she will not send the letter to her lover. She estimates, in other words, that she will have obtained sufficient emotional release from the mere writing of it to live on in obscurity. Yet she is not prepared to die, to accept the final sacrifice, without revealing herself and the nature of her sufferings and devotion. Near the end of her letter, when death seems inevitable, she alleges that she will die with a light heart only because it will not cause her lover sorrow and expresses the conviction that the love which she has so fully described will not be a burden to him (A,265,266). These remarks are by no means as unambiguously considerate as she appears to think. If she is correct in her assessment of him, they must act as a veiled accusation, a last reminder to him of the egocentric lack of sensitivity he has shown her throughout; and if she is not correct, they will bequeath to him a sense of guilt which can no longer be expiated after her death. At the very last moment, then, her conscious aim to protect her lover by means of silence is forced to yield to a long-restrained impulse to communicate something of herself and her sacrifice.

Die Mondscheingasse returns to the pattern of *Der Amokläufer*: a need for self-revelation stands in conflict with a desire for concealment which has less to do with the protection of others than with the speaker's sense of shame at his own behaviour. The abject husband is caught up in what the narrator describes as 'dieses Ringen der Scham und seelischen Not' (A,285). The shame is manifested in his repeated abortive attempts to begin his narrative; in physical symptoms such as a choking sensation which threatens to prevent him from speaking of particularly painful matters (A,285,287,290); and in the hesitations and repetitions of his delivery, which Zweig is able to maintain throughout his short narrative, but which would soon become tedious in a more extended piece. The compulsion to communicate, on the other hand, is apparent from the way in which he sticks close to the narrator as if afraid of losing his audience (A,284); from the highly-charged silence which precedes his narrative and which the narrator, in words reminiscent of the heroine of *Brief einer Unbekannten*, describes as 'voll inneren Schreis' (A,285); and from the simple fact that he does after all reveal his life-story for all the humiliation it entails. As he proceeds, moreover, it is as though the impulse to communicate were operating independently of his will, even of his listener: 'Offenbar hatte er mich vergessen. Mechanisch sprach er, wie aus dem Schlaf, mit immer lauterer Stimme' (A,288). That the impulse possesses such autonomous power is due in no small measure to the fact that he is not simply rehearsing past events, but is dealing with an experience which continues into the most painful humiliations of the here and now. When he seizes hold of the narrator at the end of his story and falls begging at his knees (A,293-4), he is no longer concerned to retain a listener; he is pleading for help in the present misery of his marital relations.

Mrs C.'s account of her volcanic experience in *Vierundzwanzig Stunden aus dem Leben einer Frau* represents the lengthiest oral narrative in any of Zweig's *Novellen*. But that does not mean that, in her urge to disclose herself, she has less resistance to overcome than the doctor of *Der Amokläufer* or the husband of *Die Mondscheingasse*. In the tense silence before she launches into her story the narrator comes to sense 'daß hier ein starker Wille gewaltsam mit einem starken Widerstand rang' (VdG,29). This struggle may be regarded as a revival of the contradictory urges which were evident in her behaviour immediately after her adventure with the young Polish gambler more than twenty years before, when, having rushed back home to her relatives, she had great difficulty in restraining the urge to blurt out ('herauszu-schreien') her betrayal of them, but then returned to France to live in obscurity and so conceal her shame (VdG,100). In the present of the narrative frame her urge to communicate is indicated first by the way in which, after the narrator's defence of Mme Henriette, she keeps returning to the theme of eruptive passion as to an obsessive preoccupation (VdG,25), then by the restlessness she displays on learning that the narrator, her potential audience, is about to leave (VdG,26), and finally, once she has got into her story, by the impression she gives of one who has prepared herself inwardly for what she wants to say (VdG,47). The contrary impulse to conceal is evident above all in the pauses in her

106

narrative, which, like those of the doctor in *Der Amokläufer*, help to divide the material into quasi-chapters, but which also serve to convey something of the speaker's psychological state. For they are usually marked by agitation on her part, the result of the difficulties she faces in speaking honestly of a particularly shameful episode in her experience (cf. VdG,47,60,67,83).

At several points, both before and after her narration, Mrs C. is portrayed as if she were a young woman during her first sexual encounter. She favours the narrator with her company in such a way that, as he puts it, 'ich auf eitle und seltsame Gedanken hätte kommen können, wäre sie nicht eine alte weißhaarige Frau gewesen' (VdG,25). Having arranged a future rendezvous in her own private room, she is 'mädchenscheu' and responds with coy embarrassment to any encounter with him in the meantime (VdG,28). And at the very end, having thanked him for listening so carefully to her story, she blushes. 'Ganz wie ein Mädchen stand sie da', he writes, 'bräutlich verwirrt von Erinnerungen und beschämt von dem eigenen Geständnis' (VdG,102-3). As Frau Irene in *Angst* would have appreciated, self-revelation in the narrative act is akin to the uncovering of the body in the first sexual act and is therefore accompanied by similar feelings of desire and shame.

Although the immediate cause of Mrs C.'s self-revelation is the sudden elopement of Mme Henriette and the ensuing discussion among the hotel-guests, it is made plain that the need has long been there, that the events of twenty and more years ago have never ceased to occupy her mind (VdG,27,29). There is a conflict within her which she has not yet been able to resolve, a conflict, moreover, which corresponds closely to that between the urge to communicate and the urge to conceal. With part of her being she affirms the actions of long ago, with part she accepts society's verdict and condemns them. That is why her response to Mme Henriette is so contradictory:

> [. . .] es schien ihr ein ganz geheimnisvolles Vergnügen zu bereiten, die Pflichtvergessene einer seelischen Haltlosigkeit und Unzuverlässigkeit zu beschuldigen. Aber gleichzeitig schien sie sich der Unerschütterlichkeit zu freuen, mit der meine Sympathien auf der Seite dieser zarten, feinen Frau verblieben. (VdG,26)

In retrospect it becomes clear that she is not really talking about Mme Henriette, but about herself. Yet she can hardly be said to be hiding her own shame behind a third person, as the doctor of *Der Amokläufer* does at the beginning of his narrative. She is rather preparing the way for an open revelation of a mind in need of confirmation and release from self-accusation.

That in turn brings us to the role in which she has cast her carefully chosen listener, the narrator: for all his relative youth he must serve her as psychiatrist.[7] It is a role for which he has no formal qualification, only the sympathy with which he has defended Mme Henriette; but it is a role which he appears to perform with some success, certainly more so than his counterpart in *Der Amokläufer*. Realising that he cannot require her to tell him more than her inner self wishes, he nevertheless asks her to be honest (VdG,27). And this she seeks to do. It might, of course, be argued that her reconciling influence on the other hotel guests betokens a well-integrated woman, who has no need of even a lay psychiatrist. Nevertheless, there is something morbid in her brooding preoccupation with events of the distant past. As she tells the narrator at the beginning of her story:

'[. . .] ich habe mir damals, als ich Sie so sachlich über den Fall Henriette reden hörte, gedacht, vielleicht würde dieses sinnlose Zurückdenken und unablässige Sich-selbst-Anklagen ein Ende haben, könnte ich mich einmal entschließen, vor irgendeinem Menschen frei über diesen einen Tag meines Lebens zu sprechen. Wäre ich nicht anglikanischer Konfession, sondern Katholikin, so hätte mir längst die Beichte Gelegenheit geboten, dies Verschwiegene im Wort zu erlösen — aber diese Tröstung ist uns versagt, und so mache ich heute diesen sonderbaren Versuch, mich selbst freizusprechen, indem ich zu Ihnen spreche.' (VdG,29-30)[8]

In several of the works considered earlier the self-revelatory impulse was expressed in the verb '(aus-)schreien'. It is a mark of Mrs C.'s more civilised manner that the same impulse in her is characterised by a less strident notion: 'sprechen', 'freisprechen', and later 'wegsprechen' (VdG,102). Yet the cathartic desire is still there — and appears finally to be satisfied.

With *Verwirrung der Gefühle* we return to the pattern of *Phantastische Nacht*. Although there is no narrative frame in the sense of an independent voice which introduces and transmits the story,[9] we are again presented with a written document,[10] which professes to have no public. The sub-title of the work indicates that these are 'private Aufzeichnungen des Geheimrates R. v. D.'[11] The writer describes the document as 'ein verschwiegenes Blatt', in which he is narrating the story of his youth to himself (VdG,157). Yet it is difficult to square this with his chief aim (which we shall consider next). In any case the whole fiction presupposes that we, as readers, have access to what he has written.

On the intellectual level Roland's document is a weapon of truth; it is an attempt to set the record straight on the matter of his academic career, which the 'Festschrift' compiled by his well-meaning colleagues and pupils has only inadequately described. In doing this, however, it also satisfies a deeper need of his affective life. The 'Festschrift' knows nothing of his earlier relations with the homosexual professor to whom alone he owes the creative impulse of his scholarly career. Hitherto he himself has kept what he regards as a cowardly silence on the subject; or to put it another way, the urge to conceal has held undisputed sway. Now, however, he is conscious of the omission as an unpaid debt (VdG,157). The difficulty is to understand how a debt of silence can be repaid by a document which is, allegedly, not intended to reach the eyes of the public. The truth is that it cannot, though it may help to diminish the debtor's sense of guilt. And in the end it is only that which matters. He describes the purpose of his tribute to the shade of his mentor as follows:

> [. . .] damit er wieder zu mir spreche und der längst schon Weggealterte bei mir, dem Alternden, sei. Ich will ein verschwiegenes Blatt legen zu den offenbaren, ein Bekenntnis des Gefühls neben das gelehrte Buch und mir selbst um seinetwillen die Wahrheit meiner Jugend erzählen. (VdG,157)

The narration is intended to satisfy his needs; its subject is his own youth as much as the problematic nature of his professor, whom, as he openly acknowledges only in the concluding sentence, he has loved as much as mother and father, wife and children. The story he tells is less an act of self-revelation than an attempt to relive the most momentous period of his life by conjuring up the presence of the man 'der mein Schicksal bestimmte und nun wieder mit doppelter Gewalt mich in meine Jugend ruft' (VdG,156-7).

The final pages of Roland's record are taken up by the confession which his professor makes to him just before they part for ever. Although the confession is not presented *verbatim*, but indirectly and in summary form, considerable attention is paid to the speaker's state of mind. His act of self-revelation is not only reserved for a very particular listener, but is inseparable from a particular moment in their relationship: the moment after he has openly confessed his love for the younger man. That too has been subject to the conflict between a restraining sense of shame and a need for declaration, the latter of which finally proved the stronger. When it comes to his revelatory explanation, the story of his life, shame still dictates that he speak in soft tones and with lights extinguished (VdG,262); but once he has begun, his pent-up desires issue in a flood of words:

> Hier aber schlug ein Mensch sich mir auf in äußerster Nacktheit, hier zerriß sich einer die innerste Brust gierig bereit, das zerhämmerte, vergiftete, verbrannte, vereiterte Herz zu entblößen. Eine wilde Wollust folterte sich flagellantisch frei in diesem durch Jahre und Jahre verhaltenen Geständnis. Nur wer ein Leben lang sich geschämt, sich geduckt und verdeckt, nur der konnte so rauschhaft überwältigt ausfahren in die Unerbittlichkeit eines solchen Gestehens. (VdG,263)

In *Vierundzwanzig Stunden aus dem Leben einer Frau* the act of self-revelation had sexual overtones. Here a brief hint of sexual deviation has been added for good measure. By the end of the professor's account, however, matters have returned to normal; self-revelation is now presented as a straightforward sexual act. The only surprising thing is that Roland is cast in the woman's role:

> Und ich nahm diese heiß vorstoßende, diese glühend eindringende Stimme in mich auf, schauernd und schmerzhaft, wie ein Weib den Mann in sich empfängt. (VdG,272)

That, however, merely confirms the suggestions of sexual ambivalence in Roland which were considered earlier.

8

The Psychology of Curiosity

The psychological curiosity of which Rolland spoke in his introduction to *Amok* was something of which Zweig himself was aware and which he openly acknowledged. 'If I had to confess which quality has been predominant to make me a writer', he once wrote for his English public, 'I believe I would have to name one which generally is not very much appreciated in private life — a great and insatiable curiosity'.[1] The multifarious psychological specimens discussed in earlier chapters are the chief evidence of this quality in his work as a story-teller; but it is also embodied in the curiosity displayed by so many of his fictional counterparts, the first person narrators. Just as there are characters with an urge to reveal themselves, so there are narrators with an urge to know, narrators who are therefore not simply devices for the introduction of a story, but psychologically interesting characters in their own right. Not all first-person narrators are given to this tendency; and the appearance of those who are does not necessarily coincide with the use of a self-revelatory inner narration. For, as we have observed, some of those narratives are written documents, which entail no personal encounter with a narrator. Furthermore, the narrator may demonstrate all his curiosity on a character who has no story to tell, or at least does not tell it.

On the face of it, curiosity of this kind might appear to be a purely intellectual matter. Nevertheless, leaving aside the Freudian contention that all curiosity has a sexual origin,[2] it must be stressed that the curiosity of Zweig's narrators derives as much as anything from their instinctive life. Predation (already implied in Roland's sobriquet 'chasseur d'âmes'), sexuality, and the gambling instinct

111

are never far away. This awareness of the instinctive component in curiosity may recall the 'anthropologischer Heißhunger' to which the narrator of Grillparzer's *Der arme Spielmann* admits, but it is present in Zweig's writing generally. Of his beloved Verhaeren, for example, he once wrote: '[. . .] wie ein Raubritter nach Abenteuern aus seiner Burg zog er dann sorglos in die Stadt hinein, sich Beute für seine große schöpferische Neugier zu erraffen'.[3] Nietzsche's restless search for knowledge he likened to Don Juan's compulsive pursuit of women.[4] Man's quest to penetrate the uncharted polar regions he depicted as a violation of virgin innocence by man's insatiable desire for knowledge.[5] And in the heroine of the story *Angst* he described the following realisation, to her a powerful cause of fear that her guilty secret will not escape her lawyer-husband, but to the reader an insight of general validity into the nature of curiosity:

> Aufspüren, Entfalten, Erklären eines kriminellen Falles konnte ihn beschäftigen wie andere Hasardspiel oder Erotik, und in solchen Tagen psychologischer Spürjagd war sein Wesen gleichsam innerlich durchglüht. (K,147)[6]

Irene probably does her husband an injustice here, but the description itself is an apt reminder of a tendency which is evident in many of Zweig's narrators. It is significant that curiosity of this kind plays virtually no part in the attitude of the narrator of *Vierundzwanzig Stunden aus dem Leben einer Frau*, where the act of self-revelation brings with it a healing catharsis, but is a prominent factor in the narrators of *Der Amokläufer* and *Die Mondscheingasse*, where self-revelation does not lead to the restoration of mental harmony.

From the very beginning the narrator of *Der Amokläufer* emerges as a man of great curiosity. He is returning to Europe from a sight-seeing trip to India, where he has, in his own words, 'rasch ineinanderstürzende Bilder in rasender Jagd in [sich] eingetrunken' (A,12). This active pursuit, with its predatory, masculine character, is counterbalanced on board ship, where he seeks to order these teeming images in his mind, by an experience of ecstatic reverie under the star-lit sky, in which he enjoys the sensual pleasure of yielding his body 'weibisch' to the surrounding softness (A,15). It is this 'feminine' passivity which is interrupted by his discovery of the mysterious stranger, the doctor. From that

112

moment his curiosity is activated once more, although it still has to contend with a contradictory impulse of an as yet unfamiliar kind. In much the same way as the doctor's urge to reveal himself is checked by shame the narrator's urge to discover more about the stranger is opposed by fear, not only at the unexplained presence of the man, but more at his state of mind, his compulsion to speak, his obsessive preoccupation with the notion of man's 'obligation to help' (A,17,21,22). It scarcely needs to be said that curiosity gets the better of the narrator. Even after the first brief meeting his sleep is disturbed by confused images. The following day finds him tormented by 'Neugier, mehr von diesem ungewöhnlichen Passagier zu wissen'; and the language in which he describes his attempts to penetrate the stranger's identity bears witness to an element of both predation and (male) sexuality in his quest:

> Rätselhafte psychologische Dinge haben über mich eine geradezu beunruhigende Macht, es reizt mich bis ins Blut, Zusammenhänge aufzuspüren, und sonderbare Menschen können mich durch ihre bloße Gegenwart zu einer Leidenschaft des Erkennenwollens entzünden, die nicht viel geringer ist als jene des Besitzenwollens bei einer Frau. (A,19)

The instinct to know becomes so powerful indeed that it operates within him as an independent 'etwas', overcoming his dread and drawing him involuntarily to a second meeting with the doctor (A,20). With that, curiosity has done its job. Although the narrator's dread has not been banished, he soon finds himself no more than a passive listener to the doctor's gripping tale, which in turn serves to satisfy the need aroused in him.

The narrator we meet at the beginning of *Die Mondscheingasse* has given himself over to a sensation of passive drift, among the crowds thronging the open boulevards of a Mediterranean port. It is a state of mind reminiscent of the ecstasy experienced by the narrator of *Der Amokläufer* as he is rocked by the ship and gazes at the stars. Before long, however, he grows weary of this noisy, intoxicating drift and escapes into the dark, narrow side-streets. His unacknowledged purpose, which nevertheless becomes clear from his reference to such districts as the 'Markt aller Leidenschaften' and from his extended and colourful description of their many temptations, is to experience some adventure of the senses, dangerous as well as pleasurable. In the event, he finds what he is looking for not in intercourse with a prostitute, but, more indirectly, in his encounter with a wretched husband in thrall to his haughty prostitute-wife. The narrator's response to their behaviour is no less contradictory than that of his counterpart in *Der Amokläufer*: he is 'gefesselt von Neugier und Grauen' (A,278); the urge to know what lies behind the present scene is opposed by a fear of what he might discover. A variation of this ambivalence characterises his departure from the brothel. Although he has been disgusted by its atmosphere and by the faded, artificial charms of the woman, his horror soon gives way to a kind of intellectual satisfaction, that of having witnessed something of the variety of human fate (A,284). The pleasure which is the object of curiosity has been at least partially realised, but the 'Neugier des Herzens', which forms part of his emotional giddiness when he is pursued by the abject husband, will be satisfied only by the latter's life-story.

The man seems eager to tell his story; the narrator's curiosity is greater than his disgust or horror. Why, then, does he not encourage the act of self-revelation? On his own admission he has been infected by the sadistic cruelty of the man's wife. Instead of helping him to unburden himself, he derives an added pleasure from observing the other's mental conflict, that struggle between shame and the need for self-disclosure discussed earlier (A,285). The purpose of the narrator's life seems therefore to consist in the accumulation of essentially aesthetic experiences, the satisfaction of a thirst for any knowledge which makes no demands on him. Consequently, when the husband reaches the end of his story, the narrator is unable to find any words of consolation; there is not even a perfunctory acknowledgement of man's 'obligation to help' such as enters the thinking of his counterpart in *Der Amokläufer*. From a man so given to the pursuit of pleasure there can be no response to cries for assistance in the reconciliation of husband and wife. The next morning finds him resuming the life of a tourist. Although he is once more drawn back to the scene of his adventure, there is no suggestion of altruism at work. The first sight of the husband, beckoning him over, renews his fear of involvement and provokes a final hasty retreat (A,295).

In the narrator of *Buchmendel* curiosity is much less pervasive. Initially, indeed, as he takes shelter from a rainstorm in an as yet unidentified Viennese café, he is in a state of mental inertia, a passivity even more profound than that experienced by the narrator of *Die Mondscheingasse* immediately after his disembarkation. Only very slowly is he roused from his somnolence by a growing awareness of having been there before. A mild unrest gives way to an inner excitement, an angry impatience to know. It is important, however, to note certain differences between his state of mind and the curiosity of other narrators. In the first place, the need to find out is directed backwards at the past. It is not therefore '*Neugier*', but the urge to unlock the secrets of his memory. Recovery rather than discovery is the aim. In the second place, his immediate object is knowledge not of a third person, a stranger, but of part of his own experience: 'hier haftete, im Unsichtbaren versteckt wie der Nagel im Holz, etwas von meinem eigenen, längst überwachsenen Ich' (K,98). And finally, if curiosity is akin to the predatory instinct to the extent that it usually entails a form of 'living off' another, then in *Buchmendel* it is rendered harmless. The imagery of angling is used extensively to describe the narrator's quest for the knowledge that eludes him (K,98-9), but his intended prey is not some other living being. He is after memories, seeking to recover the experiences of an earlier self.

It is of course true that, when the catch is finally netted, it turns out to be very much concerned with a third person, Jakob Mendel. But that comes as a surprise to the angling narrator, who is now able to depict his former acquaintance in the fullest possible detail. From the way in which he proceeds to tell of his first encounter it becomes clear that Mendel was an object not only of affectionate admiration, but also of youthful curiosity. He speaks of him in the context of a possible classification of psychological types and in such a way that the book-pedlar emerges as a rare specimen, a curiosity, one might say (K,105). The narrator derives an almost sexual pleasure from the observation of his activities: 'Bei einer solchen Konsultation Mendel zuzusehen, bereitete mir jungem neugierigen [sic] Menschen eine Wollust besonderer Art' (K,107).

The curiosity which reappears in the narrative present of the frame assumes the form of a desire to know what has become of the man who was once such an inalienable part of the Café Gluck: 'Jetzt aber, vor diesem leeren Tische, fühlte ich eine Art Scham vor ihm und eine erneuerte Neugier zugleich' (K,110). The curiosity which the narrator here experiences does certainly seek new information, but it differs from that found in his counterparts in *Der Amokläufer* and *Die Mondscheingasse* by virtue of the fact that its object is not before him as a living being, whose self-revelation will be a painful though necessary act. The shame which here accompanies his curiosity is not a contrary emotion, as though he were ashamed of wanting to find out what had become of Mendel. The context makes plain that it is rather a complementary emotion, arising from his failure to remember the man. And the story of Mendel's subsequent fate, as told by the cloakroom-attendant, not only satisfies his curiosity; it also reinforces his shame because of the loyal remembrance on her part to which it bears witness. In sum, the curiosity of the narrator in *Buchmendel* undergoes a series of transformations in both direction and content; and it issues finally not in a quasi-sexual pleasure, the satisfaction of a psychological need, but in a profounder human reflection, expressed in the concluding sentences of the work:

> Und dann ging ich und schämte mich vor dieser braven Frau, die in einfältiger und doch menschlichster Art diesem Toten treu geblieben. Denn sie, die Unbelehrte, sie hatte wenigstens ein Buch bewahrt, um seiner besser zu gedenken, ich aber, ich hatte jahrelang Buchmendel vergessen, gerade ich, der ich doch wissen sollte, daß man Bücher nur schafft, um über den eigenen Atem hinaus sich Menschen zu verbinden. (K,124)

In *Schachnovelle* the curiosity of the narrator is directed in turn, though not with equal intensity, to each of the two protagonists. It is at its most powerful in relation to Czentovic. Yet it follows a course which is the reverse of what we have by now come to expect. Here, though the setting is again an ocean-going liner, there is no encounter with a mysterious stranger, whose story the narrator feels compelled to discover. On the contrary, the narrator has already been given the biographical background of the chess-champion before his curiosity is aroused. The information he is given reacts on an innate tendency to find intellectual stimulus in psychological peculiarities. As he puts it, 'Alle Arten von monomanischen, in eine einzige Idee verschossenen Menschen haben mich zeitlebens angereizt' (S,22). He also admits that he is one of those people in whom fascination can degenerate into a passion (S,27). Accordingly, he is now unable to resist the urge to

116

make the personal acquaintance of the remarkable Czentovic, employing the tactics of the predator in his quest. Annoyed by the 'Abwehrtechnik' of his quarry (S,24), he finally hits on the well-tried method of the hunter, who lures the mountain-cock into the open by imitating its mating-call: in other words, he stages a game of chess. If his activity recalls the sobriquet 'chasseur d'âmes' which Rolland applied to Zweig himself, it also merits the same qualification, that its object is not to kill prey, but to observe a rare species (S,22), a 'Phänomen' (S,27), a 'Kuriosum' (S,35). Curiosity is rewarded by the success of his tactic; and yet he is disappointed by the encounter with Czentovic, whose uncouth and money-grubbing insensitivity is sufficient to banish his pleasure. Powerful as his curiosity may be, it will not in the end permit him to enjoy the contemplation of any fascinating phenomenon irrespective of all social and humane considerations.

In relation to Dr B. the narrator's curiosity appears far less intense. It also follows a different and more traditional course. When Dr B. intervenes in the second game of chess and saves the cause of those who are playing against the world-champion, he is still a complete stranger. It is the contradiction between his obvious ability and his assertion that he has not sat at a chess-board for twenty-five years that arouses the curiosity of both the narrator and other fellow passengers, who give themselves over to outlandish hypotheses in order to explain the provocative discrepancy and then proceed to question the steward. Nevertheless, when the narrator approaches Dr B. as spokesman of the other chess-enthusiasts, his mission is not so much to uncover the stranger's story as to ask him to play another game on their behalf. He is still curious to know the explanation of the other's prowess at chess, but not aggressively or pointedly so. Indeed Dr B. then invites him to listen to his story almost as though it were an imposition on a reluctant listener. Thereafter curiosity plays no further part in the story. Once Dr B. has reached the end of his narrative, the interest shifts to the psychological battle between the two protagonists and to the humane values embodied in the struggle.

Interesting as all these examples are of Zweig's concern to portray something of the psychology of his narrators, they pale by comparison with the extended treatment in *Unvermutete Bekanntschaft mit einem Handwerk*. It is no exaggeration to say

117

that, in terms of psychology, it is the first-person narrator himself and not his unexpected acquaintance, the pickpocket, who engages the reader's attention. The pickpocket is an 'original' and possesses a considerable skill, but it is primarily a manual skill and so falls outside the scope of our earlier discussion of intellectual feats and deficiencies. Moreover, nothing of his life-story is revealed, and he is viewed entirely from the outside. If at the end of the story the reader is left with the impression that he has shared in the tension and excitement of the pickpocket's exploits, this is merely the illusion created by the narrator's identification with his acquaintance. Essentially it is the narrator's tension and excitement projected on to the pickpocket, who may or may not experience the emotions ascribed to him.

At the heart of the narrator's experience, however, is curiosity. Having just arrived in Paris and finding himself without immediate obligation, he yields to that sensation of drift familiar to us from the narrator at the beginning of *Die Mondscheingasse* and lets chance take him where it will. At the same time he is aware of a tingling sense of expectancy, a sign that this is to be one of his 'Neugiertage' (K,9). On such days he feels empathy with everyone whose activity he observes; he can let his imagination construct a fate for each individual; he can watch the passers-by for hours, 'von Neugier magnetisch-sinnlos nachgezogen' (K,10). Before long the relative passivity of his curiosity gives way to a more active pursuit of one particular man, whose strange behaviour is a challenge to his understanding. Indeed, in a way which is reminiscent of Bob's anger at his inability to discover the identity of the young woman who embraces him in *Geschichte in der Dämmerung*, he is at first annoyed with himself for failing to satisfy his curiosity to know what the stranger is up to (K,12). The excitement aroused by his efforts to penetrate the secret of the man's stealthy movements does not abate when he has discovered the truth. Instead it develops into an increasing identification with the pickpocket at his work and remains until the climax is reached in an intimate encounter in crowded auction-rooms.

The auction-rooms are themselves an ideal location for the satisfaction of curiosity, since they offer insight not only into the range of material goods and works of art that men have created, but also into the great and captivating variety of mankind. The fascination of the place is such indeed that the narrator had allegedly resolved to go there of his own accord that morning — a surprising statement after his earlier account of aimless drifting — and, once inside, becomes caught up in the lively activity of this vanity fair, which he describes in considerable detail. For some time his attention is divided between the excitement of the auction and its many participants, on the one hand, and the skill and daring of the pickpocket, on the other. When he becomes the latter's victim, however, the crowd is forgotten; and as we shall see, curiosity ceases to be an adequate term for what he experiences.

Persistent though the narrator's curiosity may be, it does not go unchallenged by his moral sensibility. Even at an early stage, before he has correctly identified the nature of the stranger's activity, his delight at the prospect of being allowed to observe what he takes to be a plain-clothes detective at work has to contend with a somewhat sentimental feeling that it is despicable to watch an official ready to take some poor wretch off to jail. Once he has realised what the man is up to, he is not troubled in a general or conventional way by the crimes he may witness. That would scarcely be possible after his sentimental anxieties about the arrest of a criminal. Nevertheless, when the pickpocket makes to approach a poor, simple woman, something within the narrator revolts. Hitherto a kind of 'Sportfreude' (K,25) has made him wish only success for the stranger, but this is now called into question by the sight of the victim. Yet, although human sympathy seems to triumph over aesthetic pleasure, it is not allowed to become effective. His impulse to expose the thief founders from lack of conviction: aware of how fragile and ambiguous man-made justice is, he does not feel certain or courageous enough to accuse him publicly (K,26-7). Before long concern for the woman has been swallowed up by his more persistent interest in the pickpocket. His human sympathies have not been suppressed; they have been redirected. Having followed the pickpocket into a cheap restaurant and seen his greedy consumption of meagre fare, the narrator is filled with pity at such human poverty and shame at the way in which he himself has used the thief as an object of curiosity instead of trying to restrain or help him (K,31). From this point his fascination is accompanied by fear for the welfare of the stranger; instead of concern for the victims and the impulse to expose the criminal, there is concern that the criminal may lay himself open to the danger of arrest by the very acts which at the same time

119

provide such fascination.

The portrayal of the narrator's curiosity has overtones of gambling and hunting, particularly in the imagery, to which we shall return in a later chapter. But, in the end, it is the sexual overtones which come to dominate events, so much so that the climax of the story is little different from the act of coitus, in which the narrator plays the female role.[7] From the moment of his arrival in the French capital his expectancy has borne the marks of sexual excitement. He is 'aufgetan' — a word which Zweig commonly uses to describe the sexual receptivity of a woman[8] — and addresses the city in his thoughts with the words: 'alle Sinne stehen dir offen, vorwärts und vorwärts, gib dich ganz mir hin, so wie ich bereit bin, ganz mich dir hinzugeben' (K,9). Even though for much of the narrative he is no more than an observer of the pickpocket's deeds, his excitement does not lack the sexual component; it is simply that his role is more like that of the 'voyeur'. As he himself puts it: 'ich sollte einen Taschendieb in seinem charakteristischen Augenblick erspähen, [. . .] in jener knappen Sekunde, die sich so selten belauschen läßt wie Zeugung und Geburt' (K,18). Only at the auction-rooms, however, when the narrator ceases to be a mere witness and becomes the pickpocket's victim, do the latent sexual desires find their fulfilment. After allowing himself to become absorbed in the activities of the auctioneer and the crowds, he is brought back to his fundamental purpose by a jolt in the ribs from the pickpocket. Now he greets him with all the fervour of a woman reunited with a long-lost lover: 'O freundliches Wunder, er war es, der schwer Vermißte, der Langgesuchte' (K,41). Thereafter the pickpocket's attempt to steal his wallet becomes nothing less than a sexual approach which he both fears and desires.

The passage needs to be read *in toto* for one to appreciate the full extent of this, but it is too long to reproduce here. Nevertheless, particular attention may be drawn to the stress which is placed on the narrator's sensual excitement, on the intimate contact of the bodies, and on the provocative role of the pickpocket's arm with its unmistakable phallic associations, like the thrust of the dentist's drill (K,42) or the gliding of a snake as it penetrates the narrow opening of his coat (K,43). Once the phallic arm, released from the narrator's grip, has slipped back into its sleeve, there follows a sentence which might serve, without the slightest alteration, to describe the immediate after-effects of an orgasm: 'Noch spürte ich seinen Körper ganz warm angedrückt an den meinen, und als jetzt in gelöster Erregung die erstarrten Knie mir zu zittern begannen, meinte ich zu fühlen, wie dieser leichte Schauer in die seinen überlief' (K,44).

To the casual reader *Unvermutete Bekanntschaft mit einem Handwerk* might seem to belong to those later stories of Zweig which move beyond an interest in the sexual passions and concern themselves with the portrayal of individuals who have exceptional skills. Yet closer inspection reveals not only that the narrator here occupies a more central position, but also that, in some measure, he follows the pattern of those earlier protagonists such as the baron in *Phantastische Nacht* or Mrs C. in *Vierundzwanzig Stunden aus dem Leben einer Frau* who experience an unexpected eruption of passion. Moreover, just as the baron becomes caught up in passion through witnessing the frenzy of other race-goers and Mrs C. through watching the hands of other gamblers, so too the narrator of *Unvermutete Bekanntschaft mit einem Handwerk* comes to his experience of personal excitement as a result of observing the risky adventures of the pickpocket. And it is almost as though Zweig were deliberately recalling those earlier works in the metaphors of horse-racing and gambling which he employs in connection with his narrator's role as a spectator and which we shall consider in a later chapter.

Unvermutete Bekanntschaft mit einem Handwerk is an appropriate work with which to conclude an examination of Zweig's psychological approach, not because his curiosity at the remarkably varied activities of the human mind is here enacted extensively in the figure of his narrator. For the object of the narrator's curiosity is not, after all, a *psychological* rarity. The reason lies rather in the fact that the author's psychological curiosity has now, as it were, been turned in on itself. It has ceased to be merely the motive force behind the portrayal of others and become an object of interest in its own right.

121

PART TWO
THE MORAL SUPERSTRUCTURE

Psychological curiosity is morally neutral. It finds its interest in the workings of the human mind, however reprehensible their consequences may be according to given standards of behaviour. In one sense, it is true, this very indifference may be regarded as a moral act, since it implies an acceptance of all men without condemnation. Zweig himself makes much the same point near the end of his essay on Freud, when he comments on the way in which psychoanalytical therapy depends on a readiness to understand people and withhold value-judgements:

> [. . .] alles Heilen im medizinischen, alles Helfen im moralischen Sinne setzt deshalb bei Freud Erkenntnis voraus, und zwar eine jasagende, mitfühlende und dadurch wahrhaft wissende Erkenntnis. Ehrfurcht vor der Persönlichkeit, vor diesem im Goetheschen Sinne 'offenbaren Geheimnis' ist darum für ihn aller Seelenkunde und aller Seelenheilkunst unumgänglichster Anbeginn, und diese Ehrfurcht hat Freud wie kein anderer als moralisches Gebot wieder achten gelehrt.[1]

To the extent, however, that this approach declines to discriminate between good and evil, noble and ignoble, virtuous and vicious it maintains a moral neutrality.

Yet it is not for nothing that Zweig is known as a humanitarian writer. It would be an insensitive reader of his *Novellen* who failed to detect in most of them, through the voice of the narrator, through the self-assessment of the characters, or through the structure of the narrative, not just a withholding of negative judgement where others might have condemned, but a more positive commendation of certain human values. Jules Romains went so far as to imply a connection between the psychological interest and the moral quest, arguing that Zweig's curiosity about the lives of other people, real and fictional, was like a personal interrogation in which he sought to establish whether their destinies offered something which might satisfy him, whether he was right or wrong not to live like them.[2] As a general summary of Zweig's approach this may serve well enough; but it takes no account of those important occasions when psychological interpretation and moral evaluation fail to harmonise, when the psychologist Zweig undermines the intentions of the humanist Zweig, when the inmates of the human zoo resist the moral demands that are made on them.

The values in question are essentially those which the reader will find advocated elsewhere in Zweig, in the historical biographies, the essays, or the correspondence: first, an emphasis on personal freedom together with a condemnation of those forces which restrict or destroy it; second, a high regard for intensity of experience and passionate commitment as opposed to emotional indifference; third, an ideal of the rounded personality, of wide human and cultural interests, in contradistinction to narrow-mindedness of any kind; fourth, an affirmation of human brother-hood across all man-made barriers of race, creed or class.

To this list of qualities which go to make up the human ideal in Zweig's writings one must also add compassion, which always elicited from him a warm admiration, especially when translated into acts of practical philanthropy, as in the medical work of an Albert Schweitzer or a Hans Carossa or in the international relief work of the Red Cross.[3] It was a quality he considered necessary for any artist worthy of the name, a quality possessed, for example, by Romain Rolland, who realised that the true poet or artist must fulfil the role 'eines helfenden Menschen',[4] and by Joseph Roth, who, over and above his dazzling technique, dis-played 'einen immer und überall menschlich mitfühlenden Sinn'.[5]

Important as this quality of compassion is to Zweig's ideal, in the context of his *Novellen* it usually functions in a different way from those other qualities enumerated above. While they represent potentialities which are realised or thwarted, pursued or neglected in the lives of the characters, the ideal of compassion is embodied above all in the totality of each work and its understanding presentation of human fates, great and small, noble and ignoble, prosperous and calamitous. Writers as varied as Rolland, Thomas Mann and Paul Zech acknowledged that this compassion was rarely absent when Zweig's curiosity was at work.[6] That indeed is what gives his psychological approach its moral dimension.

If the ideal of compassion is implicit in each and every portrait, those other ideals, separately or in combination, provide the moral framework against which the characters and their society may be judged. Not every story is to be understood in this way. *Angst, Die Frau und die Landschaft* and *Untergang eines Herzens* yield little from the moral point of view; and in the early stories of *Erstes Erlebnis* the human values are not articulated explicitly. Even the stories which do explore the issues more openly are not to be regarded as demonstration-pieces; and no paragons are to be expected. In addition to that, however, as we examine each strand of the ideal in turn, it will be necessary to note some of the complications that arise when aspects considered in isolation then appear in combination and to confront some of the problems of which the characters, the narrators, and at times even the author, appear not to be conscious. This will not necessarily entail adverse criticism. At times the complications add a richness to the portraits and bear witness to a reassuring awareness by Zweig of life's contradictions. At times, however, it will be difficult to escape the conclusion that he did not fully realise the problematic nature of what he was presenting.

9

Personal Freedom

That personal freedom should be such a high priority for Zweig is not surprising. It is the almost inevitable consequence of his up-bringing among the wealthy, liberal bourgeoisie of late nine-teenth-century Vienna, with its indifference to political engage-ment and its emphasis on personal cultivation. The situation is well described by Hans-Albert Walter:

> Das Individuum war unbeobachtet und unreglementiert. Die private Lebenssphäre wurde nicht angetastet, dem persön-lichen Freiheitsbereich waren kaum Grenzen gezogen. Sich um die Weltläufte zu kümmern, war der Einzelne nicht aufgerufen, Politik blieb eine ferne Angelegenheit, mit der nur in Berührung kam, wer sie suchte. Jenes Bildungs-bürgertum, das Zweig repräsentiert, war aber dezidiert unpolitisch, und das verschaffte dem Einzelnen ein wahrhaft weltumspannendes Freiheitsgefühl.[1]

Throughout his life Zweig gave frequent expression to his need for personal freedom. Two examples may serve to illustrate what is in fact one of his most constant themes. In his essay 'Die Mono-tonisierung der Welt' (1925) he concludes resignedly that the individual cannot fight against the increasing uniformity of modern life, but only defend his own individuality. For, he argues, 'des geistigen Menschen höchste Leistung ist immer Freiheit, Freiheit von den Menschen, von den Meinungen, von den Dingen, Freiheit zu sich selbst'.[2] And in his late essay on Montaigne, written between 1941 and 1942, he returns to the subject time and again, most notably in these words:

In solchen Epochen, da die Edelwerte des Lebens, da unser
Friede, unsere Selbständigkeit, unser eingeborenes Recht,
alles, was unser Dasein reiner, schöner, berechtigter macht,
aufgeopfert werden der Besessenheit eines Dutzends von
Fanatikern und Ideologen, münden alle Probleme für den
Menschen, der seine Menschlichkeit nicht an die Zeit verlieren
will, in ein einziges: wo bleibe ich frei?[3]

In the *Novellen* Zweig's ideal of personal freedom is to some
extent embodied in the lives of his first-person narrators, who
travel the world, apparently free from the demands of gainful
employment, from financial worries, and from domestic
obligations. Although they undoubtedly represent a style of life
which the author sought to maintain for himself, there is nothing
to suggest that he consciously regarded them as models. Indeed,
on structural evidence, there is reason to suppose that he was also
capable of a more detached view of such ease.[4]

Elsewhere, in the lives of his central characters, the ideal is
expressed for the most part negatively, in the loss or restriction of
personal freedom. In the stories of *Erstes Erlebnis*, which take
place in a world as yet untroubled by war and which deal primarily
with those who have still not reached the age of maturity, the
problem is nowhere articulated.[5] Yet at several points the reader is
made aware that the young heroes and heroines are being treated
by the adult world in a way which fails to take proper account of
their individuality. Sometimes, as with Edgar in *Brennendes
Geheimnis*, the two sisters in *Die Gouvernante*, and, less
dramatically, the love-struck teenager in *Sommernovellette*, they
are used by older people and so denied the fundamental right of
every individual to be regarded as an end in himself.[6] Sometimes,
as with Bob in *Geschichte in der Dämmerung* and the two sisters in
Die Gouvernante, they are shut out of the adult world by their
elders in a way which limits not only their present activity and
knowledge, but also their free development towards maturity.[7]
And Edgar in *Brennendes Geheimnis*, it will be remembered, is
actually imprisoned in his room and dealt with like a little child
after receiving such encouraging signs of his individual importance
from the baron.

For commentary on these violations of adolescent freedom one
might consult the chapters of Zweig's own memoirs which deal
with his upbringing, with the authoritarian conformism of the

education system and the widespread concealment of sexual matters. Alternatively, since *Erstes Erlebnis* is dedicated to Ellen Key, one might turn to the reformist programme of her book, *Das Jahrhundert des Kindes,* with its emphasis on the child as an end in itself, on the treatment of children by parents as comrades and equals, on an educational system which is not concerned to mould children according to traditional patterns, but seeks to meet their needs and develop the potential and freedom of each individual; in short: to foster what she calls 'eine freie Selbstentwicklung'.[8] Yet even within two of the stories themselves a reference to the adverse effects which the recorded experiences have had on the social and sexual development of the adolescents concerned (EE,56 and 83) may be taken as more than a dispassionate statement of psychological cause and effect: it is also something of a warning against the dangers of dealing with young people as though they were not individuals in their own right.

The advent of the First World War represented a more acute attack on Zweig's human ideal, most obviously in its denial of a common human brotherhood — to which we shall return later — but no less painfully in the sufferings of its uncomprehending victims, Boris in *Episode am Genfer See* and Jakob Mendel. The former has been taken from home and family against his wishes and transported half way round the world to fight for his Tsar and country. Now technically a deserter, he has arrived in Switzerland with the simple desire to return home, to live and work with his wife and children. This basic human right is made impossible by the political realities of war-time Europe. The latter, having been accepted in Vienna as an unlicensed bookdealer for over thirty years, suddenly finds that the advent of war has turned him into an undesirable alien. He is arrested and taken off, in his summer clothes, to a concentration camp, where he is isolated from what is dearest to him in the world: books. Zweig describes him as 'abgetrennt wie ein Adler mit zerschnittenen Schwingen von seinem ätherischen Element' (K,117). The image seems inappropriately heroic for Mendel, but the cruelty of his treatment is aptly conveyed. When he is finally released, he is a physical wreck: his eyes have lost their sparkle; his phenomenal memory has been destroyed. In short, such is the inhumanity to which he has been subjected that Mendel is no longer Mendel (K,119). The final blow is his eviction from the Café Gluck, which may be less unequivo-

130

cally damnable than the sympathetic cloakroom-attendant makes out, but which is seen nevertheless as the violation of a sacred right, Mendel's right of access to what has been his 'Zuhaus' for thirty-six years (K,123).

In *Episode am Genfer See* and *Buchmendel* events are largely left to speak for themselves; the loss of personal freedom does not become an explicit theme. In *Der Zwang*, however, where the hero is much more intelligent and aware and is accompanied by an articulate wife, the issue is fully discussed by the characters — though that is not to say it is fully understood. Physical deprivation, on the other hand, which is a feature of the loss of personal freedom for both Boris and Mendel, plays virtually no part.

When the story opens, Ferdinand has already left behind a Germany in the grip of war, a Germany whose disregard for the individual has proved distasteful and humiliating and whose patriotic slogans he has found almost physically suffocating. His arrival in Switzerland has been marked by a renewal of vigour and willpower: 'und seine Lungen taten sich auf, Freiheit aus der Luft zu spüren. Vaterland, das hieß ihm jetzt nur mehr Gefängnis und Zwang' (VdG^2,227). As he perceives matters, the move is designed to preserve his personal freedom; and in terms of human values, this remains the central issue throughout. Whether he is able to recognise all that it entails or to meet its demands is less certain.

One strand in the personal freedom he seeks to maintain is the ability to make a free moral choice, to decide for himself what is right and wrong and not be subject to the militaristic madness of either state authority or popular sentiment. In his stronger moments, therefore, he can count it an honour 'in dieser Zeit der Sklaverei ungehorsam gewesen zu sein' (VdG^2,253). In his (more frequent) weaker moments it is left to his wife to remind him that the sort of patriotism which is being demanded of him is nothing but murderous slavery, that although the peoples of Europe have yielded to a collective madness, the individual need not comply (VdG^2,246). As she urges in her most passionate outburst:

> 'Wach doch auf, Ferdinand, spür's doch, du bist frei, ganz frei, niemand hat Macht über dich, niemand kann dir befehlen, hörst du, du bist frei, du bist frei, du bist frei!' (VdG^2,255)

A second strand is the freedom to pursue his own chosen profession undeterred by the unwelcome demands of a war-torn world. His desire to get on with his painting is disturbed by the summons to report for conscription at the consulate in Zurich, and not only when he has to take time off to make the journey. For as soon as the letter is received, images of warfare begin to obtrude themselves into the picture he is engaged on (VdG²,229). Later, on his way to the consulate, he rehearses in his mind a forceful defence against the demands of the authorities which concentrates much of its argument on the primacy of his art over matters of the moment. 'Gleich müßte der andere sehen', he reflects, 'wie gleichgültig ihm der ganze Krieg sei, wie souverän und frei er sich empfinde' (VdG²,240). Freedom here means the possibility of remaining undisturbed by the demands of the world around.

It is important to emphasise the distinction between these two strands, since the former, freedom of moral choice, has links with the wider issue of international brotherhood, while the latter remains a matter of personal satisfaction; and the difference between private and public demands proves a source of difficulty to which we must return.

Military service, which would take Ferdinand from his wife and his work and make him subordinate to superiors, would be a negation of both strands of the personal freedom he desires, a freedom which is expressly defined in the course of the narrative in terms of an opposition between what is human and what is inhuman, between that which is filled with a living spirit and has needs, wishes, responsibilities of its own and that which is soullessly mechanical or abstract. The opposition is sustained through a consistent pattern of imagery which, in its echoes of Expressionist vocabulary, represents the clearest statement of the human value which Zweig places on personal freedom. Unfortunately, his deployment of this imagery is not in the end persuasive enough to dispel some quite serious doubts about the character of the freedom which Ferdinand seeks and supposedly finds.

In discussing the psychology of Ferdinand we have already observed his sense of inner compulsion and its roots in the urge to avoid confrontation with reality, to escape moral responsibility, to yield to passivity. What we must now ask is whether such a psychological constitution is compatible with genuine personal freedom.

After his visit to the consulate and the collapse of his well-rehearsed resistance Ferdinand seeks to defend his behaviour against the criticism of his wife with some very convoluted reasoning:

'Mache mir's nicht schwer. Es wäre ja doch keine Freiheit hier. Jede Stunde würde ich spüren, daß drüben etwas ruft, nach mir tastet, an mir zieht und zerrt. Drüben wird mir leichter sein; es gibt eine Freiheit wieder im Kerker selbst. Solange man draußen ist und sich flüchtig fühlt, nur so lange ist man noch unfrei.' (VdG[2],247)

Although his use of the words 'frei' and 'unfrei' may raise an eyebrow, it is not as perverse as may at first sight appear. For to the extent that, in going into exile, he has refused to come to terms with a pressing moral problem he remains bound by it, unfree. Nevertheless, to argue that a return to Germany, submission to military authority, would grant him freedom is to be satisfied with a poor sort of freedom: freedom from the necessity (or opportunity) to think and decide for himself.

As usual, it is his wife who seeks to combat this tendency and bring him back to the truer freedom of moral choice. Even so, one should not overlook the paradox that, in order to achieve her end, she is prepared to use force. 'Ich gebe dich nicht her', she declares. 'Nie habe ich mir angemaßt, für dich zu bestimmen, aber jetzt ist es meine Pflicht, dich zu schützen' (VdG[2],246-7). Although she does not possess the physical strength to hold him back, she goes on ahead of him to try and intercept him at the station and resorts to moral blackmail, threatening to commit suicide if he returns for military service. In doing this her purpose is simple: 'Ich will dich als Menschen, als freien, lebendigen Menschen' (VdG[2],255). Such is his psychological weakness that it requires compulsion to make him free, not only in the limited sense of being relieved of responsibility, but even, it appears, in the fuller sense of being able to exercise free moral choice.

In this connection it is interesting to recall the behaviour of the heroine of *Brief einer Unbekannten*, which shares something of the same paradox. For she seeks to preserve the freedom of her lover by not allowing him to decide for himself whether he wishes to assume the responsibilities of marriage and fatherhood. There too, although the man's perspective is barely considered, and freedom is never allowed to become an issue, it is none the less pertinent to make the distinction between freedom as self-determination and freedom as exemption from responsibility.

Der Zwang ends, however, not with Ferdinand's acceptance of military service, but with his return to wife and work, preceded by a symbolic act of defiance, an assertion of freedom in the tearing up of his conscription-papers. Even so, Zweig does not manage to persuade the reader that his hero has attained full personal freedom. In that curious passage examined earlier in connection with inner conflicts freedom, it will be recalled, is said to arise within him and destroy his obedience, as though it had a separate existence of its own. There is still little evidence that he is capable of making a conscious moral choice by the exercise of his own will. And in the final scene the issue becomes obscured by a cloud of mystification, as he and his wife gaze out in ecstasy at the eternity of nature and discover there the only binding law of life: 'Aber sie schwiegen: frei schwang sich ihr Herz in die ewige Freiheit der Dinge, erlöst von der Wirrnis der Worte und der Menschen Gesetz' (VdG[2],262). It is difficult to tell quite what is supposed to be happening here. It seems clear that they are to be envisaged as having reached a state of being in which they are no longer subject to man-made laws, but the freedom they experience is an abstraction and looks suspiciously like a further escape from the pressures of the world rather than an autonomous and consciously adopted resistance to them. It is on this ecstatic note that Zweig leaves his hero and heroine. But is it churlish to ask how long such a condition could last or how this 'freedom' could be translated into action in their everyday lives?

If the First World War gave the first major impetus to Zweig's concern for personal freedom, the coming to power of the National Socialists in 1933 provided a second provocation. The growth of nationalism was, of course, a challenge to the international or European aspect of his human ideal, but the close proximity of Berchtesgaden to his Salzburg home soon appeared to threaten his personal freedom more immediately and ominously and was an important factor in his decision to go into exile.[9] *Schachnovelle*, written not long before his death, but set in that momentous year of Austrian history, 1938, is in part a product of that sense of threat, which intervening events did nothing to diminish. Personal freedom rather than human brotherhood is therefore the chief moral concern.

Unlike *Der Zwang*, the story includes no debate of the issues; it simply records violations of personal freedom in much the same way as *Episode am Genfer See* and *Buchmendel*. There is no physical brutality. Indeed, as Dr B. himself remarks, confinement in a single room of the Hotel Metropole sounds positively humane by contrast with the fate of those herded together in concentration camps (S,58-60). Yet the subtler methods of isolation and sensory deprivation are, in their way, no less inhuman and destructive; they are, in the formulation of Dr B.'s account, 'teuflisch sinnvoll, wie psychologisch mörderisch' (S,66). For they rob him of some of the very things that make him human: productive work; the intellectual stimulus of books and newspapers; contact with other people on the basis of equality and mutual trust. He might appear to have almost absolute freedom: he has unlimited time, and there are no distractions or commitments to prevent his mind from roaming where it will. But the reality is that he becomes 'der Sklave des Nichts' (S,78). The object of the mental torture is to wear down Dr B. and others in a similar position until they are ready to betray information to their captors (S,58-9). In effect, the aim is to destroy free moral choice, to force the individual into doing what his moral sensibility, of its own accord, would never allow. Although Zweig does not spell matters out in such explicit terms as these, there can be no mistaking his purpose, his implied denunciation of what was more openly, if less convincingly, rejected in *Der Zwang*.

Before we leave this aspect of Zweig's human ideal, it may be profitable to consider an extension of his notion of personal freedom which is of particular relevance to *Buchmendel*. In that veiled self-portrait, the biographical study of Erasmus, he describes the humanist as someone who, knowing so much, loves the world precisely because of its variegated manifestations and who is not alarmed by its contrasts.[10] In other words, he dislikes uniformity and welcomes what is different, out of the ordinary. Conversely, he deplores any attempt to curb originality or enforce uniformity. On this point psychological interest and moral principle coincide; 'originals' both satisfy the writer's curiosity and embody something of his ideal.

There are suggestions of this in both *Die unsichtbare Sammlung* and *Unvermutete Bekanntschaft mit einem Handwerk*. In the former the dealer goes to visit the art-collector already expecting to encounter an unusual character, 'einer jener verschollenen Menzel- oder Spitzweg-deutschen, wie sie sich noch knapp bis in unsere Zeit hinein in kleinen Provinzstädten als seltene Unika hier und da erhalten haben' (K,74). In the latter the extraordinary activity of the pickpocket is justified by the narrator, for all its criminality, on the grounds that it is his way of preserving his independence of others: 'dieser aber war einer von den Trotzigen, die lieber ihre persönliche Freiheit in gefahrvollster Weise einsetzen, statt zu betteln' (K,31). That his stealing might impinge on the freedom and well-being of others is only momentarily touched upon (K,26-7); that it might be said to make him just as dependent on the money of others as begging is not even considered.

In the portrait of Mendel the theme of individuality is worked out in much greater detail. Through his sufferings Zweig appeals to a sense of outrage at the violation of Everyman's personal freedom; through his rejection by society he also laments a failure to accommodate the individual's right to be different, even peculiar. For him the book-pedlar is a welcome exception, not only because of his phenomenal bibliographical memory, but because of his almost complete innocence of the ways of the world, his lack of interest in money, his unconscious refusal to comply with the normative classifications and categorisations of a world dominated by bureaucracy and nationalism. When the narrator learns that not one of the present waiters of the Café Gluck has even heard of Mendel, he becomes indignant at the thought that such a remarkable man can so quickly be forgotten. In this he is expressing Zweig's general conviction that unusual, exceptional, peculiar characters not only have a right to exist, but are to be cherished and fostered.

10

Intensity and Commitment

In a revealing and well-known passage from *Die Welt von Gestern*
Zweig offers his own explanation for his lifelong interest in those
who hurl themselves passionately into life:

> Vielleicht ließ mir gerade die Sphäre der Solidität, aus der ich
> kam, und die Tatsache, daß ich selbst bis zu einem gewissen
> Grade mich mit dem Komplex der 'Sicherheit' belastet fühlte,
> all jene faszinierend erscheinen, die mit ihrem Leben, ihrer
> Zeit, ihrem Geld, ihrer Gesundheit, ihrem guten Ruf
> verschwenderisch und beinahe verächtlich umgingen, diese
> Passionierten, diese Monomanen des bloßen Existierens ohne
> Ziel, und vielleicht merkt man in meinen Romanen und
> Novellen diese Vorliebe für alle intensiven und unbändigen
> Naturen.[1]

Reaction against his bourgeois background — together perhaps
with a certain dissatisfaction with the dominance of the intellect in
the modern world[2] — may be said to account for not only the
fascination of such people, but also the frequency with which they
acquire the status of the ideal. It is as though they offered a
possibility of authentic living unattainable by those who remain in
the comfortable stability of their bourgeois existence. Certainly,
they reveal their true selves in moments of passionate commitment. For Zweig, therefore, it is not in the accomplishments of
Mary Stuart that her essential character is to be seen. For as he
says, 'immer enthüllt erst die Leidenschaft in einer Frau die
innerste Seele'.[3] Later, commenting on Mary's love of adventure
and danger, he observes: 'Denn sich ganz einzusetzen mit ihrer
ganzen Kraft, ihrer ganzen Liebe, ihrer ganzen Leidenschaft, ist

das innerste Seelengeheimnis dieser entschlossenen Natur'.[4] Among his contemporaries Zweig found something akin to this in two orchestral conductors, Gustav Mahler and Arturo Toscanini. Of the latter, for example, who was able to elicit an extraordinary intensity from his players, he wrote that his rehearsals were like battlefields, 'erfüllt von dem Tumult des Auf und Nieder, durchjagt vom Fieber um das Gelingen oder Nichtgelingen, in ihnen und nur in ihnen ist der Mensch in Toscanini bis zu seiner nackten Seele entblößt'.[5]

When we turn to the *Novellen*, we find that the same view is expressed programmatically in the sonnets which stand at the beginning of the volumes *Amok* and *Verwirrung der Gefühle*. Three lines from the sestet of each will illustrate the point succinctly:

> Nur Leidenschaft, die ihren Abgrund findet,
> Läßt deine letzte Wesenheit entbrennen,
> Nur der sich ganz verliert, ist sich gegeben. *(Amok)*

> Wir sind nicht wahr, solang wir uns bewahren,
> Und nur der Blitz, von dem wir ganz entbrennen,
> Läßt Blut im Geist und Geist im Blut sich kennen.
> *(Verwirrung der Gefühle)*

In the narratives themselves the background against which intensity and commitment are set, the soil out of which they grow, is one of apathy and inner emptiness, bourgeois ease and conventionality, the cosy security of supposed moral superiority. Yet the presence of such a background, even the presence of passionate intensity, is not of itself a guarantee that the behaviour of the characters is being underwritten by the author. Quite apart from *Angst*, where the heroine's passionate adventures are understood solely in psychological terms and neither endorsed nor repudiated, we shall encounter instances where Zweig does no more than withhold negative judgement and others where he clearly depicts the destructive potential of passion. Nevertheless, although his approval is by no means universal, there remain a significant number of works in which he invites us to regard the intensity and commitment of his characters favourably, even when it leads them along the path to immorality and criminality.

The clearest expression of the ideal is to be found in *Phantastische Nacht*, where the baron does more than merely record his remarkable experience as a psychological fact; he openly affirms it as something infinitely precious to him. Looking back on his period of emotional lethargy, he now regards it as a state for which the term 'human life' hardly seems appropriate. It is rather 'etwas Totes, Leichenhaftes', little different from actual death (A,132). Later he describes himself as having been a silently functioning cog in the senseless activity of the social machine (A,168). The baron's very aloofness from society, together with a privileged position which has relieved him of the necessity to work, casts doubt on the aptness of a metaphor which might seem more justified in the case of an industrial worker. But there is no mistaking a consistency of feeling in such passages: the feeling that his earlier apathy has robbed him of something essential to true humanity.

Accordingly, the excitement that unexpectedly comes to him in the horse-race is presented as a recovery of that humanity:

> Auch ich lebte, war lebendig, war ein Mensch mit bösem und warmem Gelüst. [. . .] Und langsam — während der Wagen lässig meinen träumenden Körper durch die bürgerlich-gesellschaftliche Welt hinrollte — stieg ich, Stufe um Stufe, hinab in die Tiefe des Menschlichen in mir. (A,165-6)

The adjective 'bürgerlich', which occurs here and elsewhere in the baron's account, is to be understood not as a designation of class, but as a summary of all those standards of morality, etiquette, or dress which govern polite society. It is used in much the same sense as the English noun 'gentleman', which here represents that elegant mask behind which his present ecstasy glows (A,168-9), that correctness of behaviour and that insensitivity which he now repudiates.[6] In the rejuvenated life of the baron entirely different criteria apply. As he surveys the members of that society on which he has turned his back, he addresses them in his imagination with these words:

> Nicht mehr euch gehöre ich, nicht mehr zu euch, ich bin jetzt außen irgendwo in einer Höhe oder Tiefe, nie mehr aber, nie mehr am flachen Strand eines bürgerlichen Wohlseins. Ich habe zum erstenmal alles gefühlt, was in den Menschen an Lust im Guten und Bösen getan ist. (A,168)

Good and evil are no longer means of discriminating between what is approved and what is rejected; in a post-Nietzschean sense he

139

has moved beyond them. Instead the assessment of authentic humanity is determined by height and depth, which here quite clearly denote intensity of feeling. For that reason the hero is happy to align himself with those beyond the fringes of civilised society, to stake his entire 'bürgerliche Existenz' (A,195) as long as the quality of his feeling is not impaired.

In judging the baron's experience so positively we are of course relying very much on his own evaluation, which might be said to lack objective endorsement. The narrator's brief introduction provides endorsement only in the sense that it expresses the conviction that what follows is a factual record. That we do none the less incline to accept the baron's verdict is largely a consequence of presentation and organisation. The metaphorical language of life and death is one very persuasive factor. Another is the overall progression of the narrative, which, in taking us abruptly from cold indifference to passionate intensity, confronts us with a choice which is difficult to resist.

In *Vierundzwanzig Stunden aus dem Leben einer Frau* the first-person narrator is much more closely involved in the endorsement which Mrs C.'s volcanic experience appears to receive. This is partly a result of the role he performs in the narrative frame, where he refuses to condemn the elopement of Mme Henriette, arguing that it is more honest to follow one's instincts freely and passionately than to simulate constancy and defending the woman's right to act as she did, even though the consequences may be hard for her (VdG,19-21). In other words, he extends the ideal of personal freedom to cover the right to passion beyond what may be sanctioned by society. For the rest, his involvement arises out of his extended but more passive role as sympathetic listener to Mrs C.'s revelations.

Her relations with the young Polish gambler are characterised, as we have already seen, by a move from the sudden instinct to help, by way of the maternal instinct, to the sexual instinct. But at each stage her passionate engagement brings both rapture and despair, both height and depth, which, in their unprecedented extremity, leave her (and him) emotionally transformed, 'mit anderen Sinnen, anderem Gefühl' (VdG,61-2). Seeing the look of bliss on the face of her sleeping protégé, she feels a sense of pride at the rescue her self-abandonment has achieved (VdG,65). Remaining traces of her shame are put aside as a new will to live, a new sense of purpose pulses through her veins and, in an act of unthinking symbolism, she lays aside her mourning (VdG,67-8). She is now prepared to listen to his story, in which passion has led to criminality, without recoiling in horror, as her upbringing has taught her to do (VdG,72). By this time she is more consciously committed to a course of action which came upon her first as an irresistible, unconscious urge. Although, in recounting these events, Mrs C. is less overtly affirmative than the baron in *Phantastische Nacht*, the cumulative effect of individual detail — suggestions of vigour, rejuvenation, renewed purpose — is not to be ignored. Moreover, she now summarises her position in terms which seem to echo those of the baron: 'Ich hatte eben in jenen zehn Stunden unfaßbar mehr an Wirklichkeitswissen erlebt als vordem in vierzig bürgerlich verbrachten Jahren' (VdG,73). Compared with even fleeting passion, conventionality offers only an insipid, inauthentic kind of experience, epitomised in what she sees as the 'grauenhaft unbelebte' company of her own society (VdG,85).

It would be misleading to suggest that *Vierundzwanzig Stunden aus dem Leben einer Frau* implies a universal approval of passion. Thraldom to gambling leads the young Pole to spurn the self-sacrifice of Mrs C. in a most inhuman manner and eventually to commit suicide. She herself responds to his rejection of her with such disturbing and unbridled fury that she has to be warned about her behaviour by the casino officials. (Indeed it is the humiliation of this scene rather than the passionate self-abandonment of her earlier behaviour that causes her to return in flight to the bourgeois order.) Taken as a whole, however, her story of intensity and commitment is presented with more than an absence of condemnation; it is seen positively. When, at the end of her account, she thanks the narrator for his defence of Mme Henriette, 'weil ich zum erstenmal mich gleichsam bestätigt fühlte' (VdG,102), we may take this not only as the statement of a psychological need fulfilled, but as a more widely applicable confirmation of passionate experience. The work as a whole seems to be saying that it is better, more truly human, to live intensely than to live safely, to give oneself over to the promptings of instinct than to preserve what is ultimately only the illusion of unassailable moral superiority. And since, of all the hotel-guests present in the narrative frame, it is only Mrs C. who manages to maintain true courtesy throughout the heated debate engendered by Mme Henriette's elopement, we may judge that, in the last resort, the willingness to accept such a volcanic experience for oneself will prove a securer basis for civilised social intercourse than any attempt to deny or suppress it.

In upholding the ideal of passionate intensity in *Verwirrung der Gefühle* Zweig would seem to have set himself a more difficult task, since the eruptions of passion are here sometimes associated with what for many remains the forbidden subject of homosexuality. Despite this, and despite the fact that the main psychological emphasis is placed on the inner conflicts that ensue, *Verwirrung der Gefühle* contains some of the clearest statements of this aspect of the human ideal.

The academic method of Roland's professor achieves considerable prominence during the course of the *Novelle*. When the hero first encounters it as a young student, he is immediately struck by the way in which scholarship is combined with passion and rapture, the mechanical record of facts is replaced by an ability to inspire enthusiasm for the subject. And of his mentor's oral delivery he writes: 'Nie hatte ich dies erlebt, Rede als Ekstase, Leidenschaft des Vortrags als elementares Geschehen' (VdG,170). Although the passion of the delivery arises naturally from the physical presence of young students, the professor's pedagogic method is consciously adopted, so much so that he makes a point of explaining it openly and almost polemically to his students. The aim is not to follow the course of literary history with chronological regularity, but to fire others with enthusiasm by confronting them first with literature at its most passionate, its youthful best, before any attempt is made to analyse. For, as he puts it in words which echo those of Zweig himself when speaking of Mary Stuart and Arturo Toscanini, 'immer erkennt man ja jede Erscheinung, jeden Menschen nur in ihrer Feuerform, nur in der Leidenschaft' (VdG,174).

The principle is reinforced for him by the nature of the literary period with which he chooses to begin, the period which is to form the subject of his uncompleted *magnum opus*: Elizabethan drama. This he interprets as a single ecstatic moment which breaks through unexpectedly into the life of the nation, producing a new breed of playwrights, wild, unrestrained characters who, unlike the petty court dramatists cultivating their gentle arcadias, took

142

the theatre by storm and filled it with the wildest passions and crimes. 'Alles unbürgerliche Existenzen', he declares, 'Raufbolde, Hurentreiber, Komödianten, Betrüger, aber Dichter, Dichter sie alle' (VdG,171-3). Passion in literature has become its own justification; and, in the professor's persuasive exposition, this passion is infinitely to be preferred to the grey, pedantic puritanism that followed (VdG,173).

The experiences of Roland also speak powerfully in favour of the professor's attitude. Not only does he witness the dramatic transformation of his mentor, the difference between his tired, monotonous lecture on phonetics and his eloquent, impassioned account of the subject that is dearest to his heart. Roland himself is changed by the encounter, and permanently so. The immediate effect of their months of closest contact, when the older man dictates his scholarly masterpiece to his receptive pupil and feeling seems to stream from one to the other, is a sense of 'Selbststeigerung und Verwandlung' (VdG,221). Roland is lifted above his normal self on to a higher level of being. More important, the invigoration, the quickening of the pulse which comes to him from the moment when he first hears the professor's impassioned delivery remains with him for the rest of his life as the well-spring of his own distinguished academic career. It instils in him what he describes as 'eine neue Leidenschaft, die mir treu geblieben ist bis zum heutigen Tage: die Lust am Mitgenießen alles Irdischen im beseelten Wort' (VdG,180).

As we subsequently learn from the professor's confession, the passionate enthusiasm of Roland's response, together with his physical beauty, has in its turn a rejuvenating effect on his mentor. Without realising it, the young student has 'den quellenden Samen des Schöpferischen noch einmal in dem Verschlossenen erweckt, noch einmal die schon müd hingesunkene Fackel des Eros in seiner Seele entzündet' (VdG,271). Although the sexual element has by now been acknowledged, it still operates partly as a metaphor (even the word 'Samen' belongs here). *Eros*, moreover, has been sublimated in a creative act, the production of a literary work which has all the marks of 'Dichtung' rather than scholarship. In short, Zweig manages to rescue homosexual passion from opprobrium, to commend it even, by a kind of displacement in which the

143

process of sublimation in the professor is matched by a shift of emphasis from the literal to the metaphorical meaning of the sexual vocabulary in Roland's description.

As will already be apparent, the status of passionate intensity is inevitably enhanced by the nature of the alternatives presented: the professor's dull, lifeless lecture on phonetics after the inspiring hymn to Elizabethan drama; the grey pedantry of puritan England after the colourful explosion of talent in the age of Shakespeare. This is no doubt the reason why Zweig has chosen not to begin his story immediately with the boyhood of Roland, but to have his hero look back on events from the vantage-point of old age, provoked by the presentation of a 'Festschrift' whose thoroughness and industry not only stand in stark contrast to the passionate experiences of his youth, but, significantly, fail to uncover these experiences, which after all are the main contributory factors in his notable achievements as an academic.

It is unlikely that any one of the points just considered would of itself be sufficient warrant for accepting the ideal of passionate intensity in *Verwirrung der Gefühle*. But the reader is not allowed to view them separately; they are set against a contrastive background and are carefully interwoven with each other. Passion is at once the professor's cherished theme, the nature of his involvement in the subject and the aim of his pedagogic method; the effect on others is to inspire a similar and productive passion. The cumulative force of all this becomes even more difficult to resist when the chief obstacle, the homosexual element in the professor's passion, is converted into the more acceptable form of sublimation and metaphor. Admittedly, this does not always happen; and the story does not in the end conceal the fact that the professor has occasional recourse to male prostitutes. Nevertheless, these degrading encounters are made part of a grand, heroic struggle. The haggard, troubled look of the man who returns from them is one that springs from 'heiligerem Element' (VdG,203), that is to say, from a level of experience which is infinitely more profound than the trivial cares of Roland, who describes himself as 'kleiner Leute Sohn, aus bürgerlicher Behaglichkeit' (VdG,203). The voice that reveals the shameful secret speaks 'aus Tiefen, die mittleres Schicksal nie ertastet' (VdG,272). In short, we are confronted once more by the choice between bourgeois ease and mediocrity or noble, if flawed, passion.

In *Phantastische Nacht* and *Vierundzwanzig Stunden aus dem Leben einer Frau* the intensity experienced comes as an unexpected eruption of the unconscious which is subsequently affirmed by the character concerned. In *Verwirrung der Gefühle* intensity both arises of its own accord and is consciously pursued. In all three cases it leads to behaviour at odds with the accepted standards of society. In other stories where such behaviour occurs Zweig moves a stage further by laying much greater stress on the active commitment to it, whatever dangers may be involved, whatever disapproval may be incurred. Only towards the end of *Phantastische Nacht*, when the baron allows himself to become entangled with pimps and thieves, does he involve himself in a high risk, gambling, as he puts it, 'um den höchsten Einsatz, um meine ganze bürgerliche Existenz' (A,195). For other characters the stakes are high throughout. And this in itself seems enough to win the author's commendation.

There are moments in *Unvermutete Bekanntschaft mit einem Handwerk* when the pickpocket is seen away from his craft, consuming a simple meal. At such times, when the energies required by his occupation are relaxed, he appears like any other vulnerable human being, pitiable in the meanness and suffering of his existence (cf. K,30-1). Once at work, however, 'in seinem charakteristischen Augenblick [. . .], in der innersten Wahrheit seines Wesens', as the narrator describes it (K,18), he becomes transformed. He comes to life, as it were, and experiences an excitement ('Erregung') which he must seek to control or mask in order not to betray his criminal purpose (K,19). So, at least, the narrator interprets his action. Yet what impresses the narrator most of all is what he describes as 'ein unsinniger, ein geradezu rasender Mut' (K,19). To pick people's pockets on an open boulevard in daylight is in his estimation 'eine Mutleistung höchsten Ranges' (K,21). That it is also an expression of the man's personal freedom seems in the end to count for less than the degree to which the man engages all his energies in the act and exposes himself to great dangers, including the danger of losing the very freedom which he upholds in choosing to pick pockets rather than beg. Admiration for such commitment permits the narrator not only to suspend moral and legal judgement, but to declare the proceeds of what are after all criminal activities an insufficient

145

reward: 'viel, viel zu wenig für diesen ungeheuren Einsatz an hand-werklicher Leistung und halsbrecherischer Gefahr' (K,29). Although there is some pity for at least the poor victims, the greater value is placed on a crime which both satisfies a psychological need, curiosity, and embodies a human ideal, intensity and commitment regardless of cost.

For sustained commitment, however, there is nothing to match the heroine of *Brief einer Unbekannten*, even when due allowance is made for the psychological ambiguity of her acts discussed earlier. Her letter recounts in detail her sixteen years of unswerving devotion, the deprivation, the degradation she has endured, the personal and financial opportunities she has renounced in order to remain true to her first love. Even in the face of death from the influenza epidemic she does not repudiate her devotion. Nevertheless, there is surprisingly little overt affirmation of her behaviour as a positive value. Perhaps Zweig judged that more affirmation in his heroine's letter might introduce an unwelcome note of self-congratulation.

What she does first affirm is the animating effect of the elegant young writer's arrival. Only then, she declares, does her true life begin; what came before was merely 'etwas Trübes und Verworrenes' (A,214); and any interruptions which subsequently take him away for a time render her life 'tot und ohne Sinn' (A,225). There then follows the long catalogue of a devotion which turns its back on conventional morality, health and safety (cf. A,259) and culminates in the humiliating birth of their child in the public clinic. It is at this point that she makes her clearest declaration:

> [. . .] nie habe ich jene Nächte bereut, nie meine Liebe zu Dir gescholten, immer habe ich Dich geliebt, immer die Stunde gesegnet, da Du mir begegnet bist. Und müßte ich noch einmal durch die Hölle jener Stunden und wüßte vordem, was mich erwartet, ich täte es noch einmal, mein Geliebter, noch einmal und tausendmal! (A,250)

These words conclude the third section of her letter and so gain considerable prominence. Yet can they be taken as more than the statement of a particularly subjective attitude?

It is here that the character of her lover, the recipient of the letter, becomes very relevant. In his many amorous adventures, his carefree, non-committal treatment of women, he stands at the opposite pole to the heroine. And even when a similarity begins to suggest itself, it proves only to be the basis of a further contrast. She acknowledges that he is generous to others, but she has also to point out that it is a passive and unspecific generosity; it is motivated by weakness and shame rather than joy; and it is a means of avoiding a disturbing involvement with those in need (A,246-7). Later, when she describes their second night of love together, she shows warm admiration for the way in which he gives himself generously and passionately to his partner, but adds that it is only a momentary 'Hingabe', followed by a swift collapse into what she calls 'eine unendliche, fast unmenschliche Vergeßlichkeit' (A,260). We still of course have to rely on the woman's account, but there is nothing in the brief narrative frame to make us doubt the accuracy of her characterisation of him. Indeed the difficulty which the man experiences in recalling the woman whose letter he has just read serves rather to confirm it. And the inevitable result is that we are persuaded to regard the steadfastness of the woman's devotion, in both its invigorating intensity and its sacrificial commitment to another, as the valid expression of a human ideal.

Rejuvenating enthusiasm and single-minded devotion are the hallmarks of the old art-collector in *Die unsichtbare Sammlung* too. In this case no eruption of unconscious forces and no transgression of the bourgeois order are indicated. The emphasis is placed on a conscious commitment, though the consequence is a quasi-religious rapture, an intensity of feeling which can lift him above normal consciousness. It is this that wins the praise of the visiting dealer, in whom it also brings about a significant change of outlook. Having come in the spirit of a 'Krämer', with the intention of wheedling some valuable objects out of an unsuspecting customer, he takes away with him at the end something of greater value:

> Ich hatte wieder einmal reine Begeisterung lebendig spüren dürfen in dumpfer, freudloser Zeit, eine Art geistig durchleuchteter, ganz auf die Kunst gewandter Ekstase, wie sie unsere Menschen längst verlernt zu haben scheinen. (K,87)

Despite the dealer's unmistakable approval the critical reader will probably find this enthusiasm rather less impressive. Quite apart

147

from its egocentricity, to which we shall return in another context, it has, like the 'falsche[r] Traum seines Ruhms' which enlivens the old age of the actor in *Die spät bezahlte Schuld*,[7] an insecure basis in illusion, in this instance the illusion that the collection of prints is still intact. It is also less 'purely' concerned with art than the dealer allows. For as well as delighting in the aesthetic qualities of his supposed collection, the old man is not slow to emphasise its commercial value (K,83) or gloat over the prices it would command at a public auction (K,80). This seems a long way from that classical ideal of aesthetic contemplation which Winckelmann once upheld and which drew a sharp distinction between the pleasure of beholding a work of art and the passion to possess it.[8]

These last comments do not represent a criticism of the ideal of intensity and commitment as such. They merely challenge the quality of one intended example. Before leaving this particular ideal, however, we must also take account of some more general objections not considered in the descriptive exposition so far.

The first concerns the durability of passionate intensity. Is it not likely to be too fleeting an experience to constitute a universal ideal? As Zweig himself pointed out in his essay 'Die moralische Entgiftung Europas' (1932), it is hard to maintain intensity; 'denn nach Goethes Wort ist Begeisterung "keine Heringsware, die man einpökeln kann auf viele Jahre"; sie ist an sich nur ein kurzer Emotionszustand, ein seelendynamisches Superlative'.[9] In his *Novellen* too he seems at times to acknowledge the difficulty. Although the heroine of *Brief einer Unbekannten* manages to keep her own commitment alive through years of sacrifice, she has to admit that the passionate self-abandonment of her lover, which is such an attractive feature of their meetings, soon gives way to an almost inhuman forgetfulness (A,260). The professor of *Verwirrung der Gefühle* describes himself as 'ein Mensch der kurzen Augenblicke' (VdG,208). He is speaking moreover not of those shameful occasions when his homosexual passion takes him off to Berlin, but of his literary enthusiasm, which never lasts long enough for him to complete his *magnum opus* on the history of the Globe Theatre.

At other times, however, Zweig seems to ignore the difficulty or skirt round it. I have already hinted at this in discussing that ecstatic embrace which concludes *Der Zwang* and which leaves the two central characters in a state beyond normal consciousness,

148

without suggesting how it is to be maintained or become productive in their future lives. But the difficulty is most keenly felt in *Phantastische Nacht*, where the baron assures us that the rejuvenation that first came to him in the passionate excitement of the racecourse has remained with him in the four months that have elapsed between the event and his record of it. The sexual imagery, which is such a prominent feature of his description throughout — cf. 'ein Sich-Ergießen wie in eine Frau' (A,203) — prompts an important question: if the elation and the generosity that springs from it may be likened to copulation and ejaculation, does this not mean that they will be followed by a period of detumescence and require further stimulus if they are to be repeated? And what of the future? Can one imagine such intensity lasting a life-time? The question is neatly avoided by the author, who has his hero killed off a year later in the early months of the First World War.

The second difficulty concerns the effect which the ideal of passionate intensity, in its links with unconscious forces, might have on the ideal of personal freedom. It is a difficulty already encountered, in a modified form, in the closing passage of *Der Zwang*, where the spontaneous upsurge of a sense of freedom in the hero still gave little assurance that he had attained the freedom to exercise his will in the making of a moral choice. Taking a wider view of the matter, it is proper to ask what sort of freedom is possible where unconscious forces are involved and whether the ideals of personal freedom and passionate intensity are not, in large measure, irreconcilable. In dealing with the eruption of the unconscious in Part I we noted the frequency with which the characters concerned lost conscious control of their actions, acted at the prompting of some unspecified 'es', were subject to a kind of intoxication or possession ('Besessenheit'). To affirm the passionate intensity of such experiences is to profess a freedom from the restraints of moral conventions, but it is also, if only unwittingly, to acknowledge a degree of subordination to a force other than one's own will. For, to express the issue more sharply: can one be both possessed and free?

In the end it must be admitted that Zweig appears to have had mixed feelings about human passion. He was prepared to withhold judgement where others might have condemned, as, for example, in *Der Amokläufer* or *Die Mondscheingasse*; he was willing to imply approval, as in *Phantastische Nacht* or *Vierundzwanzig*

149

Stunden aus dem Leben einer Frau; but he was also ready to admit its destructive capability, as in the fate of the doctor in *Der Amokläufer* and the sorry end of the young Polish gambler in *Vierundzwanzig Stunden aus dem Leben einer Frau*, and to show, in his last work, *Schachnovelle*, that victory and moral freedom are possible in the renunciation of that which induces passion. Moreover, looking beyond his *Novellen* for a moment, it is worth emphasising that, as well as painting a sympathetic portrait of the passionate Mary Stuart, Zweig provided in Erasmus a no less sympathetic picture of the man who mistrusted passion and fanaticism and relied instead on the power of reason and the will, which for him were the signs of man's personal freedom.[10]

11

Wide Horizons

To consult a bibliography of Zweig's writings is to be reminded of the extraordinary breadth of his interests. A list of the visitors to his Salzburg home in the nineteen-twenties and nineteen-thirties reads like a compact *Who's Who* of modern European culture. To be fully human in his eyes it was important not only to possess a mind which was open to all man's cultural achievements, but also to be alive in every aspect of one's being. This ideal he found realised in people like Walter Rathenau, a man of varied intellectual and practical gifts, industrialist, scientist, politician, diplomat, writer, friend of art,[1] or Anton Kippenberg, a man of universal gifts and interests (music, philology, literature, business), who rescued the *Insel-Verlag* from sterility and élitism by opening its eyes to the world, beginning with Goethe, 'die universalste aller Persönlichkeiten', and spreading outwards to embrace the literature of all countries and all times.[2] Similarly, in his friend, the artist Frans Masereel, he admired the comradely spirit with which he approached all phenomena, the 'Weltbreite', the limitless horizons of his work. 'Solche Naturen', he wrote, 'und vielleicht sie allein haben die wahre Gabe der Universalität'.[3]

The repeated emphasis on universality is to be understood, in part at least, as a reaction against the increasing specialisation of modern life, a specialisation which could be a danger even for the writer. As he put it in an essay 'Pour Ramuz' (1938):

> Wer bewußt sich als Künstler einen kleinen Lebenskreis wählt und ihn bewußt nicht überschreitet, muß von vorneweg erwarten, von der großen Welt, die er doch durch Ablehnung und Gleichgültigkeit depreziert, entweder gleichgültig oder

151

bestenfalls als Kuriosum gewertet zu werden; wer ihr nicht
Liebe gibt, kann wenig Liebe von ihr erhoffen.[4]

One need delete only the words 'als Künstler' in order to be able to
apply this passage directly to fictional curiosities from the
Novellen such as Jakob Mendel, the chess-champion Czentovic,
and even the old art-collector in *Die unsichtbare Sammlung*. If one
further discards the conscious element, the relevance to the central
character of *Leporella* also becomes apparent. The significance of
this lies in the fact that, to an even greater extent than with
personal freedom, Zweig has elected to express this aspect of the
human ideal negatively. Although some of the first-person
narrators give evidence of wide human and cultural interests, they
could scarcely offer themselves as models without appearing self-
righteous and thereby alienating the reader. It is left to other
characters, therefore, to conjure up the ideal by their very denial
of it. Leporella, Mendel, and Czentovic have already been
discussed from the psychological point of view, in connection with
mental feats and deficiencies. Here we are concerned with the
degree to which their peculiarity is conceived of as a human
failing. For what satisfies psychological curiosity does not always
meet the demands of the human ideal. Moreover, a defect in this
aspect of the ideal may counterbalance or even outweigh an
advantage in another.

This is most obvious in the case of *Leporella*, where the
heroine's arousal from lethargy to a life of passion, superficially
similar to the experience of the baron in *Phantastische Nacht*,
receives no endorsement whatever for the very reason that the
narrow mentality within which the awakening takes place seems to
guarantee that her consequent actions will be horrific. From the
beginning of the story, therefore, Zweig's insistent metaphorical
language represents her as some animal or inanimate object and
thereby ensures that at every level of her existence she will be
denied the full title of human being.

Reading and writing, those specifically human activities, cause
her considerable difficulty; even thinking costs her great effort.
When she has finished work for the day therefore, or, as Zweig
himself puts it, when she is 'vom Halfter der Arbeit gelöst', there is
nothing to occupy her mind, and she dozes 'wie Tiere im Stalle
stehen' (K,46). Work, moreover, has no inherent value for her; it

is performed mechanically as if by a robot (K,47) and serves at best to accumulate the money which she hoards 'mit dem hamsterhaften Instinkt der Bäurischen und Einschichtigen' (K,47). What is more, it is suggested that, if it had not been for these narrow horizons (what are called her 'scheuklappenhaft verschlossene Sinne'), she would never have entered the service of the baron and his hysterical wife (K,49).

The narrowness of Crescenz's outlook, however, is not just a matter of intellectual impoverishment. It also extends to the affective and moral areas of her life. Zweig makes much of the fact that she has never been known to laugh:

> Auch darin war sie vollkommen tierhaft, denn, grausamer vielleicht als der Verlust der Sprache: den unbewußten Kreaturen Gottes ist das Lachen, dieser selig frei vorbrechende Ausdruck des Gefühls, nicht gegönnt. (K,47)

Laughter is an important and specifically human outlet for feelings. Whether its absence in Crescenz is to be taken as an indication that she lacks the appropriate feelings or only this particular means of expressing them is not clear. What is certain is that, when she does give vent to her feelings, the result is extreme and violent.

It is also noteworthy that, apart from her strange relations with the baron and baroness, where her extremity and violence manifest themselves, she has no proper human contact with others. Neighbours and other domestic personnel she ignores; the taunts of fellow servants make no impression on her, but 'glitschten wie Wasser an dem ledernen Fell ihrer Gleichgültigkeit ab' (K,48). One might even argue that it is her very lack of wider human contact that helps to concentrate the energy of those perversely expressed passions.

As to moral awareness, it is made clear that, in disposing of the baroness, she fails to comprehend the enormity of her deed:

> Sie saß nur und wartete mit scheuen Augen auf den ersten Pfiff ihres Herrn wie ein verprügelter Hund, der weiß, daß er Schlechtes getan hat. Ihr dumpfer Sinn verstand nicht genau, was geschehen war; nur daß ihr Gott und Herr ihr auswich und sie nicht mehr wollte, nur dies drang wuchtig in sie ein. (K,68)

The phrase 'daß er Schlechtes getan hat' should not deceive us into thinking her capable of moral judgement. The context makes plain that her awareness does not extend beyond that of an animal responding to a system of rewards and punishments. Moral sensibility of a truly human kind plays no part at all. Unlike other characters in whom unconscious forces erupt (Mrs C. or the baron of *Phantastische Nacht*), she neither affirms what she has done nor experiences shame at it. Moreover, unlike their passionate deeds, which merely transgress conventional morality or involve petty crime, her act takes the life of another human being. If that alone is sufficient to preclude the possibility of seeing her as an embodiment of the ideal of intensity and commitment, it is the narrowness of her intellectual, emotional, and moral horizons, together with their insistent animal associations, that serves to evoke, by its very deficiency, the universality which constitutes true humanity.

That is why the narrator of *Leporella* can never quite permit himself to think of Crescenz as a human being, even when she is first roused from her lethargy. Laughter may be a specifically human characteristic; and the news that the baroness is to go to a sanatorium and leave her alone with her master may provoke in Crescenz, for the first time in her life, something like laughter. But any suggestion of a positive turn is immediately subverted by the formulation of the narrator's description:

> Der Mund wurde schief, schob sich breit in die Quere, und plötzlich quoll mitten aus ihrem idiotisch erhellten Gesicht ein Grinsen dermaßen offen und tierisch hemmungslos hervor, daß der Baron [. . .] wortlos in sein Zimmer trat. (K,55)

Similarly, though the new liveliness in her manner may temporarily persuade the narrator that 'ein Mensch war erwacht in dem abgetriebenen, müden Arbeitstier' (K,60), he is soon obliged to revise his assessment in the most explicit manner and with the full weight of a quotation usually attributed to Aristotle:

> Aber die Natur macht keine Sprünge: war auch durch den Druck einer krausen und verkrümmten Leidenschaft aus diesem hartknochigen verdumpften Wesen eine gewisse geistige Bewegung herausgetrieben worden, so reichte bei Crescenz dieses neuerlernte und engstirnige Denken doch nicht über den nächsten Anlaß hinaus, darin noch immer dem kurzfristigen Instinkt der Tiere verwandt. (K,61)

After her crime she is misunderstood and rejected and becomes completely disoriented in her Viennese surroundings. Yet still the pity which the narrator's presentation of her fate allows is more like that which one might feel for a stray dog or maltreated horse. One's sense of human impoverishment is not diminished.

Even where the restriction in outlook is less severe, less radically inhuman than it is in *Leporella*, it can prove sufficient to condemn passion or call an enthusiasm into question. This is one reason why, in *Vierundzwanzig Stunden aus dem Leben einer Frau*, the young Pole's return to the gaming-table is such a sorry conclusion. It is not only destructive for him personally; it also brings to an end a meaningful relationship with Mrs C. and marks an abrupt contraction of his horizons. Gambling has now supplanted all human interest, or as Mrs C. herself expresses it: 'Die ganze Welt, die ganze Menschheit war diesem Spielsüchtigen zusammengeschmolzen in diesen viereckigen Fleck gespannten Tuches' (VdG,93). In this instance there can be little doubt that the author shares his heroine's regret at the human impoverishment of such an obsession.

In the case of *Die unsichtbare Sammlung*, on the other hand, one again has the impression that Zweig has permitted his narrator, if not to be duped by the collector's enthusiasm, then at least to be too indulgent in his assessment of it, too uncritical of the human loss it entails.[5] It is necessary, therefore, to spell out some of the implications of what the narrator sees and hears, but does not always appreciate. The daughter's explanatory account of what has happened to her father's collection contains hints that it represents for him something of a substitute for human love. He looks on his supposed prints as his 'Lieblinge' and addresses them as though they were people (K,82). As the narrator himself witnesses, the old man strokes their protective folders 'zärtlich wie über etwas Lebendiges' (K,85); and as the daughter remarks, 'er liebt jedes einzelne Blatt mit einem so fanatischen Liebe, ich glaube, das Herz würde ihm brechen, wenn er ahnte, daß alles das unter seinen Händen längst weggewandert ist' (K,81). A response of that nature would be more appropriate to the loss of a beloved relative, a point which is reinforced by the reader's knowledge that the old man has indeed lost a son-in-law in the war, but still seems interested solely in his collection. Furthermore, although he himself has certainly made sacrifices in order to build up his collection, he fails to see the sacrifices others have been obliged to make, the jewelry and holidays his wife and daughter have gone without, their more recent scrimping and saving in the vain attempt to avoid the necessity of selling his works of art (K,80). He has not only become physically blind, but has allowed his enthusiasm to blind him to the claims of the human beings closest to him.

Although the dealer-narrator is given all this information by the collector's daughter and although he is evidently moved by the quality of her and her mother's devotion, there are no clear indications that he perceives the old man's enthusiasm in the same critical light as I have just outlined. The daughter touchingly defends their secret disposal of the collection in words which might have served a programmatic purpose: 'man mußte leben . . . und Menschenleben, vier verwaiste Kinder, wie die meiner Schwester, sind doch wichtiger als bedruckte Blätter' (K,82). The narrator, however, gives the sentiment no special emphasis and certainly does not endorse it. Moreover, even if his admiration for the old man's visionary ecstasy is occasionally tinged with horror, the horror is directed not at the narrowness and human cost of such enthusiasm, but only at its illusory, ghostly basis (cf. K,84,85).

In *Buchmendel* there is never the slightest suggestion that the central character, even unwittingly, infringes the rights of others or causes them harm. He himself emerges as the victim, whose right to be is denied. Nevertheless, there is a temptation to allow sympathy with his sufferings to obscure his very real inadequacies as a human being, a temptation which is all the stronger because the narrator does not withdraw his admiration or affection from the man. On the other hand, the narrator does seem more objective than his counterpart in *Die unsichtbare Sammlung* and provides a more consciously balanced portrait of his subject. Even as he writes admiringly of the book-pedlar, the epithets he uses to conjure up the phenomenal feats of bibliographical memory betray the ambiguity of the achievement. They imply something superhuman ('ein Titan des Gedächtnisses', K,104; 'dieses Genie der Preise und Titel', K,105), or sub-human ('ein vorweltlicher Bücher-Saurier', K,101),[6] something inanimate ('ein Universalkatalog auf zwei Beinen', K,103; 'die magische Registratur aller Bücher', K,118), or even abstract ('dieses abseitige Weltwunder', K,100; 'ein Wahrzeichen des Wissens', K,100), but not what is simply human.[7]

The ambiguity of Mendel's position derives as much as anything from his powers of concentration, which form the basis of his remarkable memory, but also diminish him in human terms by their exclusion of so many areas of life. Even his interest in books is deficient in this respect, since it is concerned only with super-ficialities (price and details of publication) and ignores the great store of insight, knowledge, and beauty that may be contained between the covers, ignores, that is, those opportunities for meaningful human communication which books can provide. The richness of life holds no attraction for him unless it has been turned into print and neutralised or, to use the narrator's own word, 'sterilisiert' (K,105).

That he neither smokes nor gambles is no great loss. That he has no interest in people (K,106) is a severe and disturbing contraction of human potential. On the one hand, it inhibits relations with the opposite sex. For not only does he not have a wife; books provide a surrogate satisfaction: 'ein kostbares Buch in der Hand haben zu dürfen, bedeutete für Mendel, was für einen anderen die Begegnung mit einer Frau. Diese Augenblicke waren seine platonischen Liebesnächte' (K,108). On the other hand, it makes him indifferent to the fate of others. When war comes, he is still wrapped up in the world of books and, like the single-minded art-collector of *Die unsichtbare Sammlung*, fails to register the human losses around him: the absence of the waiter killed at Gorlice, the capture of the café-owner's son, both events which might have called forth compassion from a man with less exclusive concerns (K,112). Like his sexual impulse, Mendel's religious potential is also displaced by an unswerving bibliographical interest. Having originally come to Vienna to study for the rabbinate, he has, as Zweig puts it, 'den harten Eingott Jehovah verlassen, um sich der funkelnden und tausendfältigen Vielgötterei der Bücher zu ergeben' (K,108). Elsewhere too the story abounds with vocabulary which represents his dedicated occupation with books as if it were a solemn religious ritual.[8]

At every turn, then, we are made aware that concentration also signifies narrowness of outlook and are confronted by the human cost of Mendel's outstanding ability. Our final verdict on him must carefully weigh the claims of various aspects of the human ideal: violation of personal freedom and of the right to eccentricity, violation of human brotherhood,[9] on the one side, against a total absence of wide horizons, on the other. With Czentovic, the world chess-champion from *Schachnovelle*, it is difficult to find any cause for sympathy which might qualify the negativity of the portrait. If Dr B. is morally victorious in his defeat,[10] Czentovic displays a sad human impoverishment in all his triumphs across the chess-board. There is no need to rehearse again all the detail of his intellectual limitations, his slowness to learn the basic skills of reading, writing and arithmetic, and his alleged lack of imagination. What evidently disturbs Zweig more than these perhaps innate mental handicaps is the degree to which Czentovic seems deliberately to turn his back on wider human concerns.

In the narrator's short tribute to the 'royal game' it emerges as an activity which embraces so many opposing facets of human life, art and science, tradition and innovation, restriction and freedom, and is universal in the sense that it belongs to all nations and all ages (S,24f). Yet for Czentovic it has been reduced to a means of satisfying his twin aims: to make money and boost his ego. His admitted success in the limited field of chess, together with the financial rewards involved, has induced in him such a crass philistinism that he ignores the greater achievements, especially cultural achievements, of other men. The narrator's acquaintance concludes his biographical sketch of the chess-champion with these revealing words:

> 'Und dann, ist es nicht eigentlich verflucht leicht, sich für einen großen Menschen zu halten, wenn man nicht mit der leisesten Ahnung belastet ist, daß ein Rembrandt, ein Beethoven, ein Dante, ein Napoleon je gelebt haben? Dieser Bursche weiß in seinem vermauerten Gehirn nur das eine, daß er seit Monaten nicht eine einzige Schachpartie verloren hat, und da er eben nicht ahnt, daß es außer Schach und Geld noch andere Werte auf unserer Erde gibt, hat er allen Grund, von sich begeistert zu sein.' (S,21-2)

It may well be that there is not just ignorance, but an unacknow-ledged sense of inferiority at work here, since it is also alleged that Czentovic studiously avoids the company of educated people for fear of exposing his own weaknesses (S,23). Whatever the psycho-logical truth, it is clear that the narrowness of his concerns repre-sents for Zweig an impoverishing distortion of human values.

In his dealings with ordinary people Czentovic is more openly disdainful. In his obvious conviction that others are of no consequence he is also more unpleasant than the relatively innocent Mendel. On board ship he spends most of the time in his private cabin and keeps away from the bar and smoking lounge, what are called, significantly, the 'Gesellschaftsräume' (S,23). And when he does deign to play against a group of passengers (for money), it cannot be said that he 'joins' them in a game. He arrives on the scene without troubling to introduce himself and with a look as if to say: 'Ihr wißt, wer ich bin, und wer ihr seid, interessiert mich nicht'. Between moves, which he performs standing, he retires to a table at the opposite end of the room and leafs nonchalantly through a magazine (S,36). Essentially, other people count for no more to him than the wooden pieces he moves around the sixty-four squares of the chess-board (cf. S,37).

Although the point is nowhere made explicit, the narrowness of Czentovic's concerns, his negation of this aspect of the humane ideal, is thrown into sharper relief by the contrastive figure of Dr B. Dr B.'s concentration on chess is a more or less enforced activity, a compensation for the loss of those very things which Czentovic voluntarily avoids: culture and human contact. In stealing the book which turns out to be a chess-manual he is in fact hoping to acquire a volume of Goethe or Homer, to be stimulated by the imaginative world of great poetry (S,76). A phrase deleted from the printed version of the story speaks of the stolen book as 'einen Gefährten in meiner Einsamkeit'.[11] The words may have disappeared, but the sentiment remains, implicitly, in a later scene. For when he is finally released from his isolation and taken to hospital, his incredulity at the presence of human beings who smile and speak kindly is a clear indication of the companionship he has most sorely missed. It is not possible to accept the assertions of those who seek somehow to identify Czentovic with the brutality of the Nazis.[12] Nevertheless, it is already sufficiently disquieting that, without external provocation, he should lead the sort of restricted life which the Nazis inflict on others as a form of torture. For the ideal we must look to the opposite. 'Im Zusammenspiel aller Kräfte unter Führung des Geistes liegt für ihn [Zweig] der Ausdruck des rein Menschlichen.' This is the conclusion to which Ingrid Lent comes in her analysis of *Schachnovelle*[13] and to which the evidence of the text itself leads.

12

The Brotherhood of Man

The three main aspects of the human ideal considered so far have their roots in individualism, an individualism characteristic of the Austrian middle classes from which Zweig sprang.[1] Even where the ideal has included an interest in other people, it has been seen from the perspective of the individual, as one among several indications of the wider horizons necessary for the full life. By contrast, the aspect with which we are now concerned appears at first sight to be entirely a matter of communality, of proper relations between individuals, groups, nations. For it may be summarised quite simply as the conviction that all men belong together and should not be divided from or set against one another by differences of race, creed, class, or whatever. Nevertheless, even this more public aspect of Zweig's ideal cannot be divorced from the wish to satisfy a very personal need. Hannah Arendt goes so far as to suggest a link between his cultivation of internationalism and the social disabilities of his race, asserting that, since the international society of the famous and successful was the only one in which Jews enjoyed equal rights, Zweig sought and found there a sense of acceptance: 'Es war das immer wieder zu erneuernde Sich-in-Beziehung-setzen zu einer Welt, in welcher man seinen Namen gedruckt vorweisen mußte, um anerkannt zu werden'.[2] One need not be as sneering and cynical as that to see that Zweig's internationalism was a natural extension of the privileges (rather than disabilities) he enjoyed as a young man: an upbringing in Vienna, which he regarded as the tolerant, conciliating cultural centre of a supra-national empire;[3] extensive travel and wide reading in foreign literatures, which his means and leisure allowed. These helped to produce a man who could feel at home throughout the world, though only so long as war and nationalism did not impose their political divisions or restrict his freedom. As he wrote to Rolland in the early months of the First World War, after reading some anti-German lines of his literary mentor, Verhaeren: 'Diese Verse haben etwas in mir zerstört was zum Kostbarsten meines Lebens gehörte, das Sicherheitsgefühl der vielfachen Heimat'.[4] And as he noted in his diary on 27 September 1935, recording a journey from Paris to London which involved two irritating passport controls: 'So war unsere herrliche Welt Europa abgeteilt und verriegelt, und vergittert mit Grenzen für den frei geborenen Menschen'.[5] To some extent the ideal of human brotherhood grew out of this concern for personal freedom, which was merely projected on to other people: '[Man] soll vor allem frei bleiben und jedem anderen die Freiheit lassen, er soll, wie wir es in Wien lernten, leben und leben lassen'.[6] Tolerance of others harmonises well with the demand for personal freedom, at least until some conflict of interest emerges.

However closely related to personal satisfaction the ideal of human brotherhood may have been, it was something he constantly practised in his role as literary mediator[7] and repeatedly avowed at all stages of his life. It requires no special emphasis here. A few examples will serve to illustrate some of its different facets and some of the many people who, in his estimation, represented or promoted the ideal.

The international aspect comes out clearly in the late essay on Montaigne, who, like Erasmus, may be seen as a self-portrait of Zweig himself:

> Man wird nur sagen können, daß er durch diese Gemischtheit prädestiniert war, ein Mensch der Mitte und ein Mensch der Bindung zu werden, unbefangen nach allen Seiten blickend, ohne Borniertheit in jedem Sinne, ein 'libre penseur' und 'citoyen du monde', freigeistig und tolerant, Sohn und Bürger nicht einer Rasse und eines Vaterlandes, sondern Weltbürger jenseits von Ländern und Zeiten.[8]

Although the ideals of personal freedom and wide horizons hover in the background, it is the ability to rise above national divisions which is decisive here. It is in keeping with this that, of the many things which attracted Zweig to Brazil, the most persistent was its success in integrating different racial groups. In 1936 he wrote enthusiastically to his wife Friderike from his South American journey:

> Die Menschen bezaubernd — und Gnade auf Erden — der einzige Ort, wo es keine Rassenfrage gibt, Neger und Weiße und Indianer, Dreiviertel, Achtel, die herrlichen Mulatinnen und Kreolinnen, Juden und Christen leben in einem Frieden zusammen, den man nicht schildern kann.[9]

Towards the end of this passage racial harmony shades into religious tolerance, a virtue which he also found embodied in Albert Schweitzer. Recalling a visit made in the company of the great man to his church at Grünbach in Alsace, he emphasised one particular exemplary fact which it had brought home to him:

> Ein scheinbar Unmögliches ist also hier vollbracht, auf einer Erde, wo deutsche und französische Sprache locker ineinandergleiten — daß auch die katholische und protestantische Lehre ohne Gehässigkeit in einem gleichsam neutralen Gotteshause miteinander verbunden sein können.[10]

In this connection it is also worth noting that when, during the First World War, Zweig repeatedly reflected on his Jewishness, it was not because of the religious distinction, but because he perceived the Jews as a supra-national community.[11]

If national, racial, and religious divisions may be said to operate vertically, those which separate the different social classes may be described as horizontal. They too were deplored, while men who overcame them were applauded. One such was Maxim Gorky, whose understanding of the common folk and whose ability to write for them Zweig admired but never matched. In a tribute written on the occasion of Gorky's sixtieth birthday internationalism and the ability to bridge class-divisions are alike celebrated:

> Wir können dank seiner Werke Rußland brüderlich begreifen, nahe und nachbarlich unserer Welt, ohne Fremdheit, ohne Widerstand — damit aber ist die höchste Pflicht des Dichters erfüllt, alle Fremdheit zwischen den Menschen zu zerstören, Ferne heranzubringen und Volk und Volk, Stand und Stände zu ihrer letzten Einheit, zur allmenschlichen zu vereinen.[12]

These various elements, singly or in combination, constitute an ideal which forms the background to several *Novellen*. As with the ideals of personal freedom and wide horizons, it is more often than not conjured up negatively, commended by its lamentable absence or denial. And not unnaturally, it makes itself felt most keenly in those works which are set during the First World War, when national differences have been magnified into causes for hostility.

As we have already observed, *Der Zwang* is particularly concerned with the ideal of personal freedom. But at various points, when freedom of moral choice is at issue, there are close links with the ideal of human brotherhood. And the dedication of the story to the French pacifist Pierre J. Jouve 'in brüderlicher Freundschaft'[13] is clear confirmation that this aspect of the ideal was of particular importance to Zweig.

The purpose of Ferdinand's self-imposed exile in Switzerland is not only to preserve his individual freedom, but to escape the divisive madness of international conflict. 'Fremde,' he thinks to himself, 'sie war ihm Weltheimat, Europa die Menschheit' (VdG^2,227). For him the words 'home' and 'abroad' are defined not by geographical boundaries, but by the possibility of oneness with other people. If he manages no positive expression of this unity, then at least Switzerland seems to afford a means of avoiding its opposite, granting him the freedom not to take up arms against another man (VdG^2,230). From the psychological point of view the difficulty is that, even as he assents intellectually to his ideal, acknowledging openly, 'ich habe kein Vaterland jenseits der Menschheit' (VdG^2,231), he is subject to an inner compulsion to follow the call to conscription. For much of the time, therefore, it is left to his wife to urge the claims of human brotherhood over nationalism and heroism. It is she too who must summon up every kind of moral and physical pressure to try and prevent his submission:

'Willst du gehen, ein Mensch für die Menschheit, für das, woran du glaubst, dann halte ich dich nicht. Aber um Bestie unter Bestien zu sein, Sklave unter Sklaven, da werfe ich mich wider dich. [. . .] Sollen die für das Vaterland sterben, die daran glauben. . . ' (VdG^2,249)

In this last, powerful plea the ideals of personal freedom and common brotherhood are again interwoven. Yet they fail to deter Ferdinand; and, as we saw earlier, it is only the sight of the actual frontier and then of wounded French soldiers which brings him to the realisation of what will be involved in his submission: 'Das sollte er tun? Menschen so schänden, Brüdern nicht mehr ins Auge zu blicken als mit Haß' (VdG²,261). The parable of the Good Samaritan, which is also, among other things, an attack on national and religious divisions, provides the model, as the hero gives his last banknote to one particular wounded soldier who has no one to care for him. Thereupon, asserting both his own freedom and his refusal to abandon his international ideal, he tears up his call-up papers and returns to his wife in their Swiss refuge.

Unlike Ferdinand, the central characters of both *Episode am Genfer See* and *Buchmendel* have no awareness of human brother-hood as an ideal. Here Zweig must attain his purpose by the sympathy of his portrait of those who are victims of man-made divisions and by the occasional comment of his narrator.

In Boris he portrays a man who, without the slightest feeling of hostility towards anybody, is taken away from home to fight what is called the 'enemy' and who then simply turns his back on the fighting. Even when his naive attempt to return to his family brings him to neutral Switzerland, his welfare is temporarily threatened by the bureaucratic will to categorise, to know 'ob er als Deserteur oder als dokumentenloser Ausländer behandelt werden solle' (K,92), before a 'foreigner', again echoing the parable of the Good Samaritan, offers to pay for his keep until the authorities have settled his case. In his amusing yet challenging naiveté, however, Boris can see no reason why he should not continue immediately on his homeward journey. The meaning of the word 'Grenze', with its implications of foreign territory which he will not be allowed to pass, is beyond his imaginative grasp. What possible threat can he pose to anybody, since he has laid down his arms? The answer is that such obvious and uncompli-cated considerations no longer govern human relations. As the sympathetic hotel-manager remarks in response to the Russian's impassioned plea for help: 'Ich kann nicht, Boris. Kein Mensch kann jetzt dem andern helfen' (K,96). These words, summarising the unhappy state of affairs in which national divisions come before human need, also point to the universality of the problem. Although Boris happens to be Russian, he is clearly regarded as a representative figure; and the cross which marks his grave is described as 'eines jener kleinen Kreuze über namenlosem

Schicksal, mit denen jetzt unser Europa bedeckt ist von einem bis zum andern Ende' (K,96). With the possessive adjective of this concluding sentence the author seeks to draw the reader into his own sense of regret at the loss of that brotherhood of man which is such an important part of his ideal.

In Mendel he presents a second figure whose naiveté challenges the divisive nationalism of the world at large. When war comes, his Jewish book-pedlar is unaware that the foreign booksellers to whom he still writes are now classed as enemies. It is the narrator's task, however, to call attention to the ideal of human brotherhood in his grimly ironic observation that Mendel continues to write, 'als ob diese Grenzen seit 1914 nicht umnäht wären mit Stacheldraht und an jedem von Gott geschaffenen Tage Frankreich, Deutschland, Österreich und Rußland ihre männliche Einwohnerzahl gegenseitig um ein paar tausend Menschen kürzten' (K,114). When Mendel is arrested and interrogated, it is discovered that he is, technically, an illegal immigrant. He has come from the wrong side of the border in that grey area of Galicia; and although he has been tolerated for more than thirty years, the attitudes of wartime suddenly turn him into a 'dangerous' foreigner. There is further unmistakable irony in the narrator's account of the outraged reaction of the military authorities to the discovery of Mendel's Russian citizenship. It is as though they suspected some sinister connection between this most innocent and harmless of men and the military setbacks on the Eastern front (K,115). Absurdity has become a weapon in the author's quest to enlist the reader's sympathy with his cause. Before long, however, he will become much more direct, as his narrator, writing from the perspective of the post-war years, makes this explicit condemnation of Mendel's incarceration:

Aber allmählich weiß schon die von ihrer Tollheit ernüchterte Welt, daß von allen Grausamkeiten und verbrecherischen Übergriffen dieses Krieges keine sinnloser, überflüssiger und darum moralisch unentschuldbarer gewesen als das Zusammenfangen und Einhürden hinter Stacheldraht von ahnungslosen, längst dem Dienstalter entwachsenen Zivilpersonen, die viele Jahre in dem fremden Lande als in einer Heimat gewohnt und aus Treugläubigkeit an das selbst bei Tungusen und Araukanern geheiligte Gastrecht versäumt hatten, rechtzeitig zu fliehen — ein Verbrechen an der Zivil-

165

isation, gleich sinnlos begangen in Frankreich, Deutschland und England, auf jeder Scholle unseres irrwitzig gewordenen Europas. (K,117)

Internment, it will be noted, is here not just a violation of individual freedom, but a denial of hospitality, the very principle which welcomes strangers and so nullifies distinctions of nationality. As at the end of *Episode am Genfer See*, however, Zweig indicates that this crime against humanity is not exclusive to one nation. In his phenomenal memory Mendel is unique; but in his sufferings as a victim of narrow nationalism he is seen as typical.

If that were the complete picture, one might regard *Der Zwang, Episode am Genfer See*, and *Buchmendel* as persuasive contributions to the cause of internationalism. In fact matters are by no means as straightforward as, for clarity of exposition, I have so far presented them. It is not that there are inherent difficulties, as there were with the ideal of passionate intensity, but rather that the level of conviction and commitment which accompany the international aspect of the ideal is less high than one might wish and certainly less high than one would expect from stories which have been described as 'stirrring protests against the senselessness and barbarism of war'.[14] In both his short essay on Rolland of 1926 and his longer study of Erasmus dating from 1934 Zweig acknowledged that the ideal of a common brotherhood, for which both of these men stood, was probably incapable of realisation in a world dominated by political decisions, that it was a dream, as he described it in the former, or a utopia, as he called it in the latter.[15] That spirit of resignation seems to have infected his fictional world too, sapping the energy with which the ideal might have been presented.

The problem is not so much that the ideal is commended most by its absence as that its positive manifestations are so feeble. In this connection it is necessary to emphasise a point made previously only in passing: that although the central characters of both *Episode am Genfer See* and *Buchmendel* represent a challenge to the nationalism of the contemporary world and help to unmask some of the absurdities of frontiers, they do so unwittingly, passively, naively. Boris stands aloof from the nationalistic concerns of wartime because he *fails to understand* political and geographical realities; Mendel continues to write to 'enemy' booksellers after the outbreak of hostilities because he remains in complete *ignorance* of events in the real world. Neither man has espoused the ideal of human brotherhood; and neither can really be said to stand above the prevailing nationalism, as though its character had been weighed in the balance and found wanting. Near the end of *Der Zwang* the hero begins to reflect confusedly on the artificiality of frontiers and to wonder whether the animals and the fishes pay heed to these man-made barriers (VdG[2],259). It is essentially on this unconscious, sub-human level that Boris and Mendel come into conflict with the nationalism of their day.

Even in *Der Zwang*, where Ferdinand and his wife give conscious assent to the ideal of international brotherhood, there is little real commitment to its realisation, a serious limitation in a work which has been seen as Zweig's most tendentious narrative,[16] which is generally held to rehearse many of his own concerns and struggles,[17] and which he himself once commended to the publishers of the Russian translation as a 'Revolte gegen die Zeit und den Kriegsdienst'.[18] By the end of the story his protagonist has destroyed his call-up papers (from the safety of his Swiss exile) and gone to the aid of a wounded and neglected French soldier returning home from the battlefield. That is the extent of his revolt.

In discussing the psychology of Ferdinand I have already demonstrated his overriding tendency to escape from the uncomfortable demands of adult responsibility. I have also tried to indicate that, even when he does finally respond to the call of human brotherhood, he is yielding to an unwilled impulse rather than taking a moral decision. While all of this makes good psychological sense and fits into a coherent pattern, it provides a very shaky foundation for the advancement of an ideal. In his study of Sebastian Castellio, the humanist who did speak out clearly against the moral and spiritual dictatorship of his age and who represented an image of the author as he would like to have been,[19] Zweig wrote:

> [. . .] tatsächlich sehnt sich aus Müdigkeit angesichts der erschöpfenden Vielfalt der Probleme, angesichts der Kompliziertheit und Verantwortlichtkeit des Lebens, die große Masse nach einer Mechanisierung der Welt durch eine endgültige, eine allgütige, eine definitive Ordnung, die ihr jedwede Denkbarbeit abnimmt.[20]

From this perspective Ferdinand appears no different from the mass of people; he is certainly not the one to offer resistance to authority on behalf of tolerance and mutual understanding.

A second, though less significant, obstacle in the way of Ferdinand's commitment to the ideal of human brotherhood is his tendency to judge public issues in aesthetic rather than moral or political terms. Even his conscious reasons for leaving his native country have little to do with morality or politics. They are chiefly a matter of distaste: the 'Ekel' he feels at his treatment by the military doctors, the 'Stickluft der patriotischen Phrasen' which he finds nauseating (VdG²,226-7). Distaste is a feeble weapon against moral or political wrong, not least because it takes as its standard what is personally pleasing or unpleasing.

That brings us to a more fundamental and persistent weakness in Ferdinand's stance: the tendency to neglect the public dimension of the issues confronting him in favour of private satisfaction, a tendency which should not surprise us when we have noted the link between internationalism and personal satisfaction in Zweig himself. In discussing the ideal of personal freedom as it is worked out in the course of *Der Zwang* I drew a distinction between freedom of moral choice, on the one hand, and freedom to find one's own personal satisfaction, on the other. The importance of the distinction lies in the fact that it is only the former which leads to public involvement and it is precisely this which Ferdinand most sorely lacks, or even avoids, despite appearances to the contrary. For when he argues that to continue his painting and work for himself would be a crime while the world about him is facing destruction, he is not on the point of joining the pacifist opposition to war, but trying to justify a return to Germany and submission to the same fate as all the other conscripts (VdG²,232). On the other hand, when he does nevertheless make mental preparation for a defiance of the authorities at the consulate, the substance of his intended argument is the primacy of his own artistic work (VdG²,240), just as one later brief flickering of his resistance takes the form of an insistence that, before he goes off to war, he must first finish the picture on which he is engaged (VdG²,253). Even when he turns his back conclusively on the call of the fatherland, he commits himself to no internationalist cause, but returns to his art and his wife, in whose embrace he is removed to such an ecstatic plane that the problems of earth cannot intrude

— and cannot be tackled. The retreat of his first exile is completed in a retreat from the world altogether. And the ideal of human brotherhood yields to the claims of personal freedom, understood now only as freedom from public responsibility and freedom to seek personal satisfaction.

During his own retreat to Switzerland near the end of the First World War Zweig acknowledged in his diary that, although the only honest thing was to say a clear 'No' to war, he was not at all sure that he himself would have the strength to do this in Vienna. The entry continues: 'Refractär zu werden ist schäbig bis zum äußersten, wenn es ohne Bekenntnis geschieht. Es ist unfruchtbar, feige und klein'.[21] Judged by these words, judged even by Zweig's own ambiguous answer to the problem,[22] Ferdinand's retreat appears to be an abdication of all public responsibility.

The purpose of these critical remarks is not to question the merits of *Der Zwang* as a work of fiction, as the realisation of an interesting psychological type, but to demonstrate that its contribution to the cause of human brotherhood is much smaller than is usually supposed, smaller in comparison with a work like Leonhard Frank's cycle of anti-war stories, *Der Mensch ist gut* (1917), with all their tendentious and overblown rhetoric,[23] smaller too in comparison with the recommendation which Zweig himself made to his Russian publishers. It is true that, in depicting the weaknesses of his hero, he was not necessarily caught up in them himself. Yet the story contains little evidence of critical distance from these particular weaknesses and little indication of genuine alternatives. Even Ferdinand's wife, who is certainly more astute and strong-willed than her husband, remains entangled in many of the same inadequacies and seems content if only she can preserve his safety and personal freedom. It is significant, moreover, that, when Zweig later comes to give that thinly disguised self-portrait in Erasmus, many of Ferdinand's propensities — the avoidance of decisions, the refusal to commit himself to a common cause for fear of diminishing his independence, the concentration on his own work, the retreat to Switzerland to ensure this possibility, the final flight from the real world altogether[24] — are repeated, even if now with greater critical awareness on the part of the author.[25]

In general it seems that, in Zweig's hierarchy of values, personal freedom occupies the highest place. Ideals of a public nature therefore, which almost inevitably entail some compromise or curtailment of that freedom, are destined to suffer, or rather, they are likely to remain ideals, to be cherished but seldom realised.

The other aspects of Zweig's ideal of human brotherhood, which concern the overcoming of religious and social rather than national barriers, receive far less attention in the *Novellen*, as indeed in his writing generally. Here too, however, we shall not go far without encountering difficulties which, in their different ways, cast doubt on the level of the author's commitment to the ideal.

In *Buchmendel* the difficulties are barely apparent, but it must also be admitted that the two aspects of the ideal are in any case only briefly intimated. In her defence of the book-pedlar, when others at the Café Gluck reject or neglect him, the cloakroom attendant comes closest to fulfilling the role of Good Samaritan; and when his long absence makes it likely that he has already died, her continued concern for his welfare takes the form of a proposal to have a mass said for him (K,122). Her sublime innocence permits her to overlook religious distinctions, between Catholic and Jew, which for others might be paramount. She regards him only as a man in need. Although her response displays something of the same naiveté with which both Boris and Mendel himself challenge the absurdity of national divisions, she is the more admirable figure because of her clear disregard of intolerance of any kind and the positive, humane action she is prepared to take. Later, when the narrative frame brings her into contact with the first-person narrator, who is seeking information about the fate of Mendel, a bond is formed between them in the affectionate remembrance of this unique man, a bond strange enough to attract the attention of the customers, who stare at such an 'ungleiches Paar' (K,112), yet a bond which clearly appealed to the author, since it brings together two people from very different social and cultural backgrounds: an educated, well-read man of comfortable means and an illiterate, simple-minded working woman (cf. K,123). Although *Buchmendel* is rather gloomy in its depiction of a world in which human brotherhood has been undermined by national divisions, it does, then, allow us to glimpse rare possibilities of brotherhood across religious and social barriers.

The ideal of a human brotherhood which cuts across social barriers achieves greatest prominence and most explicit affirmation in *Phantastische Nacht*, though that is not to say it carries complete conviction even there. We are given to understand that the passionate excitement which comes to the baron not only brings with it a sense of personal rejuvenation, but also spills over into a desire for oneness with mankind at large, a desire which, according to the concluding sentences of the work, has since been fulfilled. On the basis of his private experience the baron generalises sententiously: 'Wer einmal sich selbst gefunden, kann nichts aus dieser Welt mehr verlieren. Und wer einmal den Menschen in sich begriffen, der begreift alle Menschen' (A,207).

The first stirrings of his desire take place on the animal, almost biological level. He is attracted to the crowds of ordinary folk because he senses there for the first time in his life 'im Animalischen, im Triebhaften, im Gemeinen eine Verwandtschaft mit mir selbst' (A,171), feels 'die Brunst der Millionstadt' flowing over into him (A,172). Accordingly, he seeks to immerse himself in this crowd, to transcend individuation itself by what he describes as 'Paarung mit dieser heißen, fremden, drängenden Menschheit' (A,173). Even at this early stage his quest is open to the same objection as arose in connection with the ideal of passionate intensity: that it can scarcely be expected to last. The baron would have done well to pay more regard to the implications of what he recorded earlier: that the oneness which he first witnessed at the race-course occurred only during the excitement of each race, after which the crowd subsided into a collection of individuals of different social classes (A,139-40). More seriously, if one takes him at his word ('im Animalischen', 'Brunst', 'Paarung') it is not, strictly, *human* brotherhood which he seeks, but something closer to the rutting and herding instinct of animals.

The baron's contact with others does not, however, remain on that level. In his encounter with the prostitute and her criminal associates he moves from *eros* to *caritas*, experiences pity, tenderness, generosity, and above all human kinship. His cheerful liberality with money removes the commercial basis of his contact with the prostitute and creates an experience which thrills him precisely because 'sie nach dem Menschen in mir fragte' (A,192); it also transforms the threatening behaviour of her accomplices into what he calls 'ein Zustand des Rechts, des Vertrauens, eine menschliche Beziehung' (A,198). He accepts them as 'seinesgleichen' (A,199) or, to the extent that he acknowledges the distinction that they are thieves from necessity, he from whim, feels

171

'ein brüderliches Mitleid' with them (A,196). Even after the intoxication of that first day has left him, he assures us that he is still borne along by a tide of generosity, distributing money to those on the lower fringes of society, a poor stall-holder, a road-sweeper, a lamp-lighter, and has retained a warm feeling for mankind, which makes him capable of holding genuine conversations with his servant and of responding with deep sympathy to the bereavement of the caretaker (A,205).

Fine as these sentiments are, their presentation does not entirely avoid bathos. More importantly, they leave unspoken two possible objections — as indeed does the narrative as a whole, in which, after the brief introduction, only the baron's voice is heard. First, his feeling for others is still very much designed to satisfy his own private needs: the desire to break out of his isolation and alienation (A,184), the pleasure that generosity brings to him (A,200-1). Second, his experience of human brotherhood has a doubly insecure basis. On the one hand, its origins in a sudden eruption of passion cast doubts on its durability. On the other hand, his sense of human brotherhood relies heavily on a generosity made possible by the chance winning of a considerable sum of money. Where, one wonders, would his generosity be and where the resultant sense of oneness with others, if they were dependent on the more sober realities of a hard-earned income? It is characteristic of the baron — as it is indeed of Zweig — that he has at best only a superficial understanding of the socio-economic forces that operate in his own and other people's lives.

For all his avowed sense of unity with members of the lower classes and with social outcasts, moreover, the baron never quite shakes off the snobbery which was present in his initial reaction to the crowds at the race-course and which continues to express itself above all in the fastidious or patronising tone of his narrative. Even as he gives himself gladly to the encounter with the prostitute, he experiences it as something dirty and disgusting, and his mind constructs an image of her home life which is notable for its exaggerated and lurid squalor (A,192). When her accomplices enter the scene, he experiences no fear, yet remarks on the fact that their voice, their laughter is 'ordinär' (A,193). And when his generosity leads her to obstruct attempts to extort more money from him, his gratitude for such a human response does not conceal the condescension of his attitude: 'Aus dem Gemeinen stieg Güte' (A,198). Against this background of residual snobbery it is tempting to speculate what would happen if the road-sweeper to whom he gives money with the words 'Kauf dir was Gutes dafür' (A,202) were to take this as a sign of true brotherhood and address the donor as 'Du'. The serious point behind this observation is that the baron's sense of oneness with others exists only within the framework of a rigid class-structure which it takes for granted. Jean Paul Bier has argued that on the reader of *Phantastische Nacht* in 1922 the final sentence of the work would have impressed itself as 'ein Bekenntnis zur neuen republikanischen Wirklichkeit'.[26] In the light of all that has just been noted it must be said that only an insensitive, careless or hopelessly optimistic reader could have formed such a view.

It is important not to overlook this snobbish tendency, because it occurs in other stories too and seems to correspond to something in Zweig himself which inhibited the fullest expression of his ideal of human brotherhood. The tendency can be observed, for example, in the hero of *Der Zwang*, whose sense of human brotherhood may extend horizontally to embrace men of other races, but does not always extend vertically to include those of a lower social class and who, accordingly, is most indignant at the consulate in Zurich when social rank fails to assure priority and he is forced to wait with the 'Gesindel' (VdG[2],243).[27] It is to be found in the heroine of *Vierundzwanzig Stunden aus dem Leben einer Frau*, who, somewhat surprisingly in view of the 'shameful' experiences she is about to record, begins her narrative with some disdainful comments, first, on certain elements of the casino clientèle, 'die abgefeimten Professionals und Kartenspielkokotten, jene ganze fragwürdige, zusammengeschneite Gesellschaft, die [. . .] bedeutend weniger pittoresk und romantisch ist, als sie in den elenden Romanen immer gemalt wird', and then on the difference between the good old days, when people gambled for real money, and the present, 'da in der modisch gebauten pomphaften Spielburg ein verbürgertes Cook-Reisepublikum seine charakterlosen Spielmarken langweilig verpulvert' (VdG,33). And the same snobbishness creeps into the account which Roland gives of his youthful experiences in *Verwirrung der Gefühle*. Having arrived at the difficult part of his story, where he must deal with the homosexuality of his professor, he distinguishes in a way which is difficult to justify objectively between his cultured mentor, who is allowed to keep his dignity as well as his young friend's sympathy, and the young men 'niederen Standes' with whom the professor consorts but who are treated with scornful distaste (VdG,267-9).

With regard to Zweig himself, it is probably no accident that, although he was so given to probing the mind of man, he proved unwilling or unable to present his lower-class characters from the inside. It is this indeed which most distinguishes him from his Russian friend, Maxim Gorky. Although the well-connected hero of *Der Zwang* and the peasant Boris of *Episode am Genfer See* are both victims of war who find themselves in exile, only Ferdinand's mental processes are understood and portrayed from within, while Boris is presented almost entirely in terms of what is visible to an external observer. Of the two contestants in *Schachnovelle* the educated lawyer, who has moved in imperial circles, is permitted to tell his own story from the inside,[28] while the biography of the uncultured chess-champion, brought up on public charity, is presented entirely from the outside. And when it comes to that most extended account of the peasant mind, Crescenz in *Leporella*, Zweig's limited understanding takes refuge in the pose of the non-omniscient narrator: 'vielleicht', 'möglicherweise', 'sei es [. . .]', 'war es [. . .]?' etc. (K,54,53,58).[29] It might be objected that these characters have only a limited intelligence, which makes a presentation from the inside difficult. Yet why is it that Zweig seems always to conceive the lower classes in terms of limited intelligence? This is the same Zweig whose essay 'Die Monotisierung der Welt' of 1925 is dominated not only by regret at the drab uniformity and easy superficiality of modern western culture, which can be learnt by 'das plumpste Dienstmädchen', but by a belief that it is no good appealing to the masses, who are not prepared to make an intellectual effort, but are interested only in facile entertainment.[30] It is a further symptom of Zweig's low opinion of the common people that when, in his *Novellen*, he employs the traditional narrative device of referring to his characters by initials only, rather than by a full name — a device clearly intended to promote authenticity by creating the illusion that the identity of real people is being protected — he reserves it for the socially superior such as Baron von R. or Mrs C. In *Leporella* and *Schachnovelle* indeed he discriminates pointedly between Baron F. and Dr B., on the one hand, and Crescentia

Anna Aloisia Finkenhuber and Mirko Czentovic, on the other. Some people, it seems, have no reputation and no identity worth protecting.

Having grown up among the wealthy bourgeoisie of late nineteenth-century Vienna, Zweig enjoyed a privileged social position which made it difficult for him to forge links with those of a lower social class or to appreciate their situation.[31] It also made it difficult for him, in his *Novellen*, to give unambiguous expression to the ideal of human brotherhood across social barriers, an ideal to which he did not cease to assent with at least part of his being. In his essay on Tolstoy in *Drei Dichter ihres Lebens* he writes of the Russian aristocrat's vain attempts to become one with the peasants, of his inability to reproduce their simplicity and humility in himself, of his failure to make more than a symbolic gesture of brotherhood and overcome the real social and intellectual gulf between them and him.[32] Indirectly and unintentionally, Zweig has here provided a telling commentary on the limitations of both the baron of *Phantastische Nacht* and himself.

PART THREE
TIME, PLACE, AND BEYOND

Both the psychological foundation and the moral superstructure of Zweig's *Novellen* would seem likely to reduce the importance of setting, temporal or spatial. If the proper scene of the action is the inner world of the human mind, of what interest is the place which the characters, physically, occupy? If the human ideals set forth are such as are appropriate in any age and in any place, and if one of those ideals (human brotherhood) specifically appeals to a unity beyond distinctions which are registered in geographical space, does that not make questions of 'when?' and 'where?' irrelevant? In due course we shall have to consider a number of characters who do indeed seek to live, or are forced to live, in a world cut off from time and space. Yet that is very much a response to the circumstances of a life lived at a given time in a given place. Questions of setting are no less pertinent there than elsewhere in Zweig. In general, too, it has to be recognised that mental events cannot be divorced from the dimensions of the physical world, but participate in a two-way exchange. On the one hand, the individual mind is subject to powerful influences, perhaps from the climatic environment, more frequently from the total cultural environment (itself an expression of a particular time and place), and responds to changes in that environment as well as to particular events. On the other hand, the stirrings of the mind seldom remain private and internal, but manifest themselves in gestures and actions which are perceptible in the world of time and space and may even alter that world. As to the human ideals, although they may represent the possibilities of living which are not confined to a specific time or place, it must not be forgotten that they become important to Zweig precisely at those times when they are under threat, when they fall victim to the social, economic, or political conditions of a particular age.

13

A Sense of Time

As Ingrid Lent points out,[1] it is a remarkable feature of Zweig's *Novellen* that, with the exception of a few minor works, which do not form part of our chief concern, they are all set in the contemporary world. For his biographical studies he would usually delve into the historical past; for his legends he resorted to biblical and medieval (as well as legendary) times; and for his plays he made use of all three. For his *Novellen*, however, he chose his own age. The central events recorded might lie some decades in the past, but the narrative frame usually ensured that here, as elsewhere, his first readers were granted a smooth transition from their own time to that of the fictional world.

It is not possible to detect any consistency in the degree of precision with which the author establishes the temporal setting of his *Novellen*. Sometimes he is very specific, referring to dates or to particular historical events. The dramatic death of the doctor, which begins and concludes *Der Amokläufer*, takes place in March 1912. The arrest of Dr B. in *Schachnovelle* takes place on the day before Hitler's entry into Vienna,[2] though not before he has heard Schuschnigg's farewell speech (i.e. 11 March 1938), and his release is granted after the occupation of Bohemia (29 September 1938).[3] At other times Zweig leaves matters vague, so that the reader must take his temporal bearings from incidental details such as the use of the telephone, the presence (or absence) of the motor car or the gramophone, the popularity of jazz or the cinema. Nevertheless, the degree of precision in the dating of events is no guide to the level of interest shown in the times depicted or in any significance arising out of them. *Phantastische Nacht*, which is most specific of

180

all in fixing the start of the baron's explosive experience at three minutes past three on 7 June 1913, in fact attaches no particular importance to the date. For the baron the precision acts only as an anchor, an objective, stabilising factor amid the storm of passion and excitement he seeks to relate, for which purpose almost any other date would have served equally well. By contrast, *Die unsichtbare Sammlung*, which mentions no particular date, manages to convey within its brief span considerably more of the specific quality of the inflationary times in which it is set.

Although precision of dating is no guide to the level of Zweig's interest in temporal setting, it is possible to detect a two-fold difference of approach, which, with minor exceptions, distinguishes the three volumes that form *Die Kette* from the stories which appeared in *Kleine Chronik* (and *Kaleidoskop*) and afterwards. Those in the latter group show a greater general awareness of the times, often in the explicit remarks of the narrator, and a shift of interest away from the social habits and conventions of the age towards the political and economic forces which influence the lives of the characters. The change corresponds roughly to a change in temporal setting, the change from the years before the First World War to the years of the war itself, of post-war inflation and, finally, of National Socialist dictatorship. That is not to say that Zweig immediately responded to historical developments. There was usually a lapse of time before these took shape in his narratives. Indeed he openly acknowledged that works such as *Der Amokläufer* and *Brief einer Unbekannten* were composed without regard to contemporary political realities, 'in völlig unaktivistischer Gelassenheit', as he put it in *Die Welt von Gestern*.[4] Only gradually were these realities allowed to filter through into the writing of his *Novellen*, and even there they never became as dominant as they were to become in his uncompleted novel *Rausch der Verwandlung*.[5]

In the stories which are set in the pre-war period — and that is the majority — Zweig draws on his own experiences as a child, adolescent, and young gentleman during the dying years of Habsburg Vienna, the years he was to document more fully in *Die Welt von Gestern*. Compared with that work there is little conscious attempt to present a picture of the times; attention remains focussed on individual human fates. Even so, the stories do manage to convey something of the characteristic flavour of the period[6] and, especially in *Erstes Erlebnis*, suggest a certain typicality in the lives portrayed. The aspects of the times which most frequently come to the fore are: attitudes to sexuality and marriage; bourgeois conventionality, morality, and complacency, together with the dissatisfaction that often accompanies them; superfluity and superficiality, especially in the form of aestheticism. These aspects frequently shade into one another and are in any case related to a wider cultural unease, the loss of spontaneity exposed most clearly by Nietzsche and later summarised in the title of one of Freud's most important metapsychological writings, *Civilization and its Discontents*.

In 'Eros Matutinus', the third chapter of *Die Welt von Gestern*, Zweig evidently sees attitudes towards sexuality as part of that wider complex of ideas. For, as he argues there,

> das neunzehnte Jahrhundert war redlich in dem Wahn befangen, man könne mit rationalistischer Vernunft alle Konflikte lösen, und je mehr man das Natürliche verstecke, desto mehr temperiere man seine anarchischen Kräfte; wenn man also junge Leute durch nichts über ihr Vorhandensein aufkläre, würden sie ihre eigene Sexualität vergessen. In diesem Wahn, durch Ignorieren zu temperieren, vereinten sich alle Instanzen zu einem gemeinsamen Boykott durch hermetisches Schweigen.[7]

In *Die Gouvernante* and *Brennendes Geheimnis* it is that process of concealment which emerges most clearly: the wall of silence or hushed whispers which keeps the young sisters dangerously imprisoned within their own ignorance, inhibited by the uncertainty of what little knowledge they possess; the locked doors which have kept the great secret of adult sexuality hidden from Edgar, but have also thereby increased its fascination. These difficulties are compounded by the general isolation of the young heroes and heroines, by the lack of genuine contact with their parents,[8] notably in *Brennendes Geheimnis*, and by the double standards which the adult world applies. The latter, which are fully explored in *Die Welt von Gestern*,[9] are particularly evident in *Die Gouvernante*, where the girls' mother responds with moral outrage to the governess's pregnancy, but remains ignorant that it is her own nephew who has got the young woman into trouble and — to judge from the account given in *Die Welt von Gestern* — would

182

not have reacted differently if she had known, since, unlike their female counterparts, young men who could not yet hope to marry were expected to sow their wild oats.

Although no dates are provided, it seems best to imagine at least the first three stories of the volume *Erstes Erlebnis* as being set during the period of Zweig's own adolescence, that is, nearly twenty years before their publication. Certainly, the fact that both *Geschichte in der Dämmerung* and *Brennendes Geheimnis* are able to offer at the end a brief glimpse of their heroes' later life points in that direction. The variety of the individual fates depicted and their similarity to some of the matters raised in *Die Welt von Gestern* underline the sense of typicality. Yet whether the depiction in the narratives amounts to genuine social criticism is open to question, not least because the undoubted difficulties of these young people have their roots not only in the secretive attitudes of their society, but also, as we have seen, in coincidental circumstances or in what Zweig presents as the natural process of adolescence.

The future which the narrator of *Sommernovellette* and his older companion between them predict for the teenage girl who has been the object of the latter's playful experiment is the protracted tragedy of everyday life in the provinces and marriage to some worthy 'Bürgersmann' (EE,205). Although this is no more than an unsubstantiated prophecy, it is clearly based on the assumed norm for their class, which is of a union founded on respectability rather than love, perhaps a dull marriage of convenience. This is borne out in other stories where, whether the characters are Viennese, French, or British, the conventions of the age tend to lead to some form of misalliance, or lovelessness, or both. Edgar's mother in *Brennendes Geheimnis* finds herself in a marriage which has provided for her material needs, but has offered her no love or excitement, with the result that she is particularly susceptible to the allure of erotic adventure, even while she remains aware that public scandal would be disastrous (EE,109,145). In *Vierundzwanzig Stunden aus dem Leben einer Frau* it is the narrator's contention that Mme Henriette's sudden elopement is likely to be the consequence of what he calls 'eine jahrelang enttäuschende, langweilige Ehe' (VdG,18). And although it is nowhere explicitly stated, we shall probably not go far wrong in assuming something similar in the case of the Englishwoman in *Der Amokläufer*, married to a Dutch businessman, but drawn into a fatal affair with a young officer. With the central character of *Vierundzwanzig Stunden aus dem Leben einer Frau*, Mrs C., there is no suggestion of a loveless union. Nevertheless, it is noteworthy that the pattern she has followed is that of early marriage to an older man, who has already ten years of colonial service behind him (VdG,30), a pattern which is likely to lead to early widowhood and therefore unfulfilled sexual needs.[10]

Even where there is no misalliance or unhappy marriage, even where there is no marriage at all, Zweig portrays a society which has become too confining or too comfortable to grant the individual a sense of satisfaction or fulfilment. As he implies in that passage from *Die Welt von Gestern* quoted above, the instincts embody an anarchic force which challenges the constraints and conventions that polite society has erected in the attempt to tame it. There is evidence of this not only in the immature sexual passion and aggression of Bob in *Geschichte in der Dämmerung,* which leads him into 'Inkorrektheit' and behaviour incompatible with that of a gentleman (EE,32), but also in the passionate horse-riding of the more sophisticated Margot, which, in a scene heavy with symbolism, threatens to undo her carefully ordered hair (EE,31). It is there too in the un-European excess of the doctor in *Der Amokläufer*; in the uncivil jostling of the baron in *Phantastische Nacht*; in the elemental grief of Mme Henriette's husband in *Vierundzwanzig Stunden aus dem Leben einer Frau,* which causes him to cry out loud and run about with dishevelled clothes; or in the aggressive hostility which temporarily overtakes Dr B. near the end of *Schachnovelle.*

The point of interest here, however, is not that the instincts break through the civilising restraints, but that the very existence of these restraints is itself often a source of unease. It is one important ingredient in the unrejuvenated existence of the baron of *Phantastische Nacht*, for example, that he has been brought up with a physical and moral 'Sauberkeitsempfinden' (A,155), a sense of decency appropriate to the ideal of an officer and a gentleman (A,154). In retrospect he comes more fully to realise the stifling consequences of this upbringing, to understand that 'meine Leidenschaft nur verkrümmt, nur zertreten gewesen war von dem gesellschaftlichen Wahn, von dem herrischen Ideal der Gentlemen' (A,166). In the different denominational environment that obtains in *Verwirrung der Gefühle* the young hero experiences something similar when he moves from his provincial home to Berlin and, like Zweig himself in his student days there,[11] relishes the freedom and intoxication it affords. This is evidently the Berlin of the 'Gründerjahre',[12] bustling with activity and full of a new self-confidence to match Roland's own: 'Beide, sie und ich, plötzlich aufgeschossen aus einer protestantisch ordnungshaften und umschränkten Kleinbürgerlichkeit' (VdG,160). Although the sexual licence to which this initially leads is long past by the time he writes his memoirs, his present academic pursuits are still defined by contrast with a prevailing intellectual climate which is characterised above all by industry, thoroughness, and clinical precision and is no less stultifying than the moral atmosphere of his youth (VdG,155). In other works, where the issue may not be so explicitly raised, one has only to observe the ease with which Zweig's characters (Mrs C. in *Vierundzwanzig Stunden aus dem Leben einer Frau*, the narrator in *Unvermutete Bekanntschaft mit einem Handwerk*) suspend conventional moral judgements in the face of passion and commitment to realise the discontent that lies unspoken behind it.

More pervasive than the restrictive conventionality which Zweig portrays is the superfluity and complacent ease of what Marie-Luise Welter calls the 'satte Epoche vor dem ersten Weltkrieg'.[13] For members of the aristocracy and upper middle classes, from whom most of his characters are drawn, life seems to make few demands and hold little challenge; they have no need to earn money, their wants are provided for; there is no unpleasantness to ruffle the calm surface of their daily round. These are the effete, who, in the manner of the spa guests of Baden in Hesse's *Kurgast*, populate hotels all over Europe: the gentleman from Milan who spends his day catching fish, only to throw them back in the water in the evening; the senile English ladies whose 'leise vegetative Existenz' almost passes unnoticed; the elderly sisters from North Germany who sit knitting all day, 'unerbittliche Parzen einer Welt der Langeweile und Beschränktheit' (*Sommernovellette*, EE,195-6); the guests who sit calmly eating their dinner, smoking, chatting, or playing cards, unaware of the agonies of a parched earth (*Die Frau und die Landschaft*, A,99,103); the pampered wife and daughter of the Jewish businessman, who indulge in expensive perfume and polite French conversation, take rides in fast motor cars, or sip whisky and soda through a straw (*Untergang eines Herzens*, VdG,115,123-4). In this last instance the superfluity of those depicted is judged through the puritanical eyes of a father whose motives are much less respectable than he realises; his reasons for condemning it are therefore rather special. Elsewhere, however, Zweig indicates a more general ground for dissatisfaction with the habits of this society: they are inimical to the full, authentic life. This is clearly evident in the heroine of *Angst*, who yields to the excitement of erotic adventure and its attendant dangers precisely because it takes her out of her easy, unchallenging existence. It is not that she is unhappily married. Her husband is able to meet her sexual, intellectual, and material needs; and she herself is portrayed as 'behaglich gebettet in eine breitbürgerliche, windstille Existenz' and 'von lauter satten und bürgerlichen Menschen umringt'. Zweig's suggestion is rather that the provocation lies in the very absence of difficulty. As he puts it in an undisguised narratorial reflection:

> Aber es gibt eine Schlaffheit der Atmosphäre, die ebenso sinnlich macht wie Schwüle oder Sturm, eine Wohltemperiertheit des Glückes, die aufreizender ist als Unglück. Sattheit reizt nicht minder als Hunger, und das Gefahrlose, Gesicherte ihres Lebens gab ihr Neugier auf das Abenteuer. (K,131)

In these words he manages both to characterise his own social class at a given historical period and to expose one of the roots of its unease, an unease which he himself continued to feel. For, as Strelka points out, his fiftieth birthday found him wishing that his life should not proceed so smoothly, that it should confront him rather with more restless, exciting, rejuvenating, challenging experience.[14]

In other stories Zweig isolates one particular representative type from this turn-of-the-century society: the unmarried man who has neither financial need nor family obligation, but moves easily through life in pursuit of any pleasure that will make no demands on him. In Marie-Luise Welter's classifications of Zweig's characters he corresponds most closely to the type of the dandy, that rich, well-dressed product of the 'Spätzeit des österreichischen Kaisertums' among the aristocracy and upper middle classes,[15] but his immediate literary antecedents are the aloof, narcissistic, aesthetic young hero of Hofmannsthal's *Märchen der 672. Nacht* and Schnitzler's charming, sophisticated, but ultimately trivial Anatol. Elements of both figures come together, in different combinations, in Zweig's characters. The young baron who pursues Edgar's mother in *Brennendes Geheimnis* is one such individual. He is taking a holiday at a hotel on the Semmering without knowing why he has chosen this spot or indeed why he is on holiday at all. He finds nothing to occupy him for long and so paces idly up and down, leafs absent-mindedly through the newspapers, or plays a few desultory bars on the piano. If he feels the need of other people, it is only because he dreads the prospect of being forced into intimate knowledge of himself; women are no more than interchangeable objects of predatory interest, valuable as a means of stimulation in an essentially empty life (EE,88-90). Zweig's extended description of the baron is often couched in language which unmistakably indicates his typicality ('Er war einer jener jungen Menschen [. . .]'; 'wenn man solche Menschen [. . .]'; 'sie sind immer [. . .]') and concludes with a passage which reads like an allusion to one of the characteristic figures of the age, Peter Altenberg. Among these men are said to be many

> denen sich der einzelne Tag in hundert kleine, sinnliche Erlebnisse auflöst — ein Blick im Vorübergehen, ein weghuschendes Lächeln, ein im Gegenübersitzen gestreiftes Knie — und das Jahr wieder in hundert solcher Tage, für die das sinnliche Erlebnis ewig fließende, nährende und anfeuernde Quelle des Lebens ist. (EE,90)

In the older Livonian gentleman of *Sommernovellette*, who writes fictional love-letters to the young woman, Zweig presents a minor variation of the same type, a man of wealth but with no serious interests and no real home, who passes the day observing the smoke of his own cigarettes or leafing through a book. His differences from the baron are only slight: he is not merely on holiday, he has no occupation at all; his predatory instincts are directed not so much towards women as towards works of art, which he treats, however, with the same dilettante disdain. In this as in other respects Zweig again indicates a certain typicality:

> [. . .] ohne ständigen Aufenthalt seit Jahren, war er heimatlos in dem edlen Sinne derer, die, Wikinger und Piraten der Schönheit, aller Städte Kostbarkeiten im räuberischen Flug in

187

sich versammelt haben. [. . .] Er lebte eines jener Leben, die überflüssig scheinen, weil sie sich keiner Gemeinsamkeit einketten, weil all der Reichtum, den tausend einzelne kostbare Erlebnisse in ihnen aufgespeichert haben, mit ihrem letzten Atemzug unvererbt zerrinnt. (EE,193-4)

If the aestheticism of this man is doubly unproductive, in that his involvement in art leads to no creative act and he has no heirs to whom he might pass on his artistic experiences, his younger counterpart in *Brief einer Unbekannten* appears to this extent less superfluous. He is, after all, a successful writer and has fathered a son, albeit an illegitimate son whom he never meets and who dies young. For the rest, in his wealth and nonchalant ease — exemplified once more in the familiar habits of smoking and inattentive perusal of the newspaper — in his cultivated taste and his playful, uncommitted treatment of the opposite sex, he merely conforms to type.

Where he remains locked in his aesthetic parasitism, unaware of his own inadequacy, the baron of *Phantastische Nacht*, the outstanding example of this supposed trend of the age, displays a remarkable insight into his condition, if only from the perspective of his later, rejuvenated self. He is able therefore to comment critically on his earlier existence, not only on those none too demanding moral standards discussed above, but on the inherited (that is, unearned) wealth which has relieved him of the necessity to work, on his detached contemplation of life and his casual pursuit of pleasure, on his tendency to collect beautiful objects and beautiful women without real commitment, on the emotional enervation that has resulted from lack of friction and challenge (A,128-30). And having come into contact with the lower fringes of society, he can see himself through their eyes, as the satiated parasite (A,196). More than that, he himself is aware that he is no exception, but the representative figure of what is an effete social class. Surveying the elegant ladies and gentlemen of his acquaintance at the race-course, he remarks:

Die Frauen prüften sich gegenseitig in ihren neuen Toiletten, die Männer warfen begehrliche Blicke, jene mondäne Neugier, die der Teilnahmslosen eigentliche Beschäftigung ist, begann sich zu entfalten [. . .]
Ich ging mitten durch dies laue Gewühl, grüßte und dankte, atmete wohlig — war es doch die Atmosphäre meiner

188

Existenz — den Duft von Parfüm und Eleganz. (A,140) He is fundamentally no different from those around him; in his lifestyle, as he earlier observed, he does not stand out from the rest (A,129). In some cases the representative figure of the superfluous man acts as a foil to a central character whose life embodies passion and commitment. As we shall also see, the first-person narrators of *Der Amokläufer* and *Die Mondscheingasse* share some of the same characteristics and serve a similar purpose. But if that is the most frequent means by which Zweig expresses the unease of pre-war Viennese culture, his most powerful statement is undoubtedly *Phantastische Nacht*, where the hero's sudden transformation allows us to measure full human potential against those habits of the age which deny it.

When the First World War does provide the setting for Zweig's *Novellen*, further significant differences from Leonhard Frank's *Der Mensch ist gut* emerge. The perspective is essentially that of the non-combatant: victims of the fighting, including the bereaved, are mentioned only peripherally; the sufferers are civilians or those who have escaped military service (*Der Zwang, Buchmendel, Episode am Genfer See*). Moreover, war is presented simply as a fact, with no attempt to explore its origins. In truth one could hardly expect it to be otherwise when the many pages of *Die Welt von Gestern* devoted to the First World War pay scant attention to its political and economic causes, preferring instead to picture it as some natural disaster[16] or, psychologically, following Freud, as the eruption of instinct breaking through the civilised surface of life, as an expression of 'die Unlust an [sic] der Kultur'[17] little different, one assumes, from those other manifestations considered above. To judge from the *Novellen*, what appears to concern Zweig most about the war is the general upsurge of patriotism and narrow-minded national sentiment, on the one hand, and the pervasive encroachments of bureaucracy and state authority, on the other, that is to say, those things which threaten the cherished ideals of human brotherhood and personal freedom.

Der Zwang presents a world where newspapers are full of phrases like 'Vaterland und Pflicht' (VdG^2,242), which have been robbed of all noble sentiment and, in the words of Ferdinand's wife, 'nach Blut stinken, nach warmem, lebendigem Menschenblut' (VdG^2,233), since they have become synonymous with hostility towards certain other nations. Such nationalistic propaganda has evidently been at work in *Buchmendel* too, where it is condemned by the sympathetic Frau Sporschil as 'Mordslärm' (K,112). If Mendel remains blissfully ignorant of it, he does not escape its effects. As we have already seen, the narrator writes in open condemnation of this incarceration of an alien, this denial of hospitality, which was practised in all European countries during the war and is of course an inevitable consequence of rampant nationalism, certainly no worse than the human slaughter taking place all over Europe (cf. K,114). What is also interesting, however, is that he expresses these sentiments from the vantage-point of the post-war period, of what he calls 'die von ihrer Tollheit ernüchterte Welt', thereby recalling the frequent references to 'Wahnsinn' in *Der Zwang* (VdG²,224,239,246) and implying a psychological — though not Freudian — interpretation of nationalism and war.[18]

Considerably greater space is devoted to the depiction of state authority and bureaucracy, which are everyday facts of life in times of peace too, but become more insistent and obtrusive when war breaks out.

Even allowing for the distorted perception of Ferdinand, the German state-machine, in both its military and civilian aspect, emerges from *Der Zwang* as a force which operates impersonally, takes away man's choice and individual responsibility, reduces him to an inanimate tool, a number, a case (VdG²,228,230-1,243,246-7). Similarly, in *Episode am Genfer See* tsarist authority is depicted as a force which ignores the individuality of its subjects, sending a simple-minded peasant against his will half-way round the world to fight for a cause which he does not understand and in which he has no interest. Even in the potential haven of neutral Switzerland he falls victim to the workings of the bureaucratic mind. If the immediate reaction of the local constable is that this is a deserter, who must be subjected to interrogation, subsequent discussion among the various officials turns on the question of how he is to be classified (as a deserter or a foreigner without papers) so that his case can be dispatched quickly and according to correct procedures (K,89). For the authorities do not wish to have him as a burden on the community. His representative death is brought about by state power and bureaucracy quite as much as by nationalism. His story receives its fitting conclusion, therefore, when the Swiss authorities decide to make a record of the incident ('ein Protokoll aufnehmen'; K,96). In this way the author makes a last unspoken comment on the insensitive, impersonal workings of bureaucracy.

In the case of *Buchmendel*, which is concerned solely with Austrian officialdom, a more complex picture emerges, not least because the work records what for Zweig was an important and regrettable historical development. There is a passage in Joseph Roth's *Radetzkymarsch* where the later years of the Habsburg Empire are characterised with some humour as a period when, for all the strict rules, exceptions were encouraged:

> Die Zeit war damals strenge, wie man weiß. Aber sie erkannte Ausnahmen und liebte sie sogar. Es war einer jener wenigen aristokratischen Grundsätze, denen zufolge einfache Bürger Menschen zweiter Klasse waren, aber der und jener bürger-liche Offizier Leibadjutant des Kaisers wurde; die Juden auf höhere Auszeichnungen keinen Anspruch erheben konnten, aber einzelne Juden geadelt wurden und Freunde von Erzherzögen.[19]

This relaxed attitude to what is out of the ordinary is something which Zweig obviously cherished too and which he regarded as increasingly threatened after the outbreak of the First World War. Although he does not present an entirely clear or consistent picture and has in any case a somewhat idealised view of Habsburg tolerance, he seeks to imply through the fate of Mendel that public attitudes in general and the bureaucratic mind in particular became unnecessarily intolerant with the advent of war.

When the narrator first meets Mendel, he has already been living in Vienna for some thirty years, socially disadvantaged, but nevertheless accepted. Admittedly, he does not occupy a public position commensurate with his extraordinary knowledge, but on the reasons for this we are left in some uncertainty. At one point the narrator argues that Mendel could have been much more productive in the right place — a university library, for example — but has been debarred from such an office because he received no education beyond the Talmud school (K,105). The implication, readily seized on by one Marxist commentator as evidence of wide-spread social discrimination,[20] is that society's insistence on paper qualifications and its failure to accommodate the exception have prevented a solution beneficial to both parties. Within a few pages, however, elaborating on Mendel's indifference to money, the narrator asserts that the founder of the University of Princeton in fact sought to buy his services as adviser to the library, but was refused (K,108). It seems that Zweig has not made up his mind whether responsibility for the non-integration of such an exceptional figure is to be laid at the door of the authorities or the individual himself.

In dealing with subsequent developments, on the other hand, the author emphasises the role of officialdom much more un-equivocally. After the outbreak of war the book-pedlar comes to the notice of the authorities because of the apparent absurdity of his writing to people in foreign countries. Once the censorship of mail has drawn attention to him and the police have been alerted, his naive response to questioning so baffles the officials that they simply fall back on standard bureaucratic procedure. As the narrator ironically remarks:

> In solchen unschlüssigen Verlegenheiten entschließt man sich
> bei jedem Amt fast immer, zunächst ein Protokoll
> aufzunehmen. Ein Protokoll ist immer gut. Nützt es nicht, so
> schadet es nichts, und nur ein sinnloser Papierbogen mehr
> unter Millionen ist vollgeschrieben. (K,114-15)[21]

In the event the decision does considerable harm. It leads to the discovery of Mendel's illegal immigration over thirty years previously and, since the machinery of bureaucracy acknowledges no principle of limitation and permits no individual exceptions, to his incarceration. Though he himself has not changed, the different political climate has caused a decisive hardening of official attitudes. Even so, it is worth pointing out that what brings about his eventual release is more than a typically Austrian coin-cidence — which is the narrator's overt assessment (K,117). It is a further isolated instance of that Habsburg readiness to make room for exceptions which Roth described so affectionately and which has apparently not been entirely lost even in wartime. Observing that Mendel receives letters from notable clients, the camp commandant realises that he has in this prisoner 'etwas Besonderes' and allows him to reply and beg his clients to intervene on his behalf. However unjust to other prisoners it may seem, Zweig evidently approves of this use of privilege to bend the rules and treat his central character as a special case.

Occasionally the obvious dislike of bureaucracy spills over into an attack on bureaucrats, as when, in *Der Zwang*, Ferdinand's wife deploys the somewhat irrational argument that her husband need not obey an official summons, since it was not his country which called him but merely 'ein Schreiber', 'ein gelangweilter Bureauknecht' (VdG[2],231). In general, however, individual officials emerge as no more than instruments of an impersonal force, a force which may be there all the time, but which becomes especially objectionable in times of war. Outside the world of his *Novellen* too Zweig's criticisms of bureaucracy tend to coincide with his outrage at the absurdity and inhumanity of war. For him one eloquent symptom of the madness of the First World War is the fact that, because Albert Schweitzer is an Alsatian, bureaucracy prevents him from carrying out his humanitarian mission in a French colony and instead sends him back to imprisonment in Europe.[22] Later, after the outbreak of the Second World War, the same basic conviction leads him to write from England to Max-Herrmann-Neiße that he is unable to rejoice at the war against the National Socialists, not simply because of the loss of human life, but also because of the 'Zwangswirtschaft, Beamtenallmacht' governing life in England as well.[23] Irrespective of the cause to be fought, he still finds it difficult to accept the sacrifice of personal freedom.

In the period immediately after the First World War what seems to have impressed itself most on Zweig's consciousness, more even than the problems of nutrition and the political struggles of the First Austrian Republic, is the rapid inflation. Although he himself barely felt its effects,[24] *Die Welt von Gestern* provides a vivid and detailed picture of its many manifestations, first in Austria and then in Weimar Germany.[25] As was also the case with war, he presents it as a fact, without any attempt to explore its economic and political causes. In time inflation naturally enters the world of the *Novellen* too. It forms the background to the final downfall of Mendel, who is released from the concentration camp even before the end of hostilities, but soon becomes an unwelcome parasite, whose minimal savings are 'zerpulvert in der Papiermühle der Inflation' (K,120), and more particularly to the fate of the blind art-collector and his family in *Die unsichtbare Sammlung* (sub-titled 'Eine Episode aus der deutschen Inflation'), where, blissfully ignorant of the realities of ínflation, the old man hears of the large

193

sums of money which works of art are now fetching and loses himself in the doubly illusory satisfaction of what his collection is worth, while his wife and daughter know only too well 'wie das Geld einschmilzt' (K,81) and struggle to find the bare necessities by selling off first their jewelry and then his collection, item by item.

Zweig is disturbed by the fact of inflation and expresses this metaphorically in a series of verbs denoting some radical chemical, physical, or organic change. But he is no less disturbed by the way in which inflation corrupts the social and moral life of the nation, encouraging materialism and unscrupulous business practices. That is why he devotes so much space to the décor of the refurbished Café Gluck in *Buchmendel*, which has a veneer of imitation wood and is dominated by a shiny aluminium cash-register (K,97-8). These are symptomatic innovations of the age, in which the new owner has got rich quickly from black-market dealings and has been able to buy the café 'für achtzigtausend rasch zerblätterte Papierkronen' (K,120). Under the management of such a man, who has, as the narrator puts it, 'mit den neuen Möbeln und der blanken Aluminiumkasse auch das massive Gewissen der Verdienerzeit zugelegt' (K,120), the penniless Mendel has little chance of survival. The sympathetic cloakroom attendant, who has served under both owners, is quite convinced that the first would not have thrown Mendel out for stealing a few rolls, but would have granted him free food for the rest of his life (K,122). The unmistakable implication is that the pre-war tolerance towards the non-conformist has been overthrown by the new commercial just as much as by the new bureaucratic spirit. Nevertheless, it must be conceded that, in presenting only Frau Sporschil's version of events and thereby manipulating the reader's sympathies, the author has somewhat fudged the issue. The new owner may be materialistic and unfriendly, but had he been given a voice, he might well have pointed out that the Mendel who was welcomed by the previous owner was a different person, an oddity certainly, but one who attracted other customers and so helped to pay for his privileges (cf. K,109), whereas the present Mendel has perforce become a physical embarrassment and a source of financial loss. Here, as in his depiction of bureaucracy, Zweig has observed an unwelcome social change without taking full account of the pressures that have helped to bring it about.

In *Die unsichtbare Sammlung* the art-dealer who acts as primary narrator comments most explicitly on the commercial spirit that has come to the fore in the inflationary times:

> 'Sie wissen wahrscheinlich selbst, wie es im Kunsthandel jetzt zugeht, seit sich der Wert des Geldes wie Gas verflüchtigt: die neuen Reichen haben plötzlich ihr Herz entdeckt für gotische Madonnen und Inkunabeln und alte Stiche und Bilder.' (K,73)

Art has been reduced to the level of a 'Ware', a financial investment. The old man's daughter records, as one among many unhappy attempts to raise subsistence money from the sale of her father's works of art, the deception practised by auctioneers, who may have sold an item for millions, but have held on to the money for so long that, by the time it was handed over, it was worthless paper (K,81). To the narrator, therefore, the collector becomes the representative victim of a wider trend, one among many 'dieser niederträchtig ausgeplünderten, von der Inflation hundsföttisch betrogenen Menschen [. . .], denen kostbarster, jahrhundertealter Familienbesitz um ein Butterbrot weggegaunert war' (K,82). Martha Gschiel argues that Zweig's purpose here is to establish an opposition between the old man and an age in which art collecting has been robbed of its idealism and become materialistic.[26] That, however, is to accept the word of the art-dealer too uncritically. He, too, is an unreliable narrator. In the first place, as indicated earlier, he fails to appreciate the materialistic streak in the collector; and in the second place, he is insincere, commenting disparagingly and snobbishly on the crass commercialism of the *nouveaux riches*, then letting slip that he himself has been looking through the old account books, 'um einstige Kunden aufzustöbern, denen ich vielleicht ein paar Dubletten wieder abluchsen könnte' (K,74). Commercialism is evidently more widespread and closer to home than he acknowledges.

One final feature of post-war society which clearly disturbed Zweig, its tendency towards greater and greater uniformity, can be regarded as a cultural development, less directly attributable to economic and political causes. For although his important essay on the subject, 'Die Monotonisierung der Welt' (1925), mentions the homogenising effect of both the methods of mass production derived from America and the intellectual conformity demanded

in Soviet Russia, he is more concerned with the cultural standardisation imported from beyond the Atlantic and expressed in such
phenomena as modern dance, modern fashion, the cinema, and
radio, which lead to intellectual passivity and laziness and to loss
of individuality.[27]

The stories nowhere attempt a detailed analysis of these
phenomena, but two of them, *Die unsichtbare Sammlung* and
Buchmendel, conjure up something of the broader picture. Indeed
it is the general trend towards dull uniformity which is reckoned to
enhance the special value of the central characters. The old art-
collector is first picked out as one of those rare oddities who have
barely managed to survive into the present (i.e. post-war period)
(K,74). A similar sense of loss is also present in the narrator of
Buchmendel, who laments the speed with which post-war society
has managed to forget such an original, out-of-the-way character
as Mendel and registers his own regret in relation to the wider
social development: 'weil alles Einmalige von Tag zu Tag
kostbarer wird in unserer rettungslos einförmiger werdenden Welt'
(K,110). In defence of the newly-refurbished Café Gluck,
however, it has to be said that, although it has largely yielded to
the commercial spirit of the times, it has not altogether fallen
victim to the worst cultural trends. It has retained something of the
original character of a suburban Viennese coffee-house and so
lacks what are called 'die neumodischen Attrappen der
Deutschland nachgeahmten innerstädtischen Musikdielen' (K,97).
In general, however, falseness, duplication, and lack of originality
seem to have become the tokens of the new society.

Although Zweig's *Novellen* do provide some insight into the
times about which he was writing, the picture outlined above is a
composite, perhaps even a construct. He is not a social historian.
As Alfred Pfoser observes, what Friedrich Engels once remarked
of Balzac (that knowledge of his novels made it unnecessary to
read the books of statisticians, economists, and historians)
emphatically does not apply to the *Novellen* of Zweig,[28] who may
record social, economic, and political phenomena which have a
certain typicality, but who shows little inclination to examine the
forces which have brought them about. Instead, within a limited
social range, he directs his attention to the fates of human
individuals as they are affected by those more public manifestations. Moreover, in the final analysis, the shift of interest noted

196

earlier, from the social habits of the age to its political and economic conditions, may equally well be expressed in terms of a changed emphasis in the human ideals pursued: a move from the ideal of intensity and commitment, often presented psychologically as a recovery of the hitherto inhibited instinctive self, to the ideals of personal freedom and human brotherhood, which suffer most from unfavourable political and economic conditions. It is pointless to argue whether one change pre-dates the other; what is important is that, throughout, human beings, often at some point of crisis, take precedence over historical developments and remain at the centre of Zweig's interest. It was a symptomatic yet sound piece of artistic judgement that persuaded him to delete from the final version of *Leporella* an (in its own way) interesting and extended comment on the way in which, in pre-war Austria, the aristocracy maintained an attitude of relaxed but utterly non-committal intimacy towards their servants and the common people in general.[29] In his historical works and in *Die Welt von Gestern* the lack of historical analysis may be a cause of disquiet,[30] but in the *Novellen* one could scarcely wish it to be otherwise.

14

A Sense of Place

Of itself spatial setting seems to have held little interest for Zweig. In the collection of essays, *Begegnungen mit Menschen, Büchern, Städten*, the pieces concerned with various places occupy much the smallest space; and throughout it is evident that what captures the writer's imagination in any given location is its representative quality, its ability to communicate human values: the hotels of St Moritz, high up in the Swiss Alps, embodying the attempts of the carefree rich to remain aloof from the harsh realities of war; the Panama Canal declaring the power of the human spirit to overcome the world of nature; the land of Brazil demonstrating the possibility of racial harmony in an age of racially-inspired oppression in Europe.[1] In the *Novellen*, where the locations chosen are different from those just enumerated, setting still possesses a similar, representative function. What, then, are the criteria which determine that choice?

It is not sufficient to say that the fictional works reflect Zweig's own life and travels: the Vienna of his upbringing; the holiday locations typical of his social class (the Semmering, the Tyrol, the Italian Lakes, the French Riviera);[2] his journeys to the Far East; the retreat to neutral Switzerland near the end of the First World War; the sea-journey to South America in the early years of the Second World War. For the remarkable and significant fact is that not a single work is set in Salzburg, the city which became Zweig's permanent home in 1919 and was to remain so until his final decision to continue in exile in the late nineteen-thirties. After the unsettling years of war and its aftermath his home on the Kapuzinerberg became a haven of stability and security,[3] where he

198

was able to escape the harsher socio-political realities of the capital Vienna, devote himself to his literary work, enjoy the fruits of success,[4] and share a settled domestic life with his wife, Friderike. At the same time this much-needed stability was punctuated by countless journeys, often lecture-tours, which he usually undertook without his wife, who was left at home to manage his affairs. The function of the journeys emerges quite clearly from a letter he wrote to the dutiful Friderike in October 1919: 'Wenn ich auf einer Reise bin, fällt alle Bindung plötzlich ab, ich fühle mich ganz unbeschwerlich, zusammenhanglos und frei'.[5] Since Salzburg was something of a retreat from the contemporary world and the focus of that side of Zweig's nature which sought marital stability, it was never likely to be chosen either for stories which reflected the harsh socio-economic and political realities of the time (*Buchmendel, Die unsichtbare Sammlung, Schachnovelle*) or for those accounts of people who reject or are thrust out of a life of regularity, domesticity, and conventionality (*Der Amokläufer, Phantastische Nacht, Brief einer Unbekannten, Die Mondscheingasse, Vierundzwanzig Stunden aus dem Leben einer Frau*). More suitable for the latter are settings in which the characters are temporarily or permanently removed from the sphere of normal routine, convention, or domestic obligation; and that naturally means foreign locations, holiday resorts, or places of relaxation and amusement nearer home.[6]

As to the Vienna in which Zweig grew up and which his memoirs depict as part of 'das Zeitalter der Sicherheit' which was to vanish with the First World War,[7] it is crucial to note that it was, for him, a place of only superficial security, a security already undermined by new social forces and by subconscious sexual forces which were the more dangerous for being hushed up and treated hypocritically.[8] A corollary of this security was also its insistence on state authority to the detriment of personal freedom.[9] For Vienna was not always as tolerant as the late essay 'Das Wien von Gestern' made out.[10] In short, the city of Zweig's birth represented something of a threatened and negative security, which made it an entirely suitable background for stories dealing with the rejection of a deadening social environment (*Phantastische Nacht, Brief einer Unbekannten*), with the problem of adolescents on the threshold of a world of adult sexuality which they do not understand and which fails to understand them (*Die Gouvernante,*

Brennendes Geheimnis),[11] with threats to the hypocritical veneer of civilisation (*Leporella*), or with the unfeeling exercise of bureaucratic authority (*Buchmendel*).

On the basis of his awareness of the representative function of setting it is Zweig's frequent practice to articulate the developments of his narrative in terms of changed or contrasting locations. This may be a matter of the difference between the provinces and the metropolis, between native land and foreign parts, or between domestic interiors and public places, although occasionally the categories will overlap to some degree. The functions which these differences serve may, broadly, be divided into two groups: those which help to define a dislocation or disorientation and those which express the presence or absence of normal social and moral restraints.

The dull-witted central character of *Leporella*, having been lured by the prospect of earning more money into moving from her remote Tyrolean village to the Austrian capital, is immediately lost amid the technology and speed around her and so spends most of her time indoors. Yet what proves ultimately more decisive is her disorientation in the complicated *mores* of her new surroundings. A slap on the buttocks by the baron, which in the peasant language of her home signifies 'Werbung um das Weibsbild' (K,52), but here denotes no more than a casual jest, is the source of a first misunderstanding which finally leads to the murder of the baroness, her extreme act of misjudged loyalty. The unexpected horror and rejection which this calls forth from her master lead her to take her own life, in isolation and complete mental disorientation. Had she remained in her native soil, she would have continued to be the same dull, lifeless Crescentia Anna Aloisia Finkenhuber; transplanted to Vienna, she is doomed to become the uncomprehending and uncomprehended Leporella.

A comparable sense of disorientation can be observed in *Episode am Genfer See* and *Buchmendel*, except that the presence of war gives their respective settings (Switzerland and Vienna) an added political dimension, turning the central characters into unwitting 'foreigners', homeless victims. In the latter case, as we have already noted, it is the temporal and not, strictly speaking, the geographical setting which undergoes a change. Yet the disorienting effect may sometimes be the same as when a genuine change of location is involved. Although Mendel remains static, the place he occupies unquestionably becomes different. A similar experience, moreover, forms the starting-point of *Der Zwang*, the work which provides the clearest example of Zweig's use of setting to express disorientation in a political context. Having left his native Germany because of the war and gone into exile in Switzerland, Ferdinand is brought to a painful realisation of the significance of frontiers. Because of the changed circumstances which war has brought about 'home' and 'abroad' have lost their normal meaning. At 'home' he has found the nationalistic atmosphere oppressive and restrictive; now in exile he feels himself once more fully human: 'Vaterland, das hieß ihm jetzt nur Gefängnis und Zwang. Fremde, sie war ihm Weltheimat, Europa die Menschheit' (VdG², 227). Switzerland affords the opportunity for human brotherhood across all national boundaries. And it is significant that, when nevertheless the shaky moral foundations of Ferdinand's ideal lay him open to the influence of the military authorities even here, the place where his own free will is seen to be at its feeblest is the German consulate in Zurich, that little piece of alien homeland which has a foothold in the land of exile. It is significant too that, having capitulated to the extent of boarding the train back to Germany in compliance with his call-up papers, he is finally brought to his senses by the sight of the frontier, whose physical presence brings home to him the difference it marks between peace and war, free will and compulsion. In general, however, it is characteristic of *Der Zwang* not only that home becomes alien and foreign territory a sort of home, but that all its emphasis on sharply distinguished settings in the end forms part of an attempt to plead for the abolition of all geographical distinctions.

In the majority of cases involving a shift to a new location Zweig is interested not so much in mental disorientation as in the relaxation of those civilising restraints and conventions which obtain at home, but are under threat in a different setting. The change may bring suffering, but it may also bring revitalisation and release. The contrast seems to be most dramatic where it involves the greatest geographical distance, as is the case in *Der Amokläufer* and *Die Mondscheingasse*, the former of which may serve here as our example. The setting for this depiction of the doctor's desperate struggle to preserve the guilty secret of the woman to whom he has become enthralled, of his abandonment of

201

his official post, of his rejection of medical etiquette and social convention — in short, of his running amuck — is the continent of India, not the popular, romantic India of the tourist, but that of a lonely district station, where any ideals of civilising or understanding are forgotten, where, as he puts it, one becomes soft, is cut off from one's European self, goes mad, bestial (A,25-7). It is precisely because of its distance from all civilised European influence that the woman comes to him demanding an abortion (A,38). And when, having come so much under her thrall that he pursues her everywhere, the doctor finally catches up with her, it is in one of the larger towns, along a back-street in Chinatown, among the opium-dens and brothels, where she has been given the abortion that finally kills her (A,65). Clearly, Zweig's presentation of setting goes far beyond the requirements of exotic back-cloth, as some have suggested.[12] Instead he has created his own version of Conrad's 'Heart of Darkness', Indian rather than African, but equally removed from the rational, social and moral restraints of European civilisation.

For the central character of *Der Amokläufer*, as for the couple at the heart of *Die Mondscheingasse*, the foreign setting is inextricably bound up with an all-consuming, uncivilised, passionate struggle; only for the non-committal narrators of both works, who are able to return to their native country, does it denote a source of relaxation and diversion. Yet in other works it is precisely these latter elements in the foreign locations which conduce to the abandonment of social norms and prove fateful for the central characters. Diversion can be the first step along the path to more profound and disturbing experiences.

This can be observed in a minor way in the blossoming of the young daughter of the businessman Salomonssohn in *Untergang eines Herzens*, which takes place on an Italian holiday, and more interestingly in the Parisian experiences of the narrator of *Unvermutete Bekanntschaft mit einem Handwerk*. The clearest expression, however, is to be found in the central character of *Vierundzwanzig Stunden aus dem Leben einer Frau*. Although she is first deprived of some of her social commitments when her husband dies and her sons reach the age of majority, it is not until Mrs C. goes alone on her travels that she becomes vulnerable. The French Riviera, that scene of adventure which Somerset Maugham was also fond of using for similar purposes, provides the setting for her dramatic involvement with the young Polish gambler, which reaches the point where she abandons all discretion and finds herself in bed with him in a cheap hotel. The development of the young Pole too is marked by comparable geographical changes. Having been brought up in an outlying region of the Habsburg Empire, he is preparing to assume his social obligations by training for the diplomatic service when he is taken to that well-known place of amusement, the Prater in Vienna. Once addicted to gambling, he frequents only coffee-houses and clubs and, after stealing money from an aunt, sets off impulsively for Monte Carlo, hoping to win the money he dreams of at roulette (VdG,71-2). When Mrs C. meets him there, he has, he declares, sold both clothes and possessions and has 'keine Wohnung' (VdG,53,72). In other words, he has cut off all his ties with the norms and conventions of the civilised society represented by home. Furthermore, there can be little doubt that, had Mrs C. listened to his story in her normal social surroundings rather than in this foreign resort, it would have found her much less sympathetic. For she is a woman who 'in ihrer Gesellschaft strengste, konventionelle Würdigkeit erforderte' (VdG,72).

Although an adventure involving the suspension of bourgeois norms is often associated with foreign travel, this need not always be the case. Even a move from the provinces to the metropolis can bring this about, as it does initially for the young Roland of *Verwirrung der Gefühle,* when he leaves the 'norddeutsche Kleinstadt' of his youth (VdG,157) and goes as a student to Berlin, the expanding capital of the still young Empire, a place which 'ganz überrascht von seinem eigenen Wachstum, strotzend von einer allzu plötzlich aufgeschossenen Männlichkeit aus allen Steinen und Straßen Elektrizität versprühte' (VdG,160). At the same time we have also had occasion to observe how this sort of adventure is sometimes related to more specific places of public amusement such as the Prater in Vienna or the casino at Monte Carlo. The visit to such a place can of itself entail a like adventure even when the events remain within the confines of one city.

This is particularly so in *Phantastische Nacht*, where the young baron finds inner renewal and release from the deadening norms of his high society as the result of a visit to the Prater. To the extent that he initially conforms to the patterns of an effete society, Vienna still appears to him as 'die weiche und wollüstige

Stadt', ideally suited to 'das Spazierengehen, das nichtstuerische Betrachten, das Elegantsein' (A,128). What is significant about his visit to the Prater is that the excitement of the races breaks down social barriers and neutralises the niceties of social etiquette that would elsewhere restrain behaviour. It helps, therefore, to rouse him from his aesthetic indifference to a new sense of passionate humanity, which determines his subsequent movements. He dismisses the idea of a return to 'die gewohnte Welt', to his home, or his customary fashionable eating-place, Sachers (A,169-70). Instead he moves still farther away from his social origins to the popular 'Wurstelprater', seeking a sense of human brotherhood with the mass of ordinary folk, which he finds, Zweig would have us believe, in the thrill of a dangerous encounter with prostitutes, pimps, and thieves in the dark undergrowth of these surroundings.

It will be apparent from the foregoing remarks that Zweig shows a preference for locations which are foreign, public, or recreational rather than for domestic settings. In some small measure this can be attributed to his favourite manner of narration. Public settings such as cafés, ocean-going liners, or foreign hotels are ideally suited to that predilection for narrative frames and inset narratives in the first person, since it is there that his narrators can most plausibly encounter interesting strangers and the strangers in turn feel able to reveal their gripping and often 'immoral' experiences. The weightier explanation, however, lies in the substance of what is related. For Zweig commonly places his emphasis on characters who find fulfilment or meet their destiny only when they are at a physical distance from the bourgeois norms and conventions which apply at home.[13] And although the non-committal narrators such as those of *Der Amokläufer* and *Die Mondscheingasse* may return home, for most of the central characters there can be no going back; they either die or are left to their fate in alien surroundings.

What, however, are we to make of those exceptions to this pattern, where the central characters do in the end, physically, return to their home? Do they imply the re-establishment of the old order, the abandonment of intense experience in favour of bourgeois norms or, where disorientation is involved, the recovery of a sense of belonging? We shall need to be especially careful in assessing the implications of these changes of location; and we shall discover a different answer in each case. Nevertheless, it may be noted in advance that the inference of a full return to the old world may confidently be drawn in only one such work.

Despite earlier repeated declarations that there could be no return to his usual world the hero of *Phantastische Nacht* does finally go back to his Viennese flat. Yet he assures his readers that this is only a superficial, physical return, insisting that things have changed inwardly, that he has left behind him for good the world of 'der korrekte, gefühllose, weltabgelöste Gentleman' (A,203).

With Mrs C. in *Vierundzwanzig Stunden aus dem Leben einer Frau* the change is less clear-cut, less final, but — because we are allowed to meet her years after her volcanic experience and because her account of the consequences is less insistent than the baron's — ultimately carries more conviction. After her humiliating betrayal by the young Pole she leaves as quickly as possible: 'Fort von dieser Stadt, von mir selbst, nach Hause, zu meinen Menschen, zu meinem früheren, zu meinem eigenen Leben' (VdG,99). Once at home, she takes a bath to wash away the old, soiled, passionate life (VdG,100). One could hardly wish for a clearer expression of the representative value of locations than this. Yet matters do not rest there. Her departure is, after all, as impulsive as her first decision to follow the young man. Furthermore, the narrative frame, which introduces her twenty years after these events, finds her still returning to the Riviera and joining in the heated debate about the sudden elopement of Mme Henriette not as the upholder of conventional morals, but as a tactful mediator between those who would condemn outright and a first-person narrator who defends the action too passionately. Her return home, then, is by no means final; she has been able to integrate her Riviera experience into her social and moral outlook, which has become the wiser, the maturer for it.

In neither *Phantastische Nacht* nor *Vierundzwanzig Stunden aus dem Leben einer Frau* can the central character's return to home surroundings be equated with a full reversion to the old bourgeois order. In *Angst*, however, set entirely in a modern city one assumes to be Vienna, it is precisely this rare occurrence that is recorded. And it is interesting to note that it is accompanied by a more concrete realisation of the domestic interior and by a more emphatic and explicit awareness in the mind of the heroine of the representative value of the various locations used. In depicting the conflict between Frau Irene's desire for erotic adventure and her

205

need for security within the framework of bourgeois respectability, Zweig is exploring that area of moral confusion more familiar to us from Schnitzler; and it is probably no accident that the work to which it seems to owe most, *Die Toten schweigen*,[14] should exploit the representative value of setting in a similar way. At the beginning of *Angst* Irene is at her lover's flat but, as usual, already disturbed by the fearful prospect of having to journey home through public streets: 'nur fort wollte dann immer schon alles in ihr, aus seiner Wohnung, seinem Haus, aus dem Abenteuer in ihre ruhige bürgerliche Welt zurück' (K,125). Her terror at the thought of being discovered makes the simple step 'aus fremdem Haustor auf die Straße' momentous and makes walking from 'Gasse zu Gasse' dependent on superhuman effort (K,126-8). It also renders her vulnerable to the approaches of the supposed blackmailer. An appearance of calm returns to her, therefore, only once she is back in familiar domestic surroundings, where her eyes rest on 'Eigenes [. . .], Eigentum und Geborgenheit'. To recover her composure and banish the memory of that fear which comes to her on the exposed streets it is as though she must impress the details of her home and its furnishings on her senses (K,129).

If the three important locations may be said, therefore, to embody three aspects of Irene's life (bourgeois security, personal adventure, the threat of public exposure), the progress of the story brings with it a self-imposed, protective house-arrest and then the increasing penetration of even this world by the threat from outside, which culminates in the arrival of the blackmailer in person. Suicide seems to be the only solution once her home has lost its sense of security, once her lover's flat has forfeited its adventurous appeal, and once the idea of an escape into the world of nature is recognised as only a temporary answer. It is at this point, when she is about to buy a fatal dose of drugs at the chemist's, that her knowing husband intervenes. Significantly, however, his confession of the part he has played in her experiences, the confession which paves the way for reconciliation and the restoration of the bourgeois order, comes only once the couple have returned home.

In *Untergang eines Herzens* the return home of the Jewish businessman has a rather different function. Even the holiday resort on the Italian lakes, where his daughter blossoms into full sexuality, is an alien environment, not simply because his wife and daughter converse with their male companions in a foreign language, but more because the puritanical work-ethic of his upbringing renders him completely out of place in a location devoted to the pursuit of pleasure (cf. VdG,117). When he returns to his South German home, therefore, he is doing no more than set a physical distance between himself and an already hostile environment. On the other hand, the return no longer represents the recovery of a harmony between external setting and moral purpose. Instead it completes a more radical process which takes us beyond our immediate concern and will have to be examined in a later chapter.

Except in *Angst* and in the first three stories of *Erstes Erlebnis*, which are concerned not with adults who abandon bourgeois norms and conventions, but with the problems of adolescents on the verge of a world they do not understand and which confronts them in the behaviour of parents or close relatives, Zweig places relatively little emphasis on the representative value of domestic locations. At times indeed, even when the setting is literally domestic, it is deprived of much of its significance as the locus of traditional and inherited values. We have already noted something of this in *Leporella*, where the central character enters 'domestic' service, but in a strange household, whose code of behaviour she never understands. Much the same might be said of *Verwirrung der Gefühle*, where the decisive, un-bourgeois experiences of the young hero take place at the home of his professor, yet away from the 'norddeutsche Kleinstadt' of his origins. But perhaps the clearest expression of this sort of pattern is *Brief einer Unbekannten*. Although much of the story takes place indoors, at times almost claustrophobically within the 'Vorstadthaus' in which the heroine is brought up, it is crucial to note that her most vital experiences come when she is quite literally looking beyond the confines of her mother's apartment, spying from the anteroom, or standing outside on the street looking up at the apartment of her indifferent lover. Zweig makes plain that she is something of a lone outsider in the 'kleinbürgerliche Dürftigkeit' of her own home (A,214) and is therefore particularly susceptible to the appeal of the elegant young writer and his 'Sphäre von Reichtum, Sonderbarkeit und Geheimnis' (A,217). When she becomes his lover, her surrender takes place in the young man's rooms, which she regards as a magical world, an Aladdin's cave opposed to the dull reality of her everyday surroundings (A,242). The setting may be indoors, but it certainly does not represent home or the values of home, which are thoroughly repudiated by the heroine in her profligate, all-consuming devotion.

In discussing the ways in which Zweig articulates his narratives by exploiting the different values that attach to particular locations I have deliberately avoided the problematic word 'symbolic', in order to distinguish this function from another which could equally well be subsumed under the heading 'symbolic'. This second function may be termed 'metaphorical'. Here we are not concerned with the significance which a setting may possess by virtue of the values it represents, values which are sometimes openly enunciated by the characters, sometimes recognised by the reader on the basis of general experience. We are concerned rather with values or ideas that attach to certain settings because the specific nature of their physical detail lends itself to a metaphorical interpretation which is superimposed on the literal reading. It is characteristic of most of them that they involve human beings occupying a certain position in relation to their surroundings and that there is something temporary though typical about the scene. Occasionally the character in question may sense the metaphorical import; more often this is left to the perception of the reader.

The first three stories of *Erstes Erlebnis*, which deal with the problems of adolescents on the threshold of an adult world whose standards and practices they faintly divine but do not comprehend, manage, appropriately, to capture the essence of this situation in a memorable image. In *Geschichte in der Dämmerung* the room which Bob occupies at his married sister's castle, with its atmosphere almost constantly 'schwül' (EE,15), comes to represent something of the confining world of overheated and restrained sexuality from which he seeks release in the garden. It is in the garden that he has that brief, dreamlike encounter with a girl whose identity remains as yet uncertain. In the ensuing emotional confusion Zweig describes him standing outside in the dark gazing up at a girl he thinks is the object of his love in a lighted room, seeing only puzzling signs and capable only of imagining (wrongly) her thoughts and actions. It is as though she inhabited a world of adult clarity and certainty from which he is excluded (EE,39).[15] In *Die Gouvernante* the two sisters are repeatedly depicted standing outside the door of a room in which their parents discuss the sexual misdemeanour of their governess, trying to understand what is being enacted just out of earshot and just beyond their emotional comprehension (EE,66,71,81). When Zweig coins a strange compound noun to summarise their situation ('dieses An-den-Türen-Kleben'), there can be no mistaking its metaphorical function (EE,74). In *Brennendes Geheimnis*, where the surroundings of the Semmering in general come to represent for the young hero the childhood he is soon to leave behind (EE,176), his hotel room becomes a more particular embodiment of the confining world of childhood, to which he is even banished on one occasion after an outburst of jealousy. In one especially memorable scene, however, he is pictured at night, wedged between the inner and outer doors of his room, listening for the sounds of his mother and her lover — a telling expression of his ambiguous position between the worlds of childhood and adulthood (EE,159).

A similar picture recurs several times in the later *Brief einer Unbekannten*, although the import here is somewhat different. The heroine repeatedly describes herself waiting for long periods of time at the door of her apartment, lying on the floor, or outside the house of her adored young writer, in search of a glimpse of him (A,230,234,236). Again the scene is a metaphor of exclusion, but one which, in recalling the position of a loyal dog awaiting its master or of a slave-girl keeping vigil for her sultan,[16] also provides a suitable image of her servile devotion and his haughty indifference. At times the formulation of her confessional letter suggests that she herself is aware of the metaphorical relevance of her position. On one occasion she comments: 'Am nächsten Abend stand ich schon wieder vor Deinem Hause wartend, wie ich mein ganzes Schicksal lang vor Deinem verschlossenen Leben gestanden bin' (A,236). And later, apologising even for the unsolicited intrusion of her letter, she writes: 'Ich will Dir nicht meinen Jammer hinwerfen in Dein heiteres Haus [. . .] Nur dies eine Mal mußte ich sprechen zu Dir — dann gehe ich wieder stumm in mein Dunkel zurück' (A,265). Appropriately, therefore, when we briefly return to the narrative frame at the end of the story, the metaphor which Zweig uses to describe the suave writer's chill and uncomfortable awareness of a desperate world which has previously never impinged on his consciousness is spatially defined in terms which recall those earlier vigils of the unknown young woman: 'Ihm war, als sei plötzlich eine Tür unsichtbar aufgesprungen, und kalte Zugluft ströme aus anderer Welt in seinen ruhenden Raum' (A,266). The young woman, who in her life was repeatedly left waiting outside, penetrates his sanctum posthumously through her letter.

In *Die unsichtbare Sammlung* it is a scene at the window which makes its mark as a metaphor of the admittedly illusory bliss which lifts the blind collector above the workaday world, though in this instance the formulation of the narrator makes plain that the metaphorical dimension is quite apparent to him too. The last glimpse he has of the old man is of a grey head bending out of a second-floor window, 'hoch schwebend über all den mürrischen, gehetzten, geschäftigen Menschen der Straße, sanft aufgehoben aus unserer wirklichen widerlichen Welt von der weißen Wolke eines gütigen Wahns' (K,88).

Although Zweig's view of human sexuality as a dark, irrational force operating below the surface of civilised life, which seeks to banish it from view but is constantly threatened by it, is most frequently expressed in his choice of verbal imagery, descriptions of physical setting may occasionally serve the same purpose. Near the end of *Brennendes Geheimnis* young Edgar, running away from his mother and her liaison, back to his grandmother at Baden, enters the 'Kurpark' at night. Its dark, restless, and mysterious wooded setting, which is reminiscent of the woods that provided the scene for his mother's amours and is even now peopled by courting couples, is an apt visual analogue of the disturbing labyrinth of adult sexuality which he still finds confusing and from which he consequently returns to the security and well-lit rooms of those he knows (EE,178-81).

Similarly, in *Die Mondscheingasse* the narrator's encounter with the expatriate German couple and their desperate struggle of love and hatred takes place in a port we assume to be Marseilles, that gateway to the exotic and uncivilised world.[17] More precisely, it occurs away from the spacious, well-lit boulevards lined with imposing villas, behind the shutters of an underground tavern down one of the many dark side-alleys in the 'Matrosenviertel' (A,271,273-4). The physical details of the location are an exact counterpart to the obscure, concealed, often unrecognised working of the instincts behind the facade of civilised society. And they make it a fitting setting for the passionate struggle of the man and his wife because, as the narrator somewhat colourfully puts it, such places

> so frech und aufdringlich sagen, was die hellen Häuser mit blanken Scheiben und vornehmen Menschen in hundert Masken verbergen. [. . .] Letzte phantastische Reste einer sinnlich ungeregelten Welt, wo die Triebe noch brutal und ungezügelt sich entladen, ein finsterer Wald von Leidenschaften und Dickicht und voll triebhaften Getiers sind diese unbürgerlichen Straßen. (A,273-4)

In *Der Zwang* the hero's rather defeatist attempt to maintain his pacifism against what he believes to be the ineluctable might of the military authorities passes through various stages: a loss of contact with reality (the result of his own moral abdication); self-alienation; and a sense that the world has forfeited its cohesion and order. Zweig seeks to bring these conditions to our attention through the changing physical details of the hero's surroundings, the metaphorical relevance of which the latter himself sometimes perceives. At one point, for example, Ferdinand is pictured sitting alone at night, with a lamp lighting only a small area in the middle of the room, while all around lies the darkness of the night (VdG²,251). The solitary lamp in the house and its physical distance from the rest of the world correspond neatly to the hero's spiritual isolation from both those around him and the cosmic order. The following day finds him surrendering to the compulsion of state machinery and boarding a train that will take him back to Germany and military service:

> Draußen flog [. . .] alles vorbei, was er besaß, das kleine Haus am Hügel mit seinen Bildern und Tisch und Stuhl und Bett, mit Frau und vieler Tage Glück. Und die Landschaft stob geschleudert weg, in deren Weite er sich oft strahlenden Blicks geworfen, seine Freiheit und sein ganzes Leben. (VdG²,257)

The fragmentation, even atomisation of the physical landscape, which has its natural explanation in the rapid movement of the train, also expresses the destruction of Ferdinand's spiritual links with his wife, his work, and the natural order, which his moral capitulation is bringing about. After the sight of the frontier and the wounded French soldiers has brought him to his senses, and he has gone back to his wife, she takes him to look at the night sky: 'Draußen stand, unberührt von der selbstgeschaffenen Qual einer verwirrten Menschheit, die ewige Welt und glänzte für ihn, unendliche Sterne unter unendlichem Himmel' (VdG²,262). Behind the literary cliché there can be no mistaking the metaphorical intent of the scene: after the earlier fragmentation the infinity of space (sky) and number (stars) marks the intended recovery of values that transcend man-made divisions, 'unendliche Liebe', 'die ewige Freiheit der Dinge' (VdG²,262). Here more than in any other work except *Die Frau und die Landschaft*, to which we must return in the next chapter, Zweig exploits the ability of setting to operate simultaneously on two levels: both as a physical environment in which the characters may act out their conflicts and as a translation into visible terms of their spiritual condition, a concrete manifestation of the 'landscape of the soul'.

Although Zweig's habit is to subordinate spatial setting to the human interest of his stories, it is clear that his choice of setting is not a matter of indifference or arbitrary whim. Above all it is his psychological interest and his quest for human values which govern his choice of setting. In exploiting the representative quality of certain locations he is doing no more than clarify the human issues, expressing in physical terms either the disorientation of those victims on whom he bestows his compassion or the degree of adherence to and abandonment of civilised convention in lives of passionate intensity, which for him represent something of true humanity. Even momentary or more particularised scenes can serve to reinforce the central issues by providing memorable visual images which, on the physical and metaphorical level, encapsulate characteristic human situations.

15

Weather, Climate, Atmosphere

Weather, climate, and atmosphere, which have some part to play in several of Zweig's *Novellen*, constitute an aspect of setting that belongs fully neither to time nor to place. To the extent that weather is notoriously changeable it is a function of time; and it is not for nothing that the French speak of 'le temps'. To the extent that climate denotes the prevailing atmospheric conditions of a particular region, however, it is inseparable from place. Nevertheless, more important than the participation in both time and place is the fact that, unlike most of the spatial and temporal settings considered so far, which are manifestations of man's social, economic, political, and cultural history, weather, climate, and atmosphere are natural phenomena, given conditions of life over which, for the present at least, man has no control.

Zweig appears not to have been a great lover of nature and certainly shows little inclination to indulge in extended descriptions of nature for its own sake. When he introduces weather, climate, and atmosphere into his stories, they usually serve a particular function. On the one hand, they may be used to reflect a human situation by virtue of some perceived parallel between the two realms. In such cases any suggestion of the pathetic fallacy is rarely intended to be taken seriously and — with the notable exception of *Die Frau und die Landschaft* — no very close sympathetic bond is implied between man and his natural environment. The use is simply a metaphorical reinforcement along the lines of the metaphorical function of spatial setting considered at the end of the previous chapter. Alternatively, weather, climate, and atmosphere may assume a more active role

213

and determine the behaviour of the characters in an important way. In this role they are not so much elements of a narrative strategy as formative conditions of the human lives presented.

Although there are traces of the reflective function in two of the stories from *Erstes Erlebnis*, the author's handling of the strategy as yet lacks conviction and so leaves the reader in some uncertainty. In *Geschichte in der Dämmerung* the milky whiteness of the moon and the strange twilight that persists into the summer night of the Scottish setting seem intended to complement the uncertain sexual longings of the young hero. Yet the relative brightness of the garden scene is also seen in contrast to the over-heated stuffiness of Bob's room at the castle, from which he has escaped into the garden, while the 'Schwüle' of his room finds its echo in the 'Schwüle' of the lips which kiss him — in the moonlit garden (EE,15,23). It may be true to say that the whole story is, in any case, introduced with conscious ambiguity, but that seems a feeble defence of the present confusion. Nor does it explain the lack of consistency in *Brennendes Geheimnis*, which makes no pretence to ambiguity in its narration. The restlessness of the spring weather here, where the winds send white clouds scudding across the sky and cause the trees to tremble, is clearly established from the beginning as a parallel to the inner restlessness of the three central characters. Zweig even permits himself an undisguised use of the pathetic fallacy when he speaks of the 'gärende Ungeduld' of the natural world (EE,88). Similarly, at the end of the story, the clouds that are blown across the moon, disturbing its clarity and breaking up its smooth surface, are unmistakably designed to reflect the young hero's inability to penetrate reality and perceive the whole truth, especially that of adult sexuality (EE,151,154). If that were all, a meaningful if unoriginal pattern of correspondence would have been established. But the pattern is not sustained. In between are passages in which the fresh radiance of the sunny weather bears no relation to the continued restlessness of the young hero and makes no mark on his consciousness (EE,128,163). Furthermore a chapter-heading 'Gewitter' refers solely to his inner turmoil, which is not mirrored in any atmospheric turbulence. In consequence the reader may well begin to question the significance he has elsewhere ascribed to the weather. An interpretative guide has thereby forfeited its reliability.

214

Even as late as *Phantastische Nacht* an uncertainty of purpose is apparent. For while the promise of late spring, bringing fresh green to the trees as they rise out of the lifeless asphalt of the Austrian capital, seems to point prophetically to the subsequent rejuvenation of the baron, the gentle stirring of the warm breeze as it catches the falling blossoms is felt by the hero himself, on the very next page, to correspond to his present mood of indolence ('es entsprach besser meinem lässigen Gefühl'), part of that very indifference from which he is to be roused to new life (cf. A,135-6).

In making such judgements on the lack of consistency in Zweig's purpose one must of course take care not to overlook the possibility of an intended contradiction, which may achieve an end no less meaningful than a correspondence. In *Verwirrung der Gefühle*, for example, which takes place largely indoors and uses atmosphere only sparingly, both correspondence and contradiction are exploited purposefully at the climax of the work. It is a peaceful summer's evening and the windows of the professor's flat stand open:

> und in ihrem verdunkelten Rahmen trat allmählich dämmeriger Himmel mit weißen Wolken langsam herein: ein Lindes und Klares ging von ihrem majestätisch hinschwebenden Widerleuchten wesenhaft weiter, bis tief hinab mußte mans fühlen. Wir hatten lässiger, friedfertiger, geschäftiger geplaudert, die Frau und ich, als sonst. Mein Lehrer schwieg über unser Gespräch hinweg; aber sein Schweigen stand gleichsam mit stillgefalteten Flügeln über unserem Gespräch. (VdG,222)

At this point the calm atmosphere of the summer evening seems to reflect, almost indeed to confirm, the peace of the characters. Nevertheless, there follows the scene in which the professor makes his first more overt homosexual advances, which are rejected by a confused Roland. After the young hero has returned to his room, he is full of inner restlessness, both about his mentor's advances and about the conflict between husband and wife. Yet when he opens his window, this is the picture that presents itself to his view:

> Draußen lag friedlich unter sommerlichem Gewölk die Stadt; noch leuchteten Fenster vom Scheine der Lampe, aber die dort saßen, einte friedliches Gespräch, wärmte ein Buch oder

215

häusliche Musik. Und wo hinter weißen Fensterrahmen schon Dunkel stand, gewiß, dort atmete beruhigter Schlaf. Über allen diesen ruhenden Dächern schwebte wie der Mond in silbrigem Dunste ein mildes Ruhn, eine entlocktere, sanft niedergeschwebte Stille, und die elf Schläge der Turmuhr fielen ihnen allen ohne Wucht in das zufällig lauschende oder träumende Ohr. Nur ich hier im Haus spürte noch Wachsein, böse Umlagerung fremder Gedanken. (VdG,232)

Undoubtedly a change of weather — a sudden storm perhaps — would have corresponded more closely to the hero's present state of mind, but that does not mean that Zweig has forgotten his original aim. It is quite clear that the calm of the natural world accords with the waking or sleeping peace of the population at large, a peace from which Roland feels uniquely excluded. The atmosphere outside serves to highlight his restlessness by contrast, perhaps even to mock his inner turmoil. For the reader may now recall that the whole episode was introduced with the words: 'Wie schön begann jener schicksalshafte Abend, wie verräterisch schön!' (VdG,221).

A more consistent correspondence between the weather and the state of mind of the characters is presented in *Vierundzwanzig Stunden aus dem Leben einer Frau*. That it is consciously intended by the author is confirmed not only by the explicit comments of Mrs C., but also by the widespread use of meteorological imagery and, more especially, by an occasional metaphorical inter-penetration between the human and natural spheres.

During the evening of her fateful encounter with the young Polish gambler the heavy storm-clouds have already been gathering, blown in across the Mediterranean Sea, and are now contributing to an oppressive atmosphere, which is ultimately released in a violent cloudburst. Although this has an immediate practical effect, in that it precipitates her involuntary decision to spring to the aid of the young Pole, its deeper purpose is to mirror the tumultuous passion which has seized him and will shortly take hold of his would-be protectress. In particular the way in which he sits outside, motionless, allowing himself to be drenched by what Zweig refers to as the 'Element', while ordinary men and women flee indoors, is at once a consequence of his surrender to passionate despair and a metaphorical enactment of it (VdG,50-2).

After the tumult of the night that follows the day dawns bright and calm. Interestingly, however, the unruffled radiance of the Riviera landscape or seascape is conjured up first in the vocabulary which is used to describe the features of the young Pole as he lies sleeping, the features which dispel the initial horror of Mrs C. at the compromising position in which she finds herself: 'dieser da hatte ein anderes, ein ganz kindliches, ganz knabenhaftes Gesicht, das geradezu *strahlte* von Reinheit und Heiterkeit. [. . .] und linden Wellenspiels ging ruhig der Atem von der Brust über den ruhenden Körper hin' (VdG,64-5. The emphasis is Zweig's). Shortly afterwards she notes that he has 'den Strahl dankbarer und gleichzeitig ehrerbietiger Freude in den Augen' (VdG,69).

To complement this suggestive depiction of human features Mrs C.'s account of the natural world, which is now openly linked with her own high spirits, begins to introduce explicitly anthropomorphic vocabulary:

> Und gleichsam spiegelhaft für die eigene Erhellung des Gefühles, leuchtete rings herum die Landschaft völlig entzaubert: das Meer, das gestern zornig erregte, lag so unbewegt still und hell, daß jeder Kiesel unter der kleinen Brandung weiß bis zu uns herüberglänzte. (VdG,69)

> Und dann: gleichzeitig mit diesem erschütterten, zertretenen Menschen war auch die Landschaft nach dem gestrigen Regen magisch aufgewacht. Herrlich glänzte, als wir aus dem Restaurant traten, das völlig beruhigte Meer. (VdG,75)

Moreover, just as the emotions of the characters — the gratitude of the young man, the exhilaration of Mrs C. — have a certain extravagance about them, so too the brightness of the Riviera is said to exceed its usual flat, uniform beauty and spill over into excess:

> Aber manchmal, ganz selten, gibt es dort Tage, da steht diese Schönheit auf, da bricht sie vor, da schreit sie einen gleichsam energisch an mit grellen, fanatisch funkelnden Farben, da schleudert sie einem ihre Blumenbuntheit sieghaft entgegen, da glüht, da brennt sie in Sinnlichkeit. Und ein solcher begeisterter Tag war auch damals aus dem stürmischen Chaos der Wetternacht vorgebrochen. (VdG,75)

At this point in the narrative the setting as a whole begins to assume that second function: it ceases to be merely a reflection of the emotional state of the two central characters and, briefly,

217

exerts a powerful attraction on them in its own right, provoking the wish to settle there and live in peace, shut off from the rest of the world (VdG,76).

This more active, determining role of weather, climate, and atmosphere is first encountered in *Der Zwang*, where, however, it cannot entirely be divorced from the reflective role considered so far. The dim twilight and vague mistiness of the wintry morning at the beginning of the *Novelle* may be said to mirror Ferdinand's confused state of mind, but his longing for clarity in the world of nature as a means to order his thoughts and bring a sense of peace (VdG^2,223-4) indicates that the physical atmosphere is also able to exert a decisive influence on him — or at least that, in his passivity and avoidance of responsibility, he would have it so. His wife, however, has very similar expectations, arguing shortly afterwards that the now clear March weather should make him rejoice and should hold him back from that compulsion to return to Germany and join the fighting, in short, that it should bring clarity to his mind (VdG^2,234). When he does none the less comply with the demands of the authorities and steals away from home to the consulate in Zurich, the scene is described as 'noch winterhaft dämmerig', with hoar-frost hanging over the lake (VdG^2,237), and seems again intended to reflect his clouded perception of the issues. Yet his subsequent clarity of moral purpose, when for a time he resists the compulsion to take the train back to Germany, is again more obviously dependent on favourable, springlike conditions; the compulsion is said to weigh lightly 'im hellen Tag' (VdG^2,252). His ultimate victory over the compulsion to enlist is not of course made conditional on the happy coincidence of fine weather. Although it may have disappointingly little to do with his conscious will, it does represent a response to a human predicament rather than to meteorological conditions. Even so, Ferdinand remains to the end a very impressionable man, a fact which his wife implicitly acknowledges when in that final scene she directs his attention to the myriad stars shining brightly on a clear night. It is they, it seems, that are to be the source of his faith in eternal values.

In other works where atmospheric conditions play an active role their influence is less frequently mentioned, but is more decisive. It is made clear, for example, that the doctor of *Der Amokläufer* is conditioned not simply by the location of his district station in

India, but by the oppressive climate. When the Englishwoman first appears, his mind has been softened by the effects of the monsoon, which has kept him indoors for months on end, with the rain hammering incessantly on the roof (A,29). When he seeks to explain his irrational behaviour by likening it to the native who runs amuck, he explicitly refers to the climate as a determining cause: 'Irgendwie hängt es mit dem Klima zusammen, mit dieser schwülen, geballten Atmosphäre, die auf die Nerven wie ein Gewitter drückt, bis sie einmal losspringen' (A,48). The unmistakable implication is that, if he had been living elsewhere, in a different climate, he would never have embarked on such a monomaniacal pursuit. Such is the degree to which the mind may be subject to physical influences.

Although the narrator serves as a contrast to the doctor, especially in his untroubled ease as a mere tourist returning from the East, it is interesting to observe how the ecstasy which he experiences during the opening pages and which itself forms part of the wider contrast with the desperate, earth-bound struggle of the doctor, is also induced by the very different atmosphere he encounters on deck at night in clear, calm weather. The unusual flood of light from the moon and stars, the velvet tranquillity of the sea, the mildness of the night air combine with the gentle rocking of the boat to create a voluptuous sense of lassitude, to lift him beyond himself and make him lose all sense of time (A,14-16).

In *Unvermutete Bekanntschaft mit einem Handwerk* the narrator alone is subject to the influence of the atmosphere. It should not be forgotten, however, that it is also arguably he who is the central character. Initially it seems as if the weather described at the beginning of the story — clarity and release after the oppressive gloom of a violent April storm — is to serve as an anticipatory metaphor of the sense of freedom and excitement which comes over him after his arrival in Paris. It soon emerges, however, that his excited sensitivity, his heightened receptivity to all new impressions, on which the rest of the narrative depends, may itself be a product of the change of atmosphere:

> Mag sein, daß dieser Überreiz, diese nervöse Hellsichtigkeit sehr natürlich mit der plötzlichen Ortsveränderung zusammenhängt und nur Folge ist der Umstellung des Luftdruckes und der dadurch bedingten chemischen Umschaltung des Blutes. (K,10)

Undoubtedly, the simple change of location plays its part, in that the narrator finds himself here without obligations and commitments and can for that reason alone surrender himself to the promise of adventure that such a change affords. Yet social factors are evidently not the only ones involved: there is something at work in the atmosphere of Paris which is registered first by the human body and is thence translated into a changed state of mind.

Interesting as all these various examples of both the reflective and active function of weather, climate, and atmosphere may be, they nowhere approach the significance which these attain in *Die Frau und die Landschaft*, which deserves rather special attention on that account. Their role in this work indeed transcends the categories that have applied so far. It is indissolubly linked, moreover, with the role of the landscape, which, as the title already implies, has been elevated to the status of protagonist.

Although it might be possible to speak of a metaphorical parellelism between the parched Tyrolean landscape before the storm breaks and the nervous expectancy of the young woman and the narrator before their sexual encounter, and although one might certainly argue that the meteorological atmosphere has an openly acknowledged effect on both characters,[1] this would be an inadequate account of what Zweig presents. First, there is a sustained pattern of reciprocal imagery, whereby the anthropomorphic vocabulary of the nature descriptions (1) is matched by the meteorological vocabulary of the character descriptions (2). A few brief instances from many may suffice to illustrate the point:

(1) [. . .] die dürstenden Felder, [. . .] gierige Wärme [. . .] mit tausend Lippen, [. . .] hinschmachtenden Laubes . . . (A,89)

(2) [. . .] wie ein Dunst lag um sie das weiße Nachtgewand (A,109) [. . .] als wäre diese Wärme, die von ihren Wangen glühte, der Brodem der Felder, als atmete von ihrem weichen, warmen Brüsten das schauernde Land (A,111)

Second, the parallelism of human and natural spheres frequently becomes more of a union, so that the two no longer operate alongside each other, but merge into one. Thus, to select just two passages from many, when the narrator first hears the sigh of the young woman longing for rain, he comments: 'So wild, so elementar war diese Stimme, war dieser Stoß aus einem bedrückten Gefühl, als hätte es die dürstende Erde selbst gesagt mit ihren aufgesprungenen Lippen, die gequälte, erdrosselte Landschaft' (A,93); and when the promise of rainfall is not fulfilled, he describes his own reaction in these words: 'Ich fühlte in mir die Qual der ganzen verratenen Natur, das Lechzen der kleinen Gräser war in mir, die Hitze der Straßen, der Qualm des Waldes [. . .] der Durst der ganzen betrogenen Welt' (A,96).

This widespread identification culminates in a grand sexual union. There have already been powerful suggestions that this was to come about, not least in an abortive fall of rain, which results in only a few isolated drops and is described in such a way that it bears all the marks of *coitus interruptus*:

> in ohnmächtiger, unbefriedigter Enttäuschung lag unter dem erglänzenden Horizont die lauschende Landschaft. Wie von Wut lief noch ein leises, letztes Zittern durch die Bäume, sie beugten und krümmten sich, dann aber fielen die Laubhände, die schon gierig aufgereckt waren, schlaff zurück, wie tot.
> (A,96)

The distinguishing feature of the climax, however, is not so much that the release of human instincts in sexual union is followed closely by the elemental outburst of the thunderstorm, but that this itself is seen as a sexual union of heaven and earth, which is followed by a sort of post-coital *tristesse*:

> Jetzt war [der Himmel] fern [. . .], nirgends rührte er sie mehr an, die duftende, atmende, gestillte Erde, sein Weib. Ein blauer Abgrund schimmerte kühl zwischen ihm und der Tiefe, wunschlos blickten sie einander an und fremd, der Himmel und die Landschaft. (A,119)

What has been enacted in *Die Frau und die Landschaft* is much more than a meteorological event, reflecting a human encounter; here, uniquely if not altogether convincingly, atmosphere has become a participant in a mythical act, the union of Gaea and Uranus.

16

Beyond Time and Space

It would be an incomplete examination of temporal and spatial setting in Zweig's *Novellen* which did not also take note of a remarkable tendency in some of his characters to withdraw from the concrete realities of their present surroundings, at times indeed to seek a life beyond time and space altogether. To do so, however, entails a shift of emphasis away from considerations of the function of setting or of the values ascribed to it. At most it might be possible to speak of a negative value which time and place hold for certain individuals. That also means, therefore, that the following discussion will be much less concerned with matters of narrative organisation and will instead lead us back into a consideration of character, both as the focus of Zweig's psychological interest and as the bearer of the human values he wished to commend.

Occasionally he depicts brief moments of what Marghanita Laski has called 'withdrawal ecstasy' or 'intensity ecstasy',[1] when a character is lifted out of himself and loses all sense of time and space. We have already noted this experience in the narrator of *Der Amokläufer* as he gazes at the luminous night-sky from the deck of a gently rolling liner (A,16). Similar in effect is the way in which the literary enthusiasm of the professor in *Verwirrung der Gefühle* can induce a state of *raptus*, 'das Fortgetragensein eines Menschen über sich selbst hinaus' (VdG, 170), or rob him of all awareness of those around him (VdG,203). These, however, are transient states of mind. More interesting and revealing are the cases in which the transcending of time and space or the attempt to evade their unwelcome consequences has become a way of life.

222

The phenomenon can most easily be demonstrated by resuming the account of the Jewish businessman in *Untergang eines Herzens* after his return from the Italian resort to his South German home. It might be expected that, in leaving behind him a place devoted to the pursuit of pleasure, this most puritanical of men would revert to his former mode of existence, recovering a sense of harmony between his highly-developed work-ethic and his 'proper' environment. In fact the return marks the more radical development of a different process, already initiated at the Italian resort: a withdrawal from external reality altogether into the ever-contracting world of his own heart, a withdrawal which is reflected stylistically in the unusually high frequency of interior monologue and 'erlebte Rede'. Even in Italy he increasingly avoided contact with his wife and daughter, retiring to his room, keeping his anger to himself. And even there the withdrawal into his own heart at one stage induced a loss of temporal and spatial awareness: 'er hörte nicht, daß immer wieder die Glocken vom See ihre Stunden herein in sein Zimmer schlugen' (VdG,138); he failed to notice the changes of light and their effect on the objects outside him, but 'starrte nur in das Schwarze in sich, er horchte nur in das Leere in sich hinein wie in den eigenen Tod' (VdG,139).

Once he is at home the process accelerates. He disregards the consequences of his existence in space, taking no notice of or interest in other people, refraining from looking out of the window on to the world outside (VdG,148), and allowing himself at one point, like the young Polish gambler of *Vierundzwanzig Stunden aus dem Leben einer Frau*, to become soaked by a rain-storm, which fails to impinge on his consciousness.

In much the same way, too, he disregards the implications of time, neglecting punctuality, previously so important to his commercial life (VdG,145-6), ignoring the passage of time as he addresses his long-dead parents at their graveside (VdG,149), and — introducing a motif that will recur in other works and that held a special significánce for Zweig himself — omitting to read the newspapers. In the author's own personal life this last omission was often a deliberate attempt to shun what he consistently regarded as the corrupt world of politics.[2] For Salomonssohn politics do not appear to be a problem. Nevertheless, in refusing to read the paper he too is turning his back on all those public affairs which, as the German noun 'Zeitung' reminds us, are essentially

223

temporal phenomena.

His retreat into an inner world beyond time and space may evoke some pity, but it does not emerge as a positive achievement. In the first place, it signifies not so much an attempt to confront his problems as an avoidance of the very conditions which would make confrontation possible. At the same time it is a denial of all human relationships in favour of self-absorption, just as his apparently pious intercessions and acts of charity near the end are in reality only an expression of very private concerns.[3] Perhaps the most serious implication of his retreat into himself, however, is that the logical conclusion of such denial of the world of time and space is death. From an earlier stage the imagery used in connection with Salomonssohn's withdrawal has hinted darkly at some fatal conclusion, describing him sinking back into himself, 'ertrunken in Scham und Schmerz' (VdG,125), or stealing away, 'sich vor den Menschen zu vergraben' (VdG,118).[4] It seems clear, moreover, that his serious heart condition is closely linked with the added burden placed on it by self-contraction. The 'Untergang eines Herzens' of the title denotes as much as anything the sinking of a heart under its own increased specific gravity.

In an earlier chapter a distinction was drawn between those *Novellen* which depicted something of the social habits of their period and those which involved a shift of interest towards the political and economic realities of their time. While *Untergang eines Herzens* still belongs to the former category, it is a remarkable fact, of grave significance for Zweig's outlook in general, that it is precisely in those *Novellen* which reflect a closer interest in the economic and political problems of the day that the role of this inner world beyond time and space is most pronounced. In making this judgement I am thinking not so much of the simple-minded hero of *Episode am Genfer See*, who merely lacks a proper sense of time and space, who fails to realise that serfdom has now been abolished and the Tsar assassinated, who has no concept of 'frontier' and confuses Lake Geneva with the Lake Bayal of his home (K,91-2). I am thinking rather of individuals who find or seek a form of self-protection in a world beyond time and space and of the problems involved in that quest. It will be useful to consider the relevant works in an order based not on their date of composition, but on the historical period in which they are set.

Buchmendel, which covers a period of some thirty or more years beginning in the supposed stability of the late nineteenth century,[5] is nevertheless narrated from the perspective of post-war Vienna, when economic collapse and man's quickness to forget have created in the narrator a deep sense of transitoriness: 'Wozu lebt man, wenn der Wind hinter unserem Schuh schon die letzte Spur von uns wegträgt' (K,110). Against this background he sets the portrait of a man whose very way of life is an unconscious and ultimately doomed attempt to ignore or minimise the effects of time and their spatial equivalents.

If change is at the heart of transitoriness, it is also a function of time and space, since it can only be registered in their dimensions. Significantly therefore the habits of Jakob Mendel are designed to eliminate change as much as possible. He always wears the same clothes; he occupies the same table at the Café Gluck for over thirty years, arriving and leaving at the same times each day. So immovable does he seem to be that, when the café changes hands, he is transferred to the new owner as if he were one of the fixtures (K,120). The adjectives, adverbs, and adverbial phrases which characterise his activities ('unentwegt', 'immer', 'allzeit', 'unerschütterlich', 'Tag um Tag', 'allwöchentlich') emphasise their immutability. The insert in the newspaper advertising his business appears 'allsonntäglich'; its formulation is 'stereotyp' (K,105-6). Although the unchangeable habits of Mendel are described without further comment or criticism, they represent an inhuman rigidity. In the manuscript version of *Leporella* the following passage occurs:

> Zeit und Raum, die weltgeistigen Mächte, hatten keinerlei wandelnde Kraft über ihr stumpf und regelmäßig tagwerdendes [?] Dasein, ihren traumlos totenhaften Maulwurfsschlaf: winters und sommers trug sie das gleiche angeflickte schwarze Kattunkleid über dem starren Körper gespannt, der [. . .] nichts anders begehrte als tretmühlenhaft Schritt für Schritt in die Spur des Vergangenen zu tun.[6]

Something of that dull, inanimate quality is to be found in the Jewish book-pedlar too.

Even his bibliographical memory, the very essence of his uniqueness as a character, is calculated to take him beyond time and space. The concentration required to commit so many facts to memory means, among other things, that, like Salomonssohn, he reads no newspapers and so avoids any involvement in the affairs of the times. Yet the result of his memorising is even more remarkable: it overcomes time itself. Details absorbed long ago are immediately accessible; and as the narrator puts it, 'er wußte von jedem Werk, dem gestern erschienenen wie von einem zweihundert Jahre alten, auf den ersten Hieb genau den Erscheinungsort, den Verfasser, den Preis, neu und antiquarish' (K,104).

In a similar way, spatial relations appear to mean little to Mendel. The very method he employs to impress the countless bibliographical details on his mind (a secularised application of the ways learned in the Talmud school) induces such hypnotic absorption that he is lost to his surroundings, 'wie ein Kind in Schlaf fällt und der Welt entsinkt' (K,100), and fails to register changes such as the installation of electricity (K,109) and incidents such as the burning of the carpet just a few feet away from him (K,101). Much the same applies on a wider scale too. For, as we have already seen, his continued presence in Vienna is dependent on a disregard for spatial detail (the fact that he is technically a foreigner, an illegal immigrant), while his wartime 'crime' consists in the failure to attend to the significance of territorial divisions.

The narrator invests Mendel's bibliographical interest with a superior quality, which makes it in the end not unlike that higher world of music which so inspires the central character of Grillparzer's *Der arme Spielmann*. It is 'das andere Universum der Bücher, das gleichfalls ewig kreisende und sich umgebärende, [. . .] diese Welt über unserer Welt' (K,108); it is an 'obere Welt', in which there is no war (K,116). By this he clearly intends to imply a world which is not simply spatially higher, but transcends the limitations of time and space and those petty man-made evils which grow out of them. Nevertheless, although it may be granted that Mendel's memory represents a positive conquest within its own restricted sphere, other manifestations of his world beyond time and space are more problematic. The reason why he has remained untainted by the prejudice of national divisions is, as we have seen, not that he has embraced a nobler cause, but that he has simply enjoyed the earlier casual attitude to nationality in Habsburg Vienna without appreciating its value or significance. He has not confronted time and space and overcome them, but has ignored them; and in the end this very disregard makes him defenceless against them. When his correspondence with the 'enemy' leads to the discovery of his illegal immigration, time catches up with him, and spatial relations suddenly become painfully relevant. His naive reply to a question about his failure to register, 'Wozu hätte ich mich melden sollen *auf einmal*?' (K,116; my emphasis), betrays a dangerous unwillingness to concede that circumstances do change, that time does not stand still. Even after two years in a concentration camp he returns to Vienna, behaving as though nothing were different. Now, however, the advent of inflation — for Zweig the very epitome of instability and change in the material world — and the commercialism of the new management at the Café Gluck prove his final undoing and expose the weakness of his stance. Although money has meant little to him, when he finds that he can no longer afford the little food he consumes, he resorts to stealing rolls, a pitiful act, which nevertheless unconsciously acknowledges that, even at a minimal level, he does have a place in the material world, that his inner world can never divorce itself entirely from external reality.

More devastating, however, is the fact that Mendel's experiences in the concentration camp have changed him at the essential point, robbing him of his memory, so that in a very real sense he no longer exists: 'Mendel war nicht mehr Mendel, wie die Welt nicht mehr die Welt war' (K,119). The syntactic parallelism between the individual and the world reinforces an inescapable link which Mendel has tried to ignore; it underlines the futility of responding to the world of change by acting as though its spatial and temporal preconditions did not exist.

In the case of *Der Zwang* the hero's response to the problem created by war, in which time plays a particularly insistent role, is a more deliberate withdrawal from the pressures of external reality. Even while still in Germany he has, like Salomonssohn in *Untergang eines Herzens*, locked up his sense of outrage within himself rather than directing it outwards to some individual or collective resistance (VdG²,227). He has acted only to the extent of going into self-imposed exile in neutral Switzerland, 'ein Flüchtling vor der Zeit und den Menschen' (VdG²,224). Not only is this an escape from the implications of time; it is also an attempt to find a sort of neutral space, where definitions such as frontiers are no longer in force. Even in Switzerland it is as though he wanted to deny his very existence in space, where his location might be identified. For he leaves no address and collects his mail 'postlagernd' (VdG²,227). Whenever the military authorities do none the less threaten his attempted disappearance, his defence typically follows the same pattern of escape from time and space. Like Salomonssohn and Mendel, he avoids reading newspapers; and having already chosen a house outside the town in a neutral country, he retires still further to an attic, there to concentrate on his own painting, of which the only subject-matter mentioned at this stage is, significantly, a self-portrait (VdG^2,229).

Even Ferdinand's wife, for all her greater strength of will, often resorts to tactics and arguments which could easily reinforce the flight from time and space into an inner world. 'Glaubst du an eine Gerechtigkeit', she asks him, 'außer an die unsichtbare, die wir in uns bauen' (VdG^2,233). Her conception of justice is not a public, still less a political matter, but a private, even abstract principle. Similarly, in drawing his attention to a Swiss farmer peacefully going about his work, not subject to the law of conscription, she attacks the validity of a law which is geographically (that is, spatially) bound and not universally operative. The trouble with her argument is that, if Switzerland were also at war, there would then apparently be no basis for moral resistance to war. Subsequently, after her arguments have received some intellectual assent from Ferdinand, but have failed to enlist the power of his will, she resorts to a pitiful subterfuge, which requires little comment in its implications for the present theme: she stops the clock (VdG^{2}237). It is possible that Zweig derived the motif from one of the pieces in Leonhard Frank's *Der Mensch ist gut*, where the symbolic gesture of stopping the clock denotes a mother's attempt to immobilise the inexorable machinery of war.[7] Here it expresses a powerless wish to escape from time itself.

From that moment the concept of time becomes particularly insistent and Ferdinand increasingly caught up in it. The urgency of his compulsion to submit to the war-machine is such that he arrives in Zurich absurdly early and has time to kill before he can report to the consulate. Having next devised an elaborate plan of resistance in his head, he is surprised to discover, on checking with the clock, that the exercise has taken up virtually no objective time at all (VdG^2,241). When he visits a café, however, and breaks his normal habit by reading the newspapers, it is significant that the exposure to temporal affairs upsets his imaginary plan, which, not unexpectedly, also collapses in the actual confrontation at the consulate. Although the official allows him a brief stay before he must return to enlist, it seems unlikely that even his renewed contact with his stronger wife will now be able to hold him back. This is confirmed by a strange symbolic act he performs after his return home: under an unconscious impulse he packs his knapsack and, we are told, 'darin das ganze Gewicht der Zeit' (VdG²,250). Time, however, with all the conflicts it entails, proves to be so burdensome that Ferdinand's next impulse is to seek refuge in the ultimate escape from time and space: death by drowning. Once more it is the clock which calls him back from this step, impressing urgency on him if he is to catch the train back to Germany (VdG²,254).

The reasons why Ferdinand does not in the end submit to the demands of the military authorities have already been examined. Here it is necessary only to observe the close relation between the position he finally adopts and our present concern. His wife leads him to the window of their house:

> draußen stand, unberührt von der selbstgeschaffenen Qual einer verwirrten Menschheit, die ewige Welt und glänzte für ihn, unendliche Sterne unter unendlichem Himmel. Er sah hinauf und erkannte gläubig bewegt, daß kein Gesetz für den Menschen auf Erden gilt als das ihre, daß nichts ihn wahrhaft bindet als Verbundensein. Nah seinen Lippen wogte selig der Atem seiner Frau, und manchmal zitterten ihre beiden Körper leise aneinander in der Wollust des Sichfühlens. Aber sie schwiegen: frei schwang sich ihr Herz in die ewige Freiheit der Dinge, erlöst von der Wirrnis der Worte und der Menschen Gesetz. (VdG²,262)

Not only is this a retreat once more into the private sphere ('die Wollust des Sichfühlens'). It also makes appeal to laws which are universally valid, that is, not bound by time or space, but does not seek to apply them to the world outside, contenting itself rather with a cosmic and erotic ecstasy which specifically transcends spatial and temporal limitations (note the numerous references to 'ewig' and 'unendlich'). There have been repeated references earlier in the story to the fact that Ferdinand still had time: time to reach a decision, time to catch the train, time to turn back (VdG²,250,253,259). Together they serve to emphasise that it is only within time that he can come to terms with his inner conflicts. Yet his final response is to retreat from time entirely.

The central character of *Die unsichtbare Sammlung*, which

concentrates almost exclusively on the post-war period of inflation, is like Jakob Mendel to the extent that he too inhabits an inner world, but unlike him to the extent that he does so initially out of physical necessity. He has gone blind and so lost an important means of contact with the world about him. Nevertheless, he is clearly intended to represent some sort of triumph over this limitation. Although his eyes can no longer pass to and fro across the two-dimensional space of his etchings, his inner eye is said to have preserved an image of each intact, an image so potent that it is capable of inducing in him a state of rapture and lifting him above the humdrum world (K,85-6). Appropriately, the last sight which the narrator has of him at an upper window, though spatially defined, is presented, as we have already noted, as a metaphor of spiritual elevation beyond the world of time and space. Although the illusory basis of the old man's achievement is underplayed by the narrator, its implications need to be stressed. He has been lovingly handling blank sheets of paper or worthless reproductions which his relatives encourage him to believe are original works of art. That means that his inner vision has not triumphed over the material world to such an extent that he can dispense with external support entirely. Those around him evidently judge that his mental image of all those etchings is not of itself sustaining enough for him to bear the truth of their physical loss. Furthermore, they keep him in ignorance of the true effects of inflation: 'Vater versteht nichts mehr von den Preisen und von der Zeit' (K,80). He himself cannot of course read the newspaper. But it is significant that, in reading it aloud to him, his relatives feel it necessary to exercise such strict censorship that he remains ignorant of contemporary affairs and has no idea that the war has been lost or Alsace-Lorraine ceded to France (K,81). His attitude to his collection of prints is several times likened to that of a child (K,78,86,88); and essentially he is treated like a child, kept — like the novelist in *Brief einer Unbekannten* — in a protective cocoon, as though he lacked the maturity to cope with the real world. In the final analysis his world beyond time and space does not represent a triumph over the real world, but a false utopia based on an inner contradiction: an apparent elevation above materiality and yet a heavy if unacknowledged dependence on it through the pretences and sacrificial labours of other people.

Schachnovelle stands in sharp contrast to the three works just considered, both in the portrayal of the central character and in the presentation of the world beyond time and space. As a lawyer Dr B. has been very much involved in political and economic affairs. In seeking to protect the value of clients' money in the immediate post-war period his family firm has been resisting, not evading, the most dramatic manifestations of sudden change in both spheres: revolution and inflation (S,54). His own continued involvement indeed has led to his arrest. Moreover, if he does eventually leave his native land, his exile is not voluntary, like Ferdinand's, but enforced.

The more significant contrast, however, lies in the fact that what in those other works has been a means of self-preservation — retreat from the real world with its problems and conflicts — is here transformed into a weapon to destroy the self. For the method employed by the Nazis to try and extort information from Dr B. is isolation in what he calls 'eine zeitlose, raumlose Leere' (S,62).[8] Those markers of time, clocks and newspapers, are denied him. The window of his room offers no view of the world outside, the view on which Salomonssohn turns his back, nor of a limitless cosmos such as that in which Ferdinand loses himself at the end, but looks on to a bare wall (S,61). Since change, as we have seen, is an essential product of time and space, it is noteworthy how insistently Dr B. describes the sameness of his surroundings: 'Das Schlimmste war das Zurückkommen nach dem Verhör in mein Nichts, in dasselbe Zimmer mit demselben Tisch, demselben Bett, derselben Waschschüssel, derselben Tapete' (S,64). Although he is still, strictly speaking, within the world of time and space, its manifestations are reduced to a minimum; and the reader accepts his summary of the four months' imprisonment as 'eine Zeit im Raumlosen, im Zeitlosen' (S,67) without registering the element of paradox and exaggeration in the formulation.

Dr B.'s confinement has been interpreted as a disguised representation of Zweig's own sense of monastic isolation in Petropolis shortly before his suicide during that period when nothing seemed to happen or change and when he felt a keen lack of companions.[9] It was then that he bought 'a book of the most famous chess games'[10] to help him in his seclusion. In a similar hunger for sensory and intellectual stimulus Dr B. seizes on the stolen chess-manual as a means to occupy his mind and plays through the games of the masters, first on a crudely improvised board, then in his head. He is in no position to oppose tyranny by political means. The best he can hope to do is to keep sane and not betray others; and he sees this internalised chess as a weapon against what threatens to rob him of his sanity, 'die erdrückende Monotonie des Raumes und der Zeit' (S,79). Nevertheless, it is a desperate and dangerous form of defence. One can hardly think of a game better suited, potentially, to helping him cope with his predicament, since chess relies so heavily on well-defined spatial relations and carefully planned sequences of moves and even provides the opportunity for a (surrogate) encounter with an opponent. The problem is that these very elements have been withdrawn from their proper sphere into the imagination of one man.

If his so-called schizophrenia is the most dramatic consequence of his proposed solution, the more lasting consequence, which has serious implications for our present concern, is that it becomes extremely difficult to reverse the process of internalisation. The same point is suggested in *Der Zwang*, where Ferdinand proves unable to translate his imagined resistance to officialdom into equivalent action. Here it is the lesson which Dr B. has to learn when he plays again on board the ship taking him into exile. His interference in the first match between the world champion and a team of amateurs is as much as anything a test: to see if his mental chess can be projected outwards on to a real board. Although he seems to succeed in this, the second game he agrees to play exposes the frailty of his position. In the pathological excitement that now accompanies his play he finds it increasingly difficult to relate the time and space of his imagination to those of the game taking place on the board in front of him. While his mind races ahead at its own pace to construct a pattern of play which follows his inner vision, Czentovic keeps him subject to the real game and clock-time by employing irritating delaying tactics. Eventually Dr B. becomes so engrossed in the game being played in his head, which has progressed to a much more advantageous position and may indeed have merged into another game entirely, that he calls out 'Check!' when none is present (S,113-15). Once he has been made to realise his error he resigns and renounces chess for good.

Although Dr B. emerges from this sad conclusion with dignity, as a sympathetic victim, whose confusion has its first cause in the tyranny of others, this should not blind us to the dangers implicit in his fate, above all the danger that a retreat into an inner world beyond time and space is likely to lead to an inability to deal with the conflicts that arise in time and space. This fact, which applies with equal force to Salomonssohn, Mendel, Ferdinand, and the blind art-collector, sheds further, retrospective light on the problematic nature of some of the human ideals presented in the *Novellen*. It also has a much wider relevance, providing a sobering commentary on Zweig's whole tendency to avoid concrete political realities, on what has been called his 'contemplative humanism',[11] and not least on his suicide. For the evidence of the *Novellen* suggests that the search for a world beyond time and space is at best an ambiguous matter, positive to the extent that it represents a quest for universal, unchanging, incorruptible values, negative to the extent that it is a form of escape from public involvement into the private domain, a means of avoiding commitment and conflict, and the cradle of illusion and ignorance.

The more positive aspect emerges from Zweig's early attitude to Zionism, a cause which, despite his personal admiration for Theodor Herzl, he could not for many years accept.[12] As he wrote to Martin Buber in 1917, Judaism for him was a spiritual matter, not bound to a particular place or particular customs.[13] Accordingly, when at about the same time he came to express his rejection of war through the Old Testament figure of Jeremiah, he put into the mouth of the prophet the picture of a Zion within man, not spatially and temporally bound and therefore requiring no military defence.[14]

The more negative aspects are especially apparent in repeated expressions of distaste for politics, in which he was conforming to a pattern common among intellectuals brought up in late nineteenth-century Vienna and encouraged by the government's desire to divert public attention from political affairs to cultural interests.[15] With Zweig the tendency persisted, becoming particularly marked in times of political tension. One rich source of comment on the subject is the diary he kept during the First World War, which records numerous expressions of the impulse to shut himself off from the world of public affairs, to withdraw into himself, to devote himself to his own work,[16] and rather fewer expressions of misgiving at such aloofness from the realities of war.[17] Another important source is the correspondence with the composer Richard Strauss from the period when the Nazi dictatorship threatened the fruits of their collaboration on the opera *Die schweigsame Frau.* The following short extract, with its search for neutral space and its desire to escape from the times, is typical of many: 'Ich gehe in vierzehn Tagen ins Tessin oder nach Italien zur Arbeit, um mich noch hermetischer von allem Zeitlichen abzuschließen'.[18] Since politics was a sphere in which great wrong was done and inhuman acts were performed, he chose to withdraw from it altogether, even to the extent of refusing to exercise his democratic right to vote.[19] Art, on the other hand, appeared to offer a refuge, an aesthetic haven beyond time.[20]

Towards the end of his life, as the political climate grew worse, Zweig continued to avoid public statements, preferring to express himself obliquely in veiled self-portraits such as his essays on Erasmus and Montaigne, in both of which he stressed the supremacy of inner, personal freedom as a means of preserving moral integrity and supranational tolerance, but also as a justification for not making decisions of a political nature. Significantly, the position adopted by both men is summarised in the same symbol, which Zweig took from Goethe: that of the citadel, seen as a sort of ivory tower in which the intellectual surrounds himself with books and sits high above the real world and beyond all those disturbing manifestations of time and space.[21] It is a position which will find its most grotesque literary expression in the windowless library of the scholar Peter Kien in Canetti's *Die Blendung*, a novel originally composed at much the same time as these historical portraits by Zweig.

Zweig himself was not always free from doubt on the subject of retreat from the world. The main thrust of his legend *Die Augen des ewigen Bruders* of 1922 was that withdrawal from the public sphere, even into the life of a hermit, could not prevent entanglement in human guilt and in any case bore witness to an over-valuation of the individual self. Later, even as he wrote so sympathetically about Erasmus and Montaigne, it was as if he sensed that there was no way back from such a retreat. That led him, I believe, to acknowledge that Erasmus's dream of a united mankind was a utopia (a non-place), probably incapable of achievement in the realm of reality.[22] It also led him to acknowledge that the peace Erasmus had so much desired for all men was ultimately attained only in death, in much the same way as the central character of the legend *Der begrabene Leuchter* (1936) comes to believe that the only sure way to preserve the sacred

234

candelabrum from the predations of successive political rulers is to bury it in a coffin in a secret grave.[23] For Zweig too, following a similar pattern, as well as the thinking of his earlier fictional counterpart, Ferdinand in *Der Zwang*, death was to prove the final destination along his escape route from the political turmoil of his own time and his own land. As A. Lazar puts it, his suicide was 'eine fast natürliche Tat für einen Menschen, dessen Haltung immer "ausweichend" war'.[24] And as Walter Huder writes, 'Stefan Zweigs freiwilliger Heimgang in den zeitlosen Raum war der fast verzweifelte Versuch, sich der Gewalt der Zeit zu entziehen, sich von der Angst der Unfreiheit zu befreien'.[25]

PART FOUR

NARRATIVE RHETORIC

As Wayne Booth has shown, although the writer of fiction may scrupulously avoid all open intrusions into his narrative, he cannot in the end eliminate his presence entirely, which is everywhere implied, in the sort of language he employs and in the very ordering of his material — his choice of what to include and what to omit, where to start and where to finish, what sequence to adopt, how much weight to give to each particular event or character, and so forth. Moreover, every such decision he takes has a more or less calculated influence on his reader's interest, sympathies, moral and aesthetic judgements. As Booth puts it, most succinctly, 'the author cannot choose to avoid rhetoric; he can choose only the kind of rhetoric he will employ. He cannot choose whether or not to affect his reader's evaluations by his choice of narrative manner; he can only choose whether to do it well or poorly'.[1]

Rhetoric, understood in this sense, has already formed an incidental part of our earlier discussions. We have noted the interpretative relevance of titles such as *Geschichte in der Dämmerung* or *Verwirrung der Gefühle* and of the sonnets placed at the beginning of the three volumes that go to make up the cycle *Die Kette.* We have heeded the comments of the narrator in stories as different as *Angst, Episode am Genfer See* or *Die unsichtbare Sammlung* and the self-assessment of characters with whom we tend to sympathise, such as Mrs C. and the unknown woman of *Brief einer Unbekannten.* We have observed how the central characters are set against a particular social, economic, political, cultural, or psychological background and how this affects our understanding of their behaviour. We have seen how a geographical location or a change of location can influence a character's behaviour decisively, or how the concrete details of some locations can act as a metaphorical illumination of his situation; and we have also seen how weather can govern

239

behaviour or reflect a state of mind. We have had occasion to consider the differences which may be entailed in the choice of alternatives presented to the reader (dry scholarship versus enthusiasm in *Verwirrung der Gefühle*; the progression from indifference to passion in *Phantastische Nacht*; the contrast between Czentovic and Dr B. in *Schachnovelle*) or in the perspective adopted (that of Bob rather than Margot or Elisabeth in *Geschichte in der Dämmerung*: that of the woman letter-writer of *Brief einer Unbekannten* but not that of her lover). And we have noted the effects of some of the various kinds of ending: the brief glimpses into the future provided at the end of *Geschichte in der Dämmerung, Die Gouvernante*, and *Brennendes Geheimnis* in contrast to the climactic conclusions of *Der Zwang* or *Phantastische Nacht*, which avoid any consideration of possible future outworkings.

These are just a few scattered examples of Zweig's narrative rhetoric, of the stratagems he employs to guide the reader's evaluation of the material presented. A full and systematic analysis of this rhetoric would fill an entire volume. Two particular aspects of it, however, are so prominent and so characteristic of their author that they deserve individual discussion. The one, imagery, forms part of the linguistic texture; the other, the narrative frame, is largely a matter of structure and organisation. Yet both ultimately contribute to a fuller understanding of the characters' psychology and the human values embodied in their actions and experiences.

17

Imagery and the Image of Man

Unlike Kafka, whose narratives, typically, are dominated by a central metaphor, but whose language remains factual and free of metaphorical devices, Zweig prefers plots which have a simple, contiguous relation to what we are pleased to call the real world, but employs a language exceptionally rich in imagery. So rich in metaphor is his language that it has provoked the criticism of even friends and admirers. Joseph Roth, whose own style was simple and austere,[1] drew his older friend's attention, on several occasions and in connection with both biographical and fictional works, to what he once called 'Metaphernballast'.[2] Writing of *Unvermutete Bekanntschaft mit einem Handwerk*, for example, he expressed general admiration for the story, but found the opening too sumptuous and recommended pruning: 'die Einleitung, wie diese Aussprache. Auch das Sprachliche und das Metaphorische ist dabei nicht sorgfältig genug'.[3] Hermann Kesten wrote in similar vein in his book of memoirs *Meine Freunde die Poeten*, where he summarised Zweig's language in these words: 'Seine Prosa ist nachlässig, reich an Füllseln und schiefen Bildern'.[4]

There can be little doubt that Zweig's desire to create intensity, coupled with a certain metaphorical facility, was often too seductive for him. It must also be conceded that he lacked that ability of Musil, displayed above all in *Der Mann ohne Eigenschaften*, to use metaphorical language as a cognitive tool, a means of arriving at and illuminating fresh insights; for all the richness displayed his imagery rarely leads to an equivalent sense of heightened perception. Nevertheless, it would be wrong to

241

conclude that Zweig's metaphorical language belongs simply to the decorative surface of the works and has no bearing on the substance of what is presented. Writing of language in general Terence Hawkes has convincingly argued that metaphor is not to be regarded merely as a cloak for pre-existing thought: 'A metaphor *is* thought in its own right'.[5] In Zweig's case too the metaphorical language, despite its prodigality and lack of originality, remains a valuable key to the author's understanding of the world.

There are various reasons why the reader of Zweig should pay serious attention to his use of imagery. First, he himself is aware of the cognitive possibilities of metaphor. Second, although he has a fairly constant stock of images, each work retains an individual metaphorical profile, which corresponds to the wider conception of what is presented. More particularly, the verbal imagery sometimes derives from the physical or literal details of the fictional world or operates in parallel with other concrete imagery. The point is most clearly illustrated in *Brennendes Geheimnis*. Here predatory metaphors are widely used to describe the baron's wooing of Edgar's mother as well as the young hero's watchful observation of their amorous adventures, but this language has a natural correspondence in the baron's earlier hunting expeditions in India, with accounts of which he regales the boy at one point, and in the way the latter himself actually crawls on all fours in pursuit of his mother and her would-be lover. Metaphors of doors and bolts, which serve to depict an adult world whose customs are as yet beyond Edgar's comprehension, become physically realised in those scenes noted earlier where he quite literally waits outside the door of a room occupied by the adults or is locked in his own room like a naughty child. And the metaphors of combat, which frequently characterise the relations between the three main characters, prepare the way for the real blows which are struck at critical moments.

Clearly, Zweig's verbal imagery cannot be isolated from his overall image of man and of human relations. That is why, in earlier chapters, it was not possible to discuss either his psychological presentation or his human ideals without making some reference to his imagery. As a rhetorical resource, moreover, it belongs not only to the 'propositional act', but also to the 'illocutionary act'.[6] Since its presentation of the world is not neutral but emotionally charged, it possesses considerable persuasive power, appealing to what Max Black calls a 'system of associated implications'.[7]

A central difficulty in any study of metaphor is that of determining exactly what deserves attention. Since metaphor is the very stuff of language, it could be argued that the so-called 'dead' metaphors should simply be disregarded. Yet who is to say that they may not be brought back to life again? And who possesses sufficient knowledge of linguistic medicine to pronounce them clinically dead in the first place?[8] Near the beginning of *Brennendes Geheimnis* Zweig remarks on the perceptive truth that lies concealed in the expression 'Frauenjäger' and proceeds to elaborate on the many characteristics of the hunt that are present in some men's pursuit of an attractive woman (EE,90). He at least shows himself aware of the potential life that resides in an apparently dead metaphor.

There still remains, however, the difficulty of deciding what is significant. Since metaphor is such an inalienable part of language, should one perhaps restrict the scope of the discussion to imagery which is original, consciously employed, or — to use the terminology of linguistics — 'foregrounded' in some way?[9] Even if it were possible to determine with any certainty what is original or consciously intended, it would be an impoverishing restriction to exclude out of hand all derivative or stock images, nowhere more so than in the case of Zweig. A close reading of his language indicates that the repeated or insistent use of even well-worn images is one of the most valuable sources of insight into the cast of his mind. For that reason we shall need to pay close attention not only to what appears original or is foregrounded, but to what is repeated or forms part of a pattern.

A third and rather special difficulty, which Zweig's language shares with that of the ecstatics, is that it is often impossible to be sure whether certain words or expressions are to be understood literally or metaphorically.[10] This is particularly the case where emotions and sensations are involved. In *Der Amokläufer*, to take just one example, there are frequent references to fever and feverish feelings, but it is by no means clear in every case whether the term is intended in the transferred sense to convey an impression of intensity, or whether it denotes a physical condition such as might be recorded on a thermometer, or whether both obtain simultaneously. In dealing with such cases one can do no more than apply common sense. At the same time the very difficulty calls attention to a noteworthy fact of general interest: that the link between the psychological and physiological aspects of human emotions is itself a rich source of metaphor.

Because of the sheer quantity of material it has been necessary to restrict the scope of the discussion in some way. Accordingly, I have selected for consideration a representative cross-section of the *Novellen: Geschichte in der Dämmerung, Verwirrung der Gefühle, Unvermutete Bekanntschaft mit einem Handwerk*, and *Schachnovelle*. I have also concentrated largely on what seem to be the most interesting and significant image-patterns or, to use a term derived from Caroline Spurgeon's investigation into the imagery of Shakespeare: 'image-clusters'.[11]

In imposing a further restriction I have been influenced less by the constraints of space than by the object of the investigation. Since it has been my chief aim to discover what Zweig's imagery reveals about his conception of man, that which is not concerned with human experience has been excluded. Yet in fact this represents only a minor exclusion. In his metaphorical language, as in his general approach, the inanimate, non-human world holds relatively little interest for him; and when it does appear, it often provides an indirect comment on human issues. In *Brennendes Geheimnis* the landscape around the hotel, which is described by means of sexual imagery, comes thereby to function as a projection of Edgar's own unfulfilled longings, as part of the wider mystery he seeks to uncover (EE,154). At the end of *Sommernovellette* a shooting star is likened to human life falling into the depths of an unknown fate (EE,208), but this is in reality an oblique way of suggesting the reverse: that human fate is like a shooting star, subject to hidden, irresistible forces. And in *Die Mondscheingasse*, where the setting in the backstreets of a Mediterranean port is subject to an unusual degree of personifica-tion (A,272-4), its alluring lights, the dissembling coyness of its closed blinds, its inviting posters, its masked alleyways are in a sense merely standing in for the human beings, the pimps and prostitutes, who inhabit this world.

In addition to these restrictions in scope it has also proved advisable to dispense with two possible refinements in the analysis of Zweig's metaphorical language. A complete account would no doubt make distinctions between metaphor in the narrow sense, simile, personification, analogy, and so forth. In practice, however, such distinctions reveal little of significance. As Ludwig Reiners argues, they are matters of outward form, not of substance.[12] Certainly, in the case of Zweig, whose choice of metaphorical form betrays no discernible pattern, they do not help to illuminate the image of man he presents. A complete account would also distinguish between the language of the narrator and that of his characters. Again, however, the pursuit of the distinction yields little profit. In choice of metaphor there is no significant difference between the language of the narrator and that of his characters. In view of the fact that the many inset narratives do not lay claim to literal accuracy in their reproduction of dialogue and in view of the suggestion noted earlier that these narratives by the characters have been subjected to editorial revision, this should not surprise us.

In approaching Zweig's imagery I have started from what I.A. Richards calls the 'vehicle',[13] that part of the metaphor which is applied by transference or extension to something else, and from the main areas of experience out of which the various vehicles are taken. Throughout, however, the aim has been to illuminate the writer's image of man, understood as the meaning deriving from the interaction of this vehicle with what Richards calls the 'tenor'[14] (here: some aspect of human activity). In short, I have sought to use metaphor as an interpretative tool, asking what the total image can tell us about the writer's understanding, even at moments when he is, so to speak, off his guard, not expressly concerned to communicate his image of man.

In *Geschichte in der Dämmerung* from the volume *Erstes Erlebnis* the 'Dämmerung' of the title signifies not merely that this is a story told *in* the twilight, but that its subject-matter is the ambiguous emotional world of adolescence. Not unnaturally, imagery associated with twilight achieves some prominence. It occurs most frequently to describe uncertain physical perceptions: the narrator describes himself as 'hindämmernd in Träumerei' when the story first occurs to him (EE,12); subsequently he depicts his young hero's refusal to confront reality in these words: 'Da blinzelt er heimlich zwischen den Lidern empor. Zuerst dämmert es nur purpurn rot, eine Wolke von unruhigem Licht, [. . .] ganz dämmerig sieht er sie' (EE,49). More significantly, it is used to convey that sense of mental confusion from which Bob finally begins to emerge: 'war nicht sein Leben aus einer trüben Dämmerung plötzlich in ein funkelndes und gefährliches Licht getreten [. . .]?' (EE,37).

Somewhat similar in its provenance is the imagery derived from meteorology. The verb 'stürmen' and the adverb 'stürmisch' are repeatedly used in connection with Bob's action. The noun 'Schwüle' is applied to the lips and the passion of the girl with whom he thinks he is in love (EE,23,39), while his desire appears 'wie ein roter Himmel' (EE,30). What is interesting in this pattern is not merely the degree of intensity conveyed, whether released or held in check, but the less obvious suggestion that we are dealing here with some natural phenomenon, perhaps beyond the control of man's moral decision or conscious will, as the weather itself is.

The two groups of images which occur most frequently in *Geschichte in der Dämmerung,* as indeed in Zweig's stories generally, are those concerned with fire and heat (or its opposite) and with water. While coolness of either appearance or attitude denotes indifference, flames are inevitably associated with passion: 'seine brennende Liebe zu ihr' (EE,35). At times, however, the imagery may be attached to appropriate parts of the body: 'brennende Lippen' (EE,17); 'er fühlt die Lippen wieder brennen' (EE,18). It may also be related to the lasting effects of an experience: 'jetzt hat sich [. . .] der Name Margots zu tief in ihn eingebrannt, als daß er ihn weglöschen könnte' (EE,52); or it may serve to express the intensity of passion: 'alles fühlt er auflodern' (EE,18); 'die jetzt so gedämpfte Glut ihrer Leidenschaft' (EE,52).

The water imagery is principally used to convey one of two ideas. On the one hand, it gives some impression of the emotional force to which the character is subject: 'Verlangen quillt in ihr auf' (EE,37); 'die heiße Welle der Lust [schießt] in ihm auf' (EE,35). On the other hand, it indicates a voluptuous relaxation, almost a dissolution of the harsh contours of individuality: 'Er fühlt sich irgendwie sinken und hinströmen unter diesem schwer atmenden Drängen' (EE,17); 'jetzt kann er sich wieder in die laue Flut seiner Träume badend stürzen' (EE,47). The body of the young woman with whom Bob is in love is sometimes described as a wave (EE,21) and even combines with some of the imagery just mentioned to form one extended metaphor: 'Wie gestern ist es wieder ein einziger Augenblick, da diese warme Welle unvermutet an seine Brust schlägt, daß er ohnmächtig zu werden glaubt von ihrem süßen Schlag und nur hinströmen will' (EE,22). Its immediate suggestion is that of sensuality, which plays such a prominent part in Zweig's thinking; but at a deeper level it reinforces what the water imagery in general implies: a fascination with the loss of conscious control, whether because of the power of overwhelming emotion or because of a narcotic self-abandonment. Such suggestions of a relaxing dissolution of individuality may seem appropriate to the adolescent hero of *Geschichte in der Dämmerung*, but when they are later repeated in the imagery of *Der Zwang*, where the possibility of resistance to militarism is at issue, they assume a much more disturbing quality.

The physical component in emotion, of which fire and water together also remind us, is emphasised still more by one of the most striking metaphorical patterns: that associated with eating and drinking. It appears most commonly in verbal forms such as 'saugen', 'einsaugen', or 'trinken' and is associated, not unnaturally, with kissing, since the lips are involved in both activities. The most remarkable single reference, however, is to the young woman's mouth as 'eine fremde aufgetane Frucht' (EE,17). There is no mistaking the sensuality implied. What is also note-worthy in all this is the added weight given to the instinctive aspect of what occurs. For as Zweig himself recalls in his essay on Freud, sucking at the breast ('saugen') may be regarded as the prototype of the libido.[15]

Something of the physical aspect of Bob's experience is also conveyed by the frequent recurrence of medical imagery and imagery associated with intoxication. In expressing the emotional problems of the young hero medical vocabulary occurs either in brief similes — 'geängstigt vor seiner erwachenden Leidenschaft, wie vor einem Gebrest' (EE,20) — or, most frequently in single words denoting fever, convulsion, or even dizziness: 'Neugier nach dem Zeichen fiebert in seinem Blut' (EE,24); 'das krampfig verhaltene Schluchzen der Lust' (EE,19); 'der Rausch, Schauer und Krampf des Besitzes' (EE,37); 'wie hatte er alle die beneidet, die so ruhig, so schwindelfrei und begierdelos waren' (EE,20). The overwhelming effect of the emotion is conveyed with almost equal frequency by the adjective 'trunken', the noun 'Rausch', its cognate verb 'berauschen', and — with the suggestion of still greater bodily incapacitation — by the verbs 'taumeln' and 'hintaumeln'. Over and above the intensity which Zweig again most obviously wishes to communicate, over and above the physical component in the emotion, we should not ignore the further implication that we are dealing here with a form of behaviour for which, as the meteorological vocabulary also suggests, the individual cannot be held fully responsible, behaviour which to some extent he himself suffers as a victim.

In a work like *Geschichte in der Dämmerung*, which deals with the sexual awakening of adolescence, we shall not be surprised to discover much erotic vocabulary. What does call for comment, however, is the degree to which this is used in a non-literal sense. It happens most insistently in connection with Bob's look: 'Wie ein Kuß streichelt sein Blick die runde [. . .] Linie ihrer Augenbrauen nach, [. . .] küßt die blasse, leise durchleuchtende Haut ihrer Wangen' (EE,28). This imagery is no mere ornament; it is all-too clearly intended to demonstrate the degree to which the hero's immature sexuality as yet finds only a surrogate outlet. For similar reasons, after a scene heavy with symbolism, in which Margot rides her horse so tempestuously that it leaves specks of white foam on her dress, Zweig can describe her leisurely return in language reminiscent of post-coital relaxation: 'den Körper schlaff zurückgehnt, erschöpft wie nach einer Wollust' (EE,31). Essentially, his language here is straining beyond the limits of metaphor to imply a more literal though oblique experience.

Perhaps because it does not receive satisfactory expression, the sexuality of these young people contains an unusual, even unhealthy degree of subjugation or the search for subjugation. Accordingly, the symbolic force of the riding episode, especially Margot's treatment of the horse, is confirmed by the imagery drawn from associated spheres which comes to be applied to the confused search for love. At times the vehicle of the metaphor recalls the activity of some animal-tamer, as when Bob approaches his mysterious lover with the intention 'sie zu bändigen' (EE,30), 'sie zu züchtigen' (EE,35). At other times it conjures up the world of the hunt. The verb 'locken' is repeatedly employed for Margot's powers of attraction (EE,23,24,41); Bob feels himself to be a victim ('Beute') of love in general (EE,17) or of her whim (EE,35); and when his uncertain feelings are further confused by the possibility that his mysterious lover may have been Margot's sister, Elisabeth, his meetings with *her* are said to be characterised by silence, 'einer den andern ängstlich belauernd' (EE,52). Finally, the sexual subservience of the adolescent hero is conveyed by the most insistent use of the verb 'umketten' and the cognate nouns 'Kette' and 'Umkettung' (EE,18,21,24), which conjure up a picture of either human enslavement or animal captivity.

The element of struggle and subjugation which the imagery of *Geschichte in der Dämmerung* so clearly underscores may be an understandable ingredient of immature sexuality. What is noteworthy, however, is not only that it will remain a powerful factor in many of Zweig's adult relationships, most strikingly in *Der Amokläufer* and *Die Mondscheingasse,* but also that the same image-clusters (derived from the hunt, animal captivity, enslavement) will also recur in those later works.

In *Verwirrung der Gefühle* there is a surfeit of imagery. The same is also true of *Phantastische Nacht*; and there one is tempted to take the baron's protestations that he has no literary talent more seriously than Zweig probably intended. Since, however, the narrator of the later work is a scholar, with many publications to his name, lack of literary ability can no longer provide an excuse. One is forced to the conclusion that, here as elsewhere, the densely metaphorical style is essentially the author's own.

Despite the vast quantity of metaphorical material in *Verwirrung der Gefühle* we need not dwell on what is already familiar. In terms of the vehicles used many image-clusters are little different from those already discussed, even though the tenor may sometimes vary. Fire and heat or cold again predominate, the former conveying a sense of passionate intensity which here covers intellectual enthusiasm and the hero's curiosity as well as the expected instinctive and sexual areas of life, the latter remarkable for the greater extremity of the formulations. 'Kühl' and 'kalt' are no longer always adequate to the contrastive drop in emotional temperature, which now frequently falls below zero, though not without some contravention of the laws of physics: 'Wie habe ich gelitten unter diesem [. . .] vom Heißen zum Kalten fahrenden Menschen, der mich unbewußt hitzte, um mich plötzlich mit Frost zu übergießen [!]' (VdG,204-5); 'ein einziges feiges Davonlaufen vor der Erkenntnis, daß diese fröhliche Festigkeit gar nicht so fröhlich sei und der Eisblock, der starre, mir noch ebenso schwer über dem Herzen hing' (VdG,242).

Water imagery is again second in frequency, with its suggestions of emotional force and of release after a period of retention. Its application here, however, also extends to the powerful verbal fluency of the professor, inspired by the presence of young students (VdG,171,183,185,198).

Meterological imagery is employed to express either emotional dullness (associated with clouds and mist) or intensity (usually marked by wind or storm). Elsewhere these same emotional extremes are communicated by clusters linked with death or mechanisation, on the one hand — especially as a value-judgement of what is seen as dry scholarship: e.g. 'Leichenkammer des Geistes' (VdG,159); 'anatomisieren' (VdG,174); 'Korrigier-maschine' (VdG,165); 'hier spulte ein abgenützter Professor sachlich sein Thema ab' (VdG,182) — and with intoxication or eating and drinking, on the other.

Intensity is also conveyed by much of the medical vocabulary, particularly that which speaks of fever and convulsion, though, as references to hypnosis and somnambulism also suggest — often as a description of the professor's effect on the young narrator (VdG,170,171) — the absence of rational, conscious control is a further ingredient in the conception of what is presented. Furthermore, when the professor's homosexuality is pictured as a kind of poisoning or an incurable disease (VdG,263,265), we are again being invited to regard it as something removed from the sphere of moral judgement, though not yet accepted into the world of healthy normality.

The problem of control over impulse or instinct is the chief import of the frequent and sometimes striking pattern of imagery drawn from animal-taming, which may equally well apply to the narrator as to his professor (VdG,161,184,226,265). Curiously, however, the very same image can elsewhere appear to depict the professor's own powerful hold over his pupils, which so subjugates their will: 'mit dem Worte wie mit einem Lasso sie an sich heranzog' (VdG,170); 'der mit seinem Ungestüm das eigene anstachelte, um dann plötzlich die Peitsche einer ironischen Bemerkung zu fassen' (VdG,205).

Similar in origin are those clusters whose vehicle conjures up the world of personal or military combat or that of the hunt. The tenor, however, may vary considerably. Combat is a fairly obvious way of describing the professor's unequal struggle against his own homosexuality (VdG,265,267); and its application to the immature erotic relations between the young hero and the professor's wife grows so naturally out of their actual sporting contests that one scarcely notices that it *is* often metaphor (VdG,247-50). Yet when the professor himself uses the language of combat to describe the cultural and intellectual advances of Elizabethan England (VdG,172-3), the distance between tenor and vehicle is much wider, the sense conveyed one of genuine heroism.

Predatory and venatorial images, on the other hand, especially in their suggestions of stalking, may characterise the hero's adolescent sexual forays, but they also reinforce the element of struggle in the relations between young Roland and the professor's wife (VdG,192-3) or between the watchful wife and a husband and young pupil who are growing too intimate for her liking (VdG,230). More interestingly, the idea of the hunt characterises the young hero's attempts to penetrate the fascinating secret of his admired professor: 'auf der Lauer' (VdG,189); 'dieser spürende Blick' (VdG,197); 'ein spähender, weidhafter Blick' (VdG,201). Although he is well-disposed towards his mentor, it is worth underlining this predatory element, because it is, as we have already observed, a common feature of curiosity in Zweig generally.

Remembering the links which Freud postulated between curiosity and sexuality, remembering the overtones of sexual surrender in the self-revelation of Mrs C. in *Vierundzwanzig Stunden aus dem Leben einer Frau* and remembering also that the very word 'revelation' has its origins in the removal of concealing veils, we shall not be surprised to find Roland's attempt to uncover his professor's secret depicted in sexual terms too, as though it were the undressing of a partner (VdG,197,263). Nor shall we be surprised to meet references to the professor's look in terms of physical embrace. More unusual is the way in which intellectual activity, such as the professor's lecturing, is given sexual connotations, not only in its seductive ('verführerisch') power over Roland (VdG,189) and its fertilising role ('Zeugung') in his intellectual development (VdG,156), but also in the suggestions of post-coital exhaustion in the professor himself:

wie gestern lehnte er erschöpft an dem Tisch, das Gesicht bleich, aber noch überrieselt von kleinen zuckenden Läufen und Trillern der Nerven, und im Auge glimmerte merkwürdig die weiterströmende Wollust der Ergießung wie bei einer

251

Frau, die eben sich übermächtiger Umarmung entrungen.
(VdG,186)

Much of this imagery, in which Roland implicitly performs the receptive, female role, is undoubtedly intended to make the reader aware of the sexual content of the relationship long before the hero's realisation. Its link with the intellect, however, serves also as one of several reminders of that contrast between what Zweig sees as dry scholarship and a living, emotionally satisfying kind of learning.

Since *Verwirrung der Gefühle* is in part concerned with what is presented as a duality in the professor, an inspirational gift for teaching alternating with a degrading homosexuality, we shall not be surprised to find religious and cloacal imagery reflecting that duality. Yet there is also a duality within the religious vocabulary itself, which, in its positive aspects, is usually an expression of the hero's devotion to his teacher — 'wie eines Evangelisten Wort' (VdG,189); 'bisher hatte meine knabenhaft andächtige Verehrung den vergötterten Lehrer dermaßen als Genius einer anderen Welt empfunden' (VdG,196) — and operates in harness with the frequent hints of some magical attraction in the older man, while, in its negative aspects, it describes the professor's sexual transgressions, which take him through 'Höllenwege' into some 'Unterwelt' (VdG,265). As is also the case in *Phantastische Nacht*, however, the imagery betrays a moral uncertainty. For not only does the negative religious vocabulary imply some diminution of personal responsibility, with its reference to 'dämonische Triebe' (VdG,263) and its view of the professor as 'ein Gezeichneter' (VdG,264); it occasionally seems to elevate the homosexuality to the status of sacred suffering, speaking of it, for example, in terms of 'Kreuzgang' (VdG,264).[16] The cloacal vocabulary, on the other hand, tends to be reserved for the moral depravity of those the professor meets and not for him, as though he could be soiled by the experience, but could not soil others; and if it expresses distaste, it also reveals a tendency to wallow, to enjoy the *frisson* of what it avowedly abhors. Indeed the narrator virtually admits as much at one point:

> Ist es Bequemlichkeit, Feigheit oder ein zu kurzes Gesicht,
> daß [die Schriftsteller] immer nur den obern erhellten
> Lichtsaal des Lebens zeichnen, wo die Sinne offen und
> gesetzhaft spielen, indes unten in den Kellergewölben, in den

Wurzelhöhlen und Kloaken des Herzens phosphorhaft
funkelnd die wahren, die gefährlichen Bestien der Leidenschaft umfahren [. . .]? Schreckt sie der Atem, der heiße und
zehrende der dämonischen Triebe, der Dunst des brennenden
Blutes, fürchten sie die Hände zu schmutzen [. . .] an den
Schwären der Menschheit, oder findet ihr Blick [. . .] nicht
hinab diese glitschigen, gefährlichen, von Fäulnis triefenden
Stufen? Und doch ist dem Wissenden keine Lust gleich als
jene am Verborgenen, keine Schauer so urmächtig stark, als
der das Gefährliche umfröstelt, und kein Leiden heiliger, als
das sich aus Scham nicht zu entäußern vermag. (VdG,263)

Other groups of images from *Verwirrung der Gefühle*, although
not entirely new in Zweig's language, come into consideration now
because they have not so far appeared with sufficient significance
to require comment.

In dealing with the subject of sexual confusion and homosexuality he naturally employs the language of sexual roles, often with
the suggestion of trans-sexuality. On the level of physical appearance the narrator stresses the ambiguous quality of his professor's
face, with its manly brow but feminine chin (VdG,176), and
repeatedly refers to the boyish figure of the professor's wife
(VdG,193,249). Here the degree of transference from the literal
meaning is small, the intention to provide an oblique hint of the
professor's inclinations and the reasons for his original attraction
to his wife (cf. especially VdG,266). The same sort of language,
however, may also be used of the young hero's first trembling
response to his mentor, for 'nichts ist ja leidenschaftlicher als die
Verehrung eines Jünglings, nichts scheuer, nichts frauenhafter als
ihre unruhige Scham' (VdG,186). One of the adjectives repeatedly
introduced to portray the wife's boyishness, however, seems
intended to remind us of Ancient Greece. The word is 'ephebisch'
(properly applied to Athenian youths of military age); and the
nominal form also occurs in the summarised account of the
professor's first years as a university teacher, when 'die
Versuchung [schiebt ihm] atemnah neue Blüte der Jugend her,
Epheben eines unsichtbaren Gymnasions innerhalb der
preußischen Paragraphenwelt' (VdG,267). As the context makes
clear, the whole notion of the ephebe is part of the wider attempt
to ennoble the professor's homosexuality by placing it in a
hallowed cultural tradition.

253

Ennoblement is probably also one of the motives behind the widespread use of musical imagery, which we have not encountered before *Verwirrung der Gefühle* and which is here applied almost exclusively to the professor's speech, whether he is lecturing, dictating his book to his disciple, or telling his life-story. It suggests a quality of communication which goes beyond referential discourse and attains the realm of art.[17] What is also implied, however, is power, which derives not only from the professor's dominant personality — expressed repeatedly in the image of a commanding orchestral conductor (VdG,170,174,185) — but from the emotional force of his language:

> Wie ein Zymbalschläger sich berauscht an dem immer wilderen Rhythmus seiner eifernden Händen, so wurde seine Rede immer besser, immer flammender [. . .], und je tiefer wir schwiegen [. . .], um so hymnischer schwang seine Darstellung sich auf. (VdG,185)

> und doch fühlte man gerade an dieser mühsamen Beherrschung der Leidenschaft ihre kommende Gewalt, so wie man an gewissen gewaltsam verlangsamten Takten, die einem jagenden Rhythmus vorausgehen, das Furioso schon in den Nerven vorausspürt. (VdG,263-4)

Considered together and in context, these images have an additional effect of more general significance for Zweig: they transfer the emphasis from the rational, logical aspects of speech to those qualities which appeal to the emotions and operate below the level of consciousness.

One of the most frequent image-clusters of *Verwirrung der Gefühle* is formed around the notion of torment or torture. It characterises both the professor's homosexual problems and the mental sufferings which the young hero undergoes in his confused dealings with his mentor. Much of the time the imagery does not rise above the cliché 'Qual' or 'quälen', but occasionally it takes on such colour and force that it demands more serious attention. Roland's anxious devotion makes him regard the older man as someone 'vor dem lächerlich zu erscheinen mir qualvoller ankam, als nackt auf dem offenen Marktplatz ausgepeitscht zu sein' (VdG,195). Later, picturing his professor as some 'Peiniger' (cf. VdG,239), he reacts as follows: 'Warum martert er mich, fragte meine zerrende Qual sich hundertmal, warum haßt er mich so, daß er eigens des Nachts die Treppe sich emporschleicht, nur um mir dann feindselig solche Beleidigung ins Gesicht zu schlagen?' (VdG,235). Beyond the obvious and sometimes embarrassing quest for intensity of expression, beyond the physical implications of the emotion described, the imagery of torture, when applied to the professor, may also serve to elevate the significance of his problems. Of his confession near the end of the work Roland writes: 'Eine wilde Wollust folterte sich flagellantisch frei in diesem durch Jahre und Jahre verhaltenen Geständnis' (VdG,263). His attempts to master his sexual inclinations are described as 'Qualen des Tantalus' (VdG,267). If the first of these quotations closely echoes Zweig's account of Tolstoy's tendency to self-abasing confession, his 'fanatische und flagellantische Lust an der Selbstgeißelung' after his religious crisis,[18] the second calls to mind the extended metaphor of torment and the analogies with Job, the wrestling Jacob, and a titan which he uses to characterise Dostoyevsky's life of suffering, his heroic struggle against fate.[19] Whether the world conjured up is that of the religious fanatic or of some ancient and hallowed myth, the unmistakable intention, as with the other religious and musical vocabulary considered earlier, is throughout to ennoble the subject, to raise his problems to a level beyond that which bourgeois normality can ever reach.

Revealing as all these individual images and clusters are, there remains one further source of insight into Zweig's metaphorical perceptions in *Verwirrung der Gefühle*, which has a much wider relevance. I refer to the account which the professor gives of the rise of Elizabethan drama, especially the version he dictates to the eager pen of Roland in a flood of inspired intensity. The very content of his dictation is elemental passion. For he conceives this spate of dramatic talent not as a matter of chance, but as a natural development out of England's geographical position. Surrounded by the boundless ocean, the plaything of its storms, the English nation itself became characterised by 'stürmische Leidenschaften', so that when political peace was established, it continued to desire 'das Meer, den harten Sturz des Geschehens mit seiner täglichen Gefahr', a desire which it fulfilled first in bloodsports, bear-baiting and cock-fighting, then in human combat, and finally in the drama, 'jenes andere große wogende Spiel vom Menschen, Wiederkehr all jener Abenteuer und Fahrten, nur aber auf den inneren Meeren des Herzens' (VdG,211-12). As a proposed explanation of origins this account of Elizabethan drama posits a contiguous, causal relation between the surrounding sea, man's vulnerability and love of adventure, his interest in bloodsports, combat, and human passions; but it is evident from the context that these various aspects of English experience are also conceived of as parables or metaphors of passion of varying kinds. In particular, it becomes clear that those image-patterns associated with the sea, with animal-taming, and with combat are anchored in a deeper conception of the elemental nature of all passion. Taking a more general view, one may also therefore regard the content of the professor's account as a confirmation of the inter-pretative significance of Zweig's image-patterns, however lacking in originality they may be.

In *Unvermutete Bekanntschaft mit einem Handwerk*, where interest is focussed on an encounter between the narrator and a man whom society at large would simply condemn as a criminal, the metaphorical language proves an even more powerful rhetorical weapon. In setting the 'criminal' in a wider context and establishing several unusual conceptual links, it presents a persuasive if indirect challenge to the reader's moral judgements.

The imagery of water, already familiar from earlier works, here acquires a special significance. Whether it is the sea or a river in spate that provides the vehicle, what is conjured up — often in extended metaphors — is the mass of people who pour into the streets of Paris at certain times of day or who are pressed together in an auction room: 'So war es Mittag geworden, die Stunde der großen Flut, da plötzlich die kleinen Gassen und Gäßchen, die Treppen und Höfe viele kleine einzelne Wildbäche von Menschen in das breite Strombett des Boulevards schwemmen' (K,23); 'Immer stärker wurde meine Besorgnis, je mehr wir uns dem Boulevard näherten, schon hörte man das Brausen seines ewigen Katarakts' (K,33); 'wogt jedes Mal eine zufällige Masse von bloß Neugierigen' (K,35); 'entspannte sich die zusammengekeilte Masse in einer erregten Welle' (K,41). Against this background, the collective force of the mass, the narrator emerges at first as a man rather like the adolescent hero of *Geschichte in der Dämmerung*, content to drift with the current ('treiben'), without purpose or obligation. This changes only when he discovers the pickpocket, bobbing up and down like some sea-creature (K,21,24, cf. 45), temporally isolated from the mass: 'So wie die Brandung manchmal mit unbegreiflicher Beharrlichkeit eine einzige schmutzige Alge an den Strand spült und sofort mit ihrer nassen Zunge wieder zurückschluckt [. . .], so schwemmte diese eine Gestalt immer wieder mit dem Wirbel heran' (K,11); 'die auflockende Welle hatte ihn [. . .] gerade zu mir hergeschwemmt' (K,41). There is of course a markedly visual element in this imagery, but we should not overlook its additional suggestion that this man, for all his shabbiness, has maintained some separate identity, individuality, among an undifferentiated mass, which appears, by contrast, as 'ein langweiliges Spülicht schmutzigen Menschenwassers, das immer farbloser und grauer strömte' (K,11).

One of the commonest image-clusters in *Unvermutete Bekanntschaft mit einem Handwerk* derives from the animal kingdom. Here, using a relatively high proportion of similes, Zweig deploys a considerable variety and novelty. The sense conveyed by the images is not one of sub-human intelligence, as it is, for example, in *Leporella*, nor one of instinctive, non-rational activity, as it is in parts of *Vierundzwanzig Stunden aus dem Leben einer Frau*. The images may serve to expose the foibles or pretensions of those who attend the auction: the jobbers and middlemen 'die unvermeidlichen Hyänen des Schlachtfeldes'; bespectacled librarians like 'schläfrige Tapire'; society ladies like 'bunte Paradiesvögel'; the connoisseurs still and unmoved like cranes; the self-important auctioneer like a peacock (K,35 and 38). More important, however, are the many and varied animal images associated with the pickpocket, which are devoid of any disparagement and convey instead an admiration for his qualities of lightness, speed, and elusiveness: 'Häschen' (K,12), 'Goldfisch', 'Windhund', 'Aal' (K,24), 'Wiesel' (K,26), 'Katze' (K,41), 'Schlange', 'Vogel' (K,43). Only at the very end is a more disturbing note struck, when the narrator catches the thief picking *his* pocket and could so easily hand him over to the police. Now, in closer proximity to the suggestions of the animal imagery one finds in *Der Zwang*, Zweig reveals in the pickpocket something of the suffering of the victim — here the social victim — whose pleading eyes betray 'die Urangst aller Kreatur' and who looks up to the narrator 'so hündisch' (K,44).

From the notion of elusiveness and capture it is only a short step to a whole cluster of images related to the concept of the hunt in its different forms. What is remarkable here is not the various spheres of human activity to which the vehicle of these images is severally applied, but the implications which stem from the parallelism of the application. There is nothing surprising in the use of piscatorial and venatorial images to depict the operations of the pickpocket: 'stieß zu wie mit einer Harpune' (K,13); 'indes [die] Hand die Brieftasche oder die Uhr mardert' (K,17); 'während du die gepaschte Geldbörse ausweidest' (K,29). They are also applied, however, to the curiosity with which the narrator pursues this specimen for inclusion in Zweig's human zoo, a curiosity reminiscent of that already noted in connection with Roland and his professor's secret in *Verwirrung der Gefühle*: 'Aber ich wartete mit dem leisen fröstelnden Zittern des Anglers auf jenen gewissen Ruck' (K,10); 'Was treibst du da in meinem Revier? Schärfer und schärfer nahm ich ihn aufs Korn' (K,12; cf. also K,15); 'ich [hatte] so lange und ingrimmig auf der Lauer gelegen' (K,13). This twofold application of the venatorial imagery invites the reader to ponder whether the 'criminal' is essentially any more reprehensible than the 'honest' spectator, since both, in very different ways and for different reasons, prey on their victims. Similarly, the suggestions of falconry associated with the auction, to which the public is lured ('herangelockt', K,35) and where the auctioneer hurls ever-increasing figures into the air 'wie einen Falken nach Beute' (K,40), challenge the reader, in a way which even Brecht might have applauded, to consider the revolutionary thought that so-called legitimate business may be little different from theft.

At one point, however, the imagery conjures up again the picture of a man who is no longer the hunter, nor merely an object of even predatory curiosity, but a hounded victim of social circumstance. When the narrator follows him into a café, where, in all his wretchedness and poverty, he greedily swallows a glass of milk, the pickpocket now emerges as 'einer von den unzähligen Armen und Gejagten und Kranken und Jämmerlichen dieser schief gezimmerten Welt' (K,30). Pity and shame are now the narrator's response to this 'unglücklich gejagten Menschen' (K,31).

If the military vocabulary is less pronounced than that associated with the hunt, it nevertheless fulfils a similar role, providing a further link between the activities of pickpocket, narrator and auctioneer in their search for advantage over or gain from others. It is not just the pickpocket who employs military tactics (K,36), eyeing those who enter his 'Schußfeld' (K,20), making quick movements like a torpedo (K,38). The whole auction, as we have seen, is a battlefield (K,35); and the narrator, in his fascinated pursuit, resorts to the ruse of buying a newspaper 'um mich besser hinter ihr verschanzen zu können' (K,30). The climax of the story, during which first the narrator is the victim of the pickpocket's attempted theft and then the pickpocket, once caught in the act, is subject to the narrator's power to expose him, is also pictured as a battle (K,44), at the end of which 'mein Unglücksgefährte das Feld geräumt [hatte]' (K,45). If life is a battlefield, there will be losers; but no one, it appears, may claim self-righteously to be an innocent civilian. All are involved in some way.

The most striking image-cluster of *Unvermutete Bekanntschaft mit einem Handwerk* is taken from the world of gambling. As a literal activity gambling plays a prominent part in both *Phantastische Nacht* and *Vierundzwanzig Stunden aus dem Leben einer Frau*, where it forms a paradigm of uncontrollable passion and desperate commitment.[20] As a metaphor it appears several times in the earlier *Brennendes Geheimnis*, where it serves, however, to underline especially the element of play ('Spiel') in the baron's amorous overtures to Edgar's mother. In the present work the image helps to make a significant distinction between the two contrasting aspects, between the fascinated but ultimately detached excitement of the narrator and the dangerous commitment of the pickpocket himself. The former approaches the whole encounter with a sense of 'Spiellust' (K,13)[21] or 'Sportfreude' (K,25); watching the pickpocket at work, he is like an onlooker at a game of cards ('der Kiebitz'), who is itching to intervene, but who stands to lose no money himself (K,21); or, as he later admits, in greater awareness of the realities of the pickpocket's condition, he is like a punter deriving his excitement from the effort of another: 'ich schämte mich, jetzt schon zwei Stunden diesen unglücklichen gejagten Menschen wie ein Rennpferd für meine Neugier seinen dunklen Weg laufen zu lassen' (K,31). For the thief himself the exploits entail 'Spielgefährlichkeit' (K,18); they demand the exercise of effort, courage, danger, skill, which the narrator several times describes in terms of 'Einsatz' (K,22,25,29); they are an expression of independence, not because he may suffer an occasional 'Niete' (K,29), but because they may cost him that

259

liberty he so much cherishes: 'dieser aber war einer von den Trotzigen, die lieber ihre persönliche Freiheit in gefahrvollste Weise einsetzen, statt zu betteln' (K,31).

A final group of images derives from the world of art and literature. We have already noted the elevating intention of the musical language of *Verwirrung der Gefühle*. Here the same process is extended to become a significant part of a reciprocal relation between narrator and pickpocket. The numerous references to the latter's method as 'Kunst' (K,16,18,21,33,35)[22] are not in themselves remarkable, since the word may also be used of various kinds of skill; but the noun 'Künstler', which occurs only slightly less frequently (K,18,22,27,29), has a more specialised meaning and makes more serious claims to genuine artistry. This is further confirmed by the repeated comparison with a literary artist — for which Zweig uses the word 'Dichter' rather than the less exalted 'Schriftsteller' — whose work entails creativity as well as fine judgement:

> Denn ein Dieb ist doch Dieb nur eigentlich in dem Augenblick, da er diebt, und nicht zwei Monate später, da er für seine Tat vor dem Richter steht, so wie der Dichter wesenhaft nur Dichter ist, während er schafft, und nicht etwa, wenn er ein paar Jahre hernach am Mikrophon sein Gedicht vorliest. (K,17)

> Genau wie der dichterisch Schaffende an tausend scheinbar lockenden und ergiebigen Einfällen gleichgültig vorübergeht (nur der Dilettant faßt gleich mit verwegener Hand zu), um alle Kraft für den letzten Einsatz zu sparen, so ging auch dieses kleine, miekrige Männchen an hundert einzelnen Chancen vorbei [. . .] (K,22)

It is probably no accident that, by contrast, when Zweig later comes to describe the showy, commercial activities of the auctioneer, he chooses less sublime forms of art for his vehicle, picturing him as an acrobat or 'Animiermädchen' (K,37). What all this means is that, while the predatory component in the narrator's curiosity brings him down to the level of the pickpocket, the artistic dimension in the latter's stealing raises him to the level of the narrator. In the end, therefore, the two men are linked by more than the fascination of one; a similar spirit and value are also implied. This is an important interpretative point, which can only fully be appreciated after proper attention has been paid to the metaphorical language.

In *Schachnovelle*, as in *Der Zwang*, Zweig is concerned to establish a contrast between the human and the inhuman; and as in the earlier work, he uses animal and mechanical imagery to underline the contrast. It is not the case, however, as one might have supposed, that the animal and mechanical imagery is reserved for the one-sided chess-champion Czentovic, nor that its implications are always negative.

At times, it is true, the animal imagery registers a lamentable lack of fully human imagination, intelligence, or sensitivity in Czentovic. This is so, for example, in the early account of him sitting stubbornly 'mit jenem leeren Blick, wie ihn Schafe auf der Weide haben' (S,12); in the report that, when confronted by a man of culture, he crawls back 'in sein Schneckenhaus' (S,23); and in the adjectival forms of the subsequent references to his 'dickfellige Grobheit' (S,37) or to his role as a 'kaltschnäuziger Gegner' (S,39). If that comes closer to the inhuman implications of the animal imagery in *Leporella,* other references suggest more of a patronising admiration on the part of other people, as if Czentovic were an animal of exceptional curiosity-value on account of its rarity or some peculiar ability. Even from the beginning the narrator is informed by a friend: 'Sie haben da einen raren Vogel an Bord' (S,9), which encourages him 'dieses sonderbare Spezimen [. . .] unter die Lupe zu nehmen' (S,22); and in the account of Czentovic's earlier life the first unexpected sign of his remarkable talent for chess prompts a half-jocular reference to Balaam's ass, which is explained with the words: 'schon vor zweitausend Jahren hätte sich ein ähnliches Wunder ereignet, daß ein stummes Wesen plötzlich die Sprache der Weisheit gefunden habe' (S,14).

Remarkably, the more consistently serious use of animal imagery relates to the humane Dr B. The occasions are few, but the significance all the greater. At the climax of the story, in his second game against the world champion, Dr B.'s pathological excitement becomes so great as to threaten his humanity: 'Sobald Dr B. merkte, daß Czentovic den Springer faßte [. . .], duckte er sich zusammen wie eine Katze vor dem Ansprung' (S,106); 'Erst als beim vierten Zug Czentovic wieder endlos überlegte, verließ ihn die Haltung, und er fauchte ihn plötzlich an' (S,112). Even here, however, Dr B. is not allowed to forfeit our sympathy. In the first place, we do not forget that his dangerous condition is a result of the inhuman treatment he received during his solitary confinement. Indeed the imagery seems to imply a direct link between his brutish outburst now and his earlier sensory deprivation. For the effect of that deprivation was to make him seize on the stolen chess-manual with all the instinctive ferocity of a starved animal: '[meine Augen] krallten sich gierig an jede Einzelheit' (S,71). In the second place, Dr B. is able to overcome the present threat by resigning his match with Czentovic and abandoning chess completely. The animal element in Czentovic, on the other hand, remains as a permanent deficiency.

As to the mechanical imagery, its application to Czentovic forms part of a wider cluster derived from the notion of inanimateness. To the extent that some machine is implied — as in the references to 'intellektuelle Eingleisigkeit' (S,22) and 'dieser unmenschliche Schachautomat' (S,37) — it is internal in origin and does not, as it does in *Der Zwang*, represent some force threatening man from outside. More insistent, however, is the pattern which pictures Czentovic as constituted of impervious stone. Even from an early stage his exclusive interest in obtaining financial gain from chess is said to be locked away 'in seinem vermauerten Gehirn' (S,21), where, one assumes it is inaccessible to persuasion or appeal. Yet it is above all in his encounter with Dr B. that his imperviousness appears most clearly. He remains seated facing his opponent, 'unbeweglich wie ein Block' (S,103); looks at him 'mit steinernem Blick' (S,109); and as his moves become drawn out intolerably, 'versteinte gleichsam immer mehr' (S,113). The cold insensibility of Czentovic implied in this metaphorical pattern also means that, as with that other specimen of one-sided mental prowess, Jakob Mendel, other human beings are of little concern to him. They are ignored as if they were 'tote Holzfiguren' (S,37), possessing no life or value of their own, to be manipulated presumably to serve his interests. Lack of true humanity, one is led to conclude, entails the inability to perceive humanity in others.[23]

In the case of Dr B. a single reference to a glassy stare at the end of the story represents merely a temporary loss of mental life, a brief interlude between the morbid excitement of his play and the positive assertion of his moral will in renunciation. More important, however, is the widespread mechanical imagery, sometimes in the form of an extended metaphor, which characterises certain aspects of Dr B.'s life during his confinement. What distinguishes it from the similar imagery used in *Der Zwang* is that it is here no longer applied directly to those inhuman forces which operate on man from outside, but to the effects which such forces have on the mind of the individual, reducing it to the level of some soulless machine. These are some of the outstanding statements of that process:

> Aber diese Gedanken, einmal angekurbelt im leeren Raum, hörten nicht auf, im Kopf zu rotieren. (S,65)

> Kaum ich die erste Eröffnung getan, klöppelte sich ihr Ablauf gleichsam automatisch in mir ab. (S,82)

> Ein solches Doppeldenken setzt eigentlich eine vollkommene Spaltung des Bewußtseins voraus, ein beliebiges Auf- und Abblendenkönnen der Gehirnfunktion wie bei einem mechanischen Apparat. (S,83)

Both animal and mechanical imagery, then, express a loss of true humanity. Their differentiated approach, however, serves to underline an important distinction between what is a permanent and inherent feature of the chess champion and what is an artificially imposed condition of limited duration in Dr B.

Throughout the entire story Zweig is naturally at pains to maintain a sharp contrast between the two central characters; and this is expressed nowhere more clearly than in the familiar metaphors of heat and light. While heat characterises the unhealthy excitement to which Dr B. is subject in consequence of his enforced isolation (S,73,76) and which returns in his match against the world champion (S,110,113,115), coldness is the unchanging feature of Czentovic's emotional world: 'kalte Logik' (S,19); 'kalter [. . .] Stolz' (S,21); 'diesen kühlen, verächtlichen Blick' (S,31); 'den kalten Hochmut' (S,44). The imagery of coldness and inanimateness, both of which recur in Zweig's portrait of the scheming chief police Joseph Fouché,[24] are sufficient in themselves to prevent Czentovic from ever becoming a sympathetic figure.

The intense excitement to which Dr B. is subject is also conveyed in two other familiar image-clusters, which require comment only in so far as they extend the range of either tenor or vehicle. The imagery of eating is noteworthy above all for the emphasis placed on the preceding hunger, that is, the sensory and intellectual

263

deprivation of his captivity: 'Auge, Ohr, alle Sinne bekamen von morgens bis nachts [. . .] nicht die geringste Nahrung' (S,61); 'mit meinen ausgehungerten Augen' (S,71). It is this spiritual starvation which explains and to some extent justifies the 'Unersättlichkeit' (S,89) and 'Gier' (S,72,76,78,90,91,94) with which he then seizes on any stimulus: 'wie in meinem Hunger nach Gedrucktem, nach Geschriebenem ich diese Zahl [. . .] anstarrte: ich fraß sie in mein Gehirn hinein' (S,70). At an earlier stage in Dr B.'s account the notion of eating is also applied, unusually though not insistently, to the destructive effect of his sensory deprivation: 'wie es einen zerfrißt und zerstört, dieses Nichts und Nichts und Nichts um einen' (S,68). Different as the tenor here is, it forms part of the same rhetorical defence, preparing the way for the greed with which he consumes new intellectual material by portraying him as the consumed victim.

The medical vocabulary is both more widespread and more complex. In the earlier stages of Dr B.'s confinement the predominant idea is that of choking on food, which might appear at first sight to contradict the notion of starvation just discussed. In fact, however, it reinforces the intention of that pattern, because what chokes Dr B. is not some newly-ingested material, but an unproductive rumination (concerning those whose safety depends on his secrecy) to which he is condemned in the absence of external stimulus: 'ich sollte doch würgen und würgen an meinen Gedanken, bis sie mich erstickten und ich nicht anders konnte, als sie schließlich ausspeien' (S,66); 'um dem Würgen dieses Nichts zu entkommen [. . .] in diesem Augenblick des Erstickens' (S,68-9).

Subsequently it is the familiar notion of fever which becomes most insistent as a description of the excitement that attends Dr B.'s games of chess, whether alone in his cell or, later, against Czentovic aboard ship (S,88,90,101,102,108,110,115). What is interesting about this pattern is that Zweig here provides a (metaphorical) medical cause for his hero's feverish symptoms. When the idea of stealing a book first enters his head, it acts 'wie ein starkes Gift' (S,73) and even produces physical symptoms. Thereafter, having discovered that the book is a chess-manual and having devoured its contents avidly, he is subject to what he twice describes as a 'Schachvergiftung' (S,91,102). Once, admittedly, he can refer to the effect of this renewed mental stimulus as 'heilsam' (S,87), but this merely underlines the dilemma to which he is so cruelly exposed: that of seeking a cure which may be as harmful to him as his sickness, that is, of combating the threat of insanity by a method which may simply lead to insanity in a different form.

Considered together, the language of eating (or starving) and sickness leads us beyond a perception of the intensity of Dr B.'s excitement to a sympathetic appraisal of its roots, which here go back farther than the unwilled instinct of, say, the professor of *Verwirrung der Gefühle* to the active brutality of a corrupt political system.

A further contrast by which Zweig seeks to enlist our sympathy for Dr B. is based on the relative development of imaginative powers and their alleged superiority over mere memory. Unfortunately, the musical and literary imagery which is employed in support of this conviction is not always well enough thought out to sustain a just contrast. Although one may accept as illuminating and legitimate the comparison between Dr B.'s ability to visualise games of chess from the formulae set out in a book and that of a practised musician who can recreate in his mind a full orchestral sound from the printed score (S,79), and although one may applaud his subsequent ability to play chess 'blind', the analogy which is earlier drawn to illustrate Czentovic's defective imaginative powers is not entirely appropriate. He is said to need the chess-board in front of his eyes, 'wie wenn unter Musikern ein hervorragender Virtuose oder Dirigent sich unfähig gezeigt hätte, ohne aufgeschlagene Partitur zu spielen oder zu dirigieren' (S,18). Despite the close similarity of vehicle in these analogies, which positively invites the contrast of character, careful attention to the example just quoted suggests not a want of imagination, but an inability to memorise, itself a gift which Dr B. deems inferior to imagination, when he likens his reproduction of other people's games of chess, in contrast to his growing ability to create games of his own, to the undemanding memorising of poetry (S,86). It would be easy to excuse this as a technical lapse of no further consequence. Yet just as successful metaphor can exert a powerful persuasive influence on the reader's judgements, so also a false analogy can undermine his confidence in the author's evaluation and seriously obstruct the thrust of the narrative.

By far the commonest cluster of images in *Schachnovelle* is drawn from the sphere of private or military combat. This is not at all surprising, because, on the one hand, it requires only a minor extension of meaning to speak of the 'Raublust' of the Nazis (S,59) or, with the same deliberately primitivising anachronism, of Hitler's 'Raubzüge' against ecclesiastical property (S,54) and because, on the other hand, the game of chess, which performs such a crucial role in all the major conflicts of the story, is one which is played between two individual opponents, but is at the same time a metaphor of battle, deriving much of its language from the tactics of war — cf. 'Abwehrtechnik' (S,24); 'Angriff', 'Verteidigung' (S,80) — and culminating in the symbolic death of one commander-in-chief (checkmate = the king is dead).

Although, for the narrator of this story, chess is an expression of man's intellect and imagination, an assertion of the mind's victory over mere chance — it is the royal game, 'das sich souverän jeder Tyrannis des Zufalls entzieht und seine Siegespalmen einzig dem Geist [. . .] zuteilt' (S,24) — it remains for him also a game. For others, however, chess becomes an entirely serious activity, for which Zweig invents the strange verb 'ernsten' (S,28).

This is the case above all with Czentovic, who has so concentrated his attention on chess that success within this limited sphere represents for him 'Lebenstriumphe' (S,26), but whose early victories over opponents of superior intelligence prompt the narrator to draw some remarkable historical analogies: 'Die verwegensten Champions [. . .] erlagen ebenso seiner zähen und kalten Logik, wie Napoleon dem schwerfälligen Kutusow, wie Hannibal dem Fabius Cunctator' (S,18f). It is also the case with the imprisoned Dr B., who only afterwards realises what a boon he has gained ('erobert') in the stolen chess-manual, for it proves 'eine wunderbare Waffe gegen die erdrückende Monotonie des Raumes und der Zeit' (S,79). In addition, as we noted in an earlier chapter, it becomes evident that, in his exclusion from genuine political activity, this chess provides his only means of opposition to a hated regime, an opposition which is then weakened when, having exhausted the games set out in the manual, he begins to play against himself. Now the language of combat describes an unproductive internal struggle, between the two chess opponents into which he is forced to divide himself or, in consequence of that, against his own manic obsession with chess:

> Von dem Augenblick an, da ich aber gegen mich zu spielen versuchte, begann ich mich unbewußt herauszufordern. Jedes meiner beiden Ich, mein Ich Schwarz und mein Ich Weiß

[. . .] gerieten jedes für sein Teil in einen Ehrgeiz, in eine Ungeduld, zu siegen [. . .] Jedes meiner beiden Ich triumphierte, wenn das andere einen Fehler machte. (S,87)

Etwas in mir wollte recht behalten, und ich hatte doch nur dieses andere Ich in mir, das ich bekämpfen konnte. [. . .] kaum war eine Partie beendigt, so forderte ich mich schon zur nächsten heraus, denn jedesmal war doch eines der beiden Schach-Ich von dem andern besiegt und verlangte Revanche. (S,88)

The element of genuine conflict contained in the metaphors of combat and the extent to which these inner battles represent a surrogate form of resistance to Dr B.'s external enemy are both confirmed by what happens at the critical point of his mental derangement: during the course of a game which he is playing against himself his impatience becomes so intense that he shouts out at his other self and, when a warder enters his room, seizes him by the throat as though he were the opponent — which in a representative sense he is. In this context metaphor is more than just a linguistic resource; it is part of a psychological strategy. In much the same way as an international football match may be regarded not only as a ritualised metaphor of combat, but also as a harmless substitute for actual warfare, an alternative outlet for aggression, so too the chess which Dr B. plays in his confinement, with all its metaphors of combat, may be interpreted as a (psychologically more harmful) substitute for the political opposition which is denied to him.

Above all it is the two matches between Czentovic and Dr B. in the narrative frame which see the highest concentration of images of combat. Their particular interest derives not so much from their application to the moves of what in other circumstances might be considered simply a game as from the way in which they conjure up the more serious conflict of two very different personalities. Here are just a few of many examples:

Czentovic verlängerte seine Überlegungspause; daran spürten wir, daß der eigentliche Kampf um die Vorhand einzusetzen begann. (S,104)

Czentovic hatte die Partie aufgegeben. Er hatte kapituliert, um nicht vor uns ächtbar mattgesetzt zu werden. [. . .] der Weltmeister, der Champion zahlloser Turniere hatte die

Fahne gestrichen vor einem Unbekannten. [. . .] Unser
Freund [. . .] hatte den stärksten Schachspieler der Erde in
offenem Kampfe besiegt! (S,108-9)

Es waren nicht zwei Partner mehr, die ihr Können spielhaft
aneinander proben wollten, es waren zwei Feinde, die sich
gegenseitig zu vernichten geschworen. [. . .] Offenbar hatte
der geschulte Taktiker schon herausgefunden, daß er gerade
durch seine Langsamkeit den Gegner ermüdete und irritierte.
(S,110-11)

Erst nachdem er diesen seinen uns noch unverständlichen
Triumph bis zur Neige genossen, wandte er sich mit falscher
Höflichkeit unserer Runde zu. (S,114-15)

In the penultimate example it could be argued that the language of
combat has exceeded the bounds of metaphor and assumed a
literal truth. Yet that merely underlines the purpose of the genuine
metaphors, which is to make the reader aware of the extent to
which the encounter across the chess-board represents a desperate
struggle between two opposing personalities, the one inhuman in
his cold, calculating indifference, the other fully human in his
passionate vulnerability, the one enjoying a tactical victory, the
other triumphing morally in his physical humiliation.[25] On a wider
view, however, this again means that, while technically it may be
true to say that the metaphorical language of combat is used to
describe chess, at a deeper level it is chess which provides a
metaphor of the central conflicts of the story.

Although it has been possible to consider only a small selection
of Zweig's imagery, it will be apparent how closely it reflects both
his psychological understanding and his human ideals, or, more
properly, how heavily involved it is in their presentation from the
start.

In his study of fin-de-siècle Vienna Carl Schorske describes the
typical product of this society as follows:

Traditional liberal culture had centred upon rational man,
whose scientific domination of nature and whose moral
control of himself were expected to create the good society. In
our century, rational man has had to give place to that richer
but more dangerous and mercurial creature, psychological
man. This new man is not merely a rational animal, but a
creature of feeling and instinct.[26]

Although Schorske then goes on to discuss Schnitzler and Hofmannsthal as two representative figures, he might almost have been speaking of Zweig, who in numerous *Novellen* gives a post-Nietzschean primacy to passionate intensity and commitment, in intellectual as well as emotional areas of life. While the danger and excitement of such commitment are conjured up in the recurrent image of gambling, intensity of feeling is conveyed by various clusters, none more insistent than fire or heat, water, intoxication and fever. The intensity is usually presented in contrast to emotional indifference, expressed in metaphors of death, coldness, and inanimateness, though often in such polarity as to allow no possible middle ground, the ground on which most people spend the greater part of their lives. To sharpen the polemical point, using the language of the vehicles: it sometimes seems that the only choice open to Zweig's characters is that between drunkenness and death.

It is probably no accident that much of this imagery, especially that associated with fire and water, forms part of the traditional language of mystics when describing their ecstatic experiences.[27] For Zweig clearly conceives of this intensity as both positive and elevating. At other times he may use more expressly religious vocabulary to confer the intended ennoblement on the struggles and experiences of his characters.

In presenting sexual relations, between adults as well as adolescents, in presenting certain social relations and others that entail the narrator's curiosity, Zweig displays a marked tendency to dwell on the instinctive aspect (cf. the images of eating and drinking) and especially on the aggressive instinct, expressed most commonly in images of combat, animal-taming, or the hunt. Although such patterns of behaviour are not endorsed, they are not always balanced by an equivalent awareness of more altruistic possibilities.

Zweig's emphasis on passionate intensity has important consequences. It implies a relative devaluation of man's rational faculties as well as his moral judgements and moral will. Metaphors of eating, drinking, and sexuality direct attention above all to the instinctive level of his behaviour; the language of intoxication and even religious ecstasy stresses the loss of conscious control over what he does. Moreover, although passion may lead him into conflict with the moral and even legal demands

269

of his society, the language of intoxication, the medical vocabulary, with its suggestions of fever and convulsion — as also to some extent the meteorological imagery — betoken a refusal to judge him morally, since he is implicitly regarded as less than fully responsible for his actions. This aspect of the imagery is underlined by two analogies which Zweig uses elsewhere, but which make the same point more explicitly. In his biography of Mary Stuart, commenting on Mary's uninhibited sexual passion, he argues that it would be just as senseless to sit in judgement on someone who falls prey to an overwhelming passion as it would be to call a thunderstorm to account.[28] In the novel *Ungeduld eines Herzens* Dr Condor asks: 'Haben Sie je gehört, daß man mit Logik aufkommt gegen eine Leidenschaft? Daß man dem Fieber zureden kann: "Fieber, fiebre nicht!"'[29] Only occasionally, as in *Schachnovelle*, are the consequences of passion seriously questioned; and there, exceptionally, metaphors of heat acquire a negative tone, while animal imagery serves to draw attention to a loss of proper humanity. In addition to the general devaluation of rational control one is reminded, especially by images of liquidity and childhood, of that tendency of Zweig's to grant his characters the luxury of passivity and abdication of adult responsibility, a tendency which is particularly disquieting in situations that seem to call for decision and commitment.

Since the ideal of personal freedom is most frequently commended by examples of its violation, the relevant image-clusters also tend to be negative. If we had time to examine *Der Zwang* in greater detail, we would see that metaphors of death, slavery, mechanisation, inanimateness (but also of animal vulnerability and slaughter) are one of the author's chief means of communicating his judgement on all manifestations of authority which threaten that freedom from outside or take over man's will from within. In *Unvermutete Bekanntschaft mit einem Handwerk* even the imagery of liquidity, which elsewhere possesses a positive value as a model of either emotional vigour or voluptuous drift, is presented negatively as a prototype of the undifferentiated mass against which the exceptional individual asserts his independence.

The ideal of wider horizons and sympathies, which is also commended largely by its absence, uses two of the same image-clusters to express the deficiency: those which conjure up either an animal or an inanimate object. Although the two notions, taken

270

together, contain an element of contradiction — between what is living and what is not — the important thing they have in common is their denial of true humanity.

The ideal of human brotherhood, finally, is not consistently associated with any particular image-cluster, positive or negative. Nevertheless, it is worth recalling here two points of significance: first, as several of the images imply, the conscious will, so indispensable to the realisation of this ideal, is given such little scope and its place is taken by emotions which have a strong instinctive, even sexual colouring and so provide an insecure basis for lasting communality; second, as is suggested by the cloacal language of *Phantastische Nacht* as well as *Verwirrung der Gefühle*, there is a residue of snobbery and aloofness which stands in the way of any desire for brotherhood across social barriers. In that this aloofness militates against what elsewhere appears to be a deliberate avoidance of moral judgement, there is also some evidence of moral uncertainty in Zweig.

18

The Narrative Frame

Since the nineteenth century the narrative frame has generally fallen out of favour with writers of *Novellen*. In the case of Zweig, however, it appears with such frequency — well over half the works under consideration contain some sort of frame[1] — that the reader may be inclined to dismiss it as a mere device and to agree with Klawiter, who has little good to say about it, asserting that Zweig adds nothing new to the technique and concentrates almost entirely on the atmosphere which the frame can generate.[2] The first assertion is difficult to disprove, since its chief criterion is what some other writer may or may not have done at an earlier date. On the other hand, it can be clearly demonstrated that there is very much more than atmosphere involved. We have already observed the role which the frame performs in the psychological foundation of several works: for example, when the protagonist's psychological drama is brought to a conclusion or at least continued there; when his or her very act of narration forms an integral part of the psychological picture; or when the curiosity of the narrator turns him too into an object of psychological interest. Quite apart from that Zweig treats the frame as a serious rhetorical resource, integrating it so carefully into his total narrative purpose that, without it, his meaning can only partially and inadequately be understood.[3]

His narrative frames are not, however, all of a piece. There are several recurrent formal procedures — the receipt or discovery of a document, the encounter with an interesting stranger, the shift of narrative voice between the opening situation and a narration that grows out of it — but it does not necessarily follow that the

272

presence of one of these procedures guarantees the presence of a narrative frame, nor, conversely, that the absence of one of them eliminates the possibility of a narrative frame. Moreover, even where the presence of the frame is beyond dispute, very different effects are achieved according to the relative weight it receives. In the case of *Brief einer Unbekannten* it would be absurd to think of the opening and concluding sections, in which the insouciant novelist receives and then lays down the letter from the unknown woman, as anything but a frame for the heroine's gripping narrative. In the case of *Die Gouvernante*, on the other hand, although the title might seem to imply that the main interest lay in the love-affair of the governess and the student, presented from the perspective of the two adolescent girls, it would be equally absurd to interpret this perspective as a frame enclosing an inner narrative. Zweig's chief concern is quite clearly the restless problems of the two young girls, while the fate of the governess serves merely as a focus or at most a catalyst. In their unequivocal distribution of narrative weight these two stories stand at opposite poles. Between them lie considerable areas of latitude which Zweig likes to explore and which grant him varying degrees of emphasis in the use of the narrative frame.

In *Geschichte in der Dämmerung, Der Amokläufer, Phantastische Nacht,* and *Brief einer Unbekannten* there can be no mistaking the subservient role which the frame performs. Elsewhere — though for different reasons — the position is by no means as straightforward. Despite its close thematic links with *Der Amokläufer, Die Mondscheingasse* has a noticeably different distribution of emphasis. The inner narrative occupies only about one third of the total work — an unmistakable indication that the author is as much concerned with the here and now as with past events, with the present battles of the husband and his prostitute-wife as with their antecedents. Similarly, in *Die unsichtbare Sammlung* the inset account of the old collector's earlier history and of the gradual sale of his prints is given no greater weight than the ecstasy and illusion of his present life as revealed through the visit of the narrator in the frame. And in *Schachnovelle*, where there are two inset narratives, these together emerge as no more important than the encounter of the two main characters across the chess-board in the narrative frame, the encounter which represents the outworking of those narratives in the present.

In these works it is largely the fact that Zweig is as interested in the protagonists' present activities as in their previous history that accounts for the relative expansion of the narrative frame. In other instances the chief cause lies in an increased emphasis on the attitudes and experiences of the narrator. Even in so slight a work as *Sommernovellette* the young narrator is only marginally less interesting than the elderly dilettante, not so much because it is left to him to complete the latter's story as because, by a piece of thematic integration to which we shall later return, he himself undergoes a change similar to that of his older companion. In *Buchmendel*, where the author is most obviously interested in the character and fate of the eccentric book-pedlar, a brief glance at the allocation of space will clearly indicate that he is scarcely less interested in the experiences of the narrator himself: in his struggle to remember, to recapture something of his own past; in his dissatisfaction with the commercialism and uniformity of the post-war age; in the friendship which grows out of his meeting with a woman from such a different social and cultural background. This whole process, which is reminiscent of the way in which, in Henry James, figures originally chosen as reflectors had a habit of turning into subjects in their own right,[4] reaches its farthest point in *Unvermutete Bekanntschaft mit einem Handwerk*, where, as we have seen, the first-person narrator occupies the centre of the stage, where the stranger (the pickpocket) does not tell his story and, strictly speaking, has no story to tell except as imagined by the narrator.

If — to trace the metaphor to its origins — the 'frame' has here grown to such an extent that it has, to all intents and purposes, become the 'painting', what are we to make of *Verwirrung der Gefühle*, where most of the typical formal procedures of the frame are absent — absent, that is, unless one elevates the eight brief pages of the professor's (summarised) confession to the status of inner narrative for which the other one hundred and twenty pages provide merely the frame? In fact there can be little doubt that it is the experiences of the young Roland that form the core of the work. What is less immediately apparent is that Zweig places these experiences within a frame. As the sub-title informs us, the narrative before us represents the 'Private Aufzeichnungen des Geheimrates R. v. D.'. Unlike the private papers of the baron in *Phantastische Nacht*, however, they are not communicated to us by an outsider in the shape of a primary narrator. Instead Zweig provides an internal frame, a frame that forms part of the 'Aufzeichnungen' themselves and shares the same narrative voice. In a way reminiscent of Storm's 'Erinnerungsnovellen' he isolates the main events of the story by setting them at a considerable distance of time from the narrative present, using the 'Festschrift' with which Roland is honoured on his sixtieth birthday as the occasion to have the true story of his youth recorded and as a perspective from which to judge those earlier events.

Although this wide range of procedure and emphasis should allay any suspicion that Zweig approaches the narrative frame mechanically or perfunctorily, it does not make it easier in doubtful cases to decide whether we are indeed dealing with a narrative frame or not. Nevertheless, from the point of view of rhetorical purpose, these distinctions lose much of their point. For Zweig assigns to the narrative frame a number of functions which operate irrespective of the certainty or otherwise with which the critic might allow the term 'frame'.

On the simplest rhetorical level it serves to arouse the interest of the reader, in much the same way as goods in a shop are attractively packaged in order to persuade the customer to buy them. The document which has come into the hands of the narrator, the intriguing stranger he has met, the memories set in motion by a particular setting, all provoke the reader's desire to know more. Since there can hardly be an author who does not want his readers to progress beyond the first page, there is no need to disparage a rhetorical device designed to promote that progression,[5] unless it remains too patently a device, or what follows disappoints the expectations raised. And in the latter case it is the substance of the work rather than the use of the frame which is at fault.

A second function of the narrative frame — perhaps indeed its original function — is that of authentication.[6] As W.F. Mainland ironically observes in connection with Storm: 'It is a fictitious device made to overcome the idea of fiction. If the author has taken the trouble to wrap something up, the reader will think that that something is real'.[7] In Zweig's case the need for such authentication may be seen as a particular consequence of the kind of events and characters with which he is concerned. These are so exceptional, at times even so sensational, that the reader may justifiably be expected to require some assurance of their truth, though whether any number of authenticating devices will succeed where the substance of the narrative lacks its own inner conviction must remain doubtful.

It is not the frame alone, however, but the presence there of a first-person narrator which provides the authentication. Only in the relatively early *Geschichte in der Dämmerung*, where Zweig's common patterns are not yet established, where the frame involves no encounter with a stranger, where the setting is vague, and where, uniquely, the voice of the narrator addresses an unnamed 'du' assumed to be present with him in the same room, is authenticity deliberately renounced and the inner narrative presented instead as a conflation of fact and fantasy. Elsewhere the voice of the first-person narrator guarantees the authenticity of what follows, or, more properly, the illusion of authenticity, since even the apparatus of authentication is part of the fiction. Although the reader may sometimes doubt the judgement of the narrator, he is generally prepared to accept his account of the facts, to regard him as a man who can vouch for the reality of what he himself has heard and seen. To encourage this confidence Zweig likes to place his narrator in a fairly precise setting in the real world — an ocean-going liner in Naples harbour (*Der Amokläufer*) or *en route* from New York to Buenos Aires (*Schachnovelle*), a named boulevard in Paris (*Unvermutete Bekanntschaft mit einem Handwerk*), a known café in a particular street of suburban Vienna (*Buchmendel*) — seeking thereby to increase the sense that the narrator belongs to the world we know and inhabit and is not therefore part of a fictitious invention.[8]

Authentication is most explicit in *Phantastische Nacht*, where the narrator expresses the conviction that the record which follows and which the baron's relatives take to be a work of fiction is, in fact, a piece of sincere self-revelation. Yet even an apparent denial of factual truth can serve the purpose of authentication. In *Sommernovellette*, where the older man introduces the account of his earlier experiences with the remark, 'daß es eine hübsche Novelle wäre' (EE,194), and where the narrator subsequently provides an allegedly fictional completion of the story, the former's response to the supposed fiction, whether it be a display or irony or angry repudiation, in the end confirms the truth of what is recorded, since it clearly emerges as a form of psychological self-defence.

A third function of the narrative frame is that of providing intimacy, of creating in the reader a sense of close personal contact with the writer.[9] This is not the case with the early *Geschichte in der Dämmerung*, where the prior presence of another 'du' in the frame tends rather to distance the reader, nor with *Brief einer Unbekannten*, where the recipient of the woman's letter is presented in the third person. On the other hand, where the first-person narrator introduces himself into the frame and addresses no one but the reader, the reader is encouraged to regard himself as a privileged confidant. Indeed, although there is no evidence to indicate that the author himself had any of the encounters recorded in the narrative frames,[10] the illusion he creates there is that the reader is being privileged to share a personal experience of the famous writer Stefan Zweig. That, I believe, is why the first-person narrator usually presents himself, explicitly or implicitly, as a writer and occasionally exhibits the same interests as his creator. That is also why a work as short as *Die unsichtbare Sammlung* resorts to the cumbersome stratagem of a double narrative frame — a fact on which I have so far remained silent for the sake of simplicity and clarity. The first-person narrator who has figured in earlier discussions is a dealer in antiques, as indeed he must be to explain his visit to the blind collector. Yet his is not the first voice we hear. His account is introduced by another voice, who tells us how he met the dealer, a former acquaintance, on a train travelling between Dresden and (presumably) Berlin and was told the story as a fresh experience. This first narrator, who is immediately forgotten after the opening paragraph and was wisely omitted entirely when the story was adapted for radio,[11] reveals sufficient of himself — he collects old books and autographs — for us to be easily persuaded that he is none other than Zweig himself.[12] The fact that the writer who receives the letter in *Brief einer Unbekannten* is not made into a first-person narrator in no way invalidates the present argument. For to do so would mean turning the narrator into an unsympathetic companion and would eliminate the possibility of a friendly intimacy with the reader.

If the narrative frame were intended to do no more than arouse the reader's interest, persuade him of the authenticity of what he reads, and provide a sense of intimate companionship with the writer, there would be little need for comment. In fact, however, it serves a much more important purpose in Zweig's narrative rhetoric. In a recent study concerned primarily with the nineteenth-century *Novelle* Martin Swales discusses the frame within the context of what he holds to be the central feature of the *genre*: the narration of marginal or exceptional events and the interpretative relation which these bear to the accepted norms of society. Some of his comments might almost have been written with Zweig in mind:

> [. . .] the story actually told tends to center upon experiences that are somehow unusual, unique, isolated from the common run of human affairs. The frame establishes a context around the particular inset story. That context can serve to mediate interpretatively between the isolated experience or set of experiences and the generality of the social universe, or it can serve to isolate the experiences still more.[13]

The only qualification one might wish to make in applying these remarks to Zweig's *Novellen* is to question whether the opposition between mediation and isolation is nearly as absolute as is here implied. For the narrative voice of Zweig's frames, at least where it speaks in the first person, seems to possess the paradoxical ability to set the characters or events of the inner narrative apart from the world of normal experience which we share with the narrator, by drawing attention to how extraordinary, foolish, even reprehensible they are by the standards of that world, and yet at the same time to provide a sympathetic bridge between their world and ours, introducing unexpected and sometimes uncomfortable links, questioning the very standards we might have been ready to accept unhesitatingly, provoking understanding where we might have been inclined to condemn or critical detachment where we might have been tempted to condone. In short, the frame has an important interpretative function to perform.

In order to understand this function more clearly it is necessary to examine the thematic links which Zweig so frequently establishes between frame and inner narrative, grouping the works according to whether the links are forged by means of parallelism, a simple contrast, or — with greater subtlety — a contrast in parallel.

In the relatively early *Geschichte in der Dämmerung* the

parallelism of frame and inset narrative is obvious, but its basis is scarcely thematic. After evoking an atmosphere of twilight in his frame, when time hovers uncertainly between day and night and objects lose their accustomed clarity, Zweig proceeds to tell a story which possesses something of the same ambiguity in both its origins and its content. The central narrative is presented as an undifferentiated mixture of fact and fantasy, personal and second-hand experience. As we have seen, its subject-matter is also concerned with uncertainty, the uncertainty of adolescence. In this work the links between frame and inset narrative are as yet only verbal (links between a literal and figurative understanding of the word 'Dämmerung' and its cognate forms) or at most atmospheric; they perform no further interpretative function.

It is in the final story of *Erstes Erlebnis, Sommernovellette*, that this interpretative function begins to emerge. The elderly man whose 'story' forms the interpolated narrative appears to be something of an idle dilettante, whose interest in art has taken the form of passive enjoyment without creative participation and whose treatment of an impressionable young woman has been equally casual and non-committal. Nevertheless, having played with her affections by addressing ardent but fictional love-letters to her and then observing her reaction, he then becomes much more deeply involved, as aesthetic detachment gives way to irresistible captivation. This conclusion, it will be remembered, is reported not by the man himself, but by the narrator, evidently a writer like his creator. He has accepted the account ostensibly as literary raw material, asserting that it requires aesthetic treatment before it can be moulded into a satisfying artistic whole, and now proceeds to offer an appropriate conclusion which comes provocatively close to the older man's actual experience. At this point the narrator of the frame has become like his companion: he has unthinkingly fictionalised life and played with another's feelings. The final result, moreover, is also the same, as he too comes to realise that he has been affected much more deeply than he expected by what he has witnessed of the older man's distress.

Because the frame reflects the inner narrative in this way, the older man's parting words are seen to have a double edge. 'Gute Nacht!' he says, 'Ich sehe, es ist gefährlich, jungen Leuten in Sommernächten Geschichten zu erzählen. Das gibt leicht törichte Gedanken und allerhand unnötige Träume' (EE,207). These words apply not only to the nocuous effect of his own fiction on the young woman, but also to the consequences of his reporting the events to the young narrator, who has now breached his psychological defences and disturbed his calm by confronting him with the final outcome in the form of a completed story. More important, because the circumstances of the frame reflect those of the inner narrative, Zweig is able both to underline the dangers of 'aesthetic' trifling and to forestall too hasty a judgement of others on that account. For we are made to observe how widespread it is and how easily the individual may yield to its attractions.

In *Vierundzwanzig Stunden aus dem Leben einer Frau* some degree of parallelism between frame and inner narrative will be evident from the most cursory reading, since it is the sudden elopement of a married woman with a younger man which provokes the discussion that in turn persuades Mrs C. to relate her own similar experience. But the parallelism is more extensive, more complex, and interpretatively more significant than has generally been recognised. When one otherwise astute commentator denies that there is any thematic link between the episode with Mme Henriette and the expeience of Mrs C. and concludes that the frame is unsatisfactory,[14] one suspects that detail has obscured the broader view. Obviously it makes some difference that Mme Henriette is a married woman who abandons a husband and children, while Mrs C. is already a widow, whose children have outgrown her care, when she suddenly becomes passionately involved with the young Polish gambler. Nevertheless, the wider and more important issue which the story raises is whether it is possible for the calm and civilised surface of human life to be broken suddenly by the ungovernable eruption of elemental, instinctive forces. It is a possibility denied by almost all the participants in the discussion of the frame, but upheld by the first-person narrator, who vigorously defends the existence of a psychological *coup de foudre* (VdG,18). The story which Mrs C. then proceeds to divulge to him may be seen as an endorsement of his view within the erotic sphere, but it also contains, as a further inset, a brief account of how the young Pole, just at the point in his life when he was about to settle down to a normal life in a steady job, was introduced to gambling and was immediately and irresistibly enthralled by the 'Raserei des Spiels' (VdG,70-1), an account which makes the same point in a different sphere.[15]

In the frame too, however, Zweig provides a double confirmation of his narrator's view, first in the reaction of Mme Henriette's husband, then in the behaviour of those very people who argue against the narrator. When the husband hears of his wife's disappearance, he goes to pieces socially, ranting and groaning with primitive, animal force. His grief is seen as an 'elementarer Schmerz', an 'Explosion des Gefühls'. All of this moreover, like his wife's sudden elopement, is set against a background of married regularity: she enjoying her 'allabendlichen Spaziergang', he his game of dominoes 'in gewohnter Pünktlichkeit' (VdG,15-16). Even more revealing is the argument that develops among the hitherto urbane hotel guests as a result of the elopement. It quickly becomes vehement and insulting, with the others implying that the narrator has only a fleeting knowledge of the female psyche such as philandering bachelors usually acquire, and with the narrator himself becoming (unwontedly) aggressive, defending the action of Mme Henriette more passionately than his true feelings would allow. Indeed the argument might well have ended in blows if it had not been for the tactful intervention of Mrs C. The frame, then, assumes an important interpretative function, ensuring a more sympathetic reading of Mrs C.'s story, which might otherwise have appeared wayward; it helps to demonstrate how easily the polite, conventional surface of social life can be shattered by uncontrollable passions and it questions facile assumptions about human behaviour when it presents the very woman who has earlier experienced the force of such passions as the calming, civilising influence in the present circumstances, while those who deny the possibility of these sudden passions prove just as susceptible to passion in another form.

Although it may be doubted whether *Unvermutete Bekanntschaft mit einem Handwerk* should really be reckoned among the works which possess a narrative frame, it cannot be disputed that Zweig seeks to establish a significant parallelism between the worlds of his narrator and the pickpocket who is the object of his interest. It is not just that the narrator follows the pickpocket with fascination and describes his activities with remarkable empathy. He even comes to speak of himself as the other's 'Doppelgänger und Mitgänger' (K,29); and the basis of the remark is a carefully established pattern of similarity between the activities of the artist and the thief, which is communicated above all through the image-clusters discussed in the previous chapter. In particular the venatorial associations of the narrator's curiosity tend to bring him down to the level of the predatory criminal, while the artistic dimension of the pickpocket's operations have the effect of raising him to the level of the writer. In all of this the typical rhetorical function of the frame coincides with that of the imagery. For although the similarities between artist and criminal are not given the same general significance or pursued with the same subtlety and erudition as in Thomas Mann's *Bekenntnisse des Hochstaplers Felix Krull*, they do perform the same sort of interpretative role, a role which Roth only partly recognised when he wrote to Zweig about the as yet unpublished story in 1934:

> Es ist ganz großartig, wie sich die Psychologie der erzählenden Person immer stärker identifiziert mit der Psychologie des Objektes und wie zugleich dadurch auch für jene, denen das Objekt unmoralisch erscheinen muß, dessen Moralität gehoben wird. Die originellste Art, einen Verbrecher zu verteidigen: indem das gewissenhafteste Wesen, nämlich der Dichter selbst, sich mit dem Verbrecher identifiziert.[16]

In fact the parallelism under consideration not only leads the reader to a more sympathetic assessment of the pickpocket; it also raises doubts about the propriety of the writer's profession, with its vicarious excitements, its tendency to prey on the adventures and sufferings of others.

Of the works in which the links between frame and inner narrative are based on contrast it is *Die Mondscheingasse* which demonstrates the method most clearly. The frame introduces us to a first-person narrator who is returning home to Germany from his travels, but finds himself temporarily delayed in a foreign port and so wanders the streets in search of some passing adventure. The inner narrative, on the other hand, together with its continuation in the present, concerns a couple who have abandoned everything — home, job, conventional marriage — in their native Germany, have travelled the world not as tourists in search of pleasure and relaxation, but as part of a desperate chase, and have now finished up in the brothel of a foreign port outside the confines of normal society. Furthermore, while the frame ends with the narrator returning home, unable to commit himself to help, although he has seen what could well be a dagger in the hand of the husband, the couple at the heart of the inner narrative are left in a state of impassioned but unresolved conflict. Ingrid Lent has pointed in addition to the significant stylistic difference between the measured prose of the narrator, which reflects his ordered world, and the disjointed, hesitant language of the husband, which expresses something of the intensity of his feeling.[17] In establishing this important contrast between the narrator of the frame and the characters he meets, Zweig has been able to guide his reader's responses, creating greater sympathy especially with the man, who might easily have appeared repulsive in his dog-like self-abasement, and casting doubts on the narrator's refusal to become involved. Is the greater humanity to be found in abandoning oneself to a passion, however wretched and degrading its consequences, or in preserving oneself in the security of normality and aesthetic detachment? This is the question which the frame of *Die Mondscheingasse* helps to bring inescapably to the forefront of our attention.

It is the same question which is brought into sharper focus by the contrastive frame of *Brief einer Unbekannten*, where the character who dominates the frame is again a writer, though not the first-person narrator. The central narrative is a story of all-consuming love, for the sake of which a young woman is prepared to suffer poverty, hardship, even prostitution. The forty-one-year-old novelist, on the other hand, is presented as a man with neither commitment nor profound interests, comfortably placed, wearing an air of blasé unconcern, and, one might add, lacking the critical self-awareness that characterises his counterpart, the violinist, in the early *Die Liebe der Erika Ewald*.[18] Despite the brevity of the frame the contrast is made particularly pointed. The man is introduced as 'der bekannte Romanschriftsteller R.' (A,211), which immediately recalls the 'Unbekannte' of the title. Yet it is not simply that he is a well-known public figure, while she lives and dies in obscurity. It appears that she remembers all he has ever said to her and every word of his novels, while he, even after reading her long confessional letter, with its accounts of their intimate meetings, has only the vaguest and most confused recollection of her. Even more pointedly, while the opening presents a man who knows himself so little that he is unaware it is his birthday until he looks at the newspaper, the inner narrative concerns a woman who has remembered his birthday every year and marked the occasion by sending flowers, which he has accepted casually without bothering to discover the donor. Once more, then, the frame is the means of bringing the intended interpretative issue into focus: it invites us to consider whether the greater human worth resides in the passionate, even degrading self-abandonment of an anonymous woman or in the unruffled detachment of a famous man, a writer who fails to recognise the real-life drama being enacted under his very nose. It points the contrast so persuasively, moreover, that we are in danger of sympathising with the woman too readily and overlooking those psychological ambiguities which were exposed in an earlier chapter.

In *Verwirrung der Gefühle*, where, as we have seen, the real frame is provided by the occasion of the hero's sixtieth birthday and the 'Festschrift' donated by his pupils and colleagues, contrast with the central narrative again dominates the rhetoric. The 'Festschrift' contains significant errors of fact: it includes a report by a fellow schoolboy that Roland was always interested in academic work, whereas in fact he found it sheer drudgery; the *curriculum vitae* speaks of his grounding in philology from the very first term in Berlin, whereas he initially found the university a 'Leichenkammer des Geistes' in contrast to the vitality of public life in Berlin (VdG,159-60); and the carefully compiled index omits the name of the one man who inspired him and determined his career (VdG,156-7). What Zweig is concerned to present, however, is not merely the ironic discrepancy between the official, public record and the privately experienced reality, but the confrontation of two approaches to learning and, ultimately, to life itself, such as Goethe epitomises in the figures of Faust and his famulus Wagner. On the one hand there is the 'Fleiß', the 'Gründlichkeit' of Roland's well-meaning academic colleagues, who have sought to plot his progress 'säuberlich klar, Stufe um Stufe' (VdG,155), but have missed the essence of things; and on the other hand there are the passion and enthusiasm of Roland's professor which, despite their doubtful moral links, have the power of poetic evocation, the power to inspire both friendship and learning, with the result that pupil and teacher pursue their academic work with passion rather than mere industry (cf. especially VdG,169,175,187). Zweig was well aware that he had chosen a problematic subject in this work, but he was evidently also aware that he could ensure a more sympathetic assessment of those involved if he set them within a frame which demonstrated the inadequacy of their opposites.

In some cases the contrast between frame and inner narrative is combined with an element of parallelism, which, far from confusing the interpretative issue, as one might expect, helps to define it more clearly. This is true in a relatively simple way of *Der Amokläufer*, where the primary narrator and the narrator of the inner narrative come together on board a liner bringing both of them back from India, a liner whose cabins both find unbearable like a coffin or grave, though neither wishes to associate with the other passengers (A,13,20-21). Despite these superficial similarities the doctor soon makes a distinction between himself, who has experienced the real, demoralising, debilitating India, and the primary narrator, who has only the romantic view of the tourist (A,25). It is a distinction familiar to us from the earlier discussion of *Die Mondscheingasse*, a distinction too which is reminiscent of that which was to shame Zweig into writing his biography of Magellan: the distinction between modern ocean-going travel with its safety, ease, and pleasure and the journeys of the first explorers with their dangers and their exposure to the elements.[19] In *Der Amokläufer* the distinction is again symptomatic of different approaches to life itself. Above all, however, it is a short phrase which eventually becomes a verbal leitmotif that epitomises the point at which the narrator and the doctor come close to each other yet differ so markedly. On hearing of the latter's inner sickness the primary narrator speaks of man's 'Pflicht, seine Bereitwilligkeit anzubieten', which the doctor immediately seizes upon in contemplating his own fate. Yet the crucial difference is that the narrator's readiness to help extends only to keeping quiet about the doctor's presence on board ship and listening sympathetically though passively to his story, while for the latter it brings a woman's demand to procure an abortion for her which, once declined, involves him in a desperate and humiliating pursuit of her and the sacrifice of his own life in the bid to preserve her secret. The difference comes to a head when, in describing the woman's struggle with death after a back-street abortion, the doctor implies a wide gulf between the narrator's relaxed, comfortable duty to help, which he sees as that of a 'Spazierfahrer' or 'Müßiggänger', and his own involvement in the flesh-and-blood struggle of the woman in all its horror (A,68-9).

The result is once more that we are made to look more sympathetically on the 'immoral', even criminal events of the inner narrative, on the experiences of one who, whatever else, has plumbed the depths of life, and to regard more sceptically the urbane and civil helpfulness of one who has nothing at stake, who, after listening to the other's harrowing tale, can go ashore to spend the evening at the opera, followed by a drink at a nearby café (A,85).

In terms of plot *Buchmendel* is a much simpler affair than *Der Amokläufer*, but in the subtlety with which frame and inner narrative are integrated to form one cohesive statement it represents one of Zweig's finest achievements. The basis of this integration, as I have argued in more detail elsewhere,[20] is memory, which dominates both frame and inner narrative, though in such a way that a significant contrast is set up between the two. The inset is essentially the portrait of a man whose originality resides in a memory which, despite its apparent infallibility, entails a severe limitation of human depth and breadth. This regrettable human failing might have become obscured in what remains a largely sympathetic portrait, if it were not for the fact that the portrait itself grows out of memory of a very different order. The portrait is reconstructed from the recollections of the first-person narrator, sparked off by a chance visit to the café which Mendel earlier used as his base, and those of the old cloakroom attendant whom the narrator now meets there. These recollections are no mere narrative device to introduce the story or even make it more personal; they bear a close thematic relation to the extraordinary gift of the central character. On entering the café the narrator has a considerable mental struggle before he recognises it as an earlier haunt and recalls its former *habitué*, Mendel. The difficulty is that his memory is decidedly fallible and needs some external stimulus to come to its aid. Yet this technical weakness emerges as part of a greater human richness: he is not concerned with the superficial memorising of facts; his memory of Mendel is stored at a greater mental depth along with a wide variety of other human experiences (K,98-9) and for that reason alone is not readily accessible. As to the cloakroom attendant, her memory is a matter of warm affection for and consistent loyalty to the now dead book-pedlar; in the sharpest contrast to Mendel her memory has a human content.

It is not only in the quality of the memory that Zweig creates a contrastive link between the frame and the inner narrative. It is present also in the developments that arise out of it. It is the fate of Mendel to lose his memory and thereafter to suffer increasing isolation and rejection. The frame, on the other hand, records the narrator's gradual recovery of a particular memory and his unexpected discovery of a companion in the simple, unread cloak-room attendant, who shares his affectionate remembrance. The positive developments of the frame serve, therefore, to temper the undoubted pity we feel for Mendel with an increased critical awareness of his inherent limitations as a human being.

Schachnovelle is probably best omitted from the present con-siderations, since, although certain parallels are hinted at — for example, between the manoeuvres of chess which Dr B. learns and the psychological methods of the Gestapo (S,80f) — they are not consistently pursued and never become a real part of the interpre-tative process. Nor indeed are they links between frame and inner narrative, but within each individual part. These observations are not to be understood as a criticism. It is merely that the interpre-tative function of the parallels and contrasts under discussion is already fulfilled in a different aspect of the structure: in the central opposition of Czentovic and Dr B., seen first in their separate life-stories (the inset narratives) and then in their personal encounters across the chess-board (in the frame). Frame and inner narrative are not here set against each other, but themselves, individually, embody the contrast which lies at the heart of the author's rhetoric.

So we are brought back again to what has proved the most important function of the frame. When everything has been said about authentication and the personal note, the overriding concern remains interpretative: to set up analogies and contrasts by means of which the reader may arrive at a juster assessment of the characters, the events, and the issues raised. Although it may sometimes be difficult to decide exactly what is a frame and what is not, it appears that the principle of inner reflection governs problematic cases just as much as straightforward ones and so in a sense makes the question of definition superfluous.

In 1923, when Zweig was planning the volume that was to become *Der Kampf mit dem Dämon*, a study of Hölderlin, Kleist, and Nietzsche 'als die drei Typen des dämonischen Dichters', as he told his friend Leonhardt Adelt, he also wrote:

Ein vierter ist unsichtbar dabei, aber als Gegenspieler, nämlich Goethe, der gleichfalls dämonisch veranlagt aber nicht zerstört wurde, sondern den Dämon gebändigt und — wenn man es so sagen wollte — sogar zerstört hat. Diese Zusammenstellung ergibt Analogien, die mich selber überraschen.[21]

This insight was subsequently formalised in the introduction to the volume, where he wrote:

Ich suche keine Formeln des Geistigen, sondern ich gestalte Formen des Geistes. Und wenn ich in meinen Büchern immer mehrere solcher Bilder bewußt zusammenrücke, so geschieht dies einzig in der Art eines Malers, der seinen Werken gerne den richtigen Raum sucht, wo Licht und Gegenlicht wirkend gegeneinanderströmen und durch Pendants die erst verborgene, nun aber offenbare Analogie des Typus in Erscheinung tritt. Vergleich scheint mir immer ein förderndes, ja ein gestaltendes Element, und ich liebe ihn als Methode, weil er ohne Gewaltsamkeit angewendet werden kann. Er bereichert in gleichem Maße, als die Formel verarmt, er erhöht alle Werte indem er Erhellungen durch unerwartete Reflexe schafft und eine Tiefe des Raums wie einen Rahmen um das abgelöste Bildnis stellt.[22]

In his non-fictional work Zweig was obviously conscious of the possibilities that parallels and contrasts afford for a clearer understanding of the subject. There can be no doubt that the same principle of composition informed his stories too and that it expressed itself most characteristically in the use of the narrative frame.[23] Bearing in mind that the analogy with the painter's art in the passage just quoted culminates in a reference to the function of the frame, this should not be in the least surprising.

When one considers what the issues are which these frames help to clarify and articulate, it quickly becomes apparent that, for practical purposes, they may be divided into two, which together mark the point at which the concerns of Zweig the man and Zweig the writer come together. They are, first, the question of where truly human values are to be found and, second, the position of the (literary) artist in the quest for these values.

Of the four human ideals which Zweig repeatedly advocates and which have been discussed at length in earlier chapters it is chiefly in connection with one that the rhetoric of the narrative frame is brought into play. In *Buchmendel* it endorses the value of broad human sympathies as opposed to narrow-minded specialism, but elsewhere it serves above all to enlist the reader's favourable response to either the possibility, perhaps universality, of uncontrollable passion (*Vierundzwanzig Stunden aus dem Leben einer Frau*) or the worth of passionate commitment and enthusiasm, even when they prove dangerous, immoral, or criminal, in contrast to civilised aloofness, non-committal play, or dry learning (*Der Amokläufer, Die Mondscheingasse, Brief einer Unbekannten, Verwirrung der Gefühle, Unvermutete Bekanntschaft mit einem Handwerk*).

As to the position of the writer, it is relevant to recall some of the striking similarities between Zweig's first-person narrators and their creator: they have travelled to the same places; they share his psychological curiosity; and as often as not they appear to be writers. Although it would be folly to try and construct some sort of autobiography from their collective experiences, it does seem evident that they are closer to their creator in personality than the characters they meet[24] and that, together, they articulate certain dangers which he sensed in his life as a writer: that of exploiting people as literary raw material, that of trivialising human experience by reducing it to mere aesthetic play, that of avoiding personal involvement and keeping human sympathy at a relatively harmless, superficial level. *Sommernovellette, Der Amokläufer, Die Mondscheingasse*, and *Unvermutete Bekanntschaft mit einem Handwerk* are the works in which this is most clearly expressed, but it is also worth remembering that in *Brief einer Unbekannten*, where Zweig could hardly use the blasé recipient of the woman's letter as a first-person narrator without placing his narrative in the hands of an unsympathetic person, he has nevertheless depicted this rather parasitic character as a novelist. It seems in the end that his choice of first-person narrator is not determined solely by the desire for authenticity and intimacy; it often has its origins also in a need to come to terms with his own role as a writer. Although the frame might thereby seem to imply considerable self-doubt, the very fact that Zweig is aware of the dangers, together with the general import of the inner narratives, is evidence enough that his real sympathies lie with the committed, passionate people. In raising during the course of his narrative frames matters of peculiar concern to the writer his purpose is not at all exclusive or esoteric; it is rather to underline those human values which are intelligible to all.

It is the same concern to assert human values, I believe, which underlies that other peculiarity noted earlier: the expansion of the narrative frame, often to the point where it becomes doubtful whether 'frame' is an adequate description of what is presented. The most common characteristic of this expansion is that an encounter, which in other works is made subservient to an inner narrative arising out of it, is here given added weight in its own right. Where this happens, the encounter itself initiates a humanising process, which enlarges the understanding of the narrator. He may be brought into instructive contact with a member of a different social class or someone on the fringes of society (*Die Mondscheingasse, Unvermutete Bekanntschaft mit einem Handwerk, Buchmendel*); he may find his own rather comfortable attitudes implicitly questioned; or it may be that the humanising lesson becomes explicit. In *Die unsichtbare Sammlung* it will be recalled how the chief narrator confesses near the end that, having come to visit the blind collector in the spirit of commercialism, he has experienced something of greater value: genuine intellectual enthusiasm (K,87). Unlike his counterpart in Henry James's *The Aspern Papers*, the 'publishing scoundrel', whose predatory intentions are thwarted by events but are not transformed, he is diverted from his original purpose by the apprehension of a nobler reality. Similarly, at the end of *Buchmendel* the narrator, having encountered both the memory of Mendel and the live presence of the cloakroom attendant, asserts: 'Wir verstanden einander wunderbar gut an seinem alten, verlassenen Tisch in der Gemeinschaft des vereint heraufbeschworenen Schattens; denn Erinnerung verbindet immer, und zweifach jede Erinnerung in Liebe' (K,123-4). It is not just that the encounter has brought human friendship across social and cultural barriers; it has also taught him a lesson as a writer. He has been shamed by the loyal memory of the cloakroom attendant and reflects:

> Ich aber, ich hatte jahrelang Buchmendel vergessen, gerade ich, der ich doch wissen sollte, daß man Bücher nur schafft, um über den eigenen Atem hinaus sich Menschen zu verbinden und sich so zu verteidigen gegen den unerbittlichen Widerpart alles Lebens: Vergänglichkeit und Vergessensein. (K,124)

290

The frame, then, is not only the means of clarifying human values; it can also be the place where these values are enacted. Far from being a mere literary device, it emerges as an integral part of the total meaning, demanding of the reader the same careful attention, the same willingness to respond to the call of humanity, as the narrative it embraces.

CONCLUSION

ZWEIG AND THE *NOVELLE*

After so much discussion, during which the word 'Novelle' has been used uncritically and more or less interchangeably with the looser 'story', it may seem perverse to raise at the very end the legitimacy of the term 'Novelle'. Yet to have practised utmost scrupulousness and banished the word entirely would have been both artificial and clumsy, while, on the other hand, to have prefaced the discussion with some attempt to justify its application to the works under consideration would have begged the question, assuming much that had yet to be demonstrated. It is only now, having explored so many facets of Zweig's stories, that we are in a position to judge whether they may indeed be called *Novellen*. Even so we shall approach this concluding task not with the purpose of awarding or withholding some seal of approval,[1] nor out of a compulsion to classify at all costs, but rather in the hope of uncovering the ultimate focus of Zweig's narrative art.

By temperament Zweig certainly seems to have been suited to the shorter forms of narrative. Negatively, this expresses itself in a general preference for individual fates over historical forces, which has been noted by Hans Mayer.[2] In particular it expresses itself in a lack of epic breadth in his one completed novel, *Ungeduld des Herzens*, which Harry Zohn describes as an 'over-extended novella'[3] and in which Joseph Strelka perceives an inability to match Musil and Broch in portraying a whole life, an entire age.[4] Much the same may be said of the posthumously published *Rausch der Verwandlung*, whose plot advances characteristically through a series of decisive 'Umschläge' or 'Wendepunkte'.[5] As a reader of other people's novels, moreover, Zweig confessed to a certain impatience and several times approached publishers with the proposal that they bring out the world classics from Homer to Thomas Mann's *Der Zauberberg* in an abbreviated form.[6] Positively, the temperamental affinity with shorter narrative forms expresses itself in his efforts to purge all superfluity from his own

295

works, to distil their essence. Perhaps he did not always apply the principle strictly enough to his linguistic style,[7] but in other respects he could justifiably pride himself on his art of concentration and see in it one of the reasons for his success with the public. As he put it in *Die Welt von Gestern:* 'Wenn irgend etwas, so hat mir die strenge Disziplin, mich lieber auf engere Formen, aber immer auf das unbedingt Wesentliche zu beschränken, einigermaßen die Wirkung meiner Bücher erklärt'.[8] An almost inevitable consequence of this reduction of material to its essentials was an intensification which, as he wrote to Rudolf Binding in 1928, was for him the very heart of creative writing.[9]

Nevertheless, a temperamental predisposition to shorter narrative forms does not necessarily lead to works which may be called *Novellen*. In referring to his stories collectively Zweig himself was sometimes cautious. Of the three volumes that went to make up the cycle *Die Kette* he was happy to launch the contents of *Amok* as 'Novellen einer Leidenschaft' and those of *Verwirrung der Gefühle* as 'Drei Novellen'; but those of *Erstes Erlebnis* he continued to call 'Vier Geschichten aus dem Kinderland' despite the fact that the cycle as a whole bore the subtitle 'Ein Novellenkreis'.

When we turn to the titles and sub-titles of individual works, a further hesitancy appears. Only *Schachnovelle* stakes its claim boldly, while others display varying degrees of modesty: *Geschichte in der Dämmerung, Sommernovellette, Episode am Genfer See,* 'Eine Episode aus der deutschen Inflation' (*Die unsichtbare Sammlung*). These verbal distinctions cannot be taken as a reliable guide, however, especially since they may mask an ironic purpose. The triviality and superficiality conjured up by the title *Sommernovellette* accord with the attempts of the older man to minimise the extent of his captivation by the young woman. The reality of his involvement, which the narrator uncovers, comes much closer to the definition of the *Novelle* that the latter gives when he speaks of 'Schicksale' and of the need 'sie zu Ende zu dichten' (EE,205). He recognises the presence of a profound experience taken to a significant conclusion. Although the title *Episode am Genfer See* seems to imply an incident of merely passing interest — the fisherman's discovery of the naked Russian trying to paddle across Lake Geneva is indeed described as 'eine[ ] ergötzliche[ ] Episode in der Eintönigkeit des Tages' (K,90) — this applies only to the perspective of the effete hotel-guests, who are the object of the narrator's irony. For Boris himself the events recorded mark the last and critical stage of a doomed attempt to return to the only world he understands, that of home and family. Although *Die unsichtbare Sammlung* bears the sub-title 'Eine Episode aus der deutschen Inflation', any thought that Zweig is seeking to minimise the significance of what follows is almost immediately dispelled by the excited opening of the art-dealer's account: 'Ich muß Ihnen doch erzählen, woher ich gerade komme. Denn diese Episode ist so ziemlich das Sonderbarste, was mir altem Kunstkrämer in den siebenunddreißig Jahren meiner Tätigkeit begegnet ist' (K,73). To the extent that the word 'Episode' is seriously intended in either work its likely purpose is to draw attention to those individual fates which are overlooked as unimportant in all the history-books, but which, for the author, are both interesting in themselves and representative of wider trends. Finally, even the casual, rather dismissive attitude that could be read into the title *Geschichte in der Dämmerung* has more relevance to the uncertain, non-committal manner of its introduction and conclusion in the narrative frame than to the inset account of Bob's experience.

Since titles and sub-titles are unreliable pointers, we must look to the works themselves, paying heed to the total meaning as it emerges from the interaction of the subject-matter and the manner of its presentation. To clarify our thinking on the whole vexed question of *Novelle* theory we shall for the greater part follow the balanced yet productive approach of Martin Swales,[10] who avoids the prescriptive rigour of those who would measure a given work against a checklist of supposed requirements and the scepticism of those who see no possibility of defining the *genre* or would accept as a *Novelle* anything that people have been happy to call a *Novelle*. Although he is primarily concerned with the nineteenth century, his approach has yielded insights of particular relevance to an understanding of Zweig: he has shown how the concept of the *genre* acted as a structuring principle and how the act of writing involved the author in a kind of dialogue with this concept as a 'reservoir of potentiality';[11] he has isolated as the underlying principle of the *Novelle* the presentation of the marginal or exceptional, viewed, however, in its interpretative relation to the world as commonly experienced and understood;[12] and without resorting to a checklist he has accommodated many of the familiar characteristics — the central event, the 'Wendepunkt', the role of chance or fate, symbolism, narrative frame — within the terms of that underlying principle.[13]

Bengt Sørensen has recently remarked that despite the modernity of Zweig's subject-matter (by which he means the psychological interest) the narrative technique of the stories is reminiscent of the *Novelle* theories of the nineteenth century, with their accentuation of the 'unerhörte Begebenheit', the 'Wendepunkt', and so forth.[14] One might go further and argue that Zweig probably had this theoretical framework at the back of his mind as he wrote. For it is as though he were deliberately conjuring up that classic definition of Goethe's as a point of reference. In emphasising the exceptional nature of what he is recording the narrator will sometimes use the participial adjective 'unerhört' (e.g. *Geschichte in der Dämmerung,* EE,19; *Die Frau und die Landschaft,* A,108; *Vierundzwanzig Stunden aus dem Leben einer Frau,* VdG,62; *Unvermutete Bekanntschaft mit einem Handwerk,* K,23,44; *Die unsichtbare Sammlung,* K,84); or he may choose a similar word and place it in striking proximity to another term from Goethe's definition: 'nun ereignete sich etwas Unvorhergesehenes'; 'das Unwahrscheinliche hatte sich ereignet' (*Schachnovelle,* S,47,109). It is *Phantastische Nacht,* however, which is most insistent in its implied engagement with traditional *Novelle* theory. Aware that the 'Sonderbarkeit der Vorgänge' may defy his descriptive powers, the baron has set about the task of recording his unique experience, 'um die ganze Begebenheit in ihrer natürlichen Reihenfolge einmal geordnet zu überblicken' (A,123).[15] When he reaches the decisive encounter at the race-course, which he has already referred to as the 'Drehpunkt meiner ganzen Existenz' (A,125), he introduces it with the words: 'In dieser Sekunde begann das Unerhörte, jenes einzige Erlebnis, das noch heute mein Leben bestimmt' (A,142).[16] Later, confronted by the problem of explaining his strange reaction to the unexpected winnings from a stolen betting-slip, he writes: 'Aber seltsam, wie soll ich beschreiben, was jetzt geschah, es ist ja so unerklärlich, so ganz absonderlich, und doch weiß ich, daß ich mir nichts nachträglich vortäusche' (A,164). The actual words of Goethe's definition may be absent, but their spirit is still influential. For despite the baron's alleged ignorance in literary matters he is clearly following the model of Goethe, perhaps also of Wieland, intent on persuading us that the central event of his life, though unprecedented and therefore inexplicable in terms of what he and we have previously experienced, was not imaginary, but did indeed take place in the real world.[17]

Even where the links with *Novelle* theory are less obvious Zweig's narrators repeatedly — at times monotonously — stress the unprecedented nature of what they are describing, asserting that they have experienced something for the very first time or that they have never witnessed the like before or since.[18] To this must be added the psychological, intellectual, or moral difficulties to which the central characters and chief narrators of *Phantastische Nacht, Brief einer Unbekannten, Vierundzwanzig Stunden aus dem Leben einer Frau, Verwirrung der Gefühle,* and *Unvermutete Bekanntschaft mit einem Handwerk* bear witness in the very act of narrating their experiences. They are all-too keenly aware that they are dealing with events for which neither their own past experience nor the collective experience of society provides a precedent. Yet it is in this shared context of unpreparedness that the narrative act must take place. That is the challenge of their undertaking.

In the works we have been considering the unprecedented assumes three basic forms: extraordinary events (which for Zweig means above all extraordinary psychological events); extreme or marginal situations; and exceptional, original characters. Inevitably, the lines of demarcation are fluid; and numerous overlaps occur. In outline, however, the threefold division may be accepted as a guide.

It is a feature of some of Zweig's best-known stories that they involve a volcanic psychological experience, in which the apparently calm surface of civilised life is shattered by the sudden eruption of uncontrollable forces. Whether it brings devastation, renewal, or reassessment, it is felt to be quite unique. As one reviewer of *Amok* put it, establishing a contrast between the subject of this volume and the adolescent themes of *Erstes Erlebnis,* 'Hier sind es nun Menschen auf der Höhe ihres Lebens, Menschen, denen *ein* Erlebnis, *eine* große Leidenschaft den Wendepunkt ihres Lebens — nach oben, nach unten — bringt'.[19] The clearest examples are of course *Der Amokläufer, Phantastische Nacht,* and *Vierundzwanzig Stunden aus dem Leben einer Frau,* though it should not be overlooked that the same experience forms an important element in *Leporella* and *Schachnovelle* too, while the quasi-sexual climax of *Unvermutete Bekanntschaft mit einem Handwerk* shares something of the same quality in a less radical form. In those works which do depict a radical change it may be said that the power of fate or chance, which lay at the heart of the unprecedented event in many *Novellen* of an earlier period,[20] has now been replaced by the instinctive forces of the unconscious, which are equally unamenable to rational understanding and control.[21]

Sometimes, however, the central psychological event is less sudden and eruptive. It is not so much that the individual is overwhelmed by an unexpected access of instinctive energies as that his mind becomes a battlefield of conflicting forces. In the stories of *Erstes Erlebnis* these conflicts appear to be part of the process of growing up, but from later works, notably *Angst, Der Zwang, Verwirrung der Gefühle*, and to some extent also *Schachnovelle*, it is evident that other psychological conflicts may characterise adult life. The human mind indeed is constantly being pulled in opposite directions. What is significant throughout is that Zweig does not interest himself in a random segment of some continuing mental struggle, but selects only the decisive battle, which engages all the character's energies. The adolescent heroes and heroines of his first collection are depicted at the moment of their 'erstes Erlebnis', the first experience of moment, which lifts them beyond the level of the everyday and may even determine their entire future. Yet what Alfred Pfoser observes in connection with *Brennendes Geheimnis* may be applied *mutatis mutandis* to all the stories that deal with some internal conflict: that Zweig concentrates all his attention 'auf das Erlebnis, auf das momenthafte Ausscheren aus der normalen Erfahrungswelt'.[22] To that extent the fierce struggle between Dr B. and Czentovic across the chessboard in *Schachnovelle*, which continues and in some measure externalises a conflict that took place earlier within Dr B., also forms part of the same pattern. On this occasion the battle is over in a matter of hours; but in other works it may take days (*Brennendes Geheimnis*) or may be spread over several weeks or even months (*Verwirrung der Gefühle*). In every case, however, it constitutes one event; and since it determines the individual's whole future — at times whether there will be any future for him at all — it is unique: unprecedented and unrepeated.

The sudden eruptions are inevitably more concentrated in time, but even the hero of *Verwirrung der Gefühle*, whose inner conflicts occupy the greatest length of time, introduces his account in words which seem designed to reduce the essence of his experience to the briefest span:

> Wir erleben Myriaden Sekunden, und doch wirds immer nur eine, eine einzige, die unsere ganze innere Welt in Wallung bringt, die Sekunde, da (Stendhal hat sie beschrieben) die innere, mit allen Säften schon getränkte Blüte blitzhaft in Kristallisation zusammenschießt. (VdG,156)[23]

This concentration on the decisive moment evidently appealed to Zweig's imagination, for it coloured his conception of history too. In the preface to his twelve historical miniatures *Sternstunden der Menschheit* he pictured history as a poetess, who spends most of her time amassing trivial and mundane facts and comes to creative life only at rare moments.[24] When one bears in mind that the moments chosen for depiction tend not only to reduce historical development to a series of uniquely dated and unprecedented crises, but to make each crisis dependent on the act of one individual,[25] depicted with considerable poetic licence, one must also allow that the various chapters of *Sternstunden der Menschheit* might be regarded as *Novellen* too.[26] Certainly they help to confirm Zweig's predisposition to the *genre*.

It would be surprising if the exceptional events we have just been considering did not place the individual in extreme situations. Yet even where the narrative lacks that one decisive event, Zweig continues to be fascinated by situations which occupy the desperate margins of human experience. This is most evident in *Brief einer Unbekannten*, where the driving force within the heroine is neither exhausted nor brought to a decisive climax, but nevertheless, as a constant presence, leads to the sacrifice of everything: comfort, safety, reputation; in *Die Mondscheingasse*, where the battle of the sexes is undecided at the end, but has already brought husband and wife to such squalid surroundings and shown itself to be so utterly uncompromising; and in *Untergang eines Herzens*, where the inner conflicts of the businessman are so far from resolution that they flare up even on his deathbed, but have in any case brought about such a radical and irreversible withdrawal from life. As to *Die Frau und die Landschaft*, whose sexual climax is not of itself so singular as to make it unlikely that the two central characters will have other lovers subsequently, what raises their union to the level of the extraordinary is, above all, its conjunction with extreme natural conditions: the relief of rainfall after a period of exceptionally severe drought. In *Die unsichtbare Sammlung* it is one element in the uniqueness of what is presented that, in unusually harsh times, the family of the blind collector has been driven to the desperate measure of disposing of his art-treasures secretly. Although this action is the very opposite of decisive, since it makes not the slightest difference to the attitudes and behaviour of the old man, it does nevertheless give rise to a quite extraordinary and paradoxical situation: rapturous delight over blank sheets of paper.

Introducing his professor's confession near the end of *Verwirrung der Gefühle*, Roland writes:

> Seit jenem Abend, wo dieser verehrteste Mann mir sein Schicksal wie eine harte Muschel aufschloß, seit jenem Abend vor vierzig Jahren scheint mir noch immer alles spielhaft und belanglos, was unsere Schriftsteller und Dichter in Büchern als außerordentlich erzählen. (VdG,262)

After the confession he describes the tone of his mentor's voice as one which came 'aus Tiefen, die mittleres Schicksal nie ertastet' (VdG,272). These words, which refer to an (interpolated) story that goes back a long way but never finds a proper resolution, point to the common purpose behind the many varied situations we have just been discussing: the portrayal of the extreme, the truly extraordinary in contradistinction to what is trivial or merely average.

The third form which the unprecedented assumes for Zweig is that of the exceptional, original figure. He is fascinated not only by the unique event which takes place within a limited period of time and the extreme situation with which the individual may be confronted perhaps once in a lifetime; he is also fascinated by the character whose inherent qualities or peculiar gifts set him (or her) apart from everyday experience. This is usually a matter of extra-ordinary mental powers such as memory and concentration, imagination, or learning skills (Mendel, the blind art-collector, Czentovic) or remarkable intellectual or emotional deficiencies (Boris, Crescenz), though the exceptional dexterity and daring of a

Parisian pickpocket, a man from the very fringe of society, can prove equally captivating. In each case the individual concerned becomes enmeshed in some extreme situation or participates in some extraordinary event, but that is always to some extent a product of his peculiar nature, which is itself usually sufficient to deserve the epithet 'einmalig' (K,110) and to call into question the common assumption that the *Novelle* must invariably focus its attention on a central event rather than on character.[27]

That Zweig should have taken such a consistent interest in the various aspects of the unprecedented — and that means: in the very heart of the *Novelle* — is no accident. His general outlook predisposed him to the shorter forms of narrative, but it was above all the conjunction of his psychological interest and his human ideals that led him inescapably to the *Novelle*. The sudden and unwonted eruption of unconscious forces; unparalled and unswerving commitment; inner conflicts fought out to a decisive conclusion or having a decisive influence; unrivalled mental gifts or deficiencies — all these are tailor-made for the *Novelle*, once it is allowed that psychology is not *ipso facto* an unbecoming form of dress for the *genre*. And that can no longer seriously be disputed, especially since a very good case has now been made out for the process of mutual enrichment between the *Novelle* and Freud's case histories.[28] Zweig's treatment of such subjects, moreover, was not the simple result of a passive acceptance of the psychological material randomly offered by life itself. It was an active choice, which both satisfied his psychological curiosity and accorded with the two ideals of human life that were dearest to his heart. The value he placed on passionate intensity and commitment naturally led him to favour narratives in which their expression, sudden or more extended, unbridled or in conflict with the forces of reason and morality, resulted in extraordinary events or extreme situations; and his love of personal freedom meant not only that he approved the right to such passion, even when it violated the conventions of polite society, but also that he took a special delight in those sometimes less passionate beings whose individuality manifested itself in a particularly strange, idiosyncratic, or original way.

It is possible to go still further and argue that Zweig's predilection for the *Novelle* ultimately derives from his apprehension of and response to the circumstances of his upbringing in late

303

nineteenth-century Vienna, on the one hand, and to major currents in early twentieth-century society, on the other. For the individualism fostered by his social background[29] and subsequently confirmed by his awareness of the increasing standardisation and uniformity of modern culture[30] made him particularly receptive to a form of narrative characterised by its concentration on exceptional events and characters. As Joseph Strelka remarks in explanation of Zweig's turn to the *Novelle* in the nineteen-twenties:

> Es ist nicht überraschend, sondern nur natürlich, daß die literarische Revolution Stefan Zweigs in der Hinwendung zur Novelle bestand, die einerseits den Ausschnitt aus dem Leben eines Einzelnen und andererseits — der Eintönigkeit entgegengesetzt — eine unerhörte Begebenheit aus dem Leben eines Einzelnen als Hauptmerkmale ihres inneren Struktur-prinzipes hat.[31]

Moreover, as we have already seen, a certain dissatisfaction with the solidity, security, and ease of his own social environment caused him to be especially fascinated by those who live mono-maniacally or with passionate intensity.[32] The underlying discontent was of course by no means unique to Zweig; it was widely felt both at the time and earlier. Yet the most noteworthy fact for our present considerations is that what had moved Nietzsche to a form of prophetic utterance, in which Dionysian spontaneity was celebrated as the remedy, and what led Freud to an anthropological and socio-psychological analysis, in which the 'Unlust in der Kultur' was traced to the necessary renunciation of the instincts, impelled Zweig towards a form of narrative which was peculiarly suited to recording those rare and remarkable breaches of the intellectual patterns and supposedly moral and civilising restraints that were generally regarded as the cause of the *malaise*.

One consequence of Zweig's emphasis on the exceptional nature of such events is that, although the passionate intensity is generally endorsed, he cannot readily project an appropriate future for the characters concerned, cannot indicate how they will, to quote Sørensen, 'administer this new engagement in life'.[33] Where passion leads to disaster and death, as it does in *Der Amokläufer*, the difficulty does not arise. But in *Vierundzwanzig Stunden aus dem Leben einer Frau* the volcanic experience is followed by a gap of some twenty years, about which the reader learns little except that, after an initial repudiation of its consequences, the passionate encounter has continued to occupy the heroine's mind. Although he may surmise that the experience has contributed to her subsequent tolerance, there is nothing to suggest that it has proved decisive in the sense of initiating a whole new way of life. In *Verwirrung der Gefühle* the encounter with passion and enthusiasm is said to have given a new and lifelong impulse to the hero's career, but the effects have not become fictionally real and remain obscure. And in *Phantastische Nacht*, where the greatest claims are made for the permanent and rejuvenating effects of passionate intensity, the hero is killed off before the claims can properly be put to the test. In the final analysis it seems that Zweig's interest in the uniqueness of the central event — and that means in its potential as a *Novelle* — overrides his concern for its moral outworkings.

The pursuit of the unprecedented which led Zweig to the *Novelle* simultaneously exposed him to an artistic danger which he did not always overcome: the danger of excess. If, as Pongs and others point out, the *Novelle* is designed fundamentally to answer the question, 'Was gibt's Neues?',[34] the temptation may be to respond in the sensational manner of the popular press. Joachim Müller indeed, discussing the dangers specific to the various epic *genres*, defines that of the *Novelle* as lying 'in der Übertreibung des Ereignishaften zu handfester Kolportage'.[35] Many of Zweig's *Novellen* were — and still are — popular. Novelty and excitement, two of the ingredients of the popular press, form part of the appeal of his *Novellen* too. Yet that does not of itself make them excessive or sensational. In the end it is chiefly a matter of the author's treatment and, as must also be conceded, the reader's taste, which is a variable factor. None the less, even though individual readers will continue to react differently, it may be worthwhile indicating some of those aspects which are most likely to cause disquiet.

At the simplest level there are occasional problems of credibility with some of the intellectual extremes portrayed. Can one really believe such utter naiveté and geographical ignorance as are displayed by Boris in *Episode am Genfer See*? Can one accept that an otherwise dull-witted and unimaginative man such as Czentovic might attain the position of world chess-champion from the mere

305

observation of other men's play or that, under the pressure of solitary confinement and sensory deprivation, even an imaginative man like Dr B. might learn so much from a chess-manual that he could, without the benefit of practice against an external opponent, defeat that world-champion?

In the presentation of passionate intensity similar problems of credibility occasionally arise. Could the novelist of *Brief einer Unbekannten* really have failed to recognise the woman with whom he had previously spent the night? Could the wife in *Die Mondscheingasse* really have sunk to the level of a prostitute in a foreign port? There is, however, an even more serious and fundamental difficulty to contend with. Zweig was fascinated by all forms of activity that entailed the progressive augmentation of excitement to a point of climax. In *Die Frau und die Landschaft* there is the steady accumulation of instinctive forces that eventually find release in copulation; in *Phantastische Nacht* the growth of excitement among the crowd during the course of a race, which reaches its peak as the winning horse passes the post; in *Vierundzwanzig Stunden aus dem Leben einer Frau* the nervous agitation of the gambler's hands, which mounts unbearably until it collapses at the failure of his bet; and in *Unvermutete Bekanntschaft mit einem Handwerk* the mounting tension of the public auction, as the bids increase more and more until the sudden fall of the gavel clinches the deal. These activities function in the works concerned as metaphors or paradigms of passionate intensity, but in doing so they also highlight the difficulty of the author's task. For while they are of a kind which is characterised in normal practice by repetition — in one case compulsive repetition — after an appropriate period of relaxation, the passionate event after which Zweig strives as a writer of *Novellen* has to be unprecedented and unrepeated.

One result of this is that, unlike their more sober and factual counterparts in Schnitzler, whose melancholic irony deflates the sensational and reduces the extraordinary to everyday proportions,[36] Zweig's narrators seem to feel themselves under a constant obligation to persuade the reader of the uniqueness of what they are reporting, sometimes in so many words, sometimes less explicitly, by deploying all the resources of intensifiction. I have already remarked on the sometimes wearisome assurances that the events recorded are such as have never before and never

306

since been experienced, but there are other stylistic features which bear witness to what is at bottom the same striving after maximum excitement. Among these are: the recourse to superlatives[37] and to overworked and devalued adverbs such as 'ungeheuer', 'furchtbar', 'entsetzlich'; the cumulation of imagery, the interposition of rhetorical questions; the passing use of the historic present tense.

Even beyond the linguistic level the presentation seeks to increase the drama of the decisive experience. Emotions are not simply felt; they are registered physically, so that they become quite literally sensational. As in *Sternstunden der Menschheit*, the full potential of time is exploited. Not only is the central event concentrated into a minimal span (the fantastic night, twenty-four hours in the life of a woman); its every phase is marked as an intense hour, moment, second. Bengt Sørensen calls this Zweig's 'Sekundenstil', the very opposite of the Naturalistic counterpart with its indiscriminate registering of every trivial detail, and goes on to describe it as 'a dramatising, highly artificial construction for the sake of suspense, an attempt to transform reality into a unique culmination of dramatic, sometimes even sensational events'.[38] Finally, where possible, Zweig introduces an additional urgency into the situation, perhaps by the imminent departure of a train (*Der Zwang, Vierundzwanzig Stunden aus dem Leben einer Frau*), perhaps by the threat of some impending danger (*Angst, Phantastische Nacht*), perhaps by the need for immediate medical attention (*Der Amokläufer*). Whatever the particulars, the underlying aim is to heighten the suspense, that quality which he once described as the 'Urelement' of all narrative,[39] to enable the reader to share the tension which the characters are already supposed to experience, and ultimately therefore to make him appreciate for himself how unprecedented the events really are.

That the means employed to dramatise the unprecedented event are sometimes counterproductive or fail in their aim is largely a matter of presentation. Since these matters concern the writer's powers of persuasion, however, they bring us to that final aspect of the *Novelle* isolated by Swales which we have not yet considered: its interest in the interpretative link between the exceptional or marginal event and the world as commonly experienced and understood. Particularly in the stories of his maturity, it is one of Zweig's most consistent aims to place their

307

extraordinary events and characters in some challenging relation to the generality of human experience.

This is one of the chief functions of his imagery, however unoriginal, indiscriminate, or obtrusive its use may sometimes be. As the German noun 'Vergleich' more clearly reminds us, metaphorical language is able to extend the range of what is known, understood, or accepted by providing a point of comparison with that which already lies within the common experience. Freud, who, at least in addressing Zweig himself, was more indulgent towards his metaphorical language than was Roth, agreed that, since there was no precise language available for the demonic element with which the author was dealing, he had to draw his comparisons from other areas of perception.[40] Accordingly, while much of Zweig's imagery is taken up with the task of communicating the nature and reality of extreme passion and commitment by likening it to known experiences of, for example, heat, fire, liquidity, or intoxication, or by contrasting it with their opposites, much is also designed to win acceptance for what is so extraordinary as to appear immoral or anti-social by presenting it in terms of what is widely deemed commendable (religion) or pitiable (fever, convulsion) rather than blameworthy. In this way the exceptional and marginal is brought within the intellectual, emotional, and moral grasp of ordinary society without at the same time sacrificing its special character.

Above all, however, it is Zweig's use of the narrative frame which aligns his stories with the interpretative aspect of the *Novelle.* By this means he distances the central event or character from the polite, cultured, respectable society to which both reader and narrator are assumed to belong and yet also, through parallels and contrasts, questions the values and preconceptions of that society, inviting sympathy with what might otherwise have been rejected and suspicion of what might otherwise have been accepted blindly. Like the metaphorical language, the narrative frame establishes comparisons;[41] above all through its interaction with the inset narrative it becomes an indispensable guide to a proper understanding of the 'unerhörte Begebenheit'.

If in the end there is hesitation about referring to some of Zweig's stories as *Novellen,* it is most likely in those cases where the central event does not appear sufficiently exceptional or fateful and where at the same time the interpretative challenge is not taken up. This is so in *Die Gouvernante, Geschichte in der Dämmerung*, and perhaps also *Die Frau und die Landschaft*,[42] which, significantly, are among the works which either have no narrative frame or do not use it interpretatively. In general, however, the *Novelle* appears to be so much in tune with Zweig's narrative aims that, if the *genre* had not already existed, he would have had to invent it.

List of Abbreviations used in the Notes

For the sake of brevity the following additional abbreviations have been used in the Notes:

Works by Zweig

BF	*Briefe an Freunde*
BMBS	*Begegnungen mit Menschen, Büchern, Städten*
DDL	*Drei Dichter ihres Lebens*
DM	*Drei Meister*
Erbe	*Europäisches Erbe*
GW	*Gesammelte Werke in Einzelbänden*, ed. Knut Beck
KD	*Der Kampf mit dem Dämon*
MS	*Maria Stuart*
TT	*Triumph und Tragik des Erasmus von Rotterdam*
WvG	*Die Welt von Gestern*
ZuW	*Zeit und Welt*

Secondary Literature

Gschiel	Martha Gschiel, *Das dichterische Prosawerk Stefan Zweigs*
Klawiter[1]	Randolph J. Klawiter, *Stefan Zweig's Novellen: an analysis*
Lent	Ingrid Lent, *Das Novellenwerk Stefan Zweigs*
Strelka[1]	Joseph Strelka, *Stefan Zweig: Freier Geist der Menschlichkeit*
Strelka[2]	Joseph Strelka, 'Psychoanalytische Ideen in Stefan Zweigs Novellen'
Welter	Marie-Luise Welter, *Typus und Eros: eine Untersuchung des Menschenbildes in den Novellen Stefan Zweigs*

Fuller bibliographical details will be found in the Select Bibliography.

Notes

Notes for page 3

INTRODUCTION

1. Details of the translations of Zweig's works are to be found in Randolph J. Klawiter, *Stefan Zweig: a bibliography* (University of North Carolina Studies in the Germanic Languages and Literatures no. 50, Chapel Hill, 1965).
2. Hans Vogelsang, 'Stefan Zweig', *Österreich in Geschichte und Literatur*, vol. 11 (1967) p. 95.
3. Strelka[1], p. 51.
4. Further details of sales are recorded by Alfred Pfoser, 'Verwirrung der Gefühle als Verwirrung einer Zeit: Bemerkungen zum Bestsellerautor Stefan Zweig und zur Psychologie in seinen Novellen', in: *Stefan Zweig 1881-1981: Aufsätze und Dokumente*, ed. Heinz Lunzer und Gerhard Renner (Vienna, 1981) pp. 7-17.
5. Friderike Maria Zweig, *Stefan Zweig wie ich ihn erlebte* (Stockholm, 1947), also in English as: Friderike Zweig, *Stefan Zweig* (London, 1946).
6. D.A. Prater, *European of Yesterday: a biography of Stefan Zweig* (Oxford, 1972); Donald A. Prater, *Stefan Zweig: das Leben eines Ungeduldigen* (Munich, 1981).
7. Strelka[1].
8. Of the many essays devoted to Zweig's humanism the following may be mentioned: Hanns Arens, *Stefan Zweig: der Mensch im Werk* (Vienna, 1931); Jules Romains, *Stefan Zweig: grand européen* (New York, 1941); Richard Friedenthal, *Stefan Zweig und der humanitäre Gedanke* (Eßlingen, 1948); Harry Zohn, 'Stefan Zweig as Literary Mediator', *Books Abroad*, vol. 26, no. 1/2 (1952) pp. 137-40; Kurt Böttcher, 'Humanist auf verlorener Bastion: ein Gedenken an Stefan Zweig zu seinem 75. Geburtstag', *Neue deutsche Literatur*, vol. 4 (1956) pp. 83-92; Donald G. Daviau, 'Stefan Zweig's Victors in Defeat', *Monatshefte*, vol. 51, no. 1 (1959) pp. 1-12; Hans-Albert Walter, 'Vom Liberalismus zum Eskapismus: Stefan Zweig im Exil', in: *Die deutsche Exilliteratur 1933-1945*, ed. Manfred Durzak (Stuttgart, 1973) pp. 291-311; C.E. Williams, 'Stefan Zweig: pacifist extraordinary', in: *The Broken Eagle: the politics of Austrian literature from Empire to Anschluß* (London, 1974) pp. 113-31; Klaus Jarmatz, 'Stefan Zweigs Humanismusverständnis', *Weimarer Beiträge*, vol. 21, no. 9 (1975) pp. 94-115; Lionel B. Steiman, 'The Agony of Humanism in World

Notes for pages 3-4

War I: the case of Stefan Zweig', *Journal of European Studies,* vol. 6 (1976) pp. 100-24.

9. Details of these will be found in the bibliography at the end of the volume.

10. See especially Gschiel, Lent, Welter and Klawiter[1].

11. Harry Salpeter, 'Three Powerful Stories', *New York Times Book Review,* 9 Oct. 1927, p. 14; Louis Kronenberger, 'Zweig's Tale of Guilt in the Tropics', ibid., 14 June 1931, p. 7; and 'Brilliant Tales by Stefan Zweig', ibid., 1 Apr. 1934, p. 8; Fred T. March, 'Unwavering Devotion: letter from an unknown woman', *New York Herald Tribune (Books),* 19 June 1922, p. 3. Cf. also Klawiter[1], p. 98.

12. This unpublished postcard is in the possession of the Jewish National and University Library, Jerusalem (Arc. Ms. Var. 305/58). I am grateful to the Department of Manuscripts and Archives for permission to quote from it.

13. Quoted from Klaus Jonas, 'Stefan Zweig und Thomas Mann: Versuch einer Dokumentation', *Modern Austrian Literature,* vol. 14, nos. 3-4 (1981) p. 104.

14. This unpublished letter is in the possession of the Jewish National and University Library, Jerusalem (Arc. Ms. Var. 305/41). I am grateful to the Department of Manuscripts and Archives for permission to quote from it.

15. I have been unable to trace any reference to Zweig's *Novellen* in the correspondence of Schnitzler, Hofmannsthal and Thomas Mann.

16. In an essay on 'Dichter und Dichtung' Helmut Kuhn implies a conception of 'Dichtung' as something elevated and argues that it is quite possible for both narrative and dramatic literature to part company with true 'Dichtung' by becoming, for example, merely entertaining or didactic. Nevertheless, he is forced to admit that it is a matter of degree and that no sharp distinction can be drawn between what he calls 'epische Dichtung' and 'Erzählungsliteratur'. See *Das Fischer Lexikon: Literatur II, Erster Teil,* ed. Wolf-Hartmut Friedrich and Walter Killy (Frankfurt a.M., 1965) pp. 115-51, especially p. 144.

17. *Amok ou le fou de Malaisie; Lettre d'une inconnue; La ruelle au clair de lune,* with a preface by Romain Rolland (Paris, 1930); the authorised Russian edition of Zweig's collected works (*Sobranie Sochinenij Stefana Tsweyga*) published in Leningrad between 1928 and 1930 has a foreword by Maxim Gorky, the German translation of which appears in Maxim Gorki — Stefan Zweig, *Briefwechsel,* ed. Kurt Böttcher (Frankfurt a.M., 1974) pp. 98-108; *The Royal*

Notes for pages 5-11

Game and Other Stories, with an introduction by John Fowles, translated from the German by Jill Sutcliffe (London, 1981); *Das Stefan Zweig Buch*, with a postscript by Max von der Grün (Frankfurt a.M., 1981).

18. *Das Literarische Echo*, vol. 7 (1904-1905) col. 291. Hesse expressed some of his doubts in a letter to Zweig dated 15 October 1904. See Donald Prater, 'Stefan Zweig and Hermann Hesse', *Modern Austrian Literature*, vol. 14, nos. 3-4 (1981) pp. 32-3.

19. WvG, p. 316. From a letter to Paul Zech dated 20 February 1913 it emerges that Zweig wished Zech to omit all mention of *Die Liebe der Erika Ewald* from an essay on him which he was then writing. See Stefan Zweig and Paul Zech, *Briefe 1910-1942*, ed. Donald G. Daviau (Rudolstadt, 1984) p. 35.

20. Strelka[2], p. 44, demonstrates how in *Brennendes Geheimnis* the rational understanding of the young hero fails to appreciate the depths of his own unconscious.

21. See Wayne C. Booth, *The Rhetoric of Fiction* (Chicago and London, 1961) especially pp. 158-9,175,239-40.

22. John M. Ellis, *Narration in the German Novelle: theory and interpretation* (Cambridge, 1974) p. 38.

23. Readers seeking comprehensive discussion of individual works are referred to the index, which lists together the comments from various parts of the volume.

PART ONE: THE PSYCHOLOGICAL FOUNDATION

1. Stefan Zweig, *Amok* (Paris, 1930) p. xii.

2. Ibid.

3. See Arnold Bauer, *Stefan Zweig*, (Köpfe des XX. Jahrhunderts No. 21, Berlin, 1961) p. 56.

4. Quoted from *Stefan Zweig im Zeugnis seiner Freunde*, ed. Hanns Arens (Munich and Vienna, 1968) p. 16.

5. Robert Neumann, 'Abschied von Stefan Zweig', *Blätter der internationalen Stefan-Zweig-Gesellschaft*, nos. 11/12 (Oct. 1961) pp. 2-3. A more balanced view is provided by Strelka[2], p. 45, who writes: 'Überblickt man die reifen Novellen jener Schaffensperiode, dann zeigt sich einerseits, daß sie — und zwar auch jene, in denen zahlreiche Details den Einsichten Freuds folgen — nichts weniger sind als novellistische Konstruktionen tiefenpsychologischer Anschauungen, sondern daß sie vielmehr eigene und eigenständige fiktionale Schöpfungen sind, in denen sich in vielen

Notes for pages 12-19

Fällen gewiß bewußt, psychoanalytische Ideen ausgedrückt finden'.

6. See Carl E. Schorske, *Fin-de-siècle Vienna: politics and culture* (London, 1979) pp. 5-10.

7. Letter from Freud to Schnitzler dated 14 May 1922, quoted from Ernest Jones, *Sigmund Freud: life and work*, vol. 3 (London, 1957) p. 474.

8. Eliseo Vivas, 'The Two Dimensions of Reality in *The Brothers Karamazov*', in: *Dostoevsky: a collection of critical essays*, ed. René Wellek (Englewood Cliffs, 1962) p. 74.

9. Sigmund Freud, 'Dostoevsky and Parricide', *Art and Literature* (Pelican Freud Library, vol. 14, Harmondsworth, 1985) pp. 437-60.

10. In a generally persuasive article Strelka[2] yields to this temptation in connection with *Der Amokläufer* and *Die Mondscheingasse*, especially pp. 46-7.

11. This is indeed the method theoretically espoused by Strelka.

1. The Problems of Adolescence

1. *Imago: Zeitschrift für Anwendung der Psychoanalyse auf die Geisteswissenschaften*, vol. 1 (1912) pp. 209-11.

2. See WvG, pp. 76-84.

3. Ellen Key, *Das Jahrhundert des Kindes*, (34th to 36th edition, Berlin, 1926) p. 293.

4. The same urge to dominate is to be found in the first sexual encounter of the young hero of the early story *Scharlach* (1908). Although he is already a student, he, too, is in many respects still a child.

5. In the early story *Ein Verbummelter* (1901) the young hero, a twenty-one-year-old who is still at school, vents his frustration and anger only briefly on the teacher who has prevented his advancement. In the end he can find no other outlet than to destroy himself. See Stefan Zweig, *Der Amokläufer*, GW, pp. 63-9.

6. It is in the primacy of imagination and the elevation of the beloved to unattainability rather than in 'double frustration' or 'weakness to act' that any similarities with Storm's *Immensee* lie. Cf. Klawiter[1], p. 117.

7. Cf., for example, the contrast within the same paragraph between the statement, 'Sie wissen jetzt alles', and 'Noch können sie das Furchtbare, das um sie geschehen ist, nicht fassen' (EE,82).

8. Letter dated 19 November 1911 in: *The Correspondence of Stefan*

Notes for pages 20-27

Zweig and Raoul Auernheimer, edited and with an introduction
and notes by Donald G. Daviau and Jorum B. Johns, and with
Richard Beer-Hoffmann, edited and with commentary and notes
by Jeffrey B. Berlin (Columbia, South Carolina, 1983) p. 41.
9. Cf. Welter, p. 23.
10. *Die Liebe der Erika Ewald: Novellen* (Berlin, 1904) p. 12. There is
something very similar in the young heroine of the final story of the
same volume, *Die Wunder des Lebens*, a fifteen-year-old Jewish
girl who is said to be one of those 'die Wochen und Jahre nach
Zärtlichkeit hungern'. Ibid., p. 116.
11. The inadequacy, particularly in the company of supposedly 'adult'
older students, and the confused emotional response are also to be
found in the young student of the early story *Scharlach*.
12. See Ann Clark Fehn and Ulrike S. Rettig, 'Narrative Technique
and Psychological Analysis in Two Novellas by Stefan Zweig', in:
*Stefan Zweig: the world of yesterday's humanist today:
proceedings of the Stefan Zweig symposium*, ed. Marion
Sonnenfeld (Albany, 1983) p. 174.
13. The young student of *Scharlach* also goes through a phase of
wanting to return home, to escape the problems of life, and enjoy
the carefree life of a child once more. See Stefan Zweig, *Die
Hochzeit von Lyon und andere Erzählungen* (Frankfurt a.M.,
1980) especially pp. 43,44,46.
14. Klawiter[1], pp. 121-2; and Strelka[2], p. 44, who deals with the matter
with greater differentiation. Strelka also regards the story as
evidence of a mother-fixation in Zweig himself (p. 51), a contention
which lies outside the scope of our discussion.
15. The suggestion of Fehn and Rettig, 'Narrative Technique and
Psychological Analysis', p. 175, that the ending is ambiguous in the
further sense that Edgar will in future probably adopt the
inadequate predatory sexuality of the baron is speculative.
16. Stefan Zweig, 'Das Tagebuch eines halbwüchsigen Mädchens',
Almanach der Psychoanalyse (1926) p. 142.

2. The Eruption of the Unconscious

1. *Die Heilung durch den Geist: Mesmer, Mary Baker-Eddy, Freud*
(Leipzig, 1931) pp. 323,407,444.
2. Ibid., pp. 325,333,363-4,368. Cf. also WvG, p. 437.
3. In his essay on Dostoyevsky Zweig had already used the
'Amokläufer' as a metaphor for those characters of the Russian

Notes for pages 29-47

novelist who hurl themselves into life. He also remarked there, however, that they are not linear in their journey through life. DM, pp. 130-5,139.

4. Gschiel, p. 107.
5. Cf. Welter, p. 77.
6. The encounter may be based on a similar experience of the author's. A diary entry at the end of February 1913 refers obscurely to a dangerous encounter in the Schönbornpark. Stefan Zweig, *Tagebücher*, GW, p. 41.
7. Cf. also the following passage: 'Unendliches Mitleid mit ihr, mit allen überkam mich, irgendetwas Warmes, das Zärtlichkeit war und doch keine Sinnlichkeit' (A,193).
8. Cf. Gschiel, p. 136, who points out that *Vierundzwanzig Stunden aus dem Leben einer Frau* is closest to the *Novellen* of *Amok* in its portrayal of sudden, unexpected passion which overcomes all restraints.
9. Cf. Klawiter[1], p. 140.
10. Strelka[2], p. 48, interprets the entire story in terms of the oedipal fixation.
11. See especially Freud's essay 'Dostoevsky and Parricide', pp. 459-60.
12. Klawiter[1], p. 136.
13. The manuscript is in the possession of the Deutsches Literatur-Archiv, Marbach a.N.
14. The phrase occurs at a point in the manuscript which corresponds to p. 53 of the version printed in *Kaleidoskop* (Vienna, Leipzig, Zurich, 1936).
15. Strelka[2], p. 17. One is reminded also of what Freud wrote in his essay 'Some Character-Types met with in Psychoanalytical Work': 'The practising psychoanalytic physician knows how frequently, or how invariably, a girl who enters a household as servant, companion or governess will consciously or unconsciously weave a day-dream, which derives from the Oedipus complex, of the mistress of the house disappearing and the master taking the new-comer as his wife in her place'. Freud, *Art and Literature*, p. 315.
16. Klawiter[1], p. 137.
17. Gschiel, p. 156, asserts that it is not sexual passion which is aroused. It may be true that it is not sexual passion which is directly aroused, but, however obliquely, it is aroused.
18. Donald G. Daviau and Harvey I. Dunkle, 'Stefan Zweig's *Schachnovelle'*, *Monatshefte*, vol. 65 (1973) pp. 372,382.
19. Brian Murdoch, 'Game, Image and Ambiguity in Stefan Zweig's

Notes for pages 48-51

Schachnovelle', *New German Studies*, vol. 11, no. 3 (1983) pp. 181-2, finds this prognosis 'a little optimistic'. His doubts, however, seem to be based largely on extraneous factors, particularly a supposed parallel with the conclusion of Goethe's *Torquato Tasso*.

3. Single-mindedness

1. March, 'Unwavering Devotion', p. 3.
2. A similar theme occurs in the even earlier story *Vergessene Träume* (1900), where a woman marries a wealthy count in order to escape 'die Niedrigkeit des Werkeltages'. She confesses to being 'in einem Rausch von Kunstschönheit befangen, der mich mein wirkliches Leben verachten ließ'. In her case, however, the pursuit of such elegance, art, and wealth takes her away from true love. See Stefan Zweig, *Verwirrung der Gefühle*, GW, pp. 71-8.
3. Strelka[2], p. 47, where he also suggests that the young woman's fixation determines the course of her remaining life.
4. Reprinted in *Phantastische Nacht: Erzählungen*, GW. It may be that Zweig based these portraits of teenage devotion on the infatuation of young women which he himself frequently experienced (see *Tagebücher*, p. 35), although there is something very similar in the adulation of the first letters which Friderike von Winterntiz, then a married woman with children, wrote to Zweig in the second decade of the century (see Stefan Zweig — Friderike Zweig, *Briefwechsel 1912-1942* (Berne, 1951) pp. 16-17,18-19,25-6,51,75).
5. Cf. also her reference to the child as 'Dein anderes Du' (A,250).
6. On the whole Zweig seems to present shame as an instinct. As to Freud, although he discusses it together with disgust and morality as one of the psychic dams which are constructed during the course of individual psychic development, he also describes it as an historical precipitate of the 'external inhibitions to which the sexual instinct has been subjected during the psychogenesis of the human race', a precipitate that can arise, as though spontaneously, in response to a signal from upbringing and external influence. Elsewhere he speaks of the construction of these dams as 'organically determined and fixed by heredity', as something that can occasionally occur without any help at all from education. Freud, *On Sexuality* (The Pelican Freud Library, vol. 7, Harmondsworth, 1977) pp. 109,76,93. In his *Introductory Lectures on Psychoanalysis*, on the other hand, he speaks of it as an impulse from the unconscious. *Introductory Lectures on Psychoanalysis*

Notes for pages 51-60

(The Pelican Freud Library, vol. 1, Harmondsworth, 1974) p. 452.
7. Gschiel, p. 121.

4. Inner Conflicts

1. Although one of the printed versions contains the note 'Geschrieben Wien, 1910', Zweig's diary makes clear that it was written between February and April 1913. *Tagebücher*, pp. 40,44, 67,70,71.
2. Welter, p. 41; and Lent, p. 14, who also mentions similarities with Schnitzler's *Ein Abschied*.
3. This is the interpretation of Welter, p. 40.
4. His very first recorded diary entry, dated 10 September 1912, notes that the excitement surrounding the performance of his play *Das Haus am Meer* meant less to him than one of his sexual adventures and adds: 'und die sind doch nur wertvoll durch ihre Gefahr'. *Tagebücher*, p. 9.
5. Fehn and Rettig, 'Narrative Technique and Psychological Analysis', p. 169.
6. Cf. also Gschiel, p. 97, and Welter, p. 42.
7. One might also mention that, when she has handed over her engagement ring to the blackmailer, she is painfully aware of this 'nackte Stelle' on her finger (K,160).
8. Fehn and Rettig, 'Narrative Technique and Psychological Analysis', p. 172, draw attention to the fact that Zweig writes of a scar rather than of fully healed flesh and conclude that the game between husband and wife is likely to recur in another form.
9. Kronenberger, 'Brilliant Tales by Stefan Zweig', p. 8.
10. The manuscript is in the possession of the Deutsches Literatur-Archiv, Marbach a.N. under the title *Der Refraktär*.
11. Williams, *The Broken Eagle*, p. 120, makes what I believe is an error in referring to the Austrian authorities. Although the story is not specific, the proximity of the frontier to Zurich makes it likely, on internal evidence, that Ferdinand is subject to the German authorities. The manuscript of the story makes clear that this is indeed so: the town M., where Ferdinand is ordered to report for duty, is there identified as Magdeburg.
12. Cf. the following: 'Ohne selbst um sich zu wissen, klinkte er die Türe auf' (VdG^2, 225); 'selbst unwissend um seine Hast' (VdG^2,237); 'traumwandlerisch nannte er den Grenzort als Ziel, willenlos stieg er um in einen andern Zug' (VdG^2,257).

13. Cf. the following: 'Ferdinand [. . .] hörte seine Lippen stammeln' (VdG²,244); 'er starrte auf seine eigenen Hände, die alles dies zweckmäßig taten ohne seinen Willen' (VdG²,250).
14. Cf. the following: 'Irgendetwas steht auf in mir [. . .] und zittert und gehorcht' (VdG²,234); 'aber dann riß es ihn weiter' (VdG²,237); 'aber die Maschine in seinem Blut, die nicht sprach und doch gewaltig Nerv und Glieder regte, sie stieß ihn ehern vorwärts' (VdG²,257).
15. The manuscript of the story makes the link between retreat from the world and suicide even clearer. A passage omitted from the second section describes his attempt to avoid the approaches of the military authorities in these portentous words: 'Vergebens grub er sich ein' (p. 6 of the manuscript).
16. *Die Liebe der Erika Ewald*, p. 50.
17. The phrase 'ohnmächtige Wut' is used later to describe his banging on the table, when he is seeking to justify his proposed return in contradiction of his convictions.
18. This seems to be what Klawiter has in mind when he describes Ferdinand's Swiss refuge as becoming increasingly like a cell guarded by an ever-watchful conscience that reproaches him with cowardice. Klawiter[1], p. 147.
19. I am here using the definition of prepositional object given by Karl-Dieter Bünting and Henning Bergenholtz, *Einführung in die Syntax* (Königstein, 1979) pp. 77-8.
20. Cf., for example, Anselma Heine, 'Verwirrung der Gefühle', *Die Literatur: Monatsschrift für Literaturfreunde (1926),* no. 3 (= *Das Literarische Echo*, vol. 29) p. 176.
21. It seems likely that he projects something of this idealised image of their relationship on to the beauty he perceives in the surrounding landscape: 'und hinter ihnen schroffer die Berge, streng und doch ohne Hochmut die Lieblichkeit des Sees überschauend, wie ernste Männer geliebter Kinder belangloses Spiel' (VdG,116-17).
22. To describe the daughter as 'innerlich ganz verdorben', as does Gschiel, p. 141, is to judge her too much through her father's distorted eyes.
23. Freud tended to concentrate on the incestuous component in sexuality at the stage of puberty; but he did also note the erotic element in parental affection. 'On the Universal Tendency to Debasement in the Sphere of Love', *On Sexuality*, p. 249.
24. Klawiter[1], p. 141, writes rather tentatively of the possibility of sexual jealousy.
25. Lent, p. 64, points out that, powerless against his family,

Notes for pages 70-82

Salomonssohn can only fight his fate by fighting himself, in an anger which is directed ultimately against himself.

26. Strelka[2], p. 49, regards Salomonssohn's commercial activity as an (unsuccessful) sublimation of the sexual drive. This view is speculative. The evidence of the text indicates that the signs of sexual frustration have a shorter history than his involvement in business.

27. See E. Dieckmann, '*Der Tod des Iwan Iljitsch* und *Untergang eines Herzens*: ein Vergleich zwischen Lev Tolstoj und Stefan Zweig', in: *Begegnung und Bündnis: Sowjetische und deutsche Literatur: Historische und theoretische Aspekte ihrer Beziehungen*, ed. Gerhard Ziegengeist (Berlin, 1972) pp. 418-26.

28. The former is the formulation of Welter, p. 104, the latter that of Gschiel, p. 145.

29. Cf. also the following declaration: 'Wer nicht passioniert ist, wird bestenfalls ein Schulmann — von innen her muß man an die Dinge kommen, immer, immer von der Leidenschaft her' (VdG,187).

30. 'The Sexual Aberrations', *On Sexuality*, p. 56.

31. Gschiel, p. 145.

32. Klawiter[1], pp. 142,144-5.

33. KD, pp. 182-3.

34. Welter, p. 106.

35. Strelka[2], p. 49, discusses Roland's vacillations between the professor (as a father-figure) and — 'der tiefer sitzenden Ödipusbindung folgend' — the wife; but he does not indicate any links with sexual ambivalence.

36. Reprinted in Stefan Zweig, *Die Hochzeit von Lyon und andere Erzählungen* (Frankfurt a.M., 1980).

37. A fictional example that should have been known to Zweig is the figure of Dr Skowronnek in Roth's *Radetzkymarsch*, who, once his usual partner, the 'Bezirkshauptmann', has died, sits and plays chess against himself.

38. See James Drever, *A Dictionary of Psychology* (Penguin Reference Books, Harmondsworth, 1965) p. 258. Lent, p. 109, prefers to call Dr B.'s condition a psychosis.

5. The Battle of the Sexes

1. 'The Sexual Aberrations', *On Sexuality*, pp. 70-2.
2. 'The Taboo of Virginity', *On Sexuality*, pp. 282-3.
3. It is for this reason, or perhaps out of a complementary masochistic

Notes for pages 83-90

need, that the baron, having hitherto heard only the woman's voice, pictures her first with a whip in her hand.

4. 'Infantile Sexuality', *On Sexuality*, p. 122.
5. Strelka[2], p. 46, speculates, nevertheless, on the existence of such a childhood experience and suggests that, in committing suicide, the doctor is also preserving his own psychological secret.
6. This motif plays an important role in the early story *Geschichte eines Unterganges* (1910), where the banished Mme de Prie seeks to counteract the tedium of her provincial exile in an erotic adventure with a local peasant lad in which social domination is a chief component. See Stefan Zweig, *Der Amokläufer*, GW, pp. 7-49.
7. Freud, 'The Universal Tendency to Debasement in the Sphere of Love', *On Sexuality*, pp. 256-7.
8. Kronenberger, 'Zweig's Tale of Guilt in the Tropics', p. 7.
9. This is perhaps why Klawiter[1], p. 134, speaks only in terms of masochism.
10. *Die Liebe der Erika Ewald*, p. 52.
11. Cf. also Gschiel, p. 112; Klawiter[1], p. 135; Lent, p. 34; Welter, p. 59.
12. Klawiter[1], p. 135.
13. Ibid., p. 133.
14. The following words of Dr Condor are used as the motto placed at the beginning of the novel: 'Es gibt eben zweierlei Mitleid. Das eine, das schwachmütige und sentimentale, das eigentlich nur Ungeduld des Herzens ist, sich möglichst schnell freizumachen von der peinlichen Ergriffenheit vor einem fremden Unglück, jenes Mitleid, das gar nicht Mit-leiden ist, sondern nur instinktive Abwehr des fremden Leidens von der eigenen Seele. Und das andere, das einzig zählt — das unsentimentale, aber schöpferische Mitleid, das weiß, was es will, und entschlossen ist, geduldig und mitduldend alles durchzustehen bis zum Letzten seiner Kraft und noch über dies Letzte hinaus'. Quoted from Stefan Zweig, *Ungeduld des Herzens* (Stockholm, 1939).
15. Zweig may have derived the motif from Schnitzler's story *Blumen*, where a young woman tries to repair the relations with her lover by sending him a bouquet of flowers every month.

6. Intellectual Feats and Deficiencies

1. See WvG, p. 286.
2. See DDL, p. 48; *Balzac*, ed. Richard Friedenthal (Stockholm, 1947)

Notes for pages 90-96

p. 27; WvG, p. 191; 'Walther Rathenau', Erbe, p. 234; 'Frans Masereel: der Mann und Bildner', BMBS, p. 134.

3. 'Das Buch als Eingang zur Welt', BMBS, pp. 310ff.

4. Gschiel, p. 157.

5. Among those who make the unverifiable assumption that Boris commits suicide are: Thomas Haenel, 'Die Suizidproblematik bei Stefan Zweig', *Modern Austrian Literature*, vol. 14, nos. 3-4 (1981) pp. 337-55, and Knut Beck, in his postscript to the volume *Der Amokläufer*, GW, p. 202 (a volume which the editor has assembled around the theme of suicide). Rosi Cohen, *Das Problem des Selbstmordes in Stefan Zweigs Leben und Werk* (Berne and Frankfurt a.M., 1982) allows the possibility that Boris may have been making a naive attempt to swim home (p.274), but nevertheless proceeds to consider his death as though it were suicide (pp. 320-4).

6. Cf. the reference to the 'fehllose Vision' of his recall and the assurance that he never forgets a title or a number (K,104).

7. Cf. also how, discussing the gift of memory, Zweig remarks that Balzac was able to become so absorbed in what he was reading that he lost all awareness of his physical existence and left space behind him. *Balzac*, p. 28.

8. I have discussed the distinction in greater detail in my article, 'Memory and the Humanitarian Ideal: an interpretation of Stefan Zweig's *Buchmendel*', *Modern Austrian Literature*, vol. 12, no. 1 (1979) pp. 43-62, especially pp. 51-2.

9. In problem-solving there seems to be an unavoidable creative component. According to Frank A. Geldard, *Fundamentals of Psychology* (New York, 1963) p. 225, 'suitable behaviour must be "invented" or "produced" if the problem is to be mastered. The successful problem solver accomplishes his goal by synthesising the requisite behaviour from elements already present in his repertory of responses'.

10. Jiři Veselý, 'Das Schachspiel in der *Schachnovelle*', *Österreich in Geschichte und Literatur*, vol. 13 (1969) p. 520.

11. The term 'autotelic' is used by Brian Murdoch, 'Game, Image and Ambiguity in Stefan Zweig's *Schachnovelle*'. The term he uses to describe Czentovic's interested play is 'ectotelic' (p. 178).

12. The phlegmatic element just noted makes it difficult to accept an interpretation of Czentovic as a fanatic. This is the description of D.B. Douglas, 'The Humanist Gambit: a study of Stefan Zweig's *Schachnovelle*', *AUMLA*, vol. 53 (1980) p. 18.

13. See Veselý, 'Das Schachspiel in der *Schachnovelle*', p. 521.

Notes for pages 97-112

7. The Psychology of Self-revelation

1. Kronenberger, 'Zweig's Tale of Guilt in the Tropics', p. 7.
2. Alter Brody, 'Wanted a Literary Tariff: *Conflicts* by Stefan Zweig', *The Nation*, no. 126 (11 Jan. 1928) p. 48.
3. See also Lent, p. 93.
4. Strelka[2], p. 46.
5. Ibid.
6. Cf. the following passages: 'Aber wie ich dies Wort jetzt hinschreibe, beginne ich schon zu bemerken, wie schwer es für einen Ungeübten wird, beim Schreiben die Worte in ihrem rechten Gewicht zu wählen, und welche Zweideutigkeit, welche Mißverständnismöglichkeit, sich an das einfachste Vokabel knüpft' (A,124); 'Jetzt, da ich zum ersten Male im Zusammenhange etwas erzählen soll, merke ich erst, wie schwer es ist, jenes Gleitende, das doch alles Lebendige bedeutet, in einer geballten Form zu fassen' (A,126).
7. This is a point also made by Welter, p. 52.
8. Mrs C. makes much the same point at the end of her narration, referring in particular to 'den lastenden Bann und die ewig rückblickende Starre' (VdG,102).
9. We shall consider later the way in which Zweig nevertheless places the main events within a frame.
10. This is a point overlooked by the critical American reviewer, who declares that 'a professor is moved by a presentation from his students to speak a novelette of 120 pages of concise dialogue and description'. Brody, 'Wanted a Literary Tariff', p. 7.
11. The term 'Aufzeichnungen' is also used by the narrator of *Phantastische Nacht* in his introduction to the baron's written record (A,123).

8. The Psychology of Curiosity

1. Quoted by John Fowles in his introduction to *The Royal Game and Other Stories*, p. xv. I have been unable to trace the original.
2. Cf. *Introductory Lectures*, p. 258; *On Sexuality*, pp. 109-10; 'Leonardo da Vinci and a Memory of his Childhood', *Art and Literature*, pp. 167-70.
3. 'Erinnerungen an Emil Verhaeren', BMBS, p. 23.
4. KD, p. 259.
5. *Sternstunden der Menschheit: zwölf historische Miniaturen*

Notes for pages 112-126

(Stockholm, 1945) pp. 263-4.

6. Cf. also Erwin Rieger, *Stefan Zweig: der Mann und das Werk* (Berlin, 1928) p. 143.

7. Cf. how towards the end of *Verwirrung der Gefühle* Roland casts himself in a female sexual role as he listens to his mentor's confession (VdG,272).

8. Cf. the following passages from *Phantastische Nacht*: 'Da fiel eine Frau von mir ab, [. . .] deren warmer Leib sich elastisch dem meinen aufgetan' (A,132); 'mit der Lust des Weibes war ich aufgetan jeder Berührung' (A,173). It is also worth noting that the empathy which the narrator of *Unvermutete Bekanntschaft mit einem Handwerk* displays in his observation of the pickpocket is, in Zweig's estimation, a characteristically feminine trait. In his essay on Sainte-Beuve (1923) he writes: 'Sainte-Beuve war absolut feminin als literarische Erscheinung, darum aber so unendlich, so unvergleichlich befähigt zur Hingabe, zur Anpassung, zur Einfühlung'. BMBS, p. 411.

PART TWO: THE MORAL SUPERSTRUCTURE

1. *Die Heilung durch den Geist*, p. 444.

2. Jules Romains, *Stefan Zweig: grand européen*, p. 52. Cf. also Hans Vogelsang, 'Stefan Zweig: Psychologe aus Leidenshaft — Deuter menschlichen Schicksals (Zum 25. Todestag am 22. Februar 1967)', *Österreich in Geschichte und Literatur*, vol. 11 (1967) p. 101, who sees, if not a direct connection, then at least a co-existence of psychological curiosity and humane principle.

3. Cf. 'Unvergeßliches Erlebnis: einen Tag bei Albert Schweitzer', BMBS, p. 115; 'Hans Carossa: Brief an einen französischen Freund', ibid., p. 426; 'Das Herz Europas: ein Besuch im Genfer Roten Kreuz', ibid., pp. 391-2.

4. Cf. 'Romain Rolland', Erbe, pp. 108-9.

5. Cf. 'Joseph Roth', Erbe, p. 255.

6. See Rolland's introduction to the translation of *Amok*, pp. xii-xiii; Thomas Mann's comments after Zweig's suicide, which are quoted by Klaus Jonas, 'Stefan Zweig und Thomas Mann: Versuch einer Dokumentation', p. 128; Paul Zech, *Stefan Zweig: ein Gedenkschrift* (Buenos Aires, 1943) p. 35.

9. Personal Freedom

1. Walter, 'Vom Liberalismus zum Eskapismus', p. 427.
2. 'Die Monotonisierung der Welt', BMBS, p. 161.
3. 'Montaigne', Erbe, p. 14. It is also noteworthy that his high valuation of personal freedom appears in his farewell declaration as one reason for his suicide. The document is quoted in full by Prater, *Stefan Zweig: das Leben eines Ungeduldigen*, pp. 456-7.
4. This will be discussed in a later chapter on the narrative frame.
5. An early reviewer of the volume catches the sense of what is implied throughout, but very much overstates the didacticism of Zweig's narrative method, when she writes: 'Achtung vor dem Kinde! das predigen diese Novellen; mögen wir an ihnen lernen'. Gisela Etzel, 'Neue Novellenbücher', *Die Lese: Literarische Zeitung für das deutsche Volk* (Stuttgart, 1912) p. 48. Similarly, Friderike Zweig, 'More than Literature: the legacy of Stefan Zweig', in: *Greatness Revisited*, ed. Harry Zohn (Boston, 1982) p. 91, writes: 'Freedom was his claim, and the condemnation of force was already expressed in his early works. [. . .] In his early short stories he showed the often irreparable harm done to the tender, defenseless souls of children, when thoughtless parents, disregarding their vulnerability, impose on them in a hypocritical way the cruel knowledge of the adult way of careless living'.
6. Cf. Zweig's lament at the use of people, especially children, as pawns in his biography of Mary Stuart, MS, pp. 25-8.
7. Welter, pp. 17-18, detects an element of social criticism in *Die Gouvernante*, relating it to the relevant chapter of *Die Welt von Gestern*. She also draws comparisons with Wedekind's *Frühlings Erwachen* and Halbe's *Jugend* (p. 33).
8. Ellen Key, *Das Jahrhundert des Kindes*, p. 261.
9. WvG, pp. 392-403.
10. TT, p. 111.

10. Intensity and Commitment

1. WvG, p. 126. Much the same point is made by Albert Fuchs, 'Stefan Zweig', in: *Moderne österreichische Dichter* (Vienna, n.d. [1946?]) p. 56.
2. Heinrich Meyer-Benfey, 'Stefan Zweig', in: *Welt der Dichtung, Dichter der Welt, Adel der Menschwerdung*, ed. Fritz Collatz (Hamburg, 1962) p. 408, writes: 'Sie ist ja die letzte Steigerung und

Notes for pages 137-156

Intensivierung des Lebens, die höchste Stufe der ganz unmittelbaren Lebens aus der Natur heraus, das für den modernen Intellektuellen das Ziel der Sehnsucht ist'.

3. MS, p. 40.
4. Ibid., p. 92. Cf. also Strelka[1], p. 103, who describes Mary as a typical Zweig heroine because she is defeated 'auf Grund einer großen Liebe, die er "heroisch" nannte, weil sie Gefahr und Tod nicht scheut und die Intensität des leidenschaftlichen Gefühls bis zur letzten Neige, zur Selbstauflösung und Selbstzerstörung auskostet'.
5. See 'Gustav Mahlers Wiederkehr', Erbe, pp. 172-82; and 'Arturo Toscanini: ein Bildnis', BMBS, p. 82.
6. 'Nein, nur nicht mehr dieser Mensch werden, der ich war, nicht mehr der korrekte, fühllose, weltabgelöste Gentleman von gestern', he declares (A,203).
7. See Phantastische Nacht, GW, p. 69.
8. J.J. Winckelmann, 'Abhandlung von der Fähigkeit der Empfindung des Schönen in der Kunst', Kleine Schriften und Briefe, ed. Wilhelm Senff (Weimar, 1960) especially p. 157.
9. BMBS, pp. 223-4. Zweig was evidently fond of this saying of Goethe. He used it again in a lecture, 'Geschichtsschreibung von Morgen', given in America shortly before the outbreak of the Second World War. See ZuW, p. 278. In the posthumously published Fragment einer Novelle, ed. Erich Fitzbauer (Vienna, 1961), Zweig again indicates that passion cannot be sustained in a vacuum: 'Jeder in Arbeit verbrannte Tag ließ ein paar Stäubchen Asche hinfallen in die unterirdisch wogende Glut, schließlich war der graue Belag schon dichter und dichter und nur selten sprang der Funke Erinnerung vor'.
10. TT, pp. 23-5,80-1,188.

11. Wide Horizons

1. 'Walther Rathenau', Erbe, p. 233.
2. 'Anton Kippenberg', Erbe, pp. 214-19.
3. 'Frans Masereel: der Mann und Bildner', BMBS, pp. 130-1.
4. 'Pour Ramuz', Erbe, p. 123.
5. Cf. the remarks in the previous chapter on the narrator's failure to see the problematic side of the old man's aesthetic appreciation, p. 148 above.
6. This term is used by the friend who first introduces the narrator

Notes for pages 156-166

to Mendel.

7. I have discussed this and some of the following details in my article, 'Memory and the Humanitarian Ideal'.
8. Further details will be found in my article 'Memory and the Humanitarian Ideal', pp. 45-6.
9. This aspect will be discussed in the next chapter.
10. Cf. Daviau, 'Stefan Zweig's Victors in Defeat', pp. 1-12.
11. The typescript of *Schachnovelle* is to be found in the Zweig estate in London. I am grateful to Mrs Eva Alberman for permission to quote from it.
12. This is the view of Veselý, 'Das Schachspiel in der *Schachnovelle*', p. 518. It has already been disputed by Daviau and Dunkle, 'Stefan Zweig's *Schachnovelle*', p. 378.
13. Lent, p. 110.

12. The Brotherhood of Man

1. See J.P. Stern in his introduction to: Arthur Schnitzler, *Liebelei, Leutnant Gustl, Die letzten Masken* (Cambridge, 1966) pp. 4-5; and Williams, *The Broken Eagle*, p. xx.
2. Hannah Arendt, 'Juden in der Welt von Gestern', in: *Sechs Essays* (Heidelberg, 1948) pp. 124-5.
3. 'Das Wien von Gestern', ZuW, pp. 127-50.
4. Letter dated 9 November 1914. BF, p. 41.
5. *Tagebücher*, p. 386.
6. 'Das Wien von Gestern', pp. 144-5.
7. See Harry Zohn, 'Stefan Zweig as Literary Mediator'; and 'Stefan Zweigs kulturelles Mittlertum: ein jüdischer Charakterzug?', *Bulletin des Leo Baeck Instituts*, vol. 63 (1982) pp. 19-31.
8. Erbe, p. 24.
9. Stefan Zweig — Friderike Zweig, *Briefwechsel 1912-1942*, p. 298.
10. BMBS, p. 120.
11. See especially letters to Abraham Schwadron in 1916 and 1917 and to Martin Buber at the beginning of 1917, BF, pp. 66,68,71.
12. 'Maxim Gorki: zum 60. Geburtstag des Dichters, 26. März 1928', BMBS, p. 104.
13. Towards the end of 1915 Jouve had sent Zweig a copy of his book of poems *Vous êtes des hommes* with the dedication 'Fraternellement'. See *Tagebücher*, p. 236.
14. Klawiter, *Stefan Zweig: a bibliography*, p. xxxii.
15. 'Romain Rolland', Erbe, p. 120; TT, p. 225.

Notes for pages 167-173

16. Lent, p. 183.
17. See especially Zweig's diary entries from the period of his stay in Switzerland, between November 1917 and November 1918, *Tagebücher*, pp. 255-339. See also Hans Hellwig, *Stefan Zweig: ein Lebensbild* (Lübeck, 1948) p. 67; and Prater, *European of Yesterday*, p. 104. It is also noteworthy that the woodcuts which Frans Masereel made for the edition of the story published by the Insel Verlag in 1920 took Stefan and Friderike Zweig as their models.
18. Letter dated 8 November 1926, quoted from 'Unbekannte Briefe Stefan Zweigs an den Verlag Wremja, Leningrad', *Neue deutsche Literatur*, vol. 26, no. 12 (Dec. 1978) p. 103.
19. An undated letter to Roth, probably from 1937, describes Castellio as 'das Bild des Mannes, der ich sein MÖCHTE'. Joseph Roth, *Briefe 1911-1939*, ed. Hermann Kesten (Cologne and Berlin, 1970) p. 514.
20. *Ein Gewissen gegen die Gewalt: Castellio gegen Calvin* (Berlin and Frankfurt a.M., 1954) p. 12.
21. Entry for 26 November 1917, *Tagebücher*, p. 275.
22. Zweig left a memorandum with Rolland which was to be published in the event of his being called up for active service and refusing. In it he expressed his belief in non-violence, yet also a willingness to serve his country in war as long as he did not have to bear arms. See Prater, *Stefan Zweig: das Leben eines Ungeduldigen*, pp. 145-6.
23. Leonhard Frank, *Der Mensch ist gut*, Zurich, 1917. I have discussed the links between the two works in a forthcoming article entitled 'Expressionist Pathos and Psychological Analysis: opposition to war in Leonhard Frank's *Der Mensch ist gut* and Stefan Zweig's *Der Zwang*'.
24. TT, pp. 142,145,158-9,163-4,221-2.
25. In a letter to Roth dating probably from the autumn of 1937 Zweig writes that he has depicted his own problems openly, without concealment, without any attempt to praise or defend. BF, p. 286.
26. Jean-Paul Bier, 'Der Erzähler als Chronist: *Kleine Chronik* in ihrem literarischen Kontext', in: *Stefan Zweig 1881-1941: actes du colloque tenu à l'Université de Metz (décembre 1981)*, ed. Pierre Grappin (Paris, 1982) p. 33.
27. There is something similar to this in a diary entry of Zweig's dated 4 October 1918, where he records an unpleasant train journey from Geneva to Zurich: 'langsam, entsetzlich überfüllte Züge und diese Proletarisierung der Existenz: immer dritter Classe, als ob es keine andere gäbe.' *Tagebücher*, p. 323.

Notes for pages 174-181

28. What we read is in fact presented as an edited version of Dr B.'s own account.
29. Gschiel, p. 158, also attributes the unpoetic, naturalistic (?) language of this work to Zweig's failure as an intellectual to penetrate a simple mind.
30. BMBS, p. 159-60.
31. Felix Braun, *Das musische Land: Versuche über Österreichs Landschaft und Dichtung* (Innsbruck, 1952) p. 191, notes an ambivalence in Zweig: a love of ease, yet a guilty conscience towards those who were less fortunate. This ambivalence is compared by Klawiter[1], p. 193, to the attitude of the baron in *Phantastische Nacht*.
32. DDL, pp. 304-7,333-6.

PART THREE: TIME, PLACE, AND BEYOND

13. A Sense of Time

1. Lent, p. 19.
2. His arrest is presumably intended to be part of that initial wave of arrests by the Gestapo which is estimated to have involved some seventy thousand people. See Elisabeth Barker, *Austria 1918-1972* (London, 1973) p. 114.
3. Dr B. also specifies Thursday 27 July (1938) as the day on which he discovered the chess manual. Although he is most insistent, claiming to have imprinted the date on his mind from a calendar in the room where he was kept waiting, 27 July 1938 was, in fact, a Wednesday. The error is probably Zweig's rather than an intended slip on the part of Dr B.
4. WvG, p. 316. Bier, 'Der Erzähler als Chronist', p. 31, argues that the dating of the events of *Der Amokläufer* (March 1912) is to be linked with the sinking of the *Titanic* and regarded as a symbolic signal of general decline, which would relate the socio-pathological decline of the doctor with the political state of Germany and Austria and with the Spenglerian 'Untergang des Abendlandes'. Even if the dates agreed — the *Titanic* in fact sank on 14 April 1912 — this would remain a highly speculative interpretation.
5. See my essay, 'Rausch, Ernüchterung, und die Flucht ins Private: zu Stefan Zweigs Roman aus dem Nachlaß', in: *Stefan Zweig heute*, ed. Mark H. Gelber (Berne, Frankfurt a.M., 1987),

Notes for pages 182-189

pp. 201-25.

6. Pfoser, 'Verwirrung der Gefühle als Verwirrung einer Zeit', p. 13, remarks of these works that 'ihre Schlüssellocheinblicke ins Reich der Leidenschaften benötigten als negative Folie die moralischen und ideologischen Festschreibungen des ausgehenden 19. Jahrhunderts. Ihr meist eindeutig fixierbarer historischer und sozialer Ort ist die letzte Glanzzeit des gebildeten Bürgertums'.

7. Cf. the following: 'Kinder sind immer stolz auf ihre Kränklichkeit' (EE,97); 'für alle Kinder ist das Zu-Bette-geschickt werden ein furchtbares Wort' (EE,113); 'in einen so feinen Organismus, wie den der Kinder, drückt jede Leidenschaft wie in weiches Wachs ihre Spuren' (EE,122).

8. WvG, p. 76.

9. Lack of contact between parents and children, silence on sexual matters, and the failure to appreciate the sexuality of pubescent children are also features which Zweig brings out in his analysis of the notorious case of Philippe Daudet, son of the French Royalist, Léon Daudet. See: 'Irrfahrt und Ende Pierre Bonchamps: die Tragödie Philippe Daudets' (1924), ZuW, pp. 89-102.

10. WvG, pp. 84-93.

11. In the marriage of the baron and baroness in *Leporella* Zweig depicts a four-fold misalliance: between Austrian and North German, gentry and bourgeoisie, youth and maturity, and prodigality and parsimony. He also makes clear, however, that this is not a marriage of convenience or even a conventional marriage. The baroness has contracted the misalliance against the wishes of her parents (K,49).

12. It has been suggested indeed that the portrait of the professor owes something to Felix Poppenberg, a friend from Zweig's student days in Berlin. See Knut Beck's notes to Stefan Zweig, *Tagebücher*, p. 479. Strelka[1], p. 14, also argues that the work in general is based on Zweig's experiences as a student in Berlin, when he got to know not only literary figures, but alcoholics, drug-addicts, homosexuals, and other social outcasts.

13. The temporal shift from the turn of the century, when Zweig was a student in Berlin, to the earlier 'Gründerjahre' is made to accommodate the fiction that Roland is a sixty-year-old academic when he writes the memories of his student days.

14. Welter, p. 94.

15. Strelka[1], p. 83.

16. Welter, p. 70.

17. WvG, p. 208.

Notes for pages 190-198

18. Ibid., p. 234. Even as early as the *Introductory Lectures* Freud was implying that war was an unleashing of an 'evil spirit' (i.e. the unconscious) in man. *Introductory Lectures on Psychoanalysis*, p. 179.
19. In the essay 'Die Monotonisierung der Welt' Zweig was to offer yet another psychological explanation of nationalism: it was an unconscious reaction against the increasing cultural uniformity of modern life. BMBS, p. 159.
20. Joseph Roth, *Radetzkymarsch* (Cologne, 1964) pp. 236-7.
21. See Helmut Rudolf, 'Die humanistische Position Stefan Zweigs in seiner Erzählung *Buchmendel*', *Német Filologiai Tanulmányok* (Arbeiten zur deutschen Philologie, vol. 1, Budapest, 1965) especially p. 129.
22. The opening pages of *Rausch der Verwandlung* give an extended picture of the way in which Austrian bureaucratic procedures dominate the life of a minor official.
23. BMBS, p. 117.
24. Letter dated 29 September 1939, BF, p. 303.
25. See Strelka[1], p. 48.
26. WvG, pp. 301-8,324-8.
27. Gschiel, p. 164.
28. BMBS, pp. 155-62. In his comments on the cinema Zweig adopts a rather different approach from that of his friend Joseph Roth, who tends to emphasise its propagation of falsity and illusion. See especially his novel *Zipper und sein Vater* (1928) and the polemic *Der Antichrist* (1934).
29. See Pfoser, 'Verwirrung der Gefühle als Verwirrung einer Zeit', p. 14.
30. See pp. 5b-5d of the manuscript.
31. In an essay entitled 'Heinrich Mann und Stefan Zweig', in *Literatur der Übergangszeit: Essays* (Berlin, 1949) p. 185, Hans Mayer writes: 'Darum beschränken sich seine [Zweigs] geschichtlichen Bilder auf das Individuum und die Episode: wo er geschichtliche Kräfte und Mächte darstellen sollte, versagt er, landet er im Fehlurteil'.

14. A Sense of Place

1. 'Bei den Sorglosen', BMBS, pp. 181-6; 'Die Stunde zwischen zwei Ozeanen: der Panamakanal vor seiner Beendigung', ibid., pp. 239-47; 'Kleine Reise nach Brasilien', ibid., pp. 274-305.

Notes for pages 198-220

2. In *Der Mann ohne Eigenschaften* Musil remarks in connection with a meeting of the 'Parallelaktion': 'Alles, was nicht an der Riviera oder den Oberitalienischen Seen weilte, war erschienen'. *Der Mann ohne Eigenschaften*, vol. 1, ed. Adolf Frisé (Hamburg, 1978) p. 994.
3. Zweig's younger friend and biographer, Erwin Rieger, described the Salzburg home as 'eine Rettung aus der österreichischen Sintflut in eine letzte Arche'. Rieger, *Stefan Zweig: der Mann und das Werk*, p. 120.
4. WvG, pp. 329-30.
5. Stefan Zweig — Friderike Zweig, *Briefwechsel*, pp. 125-6.
6. Welter, p. 133, remarks on Zweig's use of hotels and spas, where social ties are relaxed and a sense of adventure comes over people.
7. WvG, pp. 8-9.
8. Ibid., pp. 11,51-4,69-74,75-98.
9. Ibid., pp. 42-4.
10. ZuW, pp. 127-50.
11. Although *Brennendes Geheimnis* takes place largely in an hotel on the Semmering, its characters belong very much to Viennese society.
12. This seems to be the view of Hellwig, *Stefan Zweig: ein Lebensbild*, p. 71, who writes: 'In den Schauplätzen der Novellen gibt Zweig den Bilderreichtum seiner vielen und weiten Reisen kund'.
13. See Welter, p. 133.
14. For details of these similarities see Welter, p. 41.
15. It is as though Zweig were continuing this same metaphorical drift when he has his narrator at the end write of a young boy who 'an der Liebe vorbeiging und sich in einer Stunde für immer aus dem Garten dieses süßen Traumes verlor' (EE,58).
16. Cf. her reference to herself as a 'Sklavin' (A,229).
17. Zweig is not entirely consistent in his presentation of the setting. At first he refers to a 'kleine Hafenstadt' (A,271), but later implies a 'große Stadt' comparable with big seaports such as Hamburg and Colombo (A,273). He once described Marseilles as 'das funkelnde Tor des Orients', BMBS, p. 432. His contemporary, Bruno Frank, *Politische Novelle* (Hamburg, 1928) p. 169, described it as 'die offene Wunde des Erdteils, wo alle dunkle Barbarei einbrach in die Gesittung'.

15. Weather, Climate, and Atmosphere

1. Cf. Welter, p. 127.

Notes for pages 222-233

16. Beyond Time and Space

  1. These are the two types of ecstasy identified by Marghanita Laski, *Ecstasy: a study of some secular and religious experience* (London, 1961) pp. 19-20,32.
  2. See a letter to Frans Masereel dated 10 July 1920, BF, p. 122, and an undated letter of 1939 to Felix Braun, ibid., p. 292.
  3. When he joins in prayers for a dead person at the synagogue, he is thinking of *himself* 'wie an einen Toten' (VdG,147); and when he gives away his wedding ring and money to the poor, he is essentially breaking *his* ties with the material world in preparation for his own death (VdG,150).
  4. Cf. that reference to his thinking of himself 'wie an einen Toten' (VdG,147) and an earlier description of him as 'in sich vergraben' (VdG,145).
  5. Cf. WvG, pp. 8-9.
  6. See p. 3a of the manuscript of *Leporella*.
  7. Frank, *Der Mensch ist gut*, pp. 87,91. See also my article, 'Expressionist Pathos and Psychological Analysis'.
  8. Cf. also Dr B.'s reference to 'ein völliges Vakuum [. . .] ein Zimmer, das hermetisch von der Außenwelt abgeschlossen war' (S,60).
  9. Ingrid Schwamborn, 'Schachmatt im brasilianischen Paradies: die Entstehungsgeschichte der *Schachnovelle'*, *Germanisch-Romanische Monatsschrift*, vol. 34 (1984) pp. 404-30.
 10. See his letter to Ben Huebsch dated 6 October 1941, quoted by Jeffrey B. Berlin, 'Stefan Zweig and his American Publisher: notes on an unpublished correspondence, with reference to *Schachnovelle* and *Die Welt von Gestern'*, *Deutsche Vierteljahrsschrift für Literaturwissenschaft und Geistesgeschichte*, vol. 56, no. 2 (1982) p. 269.
 11. The term is used by Jarmatz, 'Stefan Zweigs Humanismusverständnis', p. 97.
 12. Zweig wrote in his memoirs that Herzl was happiest while his idea was still a dream in outline; as soon as he began to fix his aims in actual space, he was made to realise how divided Jews had become. WvG, p. 118. Zweig's later attitude to Judaism is discussed by Mark H. Gelber, 'Stefan Zweigs verspätete Bekehrung zum Judentum? Ein Überblick zum Zentenarium in Beer Scheva und eine Fortsetzung der Debatte', *Bulletin des Leo Baeck Instituts*, vol. 63 (1983) pp. 3-11.
 13. BF, p. 68. Cf. also a letter to Abraham Schwadron from about the

Notes for pages 233-235

same time, in which he writes: 'Für mich ist der Ruhm und die Größe des jüdischen Volkes, das einzige zu sein, das nur eine geistige Heimat, ein ewiges Jerusalem anstrebt, während es zur Wiederkehr ins reale Palästina gravitiert'. Ibid., p. 71.

14. *Jeremias: eine dramatische Dichtung in neun Bildern* (Leipzig, 1917) especially pp. 192,211,212.

15. See Schorske, *Fin-de-siècle Vienna*, pp. 5-10; L.B. Steiman, 'The Agony of Humanism in World War I', p. 102.

16. Entries for 4 January, 10 January, 13 June 1915 and 20 September 1918, *Tagebücher*, pp. 129,131,178,311.

17. Entries for 9 and 27 (= 29) January 1915, *Tagebücher*, pp. 131,136.

18. Richard Strauss — Stefan Zweig, *Briefwechsel*, ed. Willi Schuh (Frankfurt a.M., 1957) p. 53.

19. WvG, p. 403. There is no indication that his reasons for not voting were as morally scrupulous as those of Tolstoy, when he advocated an avoidance of all manifestations of the state, including elections. Zweig's account of this appears in 'Tolstoi als religiöser und sozialer Denker', ZuW, especially p. 80.

20. See Strauss — Zweig, *Briefwechsel*, especially pp. 50,56,60,62,69.

21. See TT, p. 164; 'Montaigne', Erbe, pp. 41-2. Cf. also what Zweig wrote of himself in London to Strauss on 17 May 1934: 'Mein Leben verläuft hier still, ich arbeite an meinem Buch über Maria Stuart in der Bibliothek, es ist mir — trotz der heftigsten Versuche, mich gewaltsam einzuspannen — eigentlich voll gelungen, *ganz* abseits von allen öffentlichen Discussionen und jeder Art von Politik zu bleiben'. Strauss — Zweig, *Briefwechsel*, p. 62.

22. TT, p. 225.

23. *Der begrabene Leuchter,* in: *Kaleidoskop* (Vienna, Leipzig, Zurich, 1936) pp. 228-329, especially p. 329.

24. A. Lazar, 'Zwischen Konzilianz und Verzweiflung: Gedanken einer Wienerin über den Untergang der Wiener Bürgerkultur', *Neue deutsche Literatur: Monatschrift für schöne Literatur und Kritik*, vol. 3, no. 8 (Aug. 1955) p. 103.

25. Walter Huder, 'Stefan Zweig', *Sinn und Form*, vol. 14, no. 1 (1962) p. 137. See also Matthias, 'Humanismus in der Zerreißprobe', p. 306, who refers in connection with *Der begrabene Leuchter* to 'das hier erst anklingende Todesmotiv'.

PART FOUR: NARRATIVE RHETORIC

1. Booth, *The Rhetoric of Fiction*, p. 149.

17. Imagery and the Image of Man

1. Claudio Magris, *Der habsburgische Mythos in der österreichischen Literatur* (Salzburg, 1966) p. 259, writes: 'der schmucklose Stil verzichtet auf jegliche Beigabe und jeden Kunstgriff'.
2. Letter dated 29 May 1936, Roth, *Briefe*, p. 475.
3. Letter to Zweig dated 18 February 1934, Roth *Briefe*, p. 316. Roth's editor, Hermann Kesten, mistakenly relates these comments to the much earlier story *Angst*.
4. Hermann Kesten, *Meine Freunde die Poeten* (Frankfurt a.M., 1970) p. 77.
5. Terence Hawkes, *Metaphor* (The Critical Idiom No. 25, London, 1972) p. 55.
6. These are the terms used by Paul Ricoeur, 'Metapher und das Problem der Hermeneutik', in: *Theorie der Metapher*, ed. Anselm Haverkamp (Darmstadt, 1983) p. 359.
7. Max Black, quoted from 'Mehr über die Metapher', *Theorie der Metapher*, p. 392. See also Paul Henle, 'Die Metapher', ibid., p. 99.
8. Max Black, 'Mehr über die Metapher', p. 389, is confident enough to make a distinction between: a) metaphors that are dead and beyond resuscitation; b) those that are not perceived as metaphors, but are capable of reconstruction (i.e. resuscitation); c) those that are active. There seems, however, little prospect of determining *a priori* what belongs to a) rather than b).
9. The term 'foregrounded' is an English translation of Jan Mukařovský's 'aktualisace'. See Hawkes, *Metaphor*, p. 73.
10. See Laski, *Ecstasy*, pp. 30 ff.
11. Caroline Spurgeon, *Shakespeare's Imagery and what it tells us* (Cambridge, 1935).
12. Ludwig Reiners, *Stilkunst: ein Lehrbuch deutscher Prosa* (Munich, 1961) p. 319. Cf. also Philip Wheelwright: 'The test of essential metaphor is not any rule of grammatical form, but rather the quality of semantic transformation that is brought about'. Quoted from Hawkes, *Metaphor*, p. 66.
13. I.A. Richards, *The Philosophy of Rhetoric* (Oxford, 1936) especially p. 99.

Notes for pages 245-272

14. Ibid., p. 100.
15. *Die Heilung durch den Geist*, p. 414.
16. From the context it seems clear that Zweig has chosen the wrong noun, that he intended 'Kreuzweg' rather than 'Kreuzgang' (= cloister).
17. This is confirmed by the following passage: 'Endete mein Lehrer dann in dem Diktate, wo mächtige Inspiration herrlich der wissenschaftlichen Absicht das Wort entriß und Denken zur Dichtung wurde, so taumelte ich auf' (VdG,212-13).
18. DDL, p. 287.
19. DM, pp. 96-7.
20. In his essay on Dostoyevsky Zweig describes the novelist's gambling as a symbol of his desire for intensity, of living life to the furthest extremes, of commitment to life, of staking all. See DM, p. 124.
21. Cf. also the adjective 'spiellüstern' (K,10).
22. Cf. also the reference to 'Kunstprobe' (K,42).
23. It is no accident that this same passage continues with a parallel animal image, a comparison of Czentovic's impertinent treatment of others with that with which 'man einen räudigen Hund abgewendeten Blicks einen Brocken zuwirft'. For just as the chess champion himself is likened to various animals, so too his attitude to other people reduces them to a similar level.
24. *Joseph Fouché: Bildnis eines politischen Menschen* (Leipzig, 1929).
25. Curiously, *Schachnovelle* is omitted from the list of works considered by Daviau in his article, 'Stefan Zweig's Victors in Defeat'.
26. Schorske, *Fin-de-siècle Vienna*, p. 4.
27. Laski, *Ecstasy*, especially p. 247.
28. MS, p. 223.
29. *Ungeduld des Herzens*, p. 329.

18. The Narrative Frame

1. To these must also be added the posthumously published *Die spät bezahlte Schuld*, which takes the form of a letter written by a married woman about a recent adventure and which includes a further inset narrative dealing with the antecedents of many years previously.
2. Klawiter[1], p. 43.
3. This view stands in sharp contrast to that of Strelka[2], p. 50, who

Notes for pages 274-280

equates the 'Novelle' with the 'Binnengeschichte'.

4. An account of this process is given by Booth, *The Rhetoric of Fiction*, pp. 340-7.

5. Bauer, *Stefan Zweig*, p. 53, dismisses Zweig's use of the first-person narrator (a frequent corollary of the frame) as 'meist nur ein Kunstgriff, um das Interesse des Lesers zu fesseln'.

6. Fritz Lockemann sees this as the original function of the frame: 'Die Einzelrahmung dient wohl ursprünglich dazu, die Glaubwürdigkeit der Erzählung zu stützen, den Erzähler zu legitimieren'. Fritz Lockemann, 'Die Bedeutung des Rahmens in der deutschen Novellendichtung', in: *Novelle*, ed. Josef Kunz (= Wege der Forschung 55, Darmstadt, 1968) p. 330.

7. W.F. Mainland, 'Theodor Storm', in: *German Men of Letters*, vol. 1, ed. Alex Natan (London, 1965) p. 162.

8. By contrast, the narrative frame which introduces the legend *Die gleich-ungleichen Schwestern* is given a deliberately vague setting: 'irgendwo in einer südländischen Stadt, die ich lieber nicht nennen mag' (K,334).

9. Bier, 'Der Erzähler als Chronist', p. 34, writes: 'Die erzählerischen Vermittlungsinstanzen, die in fast allen Novellen vorkommen, erfüllen eine distanzierende Funktion und wirken seiner Neigung zur sentimentalen Melodramatik entgegen, bauen aber auch eine Appellstruktur ein, die den Kontrast zum Leser als Partner fördern sollte'.

10. Friderike Zweig, *Stefan Zweig*, p. 128, insists that, despite the convincing nature of the portrayal, her husband never encountered such a whimsical figure as Jakob Mendel. An incident in Paris, when Zweig's trunk was stolen, provides only a very indirect link with the story of the pickpocket in *Unvermutete Bekanntschaft mit einem Handwerk*. See WvG, pp. 159-66.

11. A transcript of the adaptation, which was broadcast by the *Sender Freies Berlin* on 20 November 1973, is held in the Deutsches Literatur-Archiv, Marbach a.N.

12. Bier, 'Der Erzähler als Chronist', p. 35, writes that 'der Nacherzähler, der hier den Zuhörer spielt, und sich als bekannten Sammler von Autographen und alten Büchern ausgibt, kann nur der Schriftsteller Stefan Zweig selbst sein'.

13. Martin Swales, *The German Novelle* (Princeton, 1977), p. 53.

14. Lent, pp. 174-5.

15. For our purposes this may indeed be regarded as a different sphere despite those comments of Freud on the story, which are made in the context of an argument seeking to establish a link between

Notes for pages 282-295

compulsive gambling and masturbation. Freud, 'Dostoevsky and Parricide'.
16. Roth, *Briefe*, p. 315.
17. Lent, p. 32.
18. The film which Max Ophüls made from the later work, *Letter from an Unknown Woman*, in fact turns the novelist into a musician.
19. See *Magellan: der Mann und seine Tat* (Vienna, Leipzig, Zurich, 1938) pp. 5-9. See also Strelka[1], p. 115.
20. 'Memory and the Humanitarian Ideal'.
21. Unpublished letters to Leonhardt Adelt dated 31 March and 12 April 1923, in the possession of the Austrian National Library, Vienna.
22. KD, p. 7. Friderike Zweig echoes this passage, spelling out its relevance to other works such as *Drei Meister* (Balzac, Dickens, Dostoyevsky), *Drei Dichter ihres Lebens* (Casanova, Stendhal, Tolstoy) and *Die Heilung durch den Geist* (Mesmer, Mary Baker-Eddy, Freud), when she notes that 'comparisons, liberally used by him to obtain spatial depth, and reflections were facilitated by placing certain figures next to each other within a volume'. Friderike Zweig, *Stefan Zweig*, p. 113.
23. It is also interesting to observe how, in his review of Adolf Gelber's study of the *Arabian Nights*, Zweig emphasises the links that Gelber had established between the individual stories and the narrative frame, which thereby unfolded a story of its own. 'Das Drama in Tausend und einer Nacht', Erbe, pp. 157-68.
24. See also Lent, p. 18.

CONCLUSION: ZWEIG AND THE *NOVELLE*

1. This seems to be the aim of Adolf von Grolman, 'Die strenge Novellenform und die Problematik ihrer Zertrümmerung', in: *Novelle*, ed. Kunz, pp. 154-66.
2. Mayer, 'Heinrich Mann und Stefan Zweig', p. 185.
3. Harry Zohn, 'Three Austrians in German Literature: Schnitzler, Zweig, Herzl', in: *The Jews of Austria: essays on their life, history and destruction*, ed. Josef Fraenkel (London, 1967) p. 76. Huder, 'Stefan Zweig', p. 136, describes *Ungeduld des Herzens* as 'eine große Novelle'.
4. Strelka[1], pp. 118-20.
5. See my article, 'Rausch, Ernüchterung, und die Flucht ins Private'.

Notes for pages 295-299

6. WvG, p. 332. Friderike Zweig, *Stefan Zweig*, p. 129, also argues that it was impatience ('Ungeduld des Herzens') that made him so suited to the *Novelle*.
7. In an amusing attempt to expose the stylistic weaknesses of great and famous German writers Hans Weigel subjects passages of *Brief einer Unbekannten* to close scrutiny and has no difficulty in unmasking sloppiness, tautology, illogicality, and long-windedness. One would take him more seriously if his own style were more concise: 'Der Zeilenschinder Zweig braucht dazu das Doppelte dessen, was er hätte gebraucht haben können'. Hans Weigel, *Götterfunken mit Fehlzündung: ein Antilesebuch* (Zurich, Stuttgart, 1971) pp. 130-7.
8. WvG, p. 334.
9. Letter dated 13 April 1928, p. 190.
10. Swales, *The German Novelle*.
11. Ibid., p. 15.
12. Ibid., especially pp. 22-5,55. Cf. also Kunz's introduction to the volume *Novelle*, p. 8, where he writes: 'Aus der Spannung der besonderen Thematik des Novellengeschehens und der Norm der Gesellschaft wird dann auch die besondere Form der Novelle begriffen'. For Heinz Otto Bürger, 'Theorie und Wissenschaft von der deutschen Novelle', *Novelle*, p. 303, the basic situation of the *Novelle* resides in two factors: 'einem einmaligen und einzigartigen Ereignis, *von* dem gesprochen wird, und einer vorhandenen und vorgestellten Gesellschaft, *zu* der gesprochen wird'.
13. Swales, *The German Novelle*, pp. 21 f., 23 ff., 26 ff., 38 f., 45 ff.
14. Bengt Algot Sørensen, 'The Sense of Time in Stefan Zweig's Stories and *Novellen*', *The Hebrew University Studies in Literature*, vol. 10, no. 2 (Autumn 1982) p. 223.
15. The baron uses the noun 'Begebenheit' again on the next page.
16. In his subsequent encounter with the prostitute and her criminal accomplices he admits to being numbed by 'das Unerhörte, das Gemeine, das Gefährliche der Situation' (A.194).
17. Zweig has much the same in mind at the end of the little story *Die Hochzeit von Lyon*, where, after granting his hero and heroine a remarkable and unexpected reunion in the face of a cruel death, he nevertheless turns his back on a consoling happy ending. He chooses words which look back to well-known formulations of Tieck and seem intended to define the work as a *Novelle* rather than a fairy-tale: 'Aber das Leben liebt nur das Wunderbare und spart mit dem wirklichen Wunder'. *Die Hochzeit von Lyon und andere Erzählungen*, p. 182. With reference to *Phantastische Nacht*

Notes for pages 299-303

the comments of Wieland are perhaps more appropriate, when, in his preface to the *Novelle ohne Titel*, he argues that with a *Novelle*, as opposed to a fairy-tale, events take place in the real world, 'wo alles natürlich und begreiflich zugeht, und die Begebenheiten zwar nicht alltäglich sind, aber sich doch, unter denselben Umständen alle Tage allenthalben zutragen könnten'. Quoted from Benno von Wiese, *Novelle* (2nd edition, Stuttgart, 1964) p. 2.

18. Pfoser, 'Verwirrung der Gefühle als Verwirrung einer Zeit', p. 15, writes: 'Jedes Detail, und sei's noch so banal, ist bei Zweig von der innerlichen Erregtheit des Erzählers affiziert, dem ständig die Luft auszugehen droht, weil er etwas "Außergewöhnliches" und "Einzigartiges" zu berichten weiß'.

19. Hans Joachim Homann, *Das Literarische Echo*, vol. 25, nos. 19-20 (1 July 1923) col. 1636.

20. See Kunz in his introduction to the volume *Novelle*, p. 6; Wiese, *Novelle*, pp. 9,24; Musil, 'Die Novelle als Problem', quoted from *Theorie und Kritik der deutschen Novelle von Wieland bis Musil*, ed. Karl Konrad Polheim (Tübingen, 1970) p. 185.

21. Oskar Zarek's review of *Amok* argues that Zweig has here taken over the 'Urtypus der Novelle' and that Fate is here fulfilled in the psyche. In: *Die neue Rundschau*, vol. 34, no. 2 (1923) pp. 670-1. Cf. also Pfoser, 'Verwirrung der Gefühle als Verwirrung einer Zeit', p. 12, and Klawiter[1], pp. 38-40, who writes of Zweig's stories as fulfilling the criteria of the *Novelle*, though in such a way that the irrational view of the universe is related to psychoanalysis rather than the supernatural.

22. Pfoser, 'Verwirrung der Gefühle als Verwirrung einer Zeit', p. 12.

23. See also Sørensen, 'The Sense of Time in Stefan Zweig's Stories and *Novellen*', p. 221.

24. *Sternstunden der Menschheit*, p. 8.

25. This marks a further difference between Zweig and Gorky, who, as Zweig himself recognised, saw 'alles Geschehnis als Gemeinsamkeit' and, in his works, depicted the masses as bearers of power. See Zweig's introduction to Maxim Gorki, *Erzählungen* (Leipzig, 1931) p. 14.

26. Stephen Howard Garrin, 'History as Literature: Stefan Zweig's *Sternstunden der Menschheit*', in: *Stefan Zweig: the world of yesterday's humanist today*, especially p. 126, where, using a title from Cervantes, he calls them 'novellas exemplares' [*sic*]. See also Bier, 'Der Erzähler als Chronist', p. 30.

27. 'Charakteristisch für die Novelle ist der grundsätzliche Vorrang des Ereignisses vor den Personen und den Dingen.' Wiese, *Novelle*,

Notes for pages 303-309

p. 5. Elsewhere, however, Wiese is happy to discuss works such as Grillparzer's *Der arme Spielmann* and Büchner's *Lenz* as *Novellen*. Wiese, *Die deutsche Novelle von Goethe bis Kafka*, 2 vols (Düsseldorf, 1968).

28. Edward Timms, '*Novelle* and Case History: Freud in pursuit of the falcon', in: *London German Studies*, vol. 2, ed. J.P. Stern (London, 1983) pp. 115-33.
29. See Walter, 'Vom Liberalismus zum Eskapismus', p. 427.
30. See above all the essay 'Die Monotonisierung der Welt'.
31. Strelka[1], p. 51.
32. WvG, p. 126.
33. Sørensen, 'The Sense of Time in Stefan Zweig's Stories and *Novellen*', p. 215.
34. Hermann Pongs, 'Über die Novelle', in: *Novelle*, ed. Kunz, p. 138; Swales, *The German Novelle*, p. 21.
35. Joachim Müller, 'Novelle und Erzählung', in: *Novelle*, ed. Kunz, p. 475.
36. See Pfoser, 'Verwirrung der Gefühle als Verwirrung einer Zeit', p. 15.
37. See Sørensen, 'The Sense of Time in Stefan Zweig's Stories and *Novellen*', p. 220.
38. Ibid.
39. 'Jakob Wassermann', Erbe, p. 207.
40. A letter from Freud to Zweig dated 14 April 1925 includes this comment, made with immediate reference to *Der Kampf mit dem Dämon*: 'Meine Anerkennung ist umso größer, als es ja eigentlich keine exakte Darstellungsweise für das von Ihnen Beschriebene gibt und dieser Mangel durch die Verwendung der verschiedenartigsten Vergleiche aus andern Gebieten der Wahrnehmung besiegt werden muß'. The letter, in typescript, is in the possession of the Jewish National and University Library, Jerusalem (Arc. Ms. Var. 305/34). I am grateful to the Department of Manuscripts and Archives for permission to quote from the letter.
41. It is no accident that the introduction to *Der Kampf mit dem Dämon*, p. 7, uses the notion of 'Vergleich' and 'Rahmen' in close proximity.
42. Gschiel, p. 73, argues that *Geschichte in der Dämmerung* is not really a *Novelle*, but a 'psychologische Skizze'; Lent, p. 19, describes *Die Frau und die Landschaft* (together with *Sommernovellette*) as a 'Studie' or as 'psychologische Spielerei'.

Select Bibliography

I STEFAN ZWEIG

The fullest bibliography available is Randolph J. Klawiter, *Stefan Zweig: a bibliography* (University of North Carolina Studies in the Germanic Languages and Literatures, No. 50: Chapel Hill, 1965). The same author has also published a survey of more recent research, 'The State of Stefan Zweig Research: an update', in: *Stefan Zweig: the world of yesterday's humanist today: proceedings of the Stefan Zweig symposium*, ed. Marion Sonnenfeld (Albany, 1983) 324-40.

A. Narrative Fiction

Die Liebe der Erika Ewald (Berlin, 1904).
Erstes Erlebnis: vier Geschichten aus Kinderland (Die Kette: ein Novellenkreis: der erste Ring, Leipzig, 1925).
Amok: Novellen einer Leidenschaft (Die Kette: ein Novellenkreis: der zweite Ring, Leipzig 1925).
Verwirrung der Gefühle: drei Novellen (Die Kette: ein Novellenkreis: der dritte Ring, Leipzig, 1927).
Kaleidoskop (Vienna, Leipzig, Zurich, 1936).
Ungeduld des Herzens: ein Roman (Stockholm, 1939).
Schachnovelle (Stockholm, 1943).
Verwirrung der Gefühle (Frankfurt a.M., 1960). The most readily available volume to include *Der Zwang*.
Fragment einer Novelle (Special publication No. 2 of the Stefan Zweig Gesellschaft, Vienna, 1961).
Die Hochzeit von Lyon und andere Erzählungen (Frankfurt a.M., 1980). The most readily available volume to include *Scharlach* and *Die Hochzeit von Lyon*.
Rausch der Verwandlung: Roman aus dem Nachlaß (Gesammelte Werke in Einzelbänden, ed. Knut Beck, Frankfurt a.M., 1982).
Phantastische Nacht: Erzählungen (Gesammelte Werke in Einzelbänden, ed., Knut Beck, Frankfurt a.M., 1982). The most readily available volume to contain *Die spät bezahlte Schuld*.
Der Amokläufer: Erzählungen (Gesammelte Werke in Einzelbänden, ed. Knut Beck, Frankfurt a.M., 1984). The most readily available volume to contain *Geschichte eines Unterganges, Das Kreuz*, and *Ein Verbummelter*.
Verwirrung der Gefühle (Gesammelte Werke in Einzelbänden, ed. Knut Beck, Frankfurt a.M., 1984). The most readily available volume to contain *Vergessene Träume*.

B. Correspondence, Diaries, Memoirs

Stefan Zweig — Friderike Zweig, *Briefwechsel 1912-1942* (Berne, 1951).

342

Romain Rolland, *Journal des Années de Guerre 1914-1919: notes et documents pour servir à l'histoire morale de l'Europe de ce temps* (Paris, 1952). The volume includes translations into French of letters written by Zweig to Rolland.

Richard Strauss — Stefan Zweig, *Briefwechsel*, ed. Willi Schuh (Frankfurt a.M., 1957).

Victor Wittkowski, *Ewige Erinnerungen* (Rome, 1960). The volume contains at the end 'Die Briefe Stefan Zweigs an Victor Wittkowski' from Zweig's last period in Brazil.

Stefan Zweig, *Unbekannte Briefe aus der Emigration an eine Freundin*, ed. Gisella Selden-Goth (Vienna, Stuttgart, Basle, 1964).

Joseph Roth, *Briefe 1911-1939*, ed. Hermann Kesten (Cologne and Berlin, 1970). The volume includes correspondence between Roth and Zweig.

Maxim Gorki — Stefan Zweig, *Briefwechsel*, ed. Kurt Böttcher (Frankfurt a.M., 1974).

Stefan Zweig, *Briefe an Freunde*, ed. Richard Friedenthal (Frankfurt a.M., 1978).

'Unbekannte Briefe Stefan Zweigs an den Verlag Wremja, Leningrad', *Neue deutsche Literatur*, vol. 26, no. 12 (Dec. 1978) 99-120.

Donald Prater, 'Stefan Zweig and Hermann Hesse', *Modern Austrian Literature*, vol. 14, nos. 3-4 (1981) 1-70.

Ilsedore B. Jones, 'Stefan Zweig und Rainer Maria Rilke', *Modern Austrian Literature*, vol. 14, nos. 3-4 (1981) 71-98.

Klaus Jonas, 'Stefan Zweig und Thomas Mann: Versuch einer Dokumentation', *Modern Austrian Literature*, vol. 14, nos. 3-4 (1981) 99-135.

Jeffrey B. Berlin, 'Stefan Zweig and his American Publisher: notes on an unpublished correspondence with reference to *Schachnovelle* and *Die Welt von Gestern*', *Deutsche Vierteljahrsschrift für Literatur und Geistesgeschichte*, vol. 56, no. 2 (1982) 259-76.

The Correspondence of Stefan Zweig with Raoul Auernheimer, edited and with an introduction by Donald Daviau and Jorum B. Johns, and with *Richard Beer-Hoffmann*, edited and with commentary and notes by Jeffrey B. Berlin (Columbia, South Carolina, 1983).

Stefan Zweig and Paul Zech, *Briefe 1910-1942*, ed. Donald G. Daviau (Rudolstadt, 1984).

Stefan Zweig, *Tagebücher*, ed. Knut Beck (Gesammelte Werke in Einzelbänden, Frankfurt a.M., 1984).

Stefan Zweig, *Die Welt von Gestern: Erinnerungen eines Europäers* (London and Stockholm, 1941).

C. Essays and Biographies by Zweig

Drei Meister: Balzac, Dickens, Dostojewski (Leipzig, 1920).

Der Kampf mit dem Dämon: Hölderlin, Kleist, Nietzsche (Leipzig, 1925).

'Das Tagebuch eines halbwüchsigen Mädchens', *Almanach der Psychoanalyse* (1926) 140-5.

Drei Dichter ihres Lebens: Casanova, Stendhal, Tolstoi (Leipzig, 1928).

Joseph Fouché: Bildnis eines politischen Menschen (Leipzig, 1929).
Die Heilung durch den Geist: Mesmer, Mary Baker-Eddy, Freud (Leipzig, 1931).
Marie Antoinette: Bildnis eines mittleren Charakters (Leipzig, 1932).
Triumph und Tragik des Erasmus von Rotterdam (Vienna, 1935).
Maria Stuart (Vienna, Leipzig, Zurich, 1935).
Magellan: der Mann und seine Tat (Vienna, Leipzig, Zurich, 1938).
Sternstunden der Menschheit: zwölf historische Miniaturen (Stockholm, 1945).
Zeit und Welt: Gesammelte Aufsätze und Vorträge, ed. Richard Friedenthal (Stockholm, 1946).
Balzac, ed. Richard Friedenthal (Stockholm, 1947).
Ein Gewissen gegen die Gewalt: Castellio gegen Calvin (Berlin and Frankfurt a.M., 1954).
Begegnungen mit Menschen, Büchern, Städten (Frankfurt a.M., 1956).
Europäisches Erbe, ed. Richard Friedenthal (Frankfurt a.M., 1960).

D. Collections of Articles and Essays on Zweig

Arens, Hanns (ed.), *Der große Europäer Stefan Zweig* (Munich, 1956).
Arens, Hanns (ed.), *Stefan Zweig im Zeugnis seiner Freunde* (Munich and Vienna, 1968).
Fitzbauer, Erich (ed.), *Stefan Zweig: Spiegelungen einer schöpferischen Persönlichkeit* (Erste Sonderpublikation der Stefan-Zweig-Gesellschaft, Vienna, n.d.).
Gelber, Mark H. (ed.), *Stefan Zweig heute* (New Yorker Studien zur Neueren Deutschen Literaturgeschichte, vol. 7, New York, Berne, Frankfurt a.M., Paris, 1987).
Grappin, Pierre (ed.), *Stefan Zweig 1881-1941: actes du colloque tenu à l'université de Metz (déc. 1981)* (Paris, 1982).
Lunzer, Heinz and Renner, Gerhard (eds), *Stefan Zweig 1881-1981: Aufsätze und Dokumente* (Vienna, 1981).
Sonnenfeld, Marion (ed.), *Stefan Zweig: the world of yesterday's humanist today: proceedings of the Stefan Zweig symposium* (Albany, 1983).

E. Essays and Monographs on Zweig

Arendt, Hannah, 'Juden in der Welt von Gestern', in: *Sechs Essays* (Heidelberg, 1948) 112-27.
Arens, Hanns, *Stefan Zweig: der Mensch im Werk* (Vienna, 1931).
Bauer, Arnold, *Stefan Zweig* (Köpfe des XX. Jahrhunderts, Berlin, 1961).
Böttcher, Kurt, 'Humanist auf verlorener Bastion: ein Gedenken an Stefan Zweig zu seinem 75. Geburtstag', *Neue deutsche Literatur*, vol. 4 (1956) 83-92.
Cohen, Rosi, *Das Problem des Selbstmordes in Stefan Zweigs Leben und Werk* (Berne and Frankfurt a.M., 1982).
Cremerius, Johannes, 'Stefan Zweigs Beziehung zu Sigmund Freud, "eine heroische Identifizierung": zugleich ein Beispiel für die Zufälligkeit der

Rezeption der Psychoanalyse', *Jahrbuch der Psychoanalyse: Beiträge zur Theorie und Praxis*, vol. 8 (1975) 49-89.

Daviau, Donald G., 'Stefan Zweig's Victors in Defeat', *Monatshefte*, vol. 51, no. 1 (1959) 1-12.

Elster, Hanns Martin, *Deutsche Dichterhandschriften: Stefan Zweig* (Dresden, 1922). Includes a reproduction of the typescript of *Brief einer Unbekannten*.

Friedenthal, Richard, *Stefan Zweig und der humanitäre Gedanke* (Eßlingen, 1948).

Fuchs, Albert, 'Stefan Zweig', in: *Moderne österreichische Dichter* (Vienna, n.d. [1946?]) 53-9.

Gelber, Mark H., 'Stefan Zweigs verspätete Bekehrung zum Judentum? Ein Überblick zum Zentenarium in Beer Scheva und eine Fortsetzung der Debatte', *Bulletin des Leo Baeck Instituts*, vol. 63 (1983) 3-11.

Haenel, Thomas, 'Die Suizidproblematik bei Stefan Zweig', *Modern Austrian Literature* vol. 14, nos. 3-4 (1981) 337-55.

Hellwig, Hans, *Stefan Zweig: ein Lebensbild* (Lübeck, 1948).

Huder, Walter, 'Stefan Zweig', *Sinn und Form*, vol. 14, no. 1 (1962) 135-40.

Jarmatz, Klaus, 'Stefan Zweigs Humanismusverständnis', *Weimarer Beiträge*, vol. 21, no. 9 (1975) 94-115.

Kesten, Hermann, 'Stefan Zweig', in: *Meine Freunde die Poeten* (Frankfurt a.M., 1970) 74-82.

Lazar, A., 'Zwischen Konzilianz und Verzweiflung: Gedanken einer Wienerin über den Untergang der Wiener Bürgerkultur', *Neue deutsche Literatur*, vol. 3, no. 8 (Aug. 1955) 98-104.

Lucas, W.I., 'Stefan Zweig', in: *German Men of Letters*, vol. 2, ed. Alex Natan (London, 1963) 225-48.

Matthias, Klaus, 'Humanismus in der Zerreißprobe: Stefan Zweig im Exil', in: *Die deutsche Exilliteratur 1933-1945*, ed. Manfred Durzak (Stuttgart, 1973) 291-311.

Mayer, Hans, 'Heinrich Mann und Stefan Zweig', in: *Literatur der Übergangszeit: Essays* (Berlin, 1949) 182-7.

Meyer-Benfey, Heinrich, 'Stefan Zweig', in: *Welt der Dichtung, Dichter der Welt, Adel der Menschwerdung*, ed. Fritz Collatz (Hamburg, 1962) 406-11.

Prater, D.A., *European of Yesterday: a biography of Stefan Zweig* (Oxford, 1972).

Prater, Donald, A., *Stefan Zweig: das Leben eines Ungeduldigen* (Munich, 1981).

Rieger, Erwin, *Stefan Zweig: der Mann und das Werk* (Berlin, 1928).

Romains, Jules, *Stefan Zweig: grand européen* (New York, 1941).

Sardyko, G.I., 'Stefan Zweig in der sowjetischen Kritik'. *Wissenschaftliche Zeitschrift der Friedrich-Schiller-Universität Jena* (Gesellschafts- und Sprachwissenschaftliche Reihe) vol. 19, no. 3 (1970) 457-63.

Steiman, Lionel B., 'The Agony of Humanism in World War I: the case of Stefan Zweig', *Journal of European Studies*, vol. 6 (1976) 100-24.

Strelka, Joseph, *Stefan Zweig: Freier Geist der Menschlichkeit* (Vienna, 1981).

Vogelsang, Hans, 'Stefan Zweig: Psychologe aus Leidenschaft — Deuter menschlichen Schicksals (Zum 25. Todestag am. 22 Februar 1967)',

345

Österreich in Geschichte und Literatur, vol. 11 (1967) 93-102.
Walter, Hans-Albert, 'Vom Liberalismus zum Eskapismus: Stefan Zweig im Exil', *Frankfurter Hefte*, vol. 25, no. 6 (1970) 427-37.
Werman, David S., 'Stefan Zweig and his relationship with Freud and Rolland: a study of the auxiliary ego-ideal', *International Review of Psychoanalysis*, vol. 6 (1979) 77-95.
Zech, Paul, *Stefan Zweig: ein Gedenkschrift* (Buenos Aires, 1943).
Zohn, Harry, 'Three Austrians in German Literature: Schnitzler, Zweig, Herzl', in: *The Jews of Austria: essays on their life, history and destruction*, ed. Josef Fraenkel (London, 1967) 67-81.
-----------, 'Stefan Zweigs kulturelles Mittlertum: ein jüdischer Charakterzug?', *Bulletin des Leo Baeck Instituts*, vol. 63 (1982) 19-31.
Zweig, Friderike, *Stefan Zweig* (London, 1946).
-----------, *Stefan Zweig wie ich ihn erlebte* (Stockholm, 1947).

F. Articles and Dissertations on Zweig's Narrative Fiction

Bier, Jean-Paul, 'Der Erzähler als Chronist: *Kleine Chronik* in ihrem literarischen Kontext', in: *Stefan Zweig 1881-1941: actes du colloque tenu à l'université de Metz*, ed. Pierre Grappin (Paris, 1982) 27-36.
Daviau, Donald G. and Dunkle, Harvey I., 'Stefan Zweig's *Schachnovelle*', *Monatshefte*, vol. 65 (1973) 370-84.
Dieckmann, E., *'Der Tod des Iwan Iljitsch* und *Untergang eines Herzens*: ein Vergleich zwischen Lev Tolstoj und Stefan Zweig', in: *Begegnung und Bündnis: sowjetische und deutsche Literatur: historische und theoretische Aspekte ihrer Beziehungen*, ed. Gerhard Ziegengeist (Berlin, 1972) 418-26.
Douglas, D.B., 'The Humanist Gambit: a study of Stefan Zweig's *Schachnovelle*', *AUMLA*, vol. 53 (1980) 17-24.
Fehn, Ann Clark and Rettig, Ulrike S., 'Narrative Technique and Psychological Analysis in Two Novellas by Stefan Zweig', in *Stefan Zweig: the world of yesterday's humanist today: proceedings of the Stefan Zweig symposium*, ed. Marion Sonnenfeld (Albany, 1983) 168-76.
Freud, Sigmund, 'Dostoevsky and Parricide', *Art and Literature* (Pelican Freud Library, vol. 14, Harmondsworth, 1985) 441-60. This includes an analysis of *Vierundzwanzig Stunden aus dem Leben einer Frau*.
Gschiel, Martha, 'Das dichterische Prosawerk Stefan Zweigs' (University of Vienna doctoral thesis, 1953).
Klawiter, Randolph J., 'Stefan Zweig's *Novellen*: an analysis' (University of Michigan doctoral thesis, 1960).
Klein, Johannes, 'Stefan Zweig', in: *Geschichte der deutschen Novelle von Goethe bis zur Gegenwart* (4th edition, Wiesbaden, 1960) 555-64.
Lent, Ingrid, 'Das Novellenwerk Stefan Zweigs: eine Stil- und Typenuntersuchung' (University of Munich doctoral thesis, 1956).
Martens, Lorna, 'Secrets, Speech, and Silence: Stefan Zweig's concept of expressive language', *The Hebrew University Studies in Literature*, vol. 10, no. 2 (Autumn 1982) 181-207.
Meißenburg, Egbert, 'Stefan Zweigs *Schachnovelle*: eine Bibliographie der

Sekundärliteratur', *Börsenblatt für den Deutschen Buchhandel*, Frankfurter Ausgabe, no. 9 (30 January 1979) A16-19.

Murdoch, Brian, 'Game, Image and Ambiguity in Stefan Zweig's *Schachnovelle*', *New German Studies*, vol. 11, no. 3 (1983) 171-89.

Pfoser, Alfred, 'Verwirrung der Gefühle als Verwirrung einer Zeit: Bemerkungen zum Bestsellerautor Stefan Zweig und zur Psychologie in seinen Novellen', in: *Stefan Zweig 1881-1981: Aufsätze und Dokumente*, ed. Heinz Lunzer and Gerhard Renner (Vienna, 1981) 7-17.

Rolland, Romain, 'Préface' to: Stefan Zweig, *Amok: ou le fou de Malaisie, Lettre d'une Inconnue, La Ruelle au Clair de Lune*, traduit de l'allemand par Alzir Hella et Olivier Bournac (Paris, 1930) ix-xviii.

Rudolf, Helmut, 'Die humanistische Position Stefan Zweigs in seiner Erzählung *Buchmendel*', *Német Filológiai Tanulmanyok* (Arbeiten zur deutschen Philologie, vol. 1, Budapest, 1965) 122-30.

Schwamborn, Ingrid, 'Schachmatt im brasilianischen Paradies: die Entstehungsgeschichte der *Schachnovelle*', *Germanisch-Romanische Monatsschrift*, vol. 34 (1984) 404-30.

Sørensen, Bengt Algot, 'The Sense of Time in Stefan Zweig's Stories and *Novellen*', *The Hebrew University Studies in Literature*, vol. 10, no. 2 (Autumn 1982) 208-24.

Strelka, Joseph P., 'Psychoanalytische Ideen in Stefan Zweigs Novellen', *Literatur und Kritik*, Nos. 169-70 (Nov.-Dec. 1982) 42-52.

Turner, David, 'Memory and the Humanitarian Ideal: an interpretation of Stefan Zweig's *Buchmendel*', *Modern Austrian Literature*, vol. 12, no. 1 (1979) 43-62.

-----------, 'The Function of the Narrative Frame in the *Novellen* of Stefan Zweig', *Modern Language Review*, vol. 76 (1981) 116-28.

-----------, 'The Choice and Function of Setting in the *Novellen* of Stefan Zweig', *Neophilologus*, vol. 66 (1982) 574-88.

-----------, 'A World beyond Space and Time: some implications of a recurrent motif in Stefan Zweig's *Novellen*', *The Hebrew University Studies in Literature*, vol. 10, no. 2 (1982) 225-46.

-----------, 'The Humane Ideal in Stefan Zweig's *Novellen*: some complications and limitations', in: *Stefan Zweig: the world of yesterday's humanist today: proceedings of the Stefan Zweig symposium*, ed. Marion Sonnenfeld (Albany, 1983) 157-67.

-----------, 'Rausch, Ernüchterung, und die Flucht ins Private: zu Stefan Zweig's Roman aus dem Nachlaß', in: *Stefan Zweig heute*, ed. Mark H. Gelber (New York, Berne, Frankfurt a.M., Paris) 201-25.

-----------, 'Expressionist Pathos and Psychological Analysis: opposition to war in Leonhard Frank's *Der Mensch ist gut* and Stefan Zweig's *Der Zwang*', forthcoming in *Forum for Modern Language Studies*.

Veselý, Jiří, 'Das Schachspiel in der *Schachnovelle*', *Österreich in Geschichte und Literatur*, vol. 13 (1969) 517-22.

Weiß, Ernst, 'Stefan Zweig, *Ungeduld des Herzens*', *Maß und Wert*, vol. 2, no. 5 (May-June 1939) 693-6.

Welter, Marie-Luise, 'Typus und Eros: eine Untersuchung des Menschenbildes in den Novellen Stefan Zweigs' (University of Freiburg i.B. doctoral thesis,

1957).

II   LITERARY THEORY

Booth, Wayne, C., *The Rhetoric of Fiction* (Chicago and London, 1961).
Ellis, John M., *Narration in the German Novelle: theory and interpretation* (Cambridge, 1974).
Haverkamp, Anselm (ed.), *Theorie der Metapher* (Wege der Forschung, No. 389, Darmstadt, 1983).
Hawkes, Terence, *Metaphor* (The Critical Idiom No. 25, London, 1972).
Kunz, Josef (ed.), *Novelle* (Wege der Forschung, No. 55, Darmstadt, 1968).
Polheim, Karl Konrad (ed.), *Theorie und Kritik der deutschen Novelle von Wieland bis Musil* (Tübingen, 1970).
Reiners, Ludwig, *Stilkunst: ein Lehrbuch der deutschen Prosa* (Munich, 1961).
Richards, I.A., *The Philosophy of Rhetoric* (Oxford, 1936).
Spurgeon, Caroline, *Shakespeare's Imagery and what it tells us* (Cambridge, 1935).
Swales, Martin, *The German Novelle* (Princeton, 1977).
Timms, Edward, '*Novelle* and Case History: Freud in pursuit of the falcon', in: *London German Studies*, vol. 2 ed. J.P. Stern (London, 1983) 115-33.
Wiese, Benno von, *Novelle* (2nd edition; Stuttgart, 1964).
------------, *Die deutsche Novelle von Goethe bis Kafka*, 2 vols (Düsseldorf, 1968).

III   THE LITERARY AND CULTURAL BACKGROUND

Braun, Felix, *Das musische Land: Versuche über Österreichs Landschaft und Dichtung* (Innsbruck, 1952).
Magris, Claudio, *Der habsburgische Mythos in der österreichischen Literatur* (Salzburg, 1966).
Rosenthal, Friedrich, 'Jungwiener Novellistik', *Österreichische Rundschau*, vol. 38 (Jan.-Mar. 1914) 90-103.
Schorske, Carl E., *Fin de Siècle Vienna: politics and culture* (London, 1979).
Williams, C.E., *The Broken Eagle: the politics of Austrian literature from Empire to Anschluß* (London, 1974).

IV   MISCELLANEOUS

Freud, Sigmund, *Introductory Lectures on Psychoanalysis* (Pelican Freud Library, vol. 1, Harmondsworth, 1974).
------------, *New Introductory Lectures on Psychoanalysis* (Pelican Freud Library, vol. 2, Harmondsworth, 1973).
------------, *On Sexuality* (Pelican Freud Library, vol. 7, Harmondsworth, 1977).
------------, *On Metapsychology: the theory of psychoanalysis* (Pelican Freud Library, vol. 11, Harmondsworth, 1984).

------------, *Civilization, Society and Religion* (Pelican Freud Library, vol. 12, Harmondsworth, 1985).

------------, *Art and Literature* (Pelican Freud Library, vol. 14, Harmondsworth, 1985).

Key, Ellen, *Das Jahrhundert des Kindes* (34th to 36th edition, Berlin, 1926).

Laski, Marghanita, *Ecstasy: a study of some secular and religious experience* (London, 1961).

Indexes

1. General Index

Adelt, Leonhardt, 287,338n.,21
Adler, Alfred, 62
Altenberg, Peter, 187
Aristotle, 154
Auernheimer, Raoul, 19

Balzac, Honoré de, 90,196,322n.7
Binding, Rudolf, 296
Binet, Alfred, 94
Braun, Felix, 333n.2
Brecht, Bertolt, 258
Broch, Hermann, 295
Büchner, Georg, *Lenz*, 341n.27
Buber, Martin, 233,327n.11

Canetti, Elias, *Die Blendung*, 234
Carossa, Hans, 126
Casanova, Giacomo, 90
Castellio, Sebastian, 167,328n.19
Cervantes Saavedra, Miguel de, 340n.26
Conrad, Joseph, 202

Daudet, Léon, 330n.9
Daudet, Philippe, 330n.9
Dostoyevsky, Fyodor, 12,255,315n.3,
    336n.20

Engels, Friedrich, 196
Erasmus of Rotterdam, 135,150,161,166,
    169,234

Fouché, Joseph, 263
Fowles, John, 4,313n.17,323n.1
Frank, Bruno, *Politische Novelle*, 332n.17
Frank, Leonhard, *Der Mensch ist gut*,
    169,189,228
Freud, Sigmund, 11,12,14,22f.,26f.,39f.,
    43,68,73,80f.,83,111,125,182,190,247,
    303f.,308,314n.7,316n.15,317n.6,
    319n.23,337n.15,341n.40; *Civilization
    and its Discontents*, 182; 'Dostoevsky
    and Parricide', 12,316n.11;
    *Introductory Lectures on Psycho-
    analysis*, 317n.6,331n.18; 'Some
    Character-types met with in Psycho-
    analytical Work', 316n.15

Goethe, Johann Wolfgang von, 125,148,
    151,159,234,288,298f.,326n.9;
    Faust, 284; *Torquato Tasso*, 317n.19
Gorky, Maxim, 4,162,174,312n.17,
    340n.25
Grillparzer, Franz, *Der arme Spielmann*,
    93f.,112,226,341n.27
Grün, Max von der, 4,313n.17

Halbe, Max, *Jugend*, 325n.7
Hauptmann, Gerhart, *Bahnwärter Thiel*,
    43
Hebbel, Friedrich, *Maria Magdalena*,
    65f.,70
Herrmann-Neiße, Max, 193
Herzl, Theodor, 233,333n.12
Hesse, Hermann, 5,313n.18; *Heumond*
    (from *Diesseits*), 15; *Kurgast*, 185;
    Peter Camenzind, 14; *Unterm Rad*, 14
Hitler, Adolf, 3,180,266
Hofmannsthal, Hugo von, 4,6,269,
    312n.15; *Das Märchen der 672.
    Nacht*, 32,35,186
Hölderlin, Johann Christian Friedrich,
    11,287
Homer, 159,295
Huebsch, Ben, 333n.10

James, Henry, 274; *The Aspern Papers*,
    290
Jouve, Pierre J., 163,327n.13
Joyce, James, 90

Kafka, Franz, 6,241
Kesten, Hermann, 241,335n.3
Key, Ellen, 12,14f.,130; *Das Jahrhundert
    des Kindes*, 14,130
Kippenberg, Anton, 151
Kleist, Heinrich von, 11,287
Krafft-Ebing, August F.F., 80

Magellan, Ferdinand, 285
Mahler, Gustav, 138
Mann, Thomas, 4,6,126,312n.15,342n.6;
    *Bekenntnisse des Hochstaplers Felix
    Krull*, 282; *Buddenbrooks*, 14; *Der Tod
    in Venedig*, 74; *Der Zauberberg*, 295
Mary Stuart, 137,142,150,270,326n.4
Masereel, Frans, 90,151,328n.17,333n.2
Maugham, W. Somerset, 202

350

2. Index of Zweig's Works

Pages which contain a substantial discussion of the work in question are printed in bold type.

351

häusliche Musik. Und wo hinter weißen Fensterrahmen schon Dunkel stand, gewiß, dort atmete beruhigter Schlaf. Über allen diesen ruhenden Dächern schwebte wie der Mond in silbrigem Dunste ein mildes Ruhn, eine entlocktere, sanft niedergeschwebte Stille, und die elf Schläge der Turmuhr fielen ihnen allen ohne Wucht in das zufällig lauschende oder träumende Ohr. Nur ich hier im Haus spürte noch Wachsein, böse Umlagerung fremder Gedanken. (VdG,232)

Undoubtedly a change of weather — a sudden storm perhaps — would have corresponded more closely to the hero's present state of mind, but that does not mean that Zweig has forgotten his original aim. It is quite clear that the calm of the natural world accords with the waking or sleeping peace of the population at large, a peace from which Roland feels uniquely excluded. The atmosphere outside serves to highlight his restlessness by contrast, perhaps even to mock his inner turmoil. For the reader may now recall that the whole episode was introduced with the words: 'Wie schön begann jener schicksalshafte Abend, wie verräterisch schön!' (VdG,221).

A more consistent correspondence between the weather and the state of mind of the characters is presented in *Vierundzwanzig Stunden aus dem Leben einer Frau*. That it is consciously intended by the author is confirmed not only by the explicit comments of Mrs C., but also by the widespread use of meteorological imagery and, more especially, by an occasional metaphorical interpenetration between the human and natural spheres.

During the evening of her fateful encounter with the young Polish gambler the heavy storm-clouds have already been gathering, blown in across the Mediterranean Sea, and are now contributing to an oppressive atmosphere, which is ultimately released in a violent cloudburst. Although this has an immediate practical effect, in that it precipitates her involuntary decision to spring to the aid of the young Pole, its deeper purpose is to mirror the tumultuous passion which has seized him and will shortly take hold of his would-be protectress. In particular the way in which he sits outside, motionless, allowing himself to be drenched by what Zweig refers to as the 'Element', while ordinary men and women flee indoors, is at once a consequence of his surrender to passionate despair and a metaphorical enactment of it (VdG,50-2).

After the tumult of the night that follows the day dawns bright

Even as late as *Phantastische Nacht* an uncertainty of purpose is apparent. For while the promise of late spring, bringing fresh green to the trees as they rise out of the lifeless asphalt of the Austrian capital, seems to point prophetically to the subsequent rejuvenation of the baron, the gentle stirring of the warm breeze as it catches the falling blossoms is felt by the hero himself, on the very next page, to correspond to his present mood of indolence ('es entsprach besser meinem lässigen Gefühl'), part of that very indifference from which he is to be roused to new life (cf. A,135-6).

In making such judgements on the lack of consistency in Zweig's purpose one must of course take care not to overlook the possibility of an intended contradiction, which may achieve an end no less meaningful than a correspondence. In *Verwirrung der Gefühle*, for example, which takes place largely indoors and uses atmosphere only sparingly, both correspondence and contradiction are exploited purposefully at the climax of the work. It is a peaceful summer's evening and the windows of the professor's flat stand open:

> und in ihrem verdunkelten Rahmen trat allmählich dämmeriger Himmel mit weißen Wolken langsam herein: ein Lindes und Klares ging von ihrem majestätisch hinschwebenden Widerleuchten wesenhaft weiter, bis tief hinab mußte mans fühlen. Wir hatten lässiger, friedfertiger, geschäftiger geplaudert, die Frau und ich, als sonst. Mein Lehrer schwieg über unser Gespräch hinweg; aber sein Schweigen stand gleichsam mit stillgefalteten Flügeln über unserem Gespräch. (VdG,222)

At this point the calm atmosphere of the summer evening seems to reflect, almost indeed to confirm, the peace of the characters. Nevertheless, there follows the scene in which the professor makes his first more overt homosexual advances, which are rejected by a confused Roland. After the young hero has returned to his room, he is full of inner restlessness, both about his mentor's advances and about the conflict between husband and wife. Yet when he opens his window, this is the picture that presents itself to his view:

> Draußen lag friedlich unter sommerlichem Gewölk die Stadt; noch leuchteten Fenster vom Scheine der Lampe, aber die dort saßen, einte friedliches Gespräch, wärmte ein Buch oder